Dictatorship of the Air

Focusing on one of the last untold chapters in the history of human flight, *Dictatorship of the Air* is the first book to explain the true story behind twentieth-century Russia's quest for aviation prominence. Based on nearly a decade of scholarly research, but written with general readers in mind, this is the only account to answer the question "What is 'Russian' about Russian aviation?"

From the 1909 arrival of machine-powered flight in the "land of the tsars" to the USSR's victory over Hitler in 1945, *Dictatorship of the Air* describes why the airplane became the preeminent symbol of industrial progress and international power for generations of Russian statesmen and citizens. The book explains how, behind a façade of daredevil pilots, record-setting flights, and gargantuan airplanes, Russia's long-standing legacies of industrial backwardness, cultural xenophobia, and state-directed modernization prolonged the nation's dependence on western technology and ultimately ensured the USSR's demise.

Scott W. Palmer is a specialist on the history of modern Russian culture and technology. A frequent traveler to the Russian Federation, he has conducted eight extended visits to Russian archives since 1994. His research has been supported by the American Council of Learned Societies, the United States Library of Congress, the Smithsonian Institution, the Fulbright-Hays Program, the International Council for Research Exchange, and the Kennan Institute for Advanced Russian Studies. He currently resides and teaches in the Midwest.

Cambridge Centennial of Flight

Editors:

John Anderson
*Curator of Aerodynamics, National Air and Space Museum, and
Professor Emeritus, Aerospace Engineering, University of Maryland*

Von Hardesty
Smithsonian Institution

The series presents new titles dealing with the drama and historical impact of human flight. The Air Age began on December 17, 1903 with the epic powered and controlled flight by the Wright brothers at Kitty Hawk. The airplane rapidly developed into an efficient means of global travel and a lethal weapon of war. Modern rocketry has allowed heirs of the Wrights to orbit the Earth and to land on the Moon, inaugurating a new era of exploration of the solar system by humans and robotic machines. The Centennial of Flight series offers pioneering studies with fresh interpretative insights and broad appeal on key themes, events, and personalities that shaped the evolution of aerospace technology.

Dictatorship of the Air

Aviation Culture and the Fate of Modern Russia

_____

SCOTT W. PALMER

CAMBRIDGE
UNIVERSITY PRESS

CAMBRIDGE UNIVERSITY PRESS
Cambridge, New York, Melbourne, Madrid, Cape Town, Singapore, São Paulo

Cambridge University Press
40 West 20th Street, New York, NY 10011-4211, USA

www.cambridge.org
Information on this title: www.cambridge.org/9780521859578

© Scott W. Palmer 2006

This publication is in copyright. Subject to statutory exception
and to the provisions of relevant collective licensing agreements,
no reproduction of any part may take place without
the written permission of Cambridge University Press.

First published 2006

Printed in the United States of America

A catalog record for this publication is available from the British Library.

Library of Congress Cataloging in Publication Data

Palmer, Scott W., 1967–
Dictatorship of the air : aviation culture and the fate of modern Russia / Scott W. Palmer.
p. cm. – (Cambridge centennial of flight)
Includes bibliographical references and index.
ISBN-13: 978-0-521-85957-8 (hardback)
ISBN-10: 0-521-85957-3 (hardback)
1. Aeronautics – Russia (Federation) – History.   2. Aeronautics – Soviet Union – History.
3. Technology transfer – Soviet Union.   4. Technology and state – Russia (Federation)
5. Soviet Union – Politics and government.   I. Title.   II. Series.
TL526.R9P35   2006
629.1300947 – dc22   2006002826

ISBN-13   978-0-521-85957-8 hardback
ISBN-10   0-521-85957-3 hardback

Cambridge University Press has no responsibility for
the persistence or accuracy of URLs for external or
third-party Internet Web sites referred to in this publication
and does not guarantee that any content on such
Web sites is, or will remain, accurate or appropriate.

To M

But, good Lord, what do I care about the laws of nature and arithmetic if I have my reasons for disliking them, including the one about two and two making four! Of course, I won't be able to breach this wall with my head if I'm not strong enough. But I don't have to accept a stone wall just because it's there and I don't have the strength to breach it.

Fyodor Dostoevsky, *Notes from the Underground*

The author gratefully acknowledges permission to reproduce, in modified form, materials previously appearing in the following publications:

"On Wings of Courage: Public Air-Mindedness and National Identity in Late Imperial Russia." *Russian Review* 54 (1995): 209–26.

"Peasants into Pilots: Soviet Air-Mindedness as an Ideology of Dominance." *Technology and Culture* 41 (2000): 1–26.

"Icarus, East: The Symbolic Contexts of Russian Flight." *Slavic and East European Journal* 49 (2005): 19–47.

Contents

List of Illustrations

Notes on Usage

All Russian names appearing in the text have been transliterated with the Library of Congress system save those for which an alternative version is already widely known to English-speaking readers (for example, "Leon Trotsky" rather than "Lev Trotskii").

Until February 1918 Russia adhered to the Julian calendar (Old Style) that ran thirteen days behind the Gregorian calendar (New Style) used in Western Europe. Unless otherwise noted, dates before 31 January 1918 are given in the Julian style.

List of Key Terms and Abbreviations

Aviakhim	*Obshchestvo druzei aviatsionnoi i khimicheskoi oborony i promyshlennosti*, Society of Friends of Aviation and Chemical Defense and Industry
bogatyr'	warrior, hero
chastushka	a rhymed couplet or ditty
Dobrokhim	*Obshchestvo druzei khimii*, Society of Friends of Chemistry
Dobrolet	*Dobrovol'nyi vozdushnyi flot*, Voluntary Air-Fleet
ekipazh	flight crew
Gosplan	*Gosudarstvennaia planirovanaia komissiia*, State Planning Commission
GPU, OGPU	*(Ob'edinennoe) Glavnoe politicheskoe upravlenie*, (Unified) Main Political Directorate. Secret Police
Glavaviaprom	*Glavnoe upravleniie aviatsionnoi promyshlennosti*, Main Directorate of the Aviation Industry
GVF	*Grazhdanskii vozdushnyi flot*, Civilian Air Fleet
IVAK	*Imperatorskii Vserossiiskii aero-klub*, Imperial All-Russian Aero-Club
NKID	*Narodnyi komissariat inostrannykh del*, Peoples' Commissariat of Foreign Affairs
NKVD	*Narodnyi komissariat vnutrennykh del*, Peoples' Commissariat of Internal Affairs. Secret Police. Successor to the GPU
oblast'	region (an administrative unit)
ODVF	*Obshchestvo druzei vozdushnogo flota*, Society of Friends of the Air Fleet
OKB	*Opytnoe konstruktorskoe biuro*, Experimental Design Bureau
OSO	*Obshchestvo sodeistviia oborony*, Society for Assistance to Defense
Osoaviakhim	*Obshchestvo druzei oborony i aviatsionno-khimicheskogo stroitel'stvo*, Society of Friends of Defense and Avia-Chemical Construction
prostranstvo	(vast) space

Revvoensovet   *Revoliutsionnyi voennyi sovet*, Revolutionary Military
                Council. The highest decision-making body of the Red
                Army, 1918–1934
skazka   fairy-tale, fable
smychka   union, alliance
Sovnarkom   *Sovet narodnykh komissarov*, Council of Peoples'
                Commissars. Nominal government of the Soviet Union,
                functioning as a cabinet of ministers
TsAGI   *Tsentral'nyi aero-gidrodynamicheskii institut*, Central
                Aero- Hydrodynamical Institute
versty   plural of *versta*, a unit of measurement equal to
                approximately 0.63 mile
VNO   *Voennoe nauchnoe obshchestvo*, Military Scientific Society
VVF   *Voenno-vozdushnye sily*, Military Air Force

Acknowledgments

I am pleased to acknowledge those organizations and institutions whose generous financial assistance made possible the creation of this book. Fellowships from the U.S. Department of State's Fulbright-Hays Program and the International Council for Research Exchange provided significant early research support. Subsequently, individual grants from the Kennan Institute for Advanced Russian Studies, the Robert W. Tomilson Foundation, the Art Institute of Chicago, and the Western Illinois University Foundation facilitated summer archival visits to Washington, D.C., and Moscow.

Above all, I am indebted to the American Council of Learned Societies for enabling me to set aside other responsibilities and focus my full attention on Russian aviation culture during 2001–2. By granting me the simple luxury of time to research, think, and write, a year-long fellowship from the ACLS proved invaluable to the completion of this study. In addition to facilitating access to the world's largest collection of aviation-related materials, a Daniel and Florence Guggenheim Fellowship from the National Air and Space Museum in Washington, D.C., brought me into contact with many of America's leading aviation historians. Tom Crouch, Michael Neufeld, Dominick Pisano, and Robert Van der Linden were gracious and expert guides during my tenure at the Museum. Von Hardesty, who introduced me to the study of Russian aviation during my first visit to the Air and Space Museum many years ago, has been an ever-generous source of indispensable and timely support from the start to the finish of this book.

Among the friends and colleagues who offered advice, assistance, and encouragement during my work on this project, I am particularly grateful to Roger Bilstein, Jonathan Daly, Alan Holiman, Jacob Kipp, Matt Lenoe, John McCannon, David McDonald, Vladimir Pozniakov, Carl Reddel, Kurt Schultz, Sergei Shenin, Dmitrii Sobolev, Helen Sullivan, Robert Tomilson, Andrew Verner, Frank Wcislo, Elena Zheltova, and John Zukowsky. Although their individual contributions may not be immediately obvious to them, I am indebted to them all. I greatly appreciate the candor and professionalism with which the two peer readers, David Stone and Anonymous, undertook their task. Their perceptive recommendations significantly strengthened the manuscript. At Cambridge University Press, Frank Smith has proven the very model of a conscientious and forthright editor. I thank as well Larry Mortier and Larry Balsamo at WIU for their assistance with publication. Larry Dean and the staff at the Visual Production Center provided excellent and timely service in preparing the illustrative matter. Naturally, I bear responsibility for the content of this book.

On a more personal level, I am grateful for the help given me by my wife, Leesa, and my mother, Faye. In ways too numerous to count, their sacrifices and support sustained me, especially during difficult times. Without my two children, Athena and Alexander, this book would have been completed much sooner, but my life would be far poorer.

I also owe an extraordinary debt of thanks to my family in Moscow, the Dmitrievs. Vitya, Nina, Volodya, and especially Shurik played a much more important role in the creation of this book than they could possibly imagine.

Having long ago exhausted ways of expressing appreciation in words, I offer my heartfelt gratitude to M. in the form of a dedication.

Introduction

Russia's Culture of Flight in Historical Perspective

Of the twentieth century's many remarkable inventions, none exerted such powerful and lasting influence on the human imagination as the airplane. Inspiring the creative introspection of artists and intellectuals and attracting public interest through the presentation of spectacle, machine-powered flight shaped popular perceptions of the nation while simultaneously challenging states to adapt to the modern world. As mountains were conquered and continents traversed, aeronautical successes overturned conventional notions of time and space, compelling young and old, citizen and statesman alike, to reconsider their relationship with the natural order. Accompanying the physical changes that it effected, aviation produced new symbols and images that celebrated the sensations of speed and motion, communicated meanings of power and authority, and forever enriched the range of human expression. Of course, the airplane is not only a cultural symbol. It is also a military weapon, an economic instrument, and a convenient method of transportation. In fulfilling these functions aviation served as a practical device for states attempting to modernize in the course of the twentieth century. As an index of technological proficiency and human mastery over nature, the airplane has symbolized substantive progress; assisting in the development of nations, while simultaneously contributing to perceptions of "the modern."

Given its power in shaping modern sensibilities, it is not surprising that the airplane has produced a scholarly literature dedicated to exploring the image and substance of flight. In recent years, scholars of European and American culture have devoted increasing attention to the subject of aviation. Laurence Goldstein, Clive Hart, and Felix Ingold have written on the airplane's place within the modern literary canon while Stephen Pendo and Michael Paris have chronicled the portrayal of aviation in the cinema. In his pioneering work, *The Winged Gospel*, historian Joseph Corn examined American's early appropriation of flight technology as a symbol of reform and national renewal. Similarly, studies by Jonathan Vance and Peter Fritzsche have respectively explored the contours of Canadian and German flight culture. More recently, Robert Wohl has published the second installment of a projected three-volume study of "aviation and the western imagination." Focusing on the aesthetic dimensions of flight and the airplane's role as a source of cultural inspiration, Wohl's trilogy, when complete, promises to

I

become the definitive treatment of aviation culture in the twentieth-century West.[1]

Notably absent from western scholarship, however, is any account of the Russian culture of flight. Although valuable studies devoted to Russian and Soviet aviation have been produced, none consider the role of the airplane in reflecting and affecting broader patterns in Russia's development. Likewise, none have attempted to measure Russia's response to aviation within the context of then-contemporary European institutions and trends.[2] This book attempts to address this absence. Through an examination of private and public responses to the airplane, it chronicles the culture of Russian flight from its origins in the first decade of the twentieth century to the end of the Second World War. It seeks to identify the fundamental characteristics of Russian aviation and to assess their impact in shaping the images and institutions created by the country's citizens and statesmen.

Although flight devotees and aviation enthusiasts will find much to interest them in these pages, this is not a typical book about airplanes. It is not intended to provide readers with a complete account of Russia's aeronautical development, nor is it a reference work cataloging Russian contributions to the evolution of flight technology. The subject of this book is instead the historical concurrence of aviation "symbols" and "substance." It explains how successive generations of Russian and Soviet leaders understood the airplane, how they articulated that understanding through the promotion of specific images and symbols, and why they institutionalized their visions through the pursuit of particular programs and policies. In doing so, this book aims to answer a basic, but essential, question: "What is 'Russian' about Russian aviation"?

Central to this approach is my specific use of the term "air-mindedness." Initially coined by contemporary American observers to explain their nation's early, unbridled enthusiasm for the flying machine, "air-minded" has subsequently been employed by historians to describe the interest shown by any nation, group, or individual in things aeronautical.[3] In this sense, the adjective "air-minded" and the noun "air-mindedness" typically refer to an enthusiasm for machine-powered flight. My use of the term is some-what different. I have chosen to employ "air-mindedness" in reference to the particular set of cultural traditions, symbols, and markers that, combined with existing political culture and social institutions, constitute a given nation's response to the airplane. Defined in this manner, "air-minded" retains its accustomed meaning as the semantic equivalent of "enthusiastic about flight," whereas "air-mindedness" is used to communicate the specific

---

[1] Complete citations of these works appear in the bibliography.
[2] For examples of these texts, see the bibliography.
[3] Joseph Corn, *Winged Gospel: America's Romance with Aviation, 1900–1950* (New York: Oxford University Press, 1983), vii.

historical factors that revealed, expressed, and produced that enthusiasm. Put simply, I argue that both the meaning and the substance of air-mindedness are particular to the culture that one is studying. Although Americans, Britons, Germans, and French may all be said to have been enthusiastic about aviation (or, air-minded), the specific manifestations of that enthusiasm (air-mindedness) were the products of those nations' unique historical and cultural traditions. The purpose of this book is to examine air-minded Russia and to identify the cultural, social, and political conditions that contributed to the formation of a specifically Russian air-mindedness.

As scholars of western flight have convincingly demonstrated, twentieth-century Europeans and Americans communicated their separate visions of flight through reference to a shared set of cultural symbols and standards.[4] Rooted in the Hellenic tradition of the Icarus legend and shaped by the common Renaissance values of humanism and individualism, western cultures of flight focused on the accomplishments of individual pilots and endowed aeronautical successes with a supernatural bearing that typically bordered on religious reverence. In the western imagination, the advent of flight gave birth to new heroes, modern Prometheans named Wright and Blériot, Lindbergh and Earhart, whose airborne achievements spoke to the power of technology and, through it, the individual's ability to master time and space and to transcend the challenges of the human condition. Illustrative of the West's dynamism and idealism, as well as its tendencies toward conquest and self-destruction, the Icarus myth has dominated European and American consciousness and established the perceptual framework within which aviation progress, programs, and personalities are regarded by western citizens.[5]

Unknown to most audiences outside of Russia is the existence of a corresponding Icarian vision in the Russian cultural tradition. Although its origins are neither as old nor as celebrated as the western legend, the peculiar Russian variation on the ancient Greek tale likewise lends insight into Russians' unique understanding of the promise and problems posed by human flight. Recorded in obscurity and popularized in the early twentieth century, the story of the "Russian Icarus" has been retold and recast over many generations.[6] Reprinted in the general and scholarly press, transformed into

---

[4] Clive Hart, *Images of Flight* (Berkeley, CA: University of California Press, 1988); Laurence Goldstein, *Flying Machine and Modern Literature* (London: Macmillan, 1986); and Robert Wohl, *A Passion for Wings: Aviation and the Western Imagination, 1908–1918* (New Haven, CT: Yale University Press, 1994).

[5] Wohl, *Passion for Wings*, 2–3.

[6] Aleksandr Rodnykh, *Istoriia vozdukhoplavaniia i letaniia v Rossii: letanie i vozdukhoplavanie v starinu* (St. Petersburg, 1911); Vasilii Naidenov, *Russkoe vozdukhoplavanie i istoriia i uspekhi* (St. Petersburg, 1911); P. D. Duz', *Istoriia vozdukhoplavaniia i aviatsii v Rossii* (Moscow, 1979); V. A. Popov (ed.), *Vozdukhoplavanie i aviatsiia v Rossii do 1907 g.* (Moscow, 1956); and, most recently, D. A. Sobolev and Iu. V. Rychkov, *Vsemirnaia istoriia aviatsii* (Moscow: Veche, 2002), among others.

illustrative plates, and even translated to the motion-picture screen, the Russian version of the Icarus myth has attained the status of a cultural icon. As such, the tale bears retelling in its entirety.

During the reign of Ivan the Terrible, a certain serf by the name of Nikitka, belonging to the *boyar* Lupotov, devised a mechanism with which, in the presence of the Tsar and a large number of people, he intended to fly away to the Aleksandrovskii settlement. Notwithstanding a successful flight, the "inventor" Nikitka was subjected to the following decree of the Tsar: "A man is not a bird. He does not have wings. Those who attach wooden wings to themselves do so in opposition to the will of nature. Such is not a godly deed, but a deed which emanates from unclean powers. For such an association with the forces of darkness, the head of the inventor shall be cut off. The body of the enserfed [*smerdiashchago*] cur will then be thrown to swine in order that they may feed. As for the invention undertaken with demonic assistance, following a blessed liturgy, it shall be consumed by fire."[7]

The existence of this specifically Russian legend would remain a mere curiosity were it not for its recurrence in the pages of the nation's history. Another narrative, set during the reign of Tsar Peter I (1682–1725), tells a similar story, suggesting that the notion of a uniquely native Icarus speaks to larger, more enduring issues in the history of Russian flight. On 30 April 1695, a peasant [*muzhik*] by the name of Emelian Ivanov announced his intention to "fly like a crane" from the middle of Red Square. Curious to discover if the peasant could indeed fly, the tsar granted him eighteen rubles to construct a pair of wings. When the wings proved ineffective, the peasant explained that he had made them too heavy. After receiving an additional five-ruble subsidy, he refashioned the wings from leather but again failed to soar. As punishment, the peasant was beaten and his property sold to repay his incurred debts.[8]

In various guises, these two legends have served as the foundation for innumerable accounts regarding the origins of Russian flight. Throughout the nineteenth and twentieth centuries, as the country's citizens and state officials struggled to respond to European airborne successes, these stories were cited as indisputable proof of Russia's peculiar aeronautical heritage. One of the earliest (and more vociferous) efforts in this regard came from the pen of Konstantin Masal'skii, a state official and minor litterateur who lived during the reign of Tsar Nicholas I (1825–55). His 1833 rendition of the tale concerning the peasant aeronaut Emelian Ivanov consciously endeavored to establish the Russian genesis of human flight. In introductory remarks to an embellished version of the Petrine-era legend, Masal'skii warned foreign skeptics not to mistakenly attribute the invention of flight to European genius. Long

---

[7] N. Borozdin, *Zavoevanie vozdushnoi stikhi* (Warsaw, 1909), 6.

[8] I. A. Zheliabuzhskii, *Zapiski Zheliabuzhskago s 1682 g. po 2 iiulia 1709 g.* (St. Petersburg, 1840), 46–7.

FIGURE 1. *The Russian Icarus*. Reproduced from Aleksandr Rodnykh, *Kratkii ocherk po istorii russkago vozdukhoplavaniia* (St. Petersburg, 1910).

before the helium experiments of English and Italian scientists, and some eighty-eight years before the first balloon ascent of the French Montgolfier brothers, he wrote, Ivanov's 1695 effort to fly had granted to Russia the "palm of first place in aeronautics." Even before Peter the Great had begun to transform Russia from a backward Asiatic power into a modern European

nation, Masal'skii claimed, the native talent of the Russian peasantry had
"put to shame" the leading minds of Europe.[9]

Masal'skii's early attempt to exploit the Icarus legend to accord Russia
primacy in the annals of flight reveals one of the structuring motifs of the
nation's history and a characteristic trait of its aviation culture: the recurrent
effort to lay claim to distinction in the face of competition from Western
Europe. From the "Third Rome" theories of Muscovite ideologists and the
romantic reveries of nineteenth-century Slavophils, to Communist claims
of ideological supremacy and the resurgent nationalism of contemporary
politicians, Russian citizens and statesmen have long measured themselves
against the perceived standards set by Europe. Positioned on the cultural
periphery of both the East and the West, Russians have embraced ideas and
institutions imported from Europe while attempting to reconcile them with
their own native values. The alternating enthusiasm and ambivalence that
has characterized this embrace helped to produce a particular vision of the
nation and its future. Perhaps nowhere is this tendency more evident than
in the nation's response to flight.

As the quintessential marker of twentieth-century progress, the airplane,
more so than any other technology, clarified the link between nationalist
aspirations and the advent of the modern age. In promising military and
economic advantage, and in demonstrating mastery over nature, the airplane emerged as the clearest measure of nations, distinguishing not only
European civilization from those of Africa and Asia, but also the truly great
powers among the Continent's leading states.[10] Influenced by the successes
and symbols of aviation and eager to demonstrate their own technological prowess, Russians enjoined the aerial challenge emanating from Europe
by seeking to establish their own place in the heavens. Not unlike western
citizens and statesmen who came to view aerial machines as measures of
their modernity, Russians also invoked the airplane as a portent of national
progress and pride. Despite this shared recognition of the symbolic resonance of human flight, however, the Russian embrace of aviation remained
essentially distinct. Whereas Western Europeans viewed the airplane symbolically as a marker of progress and personal liberation, Russians conceived it
in iconic fashion. Like the religious images of the Russian Orthodox faith,
which are understood both to represent God's heavenly realm and to effect
salvation, the airplane served dual functions for Russians desirous of besting
the West. They saw aviation both as a sign of the future and as an instrument for collectively liberating the nation from the constraints of its past.
More than a mere symbolic representation of sought-after modernity, the

---

[9] First published in A. Smirdin (ed.), *Novosel'e* (St. Petersburg, 1833), 241–316, the story may
also be found in the recent collection, Konstantin Masal'skii, *Strel'tsy* (Moscow, 1994).

[10] Peter Fritzsche, *A Nation of Fliers: German Aviation and the Popular Imagination*
(Cambridge, MA: Harvard University Press, 1992), 3.

airplane was also seen as a means to that end, the mastery of which would make possible backward Russia's rapid transformation into the world's most advanced and powerful nation.[11]

Recognized by successive generations of Russians as both a symbol and a means of modernization, the airplane played a central, if largely overlooked, role in the efforts of twentieth-century officials to secure political legitimacy. Following the investigative lead of the late Kendall Bailes, I argue that, as the preeminent embodiments of technological modernization, aviation images and institutions were integral to Russians' views of themselves, their nation, and their place in the word.[12] Unlike Bailes, however, I propose that the airplane's influence in shaping Russian identity was not limited to the Stalinist era. Rather, it has been a continuous and essential feature of modern Russian culture, one that has structured public and private understanding of progress and legitimacy from the dawn of the air age to the present day.

Such an approach to Russia's aviation culture lends valuable insight into the continuities shared by the Imperial and the Soviet eras. As the following chapters will show, the recurrent effort to derive legitimacy through appeals to aeronautical mastery led both Imperial and Soviet political leaders to pursue polices and programs that did not always serve their country's best interests. Eager to demonstrate competency in the conquest of the air, but unable to keep pace with foreign advances, Imperial leaders focused on quantitative solutions to their aeronautical dilemmas. Revisiting long-standing patterns in Russian history, they attempted to acquire airplanes and parts abroad in a hurried effort to jump-start development and rapidly master technique. As these measures failed, tsarist-era officials and aeronautical patrons resorted to the rhetoric of "compensatory symbolism" in an effort to maintain their political legitimacy. They embellished actual accomplishments, exaggerating, and at times actively inventing, Russian achievements when, in fact, much less progress had been made. These tendencies resurfaced following the Bolsheviks' rise to power in 1917. In their efforts to foster public air-mindedness, Communist officials employed images and rhetoric derivative of those used by their Imperial predecessors. They, too, adopted compensatory symbolism as a strategy for maintaining legitimacy while relying on the West for technology and expertise. Likewise beholden to an iconic vision of flight, their understanding of the airplane and their goal of establishing a modern, air-minded nation did not differ substantially from those of their predecessors.

Still, the Soviet experience diverged from the Imperial in one critical respect. Under the influence of their Marxist ideology, Communist officials

---

[11] Scott W. Palmer, "Icarus, East: The Symbolic Contexts of Russian Flight," *Slavic and East European Journal* 49(1) (Spring 2005): 19–47.

[12] Kendall Bailes, *Technology and Society Under Lenin and Stalin: Origins of the Soviet Technical Intelligentsia, 1917–1941* (Princeton, NJ: Princeton University Press, 1978), 381–406.

imposed untold sacrifices on the country and its people in an effort to realize their modernist dreams. Unlike Imperial statesmen, they spared no expense, nor did they conserve any resources, in their totalizing campaign to transcend Russian backwardness. To be certain, they did achieve noteworthy successes in aviation, but these were sorely qualified by the injustices and inefficiencies of their authoritarian system. Ironically, while the advent of the command economy and the pursuit of crash industrialization during the 1930s made possible the rapid and impressive growth of Soviet aviation, they simultaneously institutionalized obsolescence, ensuring that the USSR would remain dependent on the acquisition of advanced technology from the more dynamic and productive West. Beholden to a static image of an industrialized utopia, but unable to make the present conform with their visions, Communist Party leaders pressed forward in an effort to engineer the future. The actions they undertook in regard to aviation revealed the inherent limitations of their modernizing agenda. They also demonstrated how the quest to create a "dictatorship of the air" ultimately abetted monumental tragedy.

Part I

Imperial Aviation, 1909–1917

From the Russian State Duma, 22 February 1910:

At a time when every country has flown by airplane and when private enterprise has taken part in [developing aviation] what have we done in Russia? Not a single one of our nation's people has flown, and yet police laws against the use of airplanes already exist and aviation is already under police surveillance. [Applause from the left]

– Vasilii Maklakov, Duma Deputy

Duma member Maklakov is indignant that no one in Russia has flown and yet laws governing aviation have already been established. What is so bad about that? We all understand that before we can allow people to fly, we must first teach the police to fly after them. [Applause from the right, laughter from all benches]

– Nikolai Mar'kov, Duma Deputy
(GARF f. 102 DPOO 1909, d. 310, ll. 241–242)

1

The Dawn of Russian Aviation

TSARS OF THE AIR IN THE LAND OF THE TSARS

On the morning of 25 July 1909, Louis Blériot piloted a twenty-four-and-a-half-horsepower Blériot XI monoplane across the English Channel from Baraques, France, toward the Shakespeare Cliff just west of Dover, England. The thirty-six-and-a-half-minute flight was not easy. Blériot's "heavier-than-air" craft was just barely so, and the wooden and canvas structure was continually buffeted by the strong air currents that swirled across the Channel. Wrestling to maintain control of his plane as it shuddered and swayed over the surface of the water, Blériot challenged his aircraft (and the force of gravity) in an attempt to bridge the narrow divide that separated England from the Continental mainland.

Blériot was not the first pilot to undertake this feat. Emboldened by a £1,000 prize offered by London's *Daily Mail*, numerous fliers had made public their intentions to become the first individual to achieve the Channel crossing. The most recent attempt had taken place six days earlier. It ended in near tragedy when an Antoinette IV flown by Englishman Hubert Latham experienced mechanical failure and plunged some 300 feet into the waters below. Miraculously, Latham survived with only minor injuries. Although he vowed to renew his efforts as soon as he could obtain a new aircraft, fate smiled on the Frenchman.

After crash-landing in a field not far from Dover Castle, Blériot was treated to a hero's welcome. Hastily assembled and well-attended receptions in London and then Paris celebrated the "miraculous flight" of the "aviator–genius" as both British and French public opinion succumbed to an air-minded delirium.[1] For weeks, French newspapers trumpeted Blériot's exploit as "a great French victory" and compared the "conqueror of the English Channel" to such cultural icons as Lavoisier, Pasteur, and Curie. Paris was "seized by a violent attack of Blériot fever." Captivated by "the most magnificent enterprise a century had ever seen," one daily proclaimed Blériot's

---

[1] For a complete account of the response to Blériot's flight see Robert Wohl, *A Passion for Wings: Aviation and the Western Imagination, 1908–1918* (New Haven, CT: Yale University Press, 1994), 57–66.

flight an expression of the "imperishable genius" of the French race. *The Times* of London was more reserved. While acknowledging the "merit" of the "plucky" Frenchman's flight, the paper observed that Blériot "had been, so to speak, shown the way by Latham." Without the example set by the English flier, the *Times* suggested, the French aeronaut would never have met with success. Even so, the glory belonged to Blériot.[2]

The feverish excitement that gripped England and France quickly spread to Russia. For weeks the St. Petersburg and Moscow press had paid only passing attention to the race for the Channel, but with word of Blériot's accomplishment the nation's newspapers rushed to cover the historic event. Reporters sent daily telegrams from London and Paris recounting details of the flight and the countless receptions held in honor of the aviator. As exhilarated newsmen proclaimed the triumph of the "Tsar of the Air," it became increasingly obvious that Blériot's flight had "opened a new chapter in the annals of human history."[3] No less so than the British or French, the Russian press acclaimed Blériot's achievement as an adventure of the ages.

The enthusiastic response to Blériot's exploit was only the most recent expression of the nation's long-standing curiosity with technologies of flight. As early as the reign of Catherine II (1762–96), Russian observers had looked with considerable interest at Western European aeronautical advances. While the brothers Étienne and Joseph Montgolfier entertained French crowds with demonstrations of their *machine aérostatique* during the summer and fall of 1783, tsarist officials stationed in Paris speculated on the political and commercial revolutions that might result once aerial travel became a practical reality. Inspired by the Montgolfiers' example and informed through lectures organized by visiting French and German scientists, Russian inventors undertook their own experiments, successfully launching a small unmanned hot-air balloon in St. Petersburg in November 1783. Although this first effort to duplicate European successes produced no new scientific advances, it testified to Russians' clear desire to participate in the emerging new field.[4]

Russian interest in things aeronautical was not confined to scientists and statesmen. In the years that followed the Montgolfiers' first ascent, thousands

[2] *Le Temps*, 26 July 1909; *The Times*, 27 July 1909; *L'Echo de Paris*, 29 July 1909; and *The Times*, 28 July 1909.

[3] *Peterburgskaia gazeta*, 14 July 1909, and *Sovremennoe slovo*, 15 July 1909. The most complete accounts of Blériot's flight can be found in the dailies *Novaia Rus'*, *Peterburgskaia gazeta*, *Rech'*, and *Sovremennoe slovo*, 16–22 July 1909.

[4] A. A. Rodnykh, *Istoriia vozdukhoplavaniia i letaniia v Rossii: letanie i vozdukhoplavanie v starinu* (St. Petersburg, 1911), 16, and P. D. Duz', *Istoriia vozdukhoplavaniia i aviatsii v Rossii* (Moscow: Mashinostroenie, 1979), 24. For a detailed account of Russians' interest in aeronautics during the late eighteenth century, see John T. Alexander, "Aeromania, 'Fire-Balloons,' and Catherine the Great's Ban of 1784," *The Historian* 58 (1996): 498–516.

turned out to witness the wonders of ballooning as touring exhibits were undertaken by Frenchmen Jean-Pierre Blanchard and Jacques Garnerin, who performed manned and unmanned launches in St. Petersburg and Moscow. Accompanying the arrival of the foreign aeronauts, publishers edified and entertained Russia's small reading public with treatises, poems, and stories dedicated to aeronautical themes. Although most of these were reproductions of recently published European texts, a few were original Russian compositions. Typical was the 1787 short story "Arrival of an Air-Balloon in Olympus," which recounted the collective effort of a group of aeronauts to ascend into the heavens by means of a balloon. Affronted by the humans' impudence, Jupiter prepares to strike them down with bolts of lighting only to be dissuaded by his daughter, the goddess Minerva. In the end, the aeronauts reach the heights of Mount Olympus, where they are feted by the gods and proclaimed the "new Argonauts." The convergence of public spectacle and popular fiction, together with the production of imported stage pieces like the German opera *Die Lufte-Bälle*, would lead one contemporary to conclude that, by 1805, aeronautics had become all the rage in the Imperial capital.[5]

As was true in the West, lighter-than-air travel was a recurrent (if not necessarily predominant) preoccupation of Russian scientists and state officials throughout the nineteenth century. Unfortunately, hampered by the nation's nonexistent industrial base and the inherent limitations of the technology itself, early Russian efforts to develop practical devices for commercial and military applications fell far short of their lofty goals.[6] By the 1860s, however, as advances in textile manufacturing and the production of hydrogen made aerostats more reliable and effective, Russian officials began to devote more attention to aeronautics. Intrigued by the appearance of tethered balloons during the American Civil War and the Franco–Prussian War, the Russian War Ministry established a series of commissions to explore the systematic use of lighter-than-air craft in battle. Within a generation these commissions had produced tangible results. In 1890 an Aeronautical Training Park was established in St. Petersburg, and manned balloons were used by the Imperial

---

[5] Notices and short summaries of public balloon demonstrations were published intermittently in the newspaper *Moskovskiia vedomosti* from October 1802 to May 1804. "Pribytie vozdushnago shara v Olimp," *Zerkalo sveta* 103 and 104 (1787): 819–23 and 819–37; and S. P. Zhikharev, *Zapiski sovremennika s 1805 po 1819 god* (St. Petersburg, 1859), 208.

[6] The most grandiose early project involving airships in Russia was the 1812 proposal of the German engineer Franz Leppich to construct an aerostat possessing a lift capacity of 12,000 pounds and a gondola capable of carrying up to forty people. Intended to deploy troops in the war against Napoleon, the aerostat, if completed, would have been by far the largest to appear up to that time. Despite the impossibility of constructing such a craft with existing technology, Leppich managed to secure Tsar Aleksandr I's support for his proposal. Following a series of spectacular failures (and amid rising expenditures), Leppich left the country, having spent more than 180,000 rubles from the state treasury. See Duz', *Istoriia*, 30–2.

armed forces to conduct aerial reconnaissance during the Russo–Japanese War (1904–5).[7]

The institutionalization of Russian aeronautics at the end of the nineteenth century meant that by the summer of 1909 residents of Russia's urban centers, like their Western European counterparts, were already familiar with the new language of flight. Still, the popular excitement generated by news of Blériot's exploit was unprecedented. As the nation's newspapers raced to keep track of the most recent developments, even casual readers in St. Petersburg or Moscow could not help but be informed of the changes taking place in the "century of speed." From regular features discussing the potential profits (and possible perils) associated with the art of flying to documentary reports on the latest technical innovations and fanciful essays on the future of flight, the nation's press devoted increasing coverage to the battles being waged for the "conquest of the air."[8] In response to the overwhelming demand for more information on the science of aviation, one major daily inaugurated a weekly column titled "Aeronautical Mail-Pouch" in which a resident aviation expert answered questions sent in by curious readers.[9] For months queries poured in from all over the Empire, requesting definitions of general terminology, explanations of specific technical problems, and clarifications concerning current world aeronautical records. The paper even received an appeal from a peasant of Novgorod province, who wrote to request technical assistance for the flying machine that he was constructing. Unfortunately, the imprecise and muddled descriptions sent in by the half-literate peasant prevented the paper's specialist from providing the finishing formulae for what might otherwise have been a native Russian airplane.[10]

The outbreak of Russia's air-minded delirium was not confined to the reading public. Vacationing in southwestern France at the time of the Channel crossing, Grand Duke Aleksandr Mikhailovich hailed the flight as an "epochal event." After telegraphing congratulations to Blériot, he sent a hastily written letter to the editors of leading Russian newspapers requesting their support in establishing a public subscription for the construction of a national air fleet.[11] Convinced that the airplane was the weapon of the future, the grand duke would labor unceasingly for this new-found cause. Ultimately, he became the central patron of Imperial aviation. Similarly, one newly appointed member of the War Ministry, General Bren, proclaimed his own optimistic faith that aviation would quickly develop into a useful

---

[7] Duz', *op cit.*

[8] See, for example, the articles titled "Peterburg cherez 50 let," *Peterburgskaia gazeta*, 16 July 1909, and "Chto dast nam pobeda nad vozdukhom," *Moskovskiia vedomosti*, 18 July 1909, among many others.

[9] See *Novaia Rus'* beginning 26 July 1909.

[10] *Novaia Rus'*, 2 August 1909.

[11] Velikii kniaz' Aleksandr Mikhailovich, *Kniga vospominanii* (Paris, 1934), Vol. 2, 233.

military resource. Interviewed shortly after the flight, Bren announced his certain belief that the airplane represented the future. Much more so than the dirigible, he noted, "the airplane promises possible service to the army as it is less vulnerable, faster, and less expensive to build." As testament to his faith in the latest technology, the minister concluded his commentary with assurances that "once they are produced in sufficient numbers, [our] army will be well equipped with airplanes. I am a man of progress."[12]

The progressive faith in the promise of flight revealed in the responses of the grand duke and the minister was not shared by every member of the Imperial state service. Less than a week after Blériot's flight, the Russian secret police [*Okhrana*] took decisive steps to forestall the introduction of flying machines into the land of the tsars. "With the goal of hindering criminal elements from accomplishing their projects with the aid of aeronautical devices," the Department of Police instructed the nation's border guards "to maintain strict surveillance in preventing the importation of aeronautical machines and their parts across the frontiers of the Russian Empire."[13] Fearful that airplanes might be employed by revolutionaries to wage a campaign of terror against the state and its representatives, the *Okhrana* established a "Special Commission on the Means of Battling the Possible Implementation of Criminal Designs With the Assistance of Aeronautical Machines."[14] The Commission convened a series of meetings during the late summer of 1909 to familiarize members of the Interior and the War Ministries with recent advances in aeronautical technology and to design a comprehensive policy for thwarting airborne crimes. Although the ban on the importation of airplanes to Russia was later overturned by the Ministry of Finance, the police did succeed in establishing a series of covert measures designed to restrict and control the Russian public's access to aeronautical technology. Among the more notable policies adopted by the state were instructions requiring all aeronautical clubs to register with police authorities in order that their members and airships might be more easily tracked. In addition, broad directives were issued to local gendarmes instructing them to "strictly monitor all flights as well as aviators and those attempting to learn to fly" within their jurisdictions. Similar commands were sent to the tsar's foreign agents, who were ordered to compile dossiers on the activities of European air clubs, especially those believed to possess ties to revolutionary organizations in

---

[12] *Novaia Rus'*, 17 July 1909.

[13] GARF f. 102 DPOO 1909, d. 310, l. 4-a.

[14] *Ibid.*, l. 19. Unknown to state officials, radicals affiliated with the terrorist wing of the Socialist Revolutionary Party had already begun drafting plans to employ an airplane in an attack on the Winter Palace. Although the terrorists' plot did not materialize, it was a prophetic indication of how airplanes would be put to use at the dawn of the twenty-first century. See K. N. Morozov, *Partiia sotsialistov-revoliutsionerov v 1907–1914 gg.* (Moscow: ROSSPEN, 1998), 376.

Russia.[15] The state's determination to impose control over private aviation was made further evident in late July 1909, when the secret police banned a newspaper advertisement that promised to deliver Blériot monoplanes ("the same plane that flew the Channel") for 5,000 rubles each to Petersburg purchasers.[16]

The contrasting responses of these individual observers to Blériot's flight were indicative of the contradictions and conflicts that beset Russian society at the dawn of the twentieth century. Overwhelmingly rural, authoritarian, and impoverished, Imperial Russia was uniquely ill-equipped to meet the challenges of the aeronautical age. The least industrialized and most illiterate of the major European powers, autocratic Russia had long been noted for its frustrating inability to overcome its history of backwardness. To many contemporaries, Imperial Russia seemed an unlikely place for the realization of a technological revolution. And yet, by the second decade of the twentieth century, technical heralds of the modern age were appearing with increasing frequency throughout the nation. Visible manifestations of dawning modernity, telephones and telegraphs, moving pictures, and electric lights added the charm of novelty and new-fangled convenience to daily life, providing Russian citizens with the same urban amenities enjoyed in the West and confirming a long-held faith in Russia's European status. Far more than these domestic technologies, however, the airplane portended a radical change in the way Russians viewed themselves and their world. In facilitating the age-old dream of human flight, the airplane opened new vistas of opportunity and created new possibilities for the unfettered imagination. Unlike the windswept balloons of the nineteenth century, the airplane conferred control over nature. In conquering channels, traversing mountains, bridging continents, and eclipsing geography, aviation technology collapsed temporal distinctions and enveloped space. It provided, or so it seemed, the means for rapidly transcending the distance that had too long prevented vast, eternal Russia from breaking with its "accursed past." At the same time, the airplane intimated the potential for refashioning customary notions of power, authority, and freedom. Inasmuch as it provided physical liberation from earthly bonds, so too might its development facilitate political liberation from autocracy by encouraging civic initiative and fostering independence on the part of its individual participants.

In this regard, the press's and public's eager embrace of Blériot's success testified to their western perspective, their faith in progress, and their desire to identify with and be defined by the cultural and scientific achievements

---

[15] GARF f. 102 DPOO 1909, d. 310, l. 80-b. For materials relating to the *Okhrana*'s surveillance of individual pilots, see GARF f. 102 DPOO 1910, d. 71 (Delo po nabliudeniiu za letatel'nami apparatami) and f. 102 DPOO 1911, d. 71.

[16] GARF f. 102 DPOO 1909, d. 310, l. 37. The advertisement appeared in *Novoe vremia*, 17 July 1909.

of Europe. Anxious to contribute to the advance of European culture in the years that followed the Channel crossing, the Russian public appropriated the airplane as defining proof of their modern heritage. Seizing on flight as a symbolic and material expression of Russia's greatness, the nation's air-minded citizenry endeavored to use aviation to demonstrate their cultural, intellectual, and technical vitality by fostering the growth of new civic institutions dedicated to the airplane and its private patrons.

In sharp contrast to the public's embrace of the airplane, the response of the Imperial secret police was de facto acknowledgment of the dangers posed by European dynamism to the antiquated tsarist system. Concerned lest this most recent product of European creativity provide new means for those challenging the autocracy's political supremacy, the state's gendarmes attempted to forestall the future, retreating inward to escape the dangers posed by western progress. Much like the ardent patriots who would later attempt to rewrite history by inventing examples of Russian greatness, these members of the state service sought escape from reality to protect their own visions of the nation they defended.

The grand duke and the military minister, for their parts, expressed the distant, though not inconceivable, hope that the autocracy might yet prove capable of harnessing Europe's most recent advances to strengthen its hand against enemies at home and abroad. In co-opting the technological fruits of European culture, they envisioned a resurgent state that would reaffirm its moral and political legitimacy by demonstrating mastery over the forces of the present. Combining the progressive optimism of the nation's public with the defensive self-interest of the nation's gendarmes, these state officials hoped to overcome Russia's legacy of backwardness by borrowing from abroad while building at home – a strategy not unprecedented in the long history of their nation.

As a common concern of government officials and private citizens alike, aviation quickly came to occupy a prominent position in the cultural landscape of late Imperial Russia. Aware of the new technology's importance to the prosperity and security of the nation and anxious that Russia not fall farther behind the rapidly developing West, representatives of Imperial state and society endowed the airplane with iconic significance, viewing it as both a metaphor and an agent of Russian modernization. However, as the contrasting views of these contemporary observers reveal, despite a shared recognition of aviation's symbolic significance and its function in facilitating the transition to modernity, the airplane would remain a contested symbol reflecting the disparate hopes held by differing social estates concerning Russia's present, future, and past. An examination of the interplay between state official and private citizens concerning the meaning and direction of aeronautical development at the dawn of flight provides unique insights into late Imperial society and culture. More important, from the standpoint of this study, it serves as a convenient window for exploring early Russian attitudes toward the airplane as well as the cultural, social, and institutional factors that shaped Russian efforts to transform erstwhile flights of fancy into the modern realities of an air-minded nation.

RUSSIA'S PASSION FOR WINGS

The heady excitement generated by word of Blériot's flight was transformed into tangible reality for Russian citizens in the fall of 1909. Eager to display the capabilities of their airplanes in the months that followed the Channel crossing, French aviators undertook public demonstrations across the European continent. Less than eight weeks after French spectators flocked to bid farewell to Blériot, Russian audiences gathered to greet the arrival of western pilots and their flying machines. On 15 September 1909, the inhabitants of Moscow saw for themselves the miracle of heavier-than-air flight as French aviator Georges Legagneux organized a public display of his Voisin biplane. Thousands of curious Muscovites flocked to Khodynka field just outside the city to witness this first-ever flight of an airplane in Russia. Although none of the five flights made by Legagneux on the 15th lasted more than a few minutes, his demonstration was a great success. He repeated his performance with an encore presentation on the 19th.[17] Subsequent demonstrations in St. Petersburg and Odessa attracted even greater numbers of spectators and generated further excitement.[18]

While French fliers entertained Russian audiences with feats of aerial daring, the Russian Ministry of War moved to establish a national aviation program. On returning from France, Grand Duke Aleksandr Mikhailovich assumed a leading role in mobilizing support for Russian aviation. As honorary chairman of the state's Special Committee for the Strengthening of the Military Fleet by Means of Voluntary Subscriptions, the grand duke had been instrumental in raising donations to rebuild the nation's navy following the disastrous losses of the Russo–Japanese War (1904–5). Hoping to capitalize on the work of the existing Committee, the grand duke petitioned Tsar Nicholas II for permission to transfer funds from the Naval Committee to a newly formed Special Committee for the Establishment of the Air-Fleet. He also requested that the tsar approve the circulation of a series of decrees intended to mobilize support for aviation construction. Overcoming the skepticism of some members of the Russian military hierarchy, the grand duke secured the tsar's approval. On 6 February 1910, Nicholas announced that 900,000 rubles of the Naval Committee's treasury be used for the development of a military air wing. The tsar subsequently

---

[17] For press coverage of Legagneux's flights, see "Polety aviatora Legan'e v Moskve," *Niva* 40 (1909): 696; *Gazeta kopeika*, 16 September 1909; *Novaia Rus'*, 16 September 1909; and *Novoe vremia*, 16 September 1909, among others.

[18] *Gazeta kopeika*, 12 October 1909.

FIGURE 2. In the second public flight of an airplane in Russia, French aviator Albert Guillaud pilots a Blériot XI monoplane at the Kolomianskoe aerodrome in St. Petersburg, November 1909.

proclaimed the inauguration of a nationwide voluntary subscription to support the Committee's goals of training military officers to fly airplanes and establishing a reserve of fully equipped aircraft for military use. In March, following the proclamation of the voluntary subscription, the Committee for the Establishment of the Air-Fleet sent six military officers to France, where two each enrolled in the pilot schools run by Henri Farman, Louis Blériot, and the Antoinette Company. Six enlisted men, who were to be trained as airplane mechanics, accompanied the officers.[19]

In addition to preparing cadres to serve in the future air corps, the Committee moved to secure necessary equipment and infrastructure. Concomitant with the decision to send officers abroad for training, the Committee placed orders with leading French airplane manufacturers for the delivery of eleven airplanes by June 1910. The Committee also established training facilities in Russia. At Gatchina, southwest of St. Petersburg, hangars were constructed to house the military's aircraft. A flight school, to be run by the French-trained Russian officers, was also established on the grounds. Unfortunately, the site proved to be a poor location. Owing to harsh winters and the region's swampy soil, training flights were limited to the summer months. As a result, having already invested a considerable sum of money

---

[19] Velikii kniaz' Aleksandr Mikhailovich, *Kniga*, 2, 237 and RGVIA f. 2000, op. 7, d. 59 (Otchet o deiatel'nosti osobogo komiteta po usiliu vozdushnogo flota), ll. 78–9.

to construct the Gatchina facilities, the Committee was compelled to find a new site capable of sustaining year-round training. A more temperate location in the Crimean city of Sevastopol' was chosen, and, following a delay in the arrival of the airplanes ordered from France, training began there in November 1910.[20]

The activity of the nation's military authorities was paralleled by that of private Russians who enlisted in the battle for the skies through participation in the ever-increasing number of aeronautical clubs, circles, and societies that blossomed in the wake of the Channel crossing. By the end of 1909, such major cities as St. Petersburg, Moscow, Odessa, and Kiev boasted their own private aeronautical organizations. Similar to automobile societies, literacy circles, and other voluntary associations, air clubs provided private enthusiasts with a forum for pursuing a common interest while facilitating the public assembly of civic-minded citizens.[21] In addition, organizations like the Moscow Society of Aeronautics and the Odessa Aero-Club produced regular journals for the nation's reading public, and, as interest increased and resources grew, they established flight schools of their own, turning the possibility of flight into a daily reality for those wealthy enough to afford the expensive training. Through generating interest in aviation and training private citizens to master mechanical flight, aeronautical clubs hoped to create a consumer demand for airplanes, thereby subsidizing the growth of the few Russian factories that could reproduce the Farman and Blériot models popular in Europe. By the fall of 1910, Russia possessed three factories capable of manufacturing airplane chassis and one enterprise equipped to build aircraft motors.[22]

Russians' passion for flight intensified during the early spring of 1910 as newspapers reported on an initial landmark in the nation's infant aviation program: the first exhibition of an airplane in Russia piloted by a native Russian. Undertaken in the Black Sea port of Odessa on 8 March before a select crowd of citizens and military representatives, Mikhail Efimov's aeronautical display aboard a Farman IV biplane was heralded as a transcendent event by the capital's journalists. Although the longest of his five demonstration flights lasted only twenty minutes, the courageous Russian aviator was credited with having "already surpassed the skill of his instructor," the pioneering French aviator and airplane designer Henri Farman.[23] According to

---

[20] RGVIA f. 2000, op. 7, d. 59. ll. 78–9.

[21] Joseph Bradley, "Voluntary Associations, Civic Culture, and *Obshchestvennost'* in Moscow," in Edith Clowes, Samuel Kassow, and James L. West (eds.), *Between Tsar and People: Educated Society and the Quest for Public Identity in Late Imperial Russia* (Princeton, NJ: Princeton University Press, 1991), 131–48.

[22] The factories were the "First Russian Association of Aeronautics" (St. Petersburg), the "Russo–Balt Carriage Factory" (St. Petersburg), the company "Aviata" (Warsaw), and the "Motor" factory (Riga). See *Vozdushnyi put'* 2 (1910): 40.

[23] *Russkoe slovo*, 9 March 1910.

FIGURE 3. Russian aviators Mikhail Efimov (*left*) and Lev Matsievich (*right*) in 1910.

one delirious reporter, Efimov's accomplishment had proven beyond doubt that "Russia was now poised to assume the world's lead in the subjugation of the heavens."[24] Like fellow countrymen Sergei Utochkin, Nikolai Popov, and the circus strongman-turned-pilot Ivan Zaikin, Efimov was a prominent early member of the emerging ranks of "sportsmen–aviators" who had honed their skills in French aviation schools before setting out to earn a living as flight instructors or participants in the Continent's burgeoning aerial shows and competitions.[25] A former locksmith and telegrapher, Efimov had borrowed money to finance flight training in Paris. Earlier in the year he had scored a spectacular coup when he set a new world record for altitude on a flight with a passenger. In keeping with all early aviation records, Efimov's mark was rapidly eclipsed. Still, it earned him considerable fame at home as an exemplar of Russian bravado and skill in the new art of flying.

[24] *Gazeta kopieka*, 10 March 1910.
[25] For an evocative, though inconsistent, account of Imperial Russia's sportsmen–aviators, see James Dimitroff, "The Confluence of Aviation and Russian Futurism, 1909–1914" (Ph.D. dissertation, University of Southern California, 1998), 77–124.

Popular excitement over Russia's very own aviator–heroes and the airplane in general was quickly manifested in the everyday customs and habits of the Empire's citizens. A reflection of producers' new efforts to market modernity to the growing ranks of the Russian middle class, "Blériot" cigarettes, "Aero-club" matches, "Aviator" candies, and "Aeronautics" chocolates appeared as brand names offered for sale to air-minded consumers.[26] Hoping to inspire interest in the development of aeronautics among Russia's far-flung inhabitants, the journal *Vestnik vozdukhoplavaniia* [*Herald of Aeronautics*] and the First Russian Association of Aeronautics jointly sponsored a mobile exposition that embarked on a fourteen-month, fifty-city tour of European and Asian Russia. Journeying as far as the Far Eastern port city of Vladivostok to "broaden provincial awareness of the successes of aeronautics," the exposition brought aviation to the nation's hinterlands. Meanwhile, in Russia's urban centers, cultured residents demonstrated their own fascination with the airplane by hosting fashionable "aeronautical balls" (complete with floating dirigibles and plane-shaped confetti) for air-conscious party goers. Others satiated their curiosity by flocking to the nation's new cinema halls. Featuring documentaries filmed from the air as well as fictional reels bearing such titles as *Experiments of the Aviator-Genius* and *Air Pirates*, cinema helped ensure the rapid dissemination of the airplane's image to audiences throughout the Empire.[27] By 1910 aviation had taken so rapid and complete a hold on the public's imagination that one leading journal could claim "interest in the question of aviation has spread like fire throughout the whole [of Russia] and throughout all classes of society . . . it has become fashionable and, as such, knowledge of [aviation] is now essential to every person who would consider himself to be a 'middling intelligent' [*srednii intelligent*]."[28] To meet the growing demand of the "aeronautical intelligentsia," leading publishers produced countless histories and studies of flight, while major newspapers sponsored special brochures and supplements devoted to aeronautics.[29] Aviation had become so popular that "the windows of almost every bookstore were peppered with the most enticing titles and covers and new books on flight appeared every week. . . ."[30]

---

[26] For reference to these products see "Aeroklub," *Smena* 3 (1934): 8–9.

[27] *Vestnik vozdukhoplavaniia* 11 (1910): 3–4; "Aero-bal," *Tiazhelee vozdukha* 8 (1911): 11–12; and *Sine-fono*, 1 December 1909 and 15 March 1911.

[28] *Aero i avtomobil'naia zhizn'* 1 (1910): 4.

[29] Among a few of the original Russian titles on aviation and aeronautics produced in the two years following Blériot's flight were N. Borozdin, *Zavoevanie vozdushnoi stikhi* (Warsaw, 1909); M. L. Frank, *Istoriia vozdukhoplavaniia i ego sovremennoe sostoianie* (St. Petersburg, 1910); Rodnykh, *Istoriia*; L. Ruzer, *Vozdukhoplavanie: ego istoriia, uspekhi i budushchee* (St. Petersburg, 1910); K. E. Veigelin, *Zavoevanie vozdushnogo okeana: istoriia i sovremennoe sostoianie vozdukhoplavaniia* (St. Petersburg, 1911); Stamat'ev, *Vozdukhoplavanie* (Odessa, 1910); and D. Dubenskii (ed.), *Vozdukhoplavanie* (St. Petersburg, 1911). The last two sources were published, respectively, by the journal *Rodina* and the newspaper *Russkoe chtenie*.

[30] *Aero i avtomobil'naia zhizn'* 4 (1910): 5. The ellipses appear in the original.

To all appearances the Russian public's embrace of all things aeronautical differed very little from the airplane-induced delirium simultaneously sweeping Europe and the United States. In London, Paris, Berlin, and New York (as well as backwaters like Milan, Vienna, and Los Angeles), citizens of all western nations and from all walks of life greeted the arrival of machine-powered flight with an enthusiasm bordering on religious fervor. Transfixed by the spectacle of twentieth-century technology, Europeans flocked to airfields and air shows in the tens of thousands to marvel at the mechanical magic effected by flying machines. They reveled in the modern aesthetic of the airplane's image that quickly came to prominence in newspapers, paintings, newsreels, and postcards. They celebrated as their own the accomplishments of their nation's flying heroes. And, soon, they came to envy the success of foreigners who outperformed native favorite sons.

In spite of the latent competition among such long-standing rivals as France, Germany, and Great Britain, citizens of these European states communicated their mutual passion for wings through a shared language rooted in the symbols and traditions of western civilization. The existence of this common air-minded culture has been ably portrayed by Robert Wohl, who describes the airplane as an exemplar of the West's dynamism and idealism, a unique and influential instrument in reflecting "the human psyche and the sensibility of the twentieth-century West."[31] As we have seen, the airplane engendered among Russians kindred responses. Similar to their western neighbors, Russian citizens embraced the airplane as a portent of modernity and national might. They, too, excitedly followed the new sport of flying while consuming the products of the aeronautical age with the same zeal as that evinced by the French and British. Such sentiments notwithstanding, Russians' initial enthusiasm with flight obscured underlying social and cultural differences that would profoundly affect the nation's response to the airplane as efforts began in earnest to match western aeronautical success. Dependent on a hierarchical autocratic system, hampered by a legacy of economic and industrial backwardness, and influenced by cultural traditions that eschewed entrepreneurship and personal profit, Russia's drive to emerge as a preeminent aeronautical power would assume its own character and adopt its own forms. These would be revealed in the first decade of the airplane age and the last of the Imperial order.

PUBLIC AIR-MINDEDNESS AND NATIONAL IDENTITY IN LATE IMPERIAL RUSSIA

Of the airplane's many material manifestations in the Russian Empire, none was more indicative of the public's growing interest than the proliferation of private voluntary associations dedicated to aviation. By the middle of

---

[31] Wohl, *Passion for Wings*, 3.

1910, the most prominent of these was the Imperial All-Russian Aero-Club [*Imperatorskii Vserossiiskii Aero-Klub*, or IVAK]. A native version of the highly effective Aéro-Club de France, IVAK had been established in St. Petersburg in 1907.[32] Expected to serve as the leading private promoter of Russian aviation, it quickly came to be dominated by the Russian capital's social elite. Within two years of its founding, the organization counted among its roster members of the Imperial family, high-ranking state officials, leading nobles, military officers, and wealthy merchants as well as opera singers, ballerinas, actors, and numerous other celebrities.[33] By the end of 1910, the less esteemed (though decidedly more professional and technically proficient) Moscow Society of Aeronautics and Odessa Aero-Club, as well as scores of small provincial organizations, had joined IVAK as established aviation associations.

In addition to publishing journals and raising donations for airplane construction, aeronautical clubs worked to increase the public's contact with aviation by sponsoring expositions, exhibitions, lectures, and flights. Modeled after similar events made popular in Western Europe, these spectacles showcased the new technology in the hope of both educating spectators and instilling in them a passion for flight. Typical of such undertakings was Russia's first major aeronautical event, the St. Petersburg "Aviation Week." Sponsored by IVAK, the "First International Week of Aviation" (like the German programs after which it was patterned) was intended to develop public support for the cause of aeronautics by demonstrating the capabilities of the nation's aeronauts. Before the festival's opening on 15 April 1910, Russians' personal encounters with aviation had retained a distinctly foreign air, consisting largely of the demonstration flights undertaken by visiting French and English pilots. The International Aviation Week changed that. Opening less than one month after Mikhail Efimov's triumphal flight in Odessa and running concurrently with the public exhibit of the first airplane constructed in Russia, the St. Petersburg Aviation Week offered the nation's citizens initial proof of their countrymen's ability to master the heavens.[34] Accompanying the five foreign fliers who took part in the spectacle,

---

[32] The Aero-Club received official sanction in the spring of 1909 when Tsar Nicholas II granted its members the honor of affixing "Imperial" to the club's title. See *Imperatorskii Vserossiiskii Aero-Klub. Zhurnal.* 16 zasedaniia soveta IVAK, 3 April 1909.

[33] Although no statistical analysis of air-club membership in Imperial Russia has yet been undertaken, a cursory survey of IVAK's roster makes clear that the organization was dominated by state dignitaries and the well-to-do. The club included several members of the Imperial household as well as such state luminaries as P. A. Stolypin, S. Iu. Witte, P. N. Trubetskoi, and more than two dozen members of the State Duma. The Aero-Club's membership rolls were regularly published between 1908 and 1914 in an addendum to the club's journal *Vozdukhoplavatel'*, titled *Imperatorskii Vserossiiskii Aero-Klub Zhurnal.*

[34] For newspaper coverage of Efimov's first flight, see *Gazeta kopeika, Sankt Peterburgskiia vedomosti,* and *Novoe vremia,* 23–26 March 1910, among others. The first serviceable

Nikolai Popov thrilled St. Petersburg spectators with a series of flights in the first performance by a Russian aviator open to the general public. By any measure, the International Aviation Week achieved its goals of captivating Russians' interest and increasing excitement in the cause of aeronautics. During its course the Aviation Week (which, in response to public interest, actually ran for some two-and-a-half weeks) attracted no fewer than 160,000 spectators.[35]

Hoping to capitalize on the enthusiasm generated by the First International Week of Aviation, IVAK scheduled a second public event for the fall of the year. Held at the recently completed Komendantskoe Aerodrome in St. Petersburg, the first "All-Russian Festival of Aeronautics" was intended to strengthen public interest in aviation by highlighting recent Russian achievements in the field. In addition to lectures, exhibits, and displays similar to those presented during the International Aviation Week, the All-Russian Festival of Aeronautics offered spectators a first-hand glimpse of the future in the form of airplane and balloon rides. Adding to the excitement, the three-week festival featured daily demonstration flights in which aviators competed for cash prizes in categories such as flight duration, altitude, and accuracy of landing. Participating alongside familiar "sportsmen–aviators," including Mikhail Efimov and Sergei Utochkin, the nation's handful of military aviators (newly trained and recently returned from France) gave compelling evidence of the state's efforts to establish a Russian air fleet. In total, thirteen fliers competed for prize money that exceeded 20,000 rubles. The most prominent manifestation of Russian air-mindedness to date, the All-Russian Festival of Aeronautics was an early demonstration of the nation's ability to master new flight technology.[36]

Despite the early autumn's inclement weather, which restricted all flights on eight separate occasions and weekday activities that required many spectators to skip work, the Aeronautical Festival attracted an audience in excess of 140,000. Day after day, crowds flocked to the aerodrome to witness "the greatest miracle of the twentieth century."[37] For those fortunate (and

airplane constructed in Russia was dubbed the Rossiia-A. Assembled by the First Russian Association of Aeronautics, the plane was modeled after the French Farman III biplane and was equipped with a fifty-horsepower Gnome motor imported from the West. See V. B. Shavrov, *Istoriia konstruktsii samoletov v SSSR do 1938 g.* (Moscow, 1986), 57–9.

[35] For extensive coverage of the Aviation Week see *Russkoe slovo*, 16 April–2 May 1910. Popov's flights were quickly followed by a series of well-publicized demonstrations in Moscow by the aviator Sergei Utochkin. The attendance figures are reported in V. E. Sankov, *U istokov aviatsii* (Moscow, 1976), 84.

[36] The festival ran from 8 September to 1 October 1910. Owing to the event's popularity, unofficial demonstrations continued at the airfield until 5 October. For a complete account of the festival and its related activities, see N. A. Rynin, *Vserossiiskii prazdnik vozdukhoplavaniia* (St. Petersburg, 1910).

[37] *Novoe vremia*, 8 October 1910 and *Niva* 39 (1910): 681.

wealthy) enough to purchase a ride in an airplane, the experience provided lifelong memories and helped to convince them of aviation's vital role in serving the nation. For one such individual, the Chairman of the Council of Ministers, Peter Stolypin, an airplane ride with Captain Lev Matsievich proved the decisive factor in winning his unconditional support for the air fleet. "Prior to today," the prime minister was quoted as saying, "I only believed in the technical possibility of flight. Now I am convinced of its practicality. And I predict that [Russian aviation] will enjoy a great future."[38]

Although dignitaries and state officials played an important part in lending the festival a proper decorum, the overwhelming majority of observers came from the city's lower and middle classes. This fact was not lost on the director of the aeronautical society "Wings." Lamenting the absence of St. Petersburg's well-to-do in attendance at the aerodrome, the director noted that, by and large, individuals who could not lend material support to the aeronautical cause were those who frequented the festival. If Russia was to match the success of the leading European states, he continued, the more economically advantaged members of society as well as the government would have to contribute their active, financial support.[39] A closer examination of the festival's ticket sales bears out the director's commentary. Of the approximately 140,000 tickets sold during the course of the festival, the vast majority (104,000) were purchased by those of more modest means.[40]

In addition to appealing to the capital's citizenry, aviation captured the imagination of the St. Petersburg underworld. While being escorted to jail on the night of 6 October 1910 for questioning in relation to a murder investigation, an unidentified subject suddenly stopped near the Aleksandrov Bridge, looked skyward, and began shouting, "He's flying! He's flying!" As his police escort looked to the heavens to view the spectacle, the suspect pushed him to the ground and escaped into the fog. That same evening, in a different part of the city, Vasilii Mel'nikov and Ivan Maksimov were taken into custody for their part in the burglary of a perfumery. On the road to the police station, Mel'nikov "started acting crazy." Once jailed, his mental condition became more acute. Identifying himself as the aviator Matsievich, Mel'nikov began banging his head against his cell wall and demanded to be released, in

---

[38] *Rech'*, 23 September 1910.

[39] *Novoe vremia*, 8 October 1910.

[40] Tickets were divided into four pricing categories: five rubles, three rubles, one ruble, and twenty kopecks. The most expensive permitted one access to the airfield's main grandstand and accorded one, obviously, the best view of the events. The twenty-kopeck tickets provided access to the "commons area" that surrounded the field. Although space permitted the sponsors to sell far more cheap tickets (which may, in part, explain the increased volume), daily reports indicate that these areas were far more consistently filled with spectators than the more expensive sections. The most extensive coverage of the festival appears in *Gazeta kopeika*, from 8 September to 4 October 1910.

order that he could fly his airplane.[41] Although most criminals, presumably, did not look to aviation as a means of escaping state justice, such incidents testify to the widespread appeal of aeronautics among Russia's many social and economic estates. Far from a foppish sport restricted to an isolated and privileged minority, aviation belonged to the popular imagination.

The prevalent public concern for aeronautics revealed in these anecdotal accounts was confirmed following a tragedy at the Aeronautical Festival. On the afternoon of 24 September the young naval captain and newly trained pilot Lev Matsievich was killed while attempting to establish a Russian altitude record. In the wake of the accident, the nation's newspapers and journals were filled with stories dedicated to Matsievich's memory and the meaning of his death. Meanwhile, scores of Russians, from statesmen to factory workers, sent personal letters to popular publications testifying to the ways in which the pilot's death had touched their lives. Through his participation in the All-Russian Festival of Aeronautics, the young pilot had earned the respect and admiration of the nation's public. And, in honor of the fallen flier, tens of thousands of St. Petersburg residents took to the streets on the day of his funeral, to pay their respects to an individual whose activity they viewed as truly heroic. In the weeks that followed, articles and editorials appeared hailing Russia's aviators as the nation's best and brightest, the Empire's greatest assets in asserting its collective might and power. Particular reverence was reserved for Matsievich. As the nation's first airplane casualty, the young pilot was lionized as a "hero" and "martyr," a fighter in the tradition of the folkloric Russian *bogatyr'* [warrior].

Typical of the hagiography that materialized around Matsievich's memory was an editorial titled "To the Sun! . . ." written by Ol'ga Gridina, a staff writer for one of the Russian capital's most popular newspapers. Testifying to the personal loss that she felt on reading of Matsievich's misfortune, Gridina's essay endowed the flier's death with national and historic significance. Contrasting the young pilot's selfless simplicity to the "contemporary age of egoism and greed," Gridina praised Matsievich for giving new sustenance to Russia's depleted pride. Unlike the typical state servant who "risked nothing writing his daily proclamations," Matsievich's service required that he constantly "flirt with a ravenous death." Yet, "in sacrificing everything to conquer the elements," Matsievich had helped to "strengthen the fatherland" by advancing the aviation program. For this contribution, Gridina argued, Matsievich's name should not be allowed to pass from memory, and she took up a call, repeated in all of the nation's major publications, that a fund be established to construct a memorial for the dead pilot. In an emotional appeal to the Russian people, Gridina proclaimed the nation's moral obligation to honor its fallen hero. She urged that a monument be established,

---

[41] Both incidents are reported in *Gazeta kopeika*, 8 October 1910.

FIGURE 4. The public funeral of Lev Matsievich in St. Petersburg, 28 September 1910.

not on the "accursed spot" of Matsievich's crash (as one newspaper had suggested), but on "one of the liveliest sites in the nation's capital" as such a location would provide a "constant and distinct" reminder to Russians of the "sacrifice made by one of their own for the greater good of all."[42]

Gridina's hagiographic treatment of Matsievich and her attempt to win popular participation in the construction of a monument to the pilot were typical responses to the aviator's death. Similar appeals appeared in all of the nation's leading newspapers and journals. Likewise, all accorded the fallen pilot a degree of honor and respect usually reserved for the most august personages. A lengthy article published in the weekly journal *Niva* echoed these sentiments. Acknowledging Matsievich's activity as "an attempt to ennoble and advance the decrepit and impoverished forces of man and to grant humanity new, powerful resources for victory over nature," *Niva* celebrated the heroism and courage of the Russian pilot and pointed to his selfless interest in advancing aviation as a model to be emulated by others.[43] More than a simple aviator fulfilling his duty to the state, Matsievich was one of his country's "conquerors of the air," esteemed as a modern Prometheus whose suprahuman abilities were helping humanity to triumph over nature.

Indeed, of the numerous themes that emerged in contemporary literature following Matsievich's death, the aviator's role as a victor over nature was one of the most compelling. Some two-and-a-half decades before the

[42] Ol'ga Gridina, "K solntsu!...," *Gazeta kopeika*, 26 September 1910.
[43] *Niva* 41 (1910): 714

Soviet press would hail the victories of the nation's fliers over the harsh polar environment, Imperial observers looked to aviation as proof of humanity's inevitable triumph over the forces of the natural world. Although Matsievich's flight had demonstrated the frailty of the aeronautical enterprise, articles, essays, and poems celebrated the vital role of the pilot in helping to tame the chaotic elements [*stikhiia*]. One short story, written in the form of a peasant fairly tale [*skazka*], described the efforts of "Tsar-Air" and his offspring "Clouds," "Wind," and "Storm" to thwart an aviator's unwelcome intrusion into their aerial kingdom. After successfully defending their heavenly abode by casting down a lone pilot (Matsievich), the forces of nature "humbly succumb" to the flock of aviators that follow in his wake.[44] The subject of *stikhiia* frequently appeared in articles published after Matsievich's accident. Whereas one editorial warned that it was still too early for Russians to "lose respect for nature," another expressed happiness at the reality of the airplane's conquest over the "heretofore unconquerable elements," while yet another marveled at the ability of Russia's aviators to master the natural world.[45] In each instance *stikhiia*, elemental and chaotic, was the object of the authors' reflections.

For contemporary observers, this close association of aviation with mastery over the elements suggested the possibility of Russia's corresponding mastery over the forces of history and the present. For, if the airplane could grant the nation the keys to fulfilling the dream of centuries, might it not also assist the country in overcoming the obstacles to its own modernization? In contemplating the potential benefits that aviation might provide the nation, several observers contrasted the modern realities of aeronautical technology with the "barbarism" [*nekul'turnost'*] and "savagery" [*dikost'*] of their native Russia. Reporting on an unsuccessful balloon flight, scheduled to traverse the region between St. Petersburg and the Azov Sea during early October 1910, one newspaper proclaimed the undeniable importance of the attempt for taking place "over the most uncivilized and picturesque portion of the Russian land [inhabited by] dark and ignorant people."[46] Delighting in the cultural superiority accrued by flight, several publications printed the story of an encounter that took place between the "dark masses" and the passengers of the balloon. Terrified at the sight of the floating airship and "convinced that [it] was nothing other than the Devil,"[47] local peasants of the Perm-Kotlasskoi region "fell to their knees and made the sign of the

---

[44] "Nad zemlei," *Gazeta kopeika*, 28 September 1910.

[45] "Kapitan Matsievich," *Rech'*, 25 September 1910; *Gazeta kopeika*, 25 September 1910; and *Russkoe slovo*, 25 September 1910.

[46] *Novoe vremia*, 7 October 1910.

[47] "Mezhdu nebom i zemlei," *Niva* 43 (1910): 760. Similar encounters between peasants and aviators were often published in the Russian press. See also "Aviator," *Gazeta kopeika*, 6 April 1910 and "Polineziiskii vozhd' na aeroplane," *Niva* 11 (1913): 220.

cross in expectation of the final hour."[48] After meeting with the balloon's
two occupants, they were only reluctantly assured that their airborne visitors had not been sent from the nether regions to unleash the Apocalypse.
The peasants' ultimate acceptance of the aerial invader demonstrated to contemporary observers the ability of aeronautical technology to transcend the
backwardness and ignorance of Russia's hinterlands.

As the "conquest of the air" had made possible a corresponding "conquest of barbarism," many observers looked to the airplane as the means
by which Russia would transcend the cultural backwardness that had long
distinguished it from the states of Western Europe. Daily reports from the
nation's airfields routinely compared Russian accomplishments with the
achievements of France and Germany. Elated reporters frequently alluded
to the inevitable day when Russia would emerge as the preeminent leader
in all aspects of the aeronautical race. Each new day "revealed new talents
and new heroes in [Russian] aviation" and produced "brilliant successes"
that demonstrated that "the Russian Bear" was the equal of its French and
German counterparts. As early as the fall of 1910, "it had become obvious"
to every observer that Russian aviation was "on a proper and firm path,"
and that the nation had "made colossal strides, matching, in many respects,
the achievements of European neighbors."[49]

These histrionic ruminations are important not only for what they say
about Russian views of aviation but also for what they imply about Russians'
views of their own nation. All too eager to contrast clichéd images of rural
Russia's peasant inhabitants with the technological advances encountered
in the nation's urban centers, the commentaries of contemporary observers
indicate the extent to which the long-standing dichotomy of Russia versus the
West, which had dominated the nation's cultural landscape throughout the
previous two centuries, was an integral component of the nation's emerging
aeronautical culture. By the second decade of the twentieth century, a vision
had emerged within educated society that acknowledged (and criticized)
those elements of national life that did not live up to perceived European
standards, yet insisted on Russia's rightful place alongside the other nations
of Europe. Thus, if "the sense of cultural inferiority that had haunted Russian
artists and intellectuals for generations" had indeed begun to fade in the years
following 1905, the self-stylized vision of an advanced Europe remained a
vital reference in the process by which contemporary Russians fashioned
their national identity.[50] Characterized by the technical accomplishments

---

[48] *Novoe vremia*, 7 October 1910.

[49] M. Kochergin, "Est' u nas liudi!," *Rossiia*, 20 October 1910; "Uspekhi Russkago vozdukhoplavaniia," *Zhurnal aerodroma* 1 (1910): 13; *Niva* 41 (1910): 715 and *Aero i avtomobil'naia
zhizn'* 17 (1910): 5–6.

[50] Samuel D. Kassow, James L. West and Edith W. Clowes, "Introduction: The Problem of
the Middle in Late Imperial Russian Society," in Clowes et al. (eds.), *Between Tsar and
People*, 9.

that accompanied Russia's conquest of the air, aviation served as demonstrable proof for contemporary observers that Russia belonged to Europe. And if Russia could match European nations in the race to conquer the skies, might it not also match the cultural and political vitality of the West and its institutions?

The European subtext that structured public discourse on Russian aviation had been first articulated in late 1907 by the founder of IVAK, Vasilii Korn. In letters to the newspaper *Novoe vremia* [*New Times*] and the journal *Vozdukhoplavatel'* [*The Aeronaut*], Korn lamented the sorry state of Russian aeronautics and questioned the ability of the nation to meet the social and technical challenges posed by flight. Hoping to inspire others to support his call for a national aviation club, Korn measured Russia's future aeronautical endeavors against the yardstick of European advances:

How can we explain the fact that we have developed [our flight technology] only to a level comparable to France during the age of the Montgolfier brothers? Is it really true that Russian genius exists in such an embryonic state that it is impossible to establish something of our own, even something of the most feeble nature? Is it really so difficult for us to measure up to Europe and, indeed, the entire cultured world?[51]

Arguing that Russia's aeronautical "primitiveness" stemmed from its failure to develop social organizations that would "popularize the idea of aviation as a sport, and that might accommodate that sport to society," Korn advanced West European aviation circles as models for Russian emulation. By mobilizing popular support for aeronautical endeavors, he argued, western air clubs had been successfully able to "[attract the broader] interests of society and to win over its sympathy to the bold and productive venture of humanity's conquest of the air."[52] As a direct result, European aeronautics had achieved "spectacular successes." In stark contrast, Russia's failure to develop a national program raised serious questions concerning its technical and cultural standing.

Aside from highlighting the important role of a stylized Europe in the formation of Russian aeronautical culture, Korn's proposals indicate a belief that late Imperial society was indeed capable of evolving forms of social association similar to those present in Western Europe. In urging that Russia develop western social organizations to "attract the broader interests of society," Korn explicitly acknowledged the vital importance of the civic arena as a key element in the solution of the nation's aeronautical dilemma. To this end, his sentiments support the view that prewar Russians were developing the sense of civic consciousness necessary for the evolution of a civil society

[51] V. Korn, "Russkii aero-klub (pis'mo v redaktsiiu)," *Vozdukhoplavatel'* 12 (1907): 480.
[52] V. Korn, "Organizatsiia i zadachi russkago aero-kluba (pis'mo v redaktsiiu)," *Vozdukho-plavatel'* 1 (1908): 39.

independent of the tsarist state.[53] Significantly, Korn's attempt to enlist public support for the development of aeronautics was not motivated simply by
a desire to see Russia match its competitors' successes. Instead, he argued,
Russia's late entry into the field had afforded the nation with a favorable
opportunity to overtake the Europeans in all things aeronautical. If Russia
could only follow the European model, Korn patriotically proclaimed, it
would at worst be guaranteed the same success garnered by Europe. At best,
the nation would rapidly pass over Western European mistakes on its way
to establishing the most prominent aviation program on the Continent.[54]
Through such an acknowledgment of European achievements, Korn presented the nation with an aeronautical policy that exhorted his readers to
meet the European challenge while reassuring their faith in the certainty of
a great Russian future.

The connection between aviation and culture alluded to in Korn's letters
was stated more explicitly in IVAK's subsequent appeals for public support
in the establishment of a national air fleet. Issued in early 1909, the club's
appeals warned that Russia was in danger of falling further behind Europe
and argued that only active, public support of aviation could save the nation
from the continued ignominy of backwardness and barbarism. According
to IVAK, the advent of aviation had inaugurated a new epoch in the history of humanity. Echoing the harshly critical tones of Peter Chadaaev's
First Philosophical Letter (1836) that had condemned Russia for failing to
contribute to broader European culture, IVAK announced that while "all
cultured peoples of the world" had begun to mobilize support for their
nations' aeronautical needs, Russia "remained only an observer and [had]
not contributed a single thing to the treasure house of human knowledge."
As European states made great strides toward developing national aviation
programs, "the productive forces of [our] huge country, a first-class power,"
continued one appeal, "have been utterly absent from this common cause
of humanity." While others, "even the smallest states, have not spared any
effort or any expense regarding this concern of colossal importance, [our]
enormous country has remained silent and has decisively done nothing."[55]
Unless Russia acted quickly, it would have little to contribute to the advance
of aviation and the development of European culture.

COMPENSATORY RHETORIC AND
AERONAUTICAL TRANSCENDENCE

The equation of the airplane with cultural standing was a dominant theme
in Imperial Russian discourse. In charting the progress of the nation's

[53] Bradley, "Voluntary Associations," 131–48.
[54] V. Korn, "Organizatsiia," 41.
[55] RGVIA f. 1, op. 1, d. 74101 (Bumagi po raznym predmetam), l. 112.

accomplishments, popular publications repeatedly measured success against European standards. Newspapers and journals routinely reported on western aeronautical festivals and air shows, and they took every opportunity to compare Russian efforts with those already underway in the West.[56] In essays, short stories, and poetry, Russian readers were introduced to pilots Hubert Latham, Louis Blériot, and Alphonse Pégoud, whose exploits were chronicled as closely as those of native fliers. At festivals and exhibitions, Russian spectators became familiar with the names "Voisin," "Gnome," and "Farman," the leading European manufacturers of airplane engines and equipment, while in public lectures Russian spokesmen reported on the stunning progress made by Germany and France.[57] In each instance, Western Europe was cited as a standard to be emulated, the leading force in the technical and cultural race to dominate the heavens.

In spite of a sincere desire to see their state attain a level of competence equal to that of the West, most Russians could not help but recognize that their aviation program did not yet match European standards. Notwithstanding Russia's achievements, western nations continued to develop their aerial prowess at a time when Russia was struggling to duplicate their earlier accomplishments. Faced with the continuing progress of states like France and Germany, observers increasingly attributed signs of Russian success to airborne exploits of only marginal significance. Oftentimes the importance of Russian aeronautical feats was exaggerated by the nation's press as a means of affirming Russia's contributions to the development of world aviation. Typical was the attention given to the inaugural flight of Russia's first military dirigible, the *Lebed'*. Constructed in France and purchased by Russia in 1909, the *Lebed'* could hardly be called "Russian."[58] Even the name of the airship (which means "swan" in Russian) was derived from its French manufacturer, Leboud. Still, detailed accounts of the dirigible's twenty-two-minute flight were widely reported.[59] At a time when "the questions of aviation concerned each and every individual" (and when zeppelins were undertaking extended tours of southern Germany!), the seven-mile journey of the *Lebed'* was hailed as a "major development in the aeronautical world." By demonstrating Russia's ability to launch a rigid airship, the *Lebed'*, supposedly, had "inaugurated a new era" in the history of the nation.[60]

---

[56] Particular attention was given to the German zeppelin flights that took place during the summer of 1909. Lengthy reports, detailing these flights and providing extensive histories of the craft and their creator, appeared in many Russian dailies. See "Zeppeliny na bol'shikh nemetskikh manevrakh," *Novaia Rus'*, 21 July 1909; "Zeppelinovskie dni," *Moskovskiia vedomosti*, 29 August 1909; and the two-part story, "Berlinskiia pis'ma," *Rossiia*, 29–30 August 1909.

[57] *Novoe vremia*, 10 October 1910 and 18 October 1910.

[58] The construction and service history of the *Lebed'* is summarized in Duz', *Istoriia*, 246–7.

[59] See, for example, *Peterburgskaia gazeta*, 27 August 1909, and *Rech'*, 26 August 1909.

[60] "Pervyi polet Lebedia," *Niva* 36 (1909): 629.

Similar hyperbole accompanied Lieutenant Georgii Piotrovskii's flight from St. Petersburg to Kronstadt on 22 September 1910 aboard a Blériot XI monoplane. Recognized for the importance of his "historic" accomplishment, Piotrovskii was roundly praised for the "heroism" and "courage" that he had demonstrated in completing the eighteen-mile journey.[61] Moved to tears by the news of the pilot's successful landing, one reader proclaimed Piotrovskii was proof that "the warrior spirit ha[d] not died out in Russia," and he compared the forty-minute flight to the nation's eighteenth-century naval victory against the Turks at Chesme. As a demonstration of the country's might and strength, the flight to Kronstadt had "comforted a Mother Russia still grieving over the loss at Tsushima" and had "astonished the whole world" by confirming Russia's aviation prowess. "After so many bitter defeats," the writer continued, "a worthy son of Russia has renewed a bright hope in the hearts of our countrymen." More important, he concluded, Piotrovskii's flight, "has shown the world that Russia is no less than Germany."[62]

The exaggerated excitement that accompanied marginal accomplishments such as the launch of the *Lebed'* and Piotrovskii's flight reveals one of the more peculiar characteristics of Russians' response to the airplane and, indeed, to technological development in general. Confronted with the reality of their nation's backwardness vis-à-vis the more advanced states of Western Europe, native observers cultivated a deep-seated faith that a single, transcendent event would transform Russia from its current state of underdevelopment and dependence into a position of dominance as the world's leading air power. Not unlike biblical eschatology that preached the last would be first and the first would be last in the kingdom to come (or the folkloric narrative that told of the lowly peasant's sudden permutation into heroic guise), the language employed by Russian officials and patrons disclosed an ardent faith that the future belonged to those currently dispossessed of technological fortune. All that Russia required to make the leap into the kingdom of the air was a breakthrough event or a crash-course campaign. While this fanciful notion assuaged national pride by implicitly downplaying the scope of the technological gap separating Russia from the West, it obscured the reality that aviation programs could not succeed in the absence of a modern, proficient, and technically advanced industrial infrastructure. Susceptible to belief in the coming transcendent act, Russians continually looked toward a quick fix that would provide an immediate and decisive payoff in their quest to overtake and then surpass Western Europe. The prominence of this peculiar trait in Russian technological culture would have a recurrent, deleterious impact on the nation's long-term aeronautical fortunes.

---

[61] *Rech'*, 23 September 1910. Piotrovskii's flight was widely reported in all of the major dailies of St. Petersburg and Moscow. Celebration of the event was quickly overshadowed by the death of Captain Matsievich two days later.

[62] S. Bashmakov, "Pis'mo v redaktsiiu," *Novoe vremia*, 24 September 1910.

In addition to embracing the false hope that a single, transcendent event would propel the nation to the heights of aeronautical greatness, Russian aviation patrons adopted the rhetoric of compensatory symbolism as a means of prognosticating future success. Presaging the national chauvinism and historical myth-making of the Soviet era, Imperial observers rewrote language and history as a means of demonstrating Russian contributions to the development of world aeronautics. Arguing that a widespread understanding of aviation terminology was essential to the successful proliferation of air-consciousness in Russia, one commentator took up the call to establish a purely Russian lexicon of aeronautical terms.[63] Hoping to "cleanse" Russian aeronautical literature of "unintelligible foreign and ancient words," another writer proposed a list of some 100 alternative designations, "purely derived from Russian," as a means of facilitating public understanding of aeronautical terminology.[64] Others looked to an imagined past in order to validate Russia's claim to aeronautical and cultural greatness. As a means of compensating for Russia's present failings, many writers turned to history in the hope of establishing Russia's airborne credentials. In newspapers, journals, and popular pamphlets, fanciful stories of early Russian "aviators" were often repeated to lend authority to a belief in Russia's long-established aeronautical tradition.[65] Similarly, works such as Aleksandr Rodnykh's *History of Aeronautics and Flight in Russia* and Vasilii Naidenov's *Russian Aeronautics: History and Successes* were published with the intention of providing "a complete account of what Russians have done on behalf of aviation."[66]

Typically, these historical claims to aeronautical mastery were based on the recitation and embellishment of the stories involving Emelian Ivanov and the peasant Nikitka. More intrepid authors advanced the idea that Russians had invented both balloons and parachutes.[67] Yet, if these precedents were not enough to convince contemporaries of their nation's historical claim to having pioneered flight, then the oft-cited exploits of the tenth-century Kievan prince, Oleg, were certain to establish Russia's aeronautical lineage. In an attempt to capture a besieged city in A.D. 906, the prince ordered an entire cavalry regiment, constructed out of gilded paper, to be carried by the wind into the enemy's camp. The confusion and turmoil caused by the airborne distraction proved the decisive edge in the prince's conquest

---

[63] F. Kupchinksii, "Prakticheskie terminy vozdukhoplavaniia," *Novaia Rus'*, 12 November 1909. Kupchinskii's article was reprinted, accompanied by a supportive rejoinder, in *Vozdukhoplavatel'* 11 (1909): 737–47.

[64] *Vozdukhoplavatel'* 11 (1909): 737–8.

[65] See, for example, N. Dneprov, "Pervye russkie tseppeliny," *Gazeta kopeika*, 31 August 1909. Note should be made of the title and date, as this story appeared at a time when the Russian press was devoting extensive coverage to German zeppelin flights.

[66] Rodnykh, *Istoriia*, and Vasilii Naidenov, *Russkoe vozdukhoplavanie i istoriia i uspekhi* (St. Petersburg, 1911). The quotation appears in Aleksandr Rodnykh, *Kratkii ocherk po istorii russkago vozdukhoplavaniia*, 2nd ed. (St. Petersburg, 1910), 1.

[67] Rodnykh, *Kratkii*, 4–5.

of the city and provided a pretext for later Russian claims to having pioneered flight.[68] Russians, it seems, had flown even before there was a Russia.

In addition to advancing such tenuous claims as having been the first nation to experiment with flight, Russia's compensatory symbolism led to the refashioning of more familiar aviation history. According to an article titled "The First Aviators," published in *Novoe vremia* in September 1910, the public was to believe that Russia was at one point "the leader of the world in the conquest of the air."[69] Citing manuscripts studied by the curator of a recently opened Munich museum, the newspaper proclaimed the invention of the world's first airplanes to have been the product of Russian genius. Secretly constructed by the naval officer Aleksandr Mozhaiskii and engineer Pavel Kuz'minskii during the 1880s, a steam-powered Russian aircraft had preceded the Wright brothers' efforts by nearly two decades. A later model, constructed in St. Petersburg during the 1890s, was likewise heralded as the world's first biplane. However, similar to earlier Russian showpiece technologies such as the sixteenth-century "tsar-cannon" (which could not fire) and the eighteenth-century "tsar-bell" (which could not sound), Mozhaiskii's nineteenth-century airplane could not fly. This fact did not discourage the paper from arguing that the nation had pioneered the science of aviation. Encouraging to contemporary readers, the article was important for holding out the hope of future Russian success. Arguing that recent aeronautical accomplishments had demonstrated that Russia "is not very far behind Europe in matters of aviation," the paper challenged disbelief in the ability of the nation to overtake quickly its western competitors. In citing the incredible examples of Mozhaiskii and Kuz'minskii (as well as laying claim to Russia's invention, in 1731, of the world's first balloon), the article made more easily imaginable a belief in the glorious future of Russian aviation. In light of these alleged accomplishments proclaimed by scholars and the press, the challenge posed by the West appeared a less exotic and more manageable problem. Historically, Russia had already demonstrated its ability to fly. All that remained was to await the transcendent event that would lift the nation past its European competitors.

---

[68] See A. I. Sulakadzev, "O vozdushnom letanii i Rossii s 906 leta po R. Kh.," in V. A. Popov, *Vozdukhoplavanie i aviatsiia v Rossii do 1907 g.: sbornik dokumentov i materialov* (Moscow, 1956), 13–15. Sulakadze's account is a modified version of a story from the *Russian Primary Chronicle*. See *Povest' vremmenykh let* (Petrograd 1916), Vol. 1, 30–1. The tale has been printed innumerable times in Russian histories of the nation's aeronautical development. Most recently, it appeared in Duz', *Istoriia*, 17.

[69] *Novoe vremia*, 30 September 1910.

2

"The Air Fleet is the Strength of Russia"

JOURNEY FROM ST. PETERSBURG TO MOSCOW

Russian aviation patrons staked yet another claim to aeronautical fame in the summer of 1911. Hoping to win further public support by demonstrating the practicality of airplanes outside of the confines of an aerodrome, the Imperial All-Russian Aero-Club organized an airborne race between the nation's two most important urban centers, St. Petersburg and Moscow. Patterned after recent contests held in Western Europe, the premise of the race was simple: Participating pilots would travel from St. Petersburg to Moscow along a prescribed route, passing over mandatory checkpoints and landing (when necessary) at established sites equipped to service their planes. The first pilot to reach Moscow was to receive a small cash sum while the remainder of the competition's prize money (which approached 75,000 rubles) was divided into categories for those pilots flying alone and those accompanied by a passenger. Additional prizes were to be awarded for the longest flights without a stop and to pilots who made the fewest stops en route to Moscow. The largest single prize was reserved for the flier who reached Moscow with the fastest time.[1]

Held in the wake of successful Paris–Rome and Paris–Madrid races, the St. Petersburg–Moscow competition was a daring attempt to demonstrate that Russia could match the organizational and technical accomplishments of the Continent's leading aeronautical powers. Accompanying the routine difficulties faced by their western contemporaries in planning such an event, IVAK's organizational committee was forced to contend with the isolated expanse of the Russian hinterlands. To guard the safety and success of the nine participating pilots, the race was run along the highway connecting Moscow to the Imperial capital. Entrants were provided with maps of the region to assist in navigating their journeys. IVAK also attempted to mobilize resources along the planes' path by calling on local officials to have medical teams standing by in the not-unlikely event that misfortune occurred.[2]

---

[1] K. E. Veigelin, *10–15 iiulia 1911 g. Perelet S. Peterburg–Moskva* (St. Petersburg, 1911).

[2] A. V. Kaul'bars, "Otchet ob organizatsii pervago v Rossii pereleta SpB.–Moskva," *Vozdukhoplavatel'* 8 (1911): 524–39.

FIGURE 5. Villagers greet a passing aviator during the St. Petersburg–Moscow air race, July 1911.

Despite these safety precautions the race was beset by numerous accidents that quickly overshadowed the event and earned IVAK the enmity of the press. Early in the morning on 12 July, a sizable crowd gathered at the airfield in Moscow to greet Aleksandr Vasil'ev, the fourth competitor to take off from St. Petersburg and the first to complete the 450-mile flight. Having done battle with the "savagery and barbarity of the Russian countryside," Vasil'ev and his aircraft had emerged victorious "in spite of the obstacles placed before him by Russia."[3] The expected air of celebratory triumph was quickly dispelled, however, by news of the aviator's travails. Vasil'ev reported that the maps provided by the organizational committee were riddled with mistakes and that, as a result, he had lost his way twice (in one instance flying some sixty miles out of the way in a vain search for the checkpoint at Tver'). Forced to land his plane to ask for directions, Vasil'ev corrected the mistake and returned to the proper route only to encounter engine trouble forty miles short of Moscow. There, the pilot was compelled to wait overnight in a small barn following the delayed arrival of spare parts. He completed his journey only on the morning of the 12th, arriving more than twenty-four hours after his departure from St. Petersburg.

After landing at the Moscow aerodrome, an extremely agitated and fatigued Vasil'ev castigated the coterie of IVAK officials and city dignitaries

---

[3] "Perelet Peterburg–Moskva," *Niva* 30 (1911): 558.

gathered to greet him. Complaining of the disorder and dereliction that the club's organizers had demonstrated in arranging the competition, Vasil'ev publicly decried the pitiful conditions that he had encountered at the race's checkpoints as well as the poor signaling system and shoddy maps that he had been forced to endure. Likening his flight to "penal servitude," Vasil'ev warned that the journey was "a summons to die" and suggested that "if the race doesn't end with the death of an aviator, then we will have only God to thank."[4] What was intended to serve as a celebration of technological ascendancy quickly turned into a public-relations fiasco as Vasil'ev repeated his criticisms in an open letter published less than a week after the conclusion of the race.[5]

Vasil'ev's critical tone was echoed by the press as word of accidents involving the pilots Utochkin, Agafonov, and Maslennikov soon reached St. Petersburg and Moscow. Public concern quickly escalated into a crescendo of indignation following the crash of the pilot Vladimir Sliusarenko in which his passenger, the twenty-six-year-old aviation student Konstantin Shimanskii, was killed. The press exploded. Proclaiming the race the "saddest moment in the history of Russian flight," news publications pointed to the "stupidity, arrogance, and pure Russian 'know-it-all-ism'" of the organizing committee for having failed to foresee the "colossal defects" that had plagued the race.[6] The celebration of Vasil'ev's triumphant arrival in Moscow quickly gave way to "nightmarish days" in which newspaper headlines screamed "Enough Blood!" and impassioned editorials demanded an end to the "airborne butchery" taking place in the skies between St. Petersburg and Moscow.[7]

Although Vasil'ev inaugurated public debate concerning the (in)competence of IVAK's organizational committee, it cannot be said that the pilot's words had inspired popular skepticism of the race in particular or the cause of aviation in general.[8] Such misgivings had been manifest even before the start of the competition. One indication of growing concern with the status of the nation's aeronautical endeavors was revealed in a lengthy editorial published to coincide with the start of the race. The editorial railed against the ever-increasing number of aeronautical accidents and fatalities both in Russia and abroad and attacked competitions like the St. Petersburg–Moscow Race for providing monetary incentives for pilots to risk their lives. Employing bitter

---

[4] *Vestnik vozdukhoplavaniia* 11 (1911): 9 and *Svet*, 12 July 1911, 2.

[5] A. Vasil'ev, "Moi perelet," *Sinii zhurnal* 31 (1911): 5.

[6] *Svet*, 15 July, 1911; *Sinii zhurnal* 31 (1911): 6–7; and *Utro Rossii*, 13 July 1911.

[7] "Koshmarnye dni," *Utro Rossii*, 13 July 1911; "Ne nuzhno stol'ko krovi," *Ranee utro*, 13 July 1911; and "Aviatsionnaia boinia," *Peterburgskii listok*, 13 July 1911.

[8] In a spirited defense of the race and the Aero-Club, Konstantin Veigelin invoked biblical imagery in suggesting that Vasil'ev's public castigation of the organizational committee was a "lance thrust with anger into the side of the nation's aeronautical program," and he blamed the aviator for spearheading criticism of the Aero-Club after the race. See Veigelin, *Perelet*, 56.

sarcasm, the author compared the social phenomenon [*bytovoe iavlenie*] of the aeronautical competition to society's earlier fascination with capital punishment. With the aid of advertisements and press coverage, the writer argued, the public's blood-lust was whetted, just as it had been by the published notices that recounted the executions of the condemned. In fact, the article suggested, the aeronautical race was in many respects more disreputable than the individual condemnation notice as "everyone knows that from among these pilots some have been condemned to death and an even greater number to mutilation." Lending statistical support to his moral indignation, the author announced that during the previous year more than thirty victims had died worldwide in airplane accidents. But, he added wryly, "as proof of the great successes in aviation, experienced people have promised us simpletons that this year there should *only* be around 100 deaths."[9] The "experienced people" proved right on the mark. In 1911, there would be ninety-six reported fatalities.[10]

Reactions to the death of Shimanskii and the numerous accidents that plagued the St. Petersburg–Moscow Race cannot be explained, however, as simple, spontaneous responses to the mounting casualties resulting from Russian aeronautical activities. During the previous two decades, as the popularity of ballooning had increased, airborne accidents had multiplied, conditioning the Russian public to the dangers associated with flight. Moreover, the number of Russian fatalities in no way compared with those in Western Europe. Of the ninety-six fatalities that were to occur throughout the world in 1911, only five (including Shimanskii) were numbered from among Russian fliers. Although this was a fivefold increase over the lone death of Matsievich in 1910, Russian casualties remained only a third of those occurring in either Germany or the United States and were more than seven times fewer than those in France during the same year.[11] Nevertheless, public criticism over the outcome of the race and the rising tide of concern for aeronautical victims indicated that by the summer of 1911 Russian attitudes toward aviation had undergone an important shift.[12] If, in the fall of 1910, the press had been willing to dismiss fatalities as the "unavoidable risk" of a great, new venture and had boldly declared that the "genius of man" should

---

[9] A. Marker, "Aviatsiia," *Zhizn' dlia vsekh* 7 (1911): 957–63. The italics appear in the original.

[10] *Tiazhelee vozdukha* 1 (1912): 16.

[11] The *Tiazhelee vozdukha* article cited above incorrectly lists the number of Russian aeronautical casualties in 1911 as seven. For correct assessments, including the names of the deceased, see *Vechernee vremia*, 10 December 1911; *Vestnik vozdukhoplavaniia* 4 (1912): 15; and *Sevastopol'skii aviatsionnyi illiustrirovannyi zhurnal* 2–3 (50–51) (1912): 2.

[12] For a sample of press commentary on accidents at this time, see *Ranee utro*, 13 July 1911; *Vestnik znaniia* 8 (1911): 732–4; and *Sinii zhurnal* 19 (1911): 13, in addition to the sources cited above. On the growing concern over accidents in the contemporary American press, see Roger E. Bilstein, *Flight in America: From the Wrights to the Astronauts* (Baltimore: Johns Hopkins University Press, 1984), 24–6.

not halt before the bodies of "the brave and daring victims" of aviation accidents, by mid-1911, it was sounding a much more critical tone.[13]

Heightened sensitivity to these losses of life was a reflection of the growing awareness that aviation itself was undergoing a fundamental transformation. During the earliest years of the decade, Russian newsmen, much like their West European counterparts, had been content to proclaim the marvels of humanity's latest invention and to praise the temerity of the flying "tsars of the skies" whose feats of technical skill promised to usher in a "new era of human history."[14] Celebrating pilots as modern incarnations of the ancient Prometheus, the press had extolled these men and their machines for subjugating the laws of nature to the interests of progress. Enamored of the daring displayed by the airborne aviator, early accounts of aeronautical exploits employed romantic imagery of the individual pilot to promote a general faith in the hero of the skies.

However, as engines grew more powerful and fuselages more sturdy and as once-small bands of amateur fliers were transformed into cadres of professional pilots, idyllic visions of nature's conquest rapidly gave way to nervous expectations that aviation would soon be employed in the pursuit of less noble, more martial goals. True, commentators at both ends of the Continent had ruminated on the military potential of the airplane as early as 1909. But, in the intervening two years, European governments had taken practical steps in developing aviation to serve recognizable military objectives.[15] As these efforts intensified it became increasingly obvious to concerned individuals that Russian approaches to developing aviation needed to undergo a marked transition.

AVIATION BETWEEN STATE AND SOCIETY

In the weeks that followed the St. Petersburg–Moscow Race, leading publications called attention to the changing circumstances of Russian aviation and urged the tsarist government to take appropriate measures to meet the challenge posed by European advances. During the fall of 1911, the press closely documented the expanding role of airplanes and dirigibles in the military maneuvers of western neighbors and used these events as springboards for mounting criticisms of Russia's preparedness. Announcing that "the incredible influence of the airplane in military affairs and in the conduct

---

[13] *Novoe vremia*, 28 September 1910, and K. Priural'skii, "V tsarstve vozdukha," in *Aero i avtomobil'naia zhizn'* 13 (1910): 12, among many others.

[14] *Peterburgskaia gazeta*, 14 July 1909, and *Russkoe znamia*, 14 July 1909. For a discussion of the excitement that surrounded the earliest flights in Europe see Robert Wohl, *A Passion for Wings: Aviation and the Western Imagination, 1908–1918* (New Haven, CT: Yale University Press, 1994), 33–68.

[15] John H. Morrow, Jr., *The Great War in the Air: Military Aviation from 1909 to 1921* (Washington, D.C.: Smithsonian Institution Press, 1993), 11–29.

of battle" had already "been proclaimed with heated enthusiasm not only in France, but amid the social opinion and military circles of Germany and England," the press warned of the rapid growth of military aviation in Europe and evinced growing concern for the status of Russian aeronautical endeavors.[16]

The outbreak of war between Italy and the Ottoman Empire on 29 October 1911 [n.s.] proved these concerns well founded. Armed with a contingent of nine planes purchased from France, the Italian army employed its aircraft for assisting with troop reconnaissance and conducting limited bombing raids against enemy positions. Although the airplanes did not provide an overwhelming tactical or strategic advantage, they retained powerful symbolic significance as the first application of aviation in military combat.[17] The Russian press followed the events in North Africa with keen interest, publishing accounts of each new appearance by "the weapon of the future" and reporting on Italian efforts to augment their aeronautical capabilities by purchasing more planes from the French.[18] Such measures seemed highly appropriate. Although the war in Tripoli did not elucidate every aspect of the future of military aviation, it had proven the importance of possessing a military air fleet and had demonstrated the vital significance of such a fleet to a nation's armed forces.[19]

While Italian pilots applied their skills to tormenting the Turks from the skies over Africa, the French government provided European rivals with another demonstration of its unsurpassed aeronautical might. Supported by a state subsidy of some 1 million francs, military maneuvers at Reims in October 1911 again confirmed the enviable progress being made by the French. In the course of the event, some 140 planes (representing no fewer than thirty different models) were displayed: a striking testament to the French commitment to developing military aviation.[20] In contrast to this showcase (and the continuing success of the German zeppelin program), the Russian military's effort to organize a September air exposition of its own had proven a failure. Of the four planes that applied to enter the competition, one was immediately disqualified for failing to meet the military's basic specifications, while another was destroyed when a temporary hangar collapsed in high winds. The ill-fated competition met a premature end when the final two entries crashed during their initial flights.[21] At a time when the French were flexing their aeronautical muscle within the context of organized military

[16] *Vestnik vozdukhoplavaniia* 13–14 (1911): 4.

[17] Morrow, *Great War*, 25.

[18] See, for example, *Peterburgskii listok*, 16 October 1911; *Ranee utro*, 19 October 1911; *Birzhevyia vedomosti*, 21 October 1911 (evening edition); and *Peterburgskaia gazeta*, 14–16 October 1911, among many others.

[19] *K sportu!* 3 (1911): 5.

[20] *Vozdukhoplavatel'* 10 (1911): 678–681.

[21] *Birzhevyia vedomosti*, 23 September 1911; *Peterburgskaia gazeta*, 10 September 1911; and *Sankt Peterburgskiia vedomosti*, 23 September 1911.

maneuvers and the Italians were gaining valuable experience in aerial warfare, such failures were the cause of considerable public concern. One leading
journal voiced its anxiety by castigating the state for not doing enough to
advance the nation's aviation interests. By means of comparison with the
spectacular French demonstration at Reims, it ridiculed the Russian "air
fleet" as consisting of no more than "a dozen or so old training planes worn
out from over-use." While acknowledging that Russia could take pride in
the collective achievements of its pilots, the journal chastised the government for the lack of foresight and planning demonstrated in its handling
of the military aviation program. As a result of state bungling, the journal
concluded, "haphazardness and insufficiency" had emerged as "the distinc-
tive characteristics of Russian aviation." Without fundamental reform of the
military's aeronautical sections Russia would not prove capable of meeting
foreign challenges.[22]

The government agreed. During the winter and spring of 1911–12, the
Russian Ministry of War undertook an internal examination of its aeronautical sections to determine what measures might be adopted to correct existing inadequacies. The results of the investigation, first circulated in summer
of 1912, indicated that press criticism had been well founded. In his introductory cover letter to the Ministry report, the commander of the Officers'
Aeronautical School, Major-General Aleksandr Kovan'ko, acknowledged
that the heretofore haphazard attention paid by the military to the development of Russian aviation had prevented the government from best exploiting
the new technology to its own advantage. Kovan'ko urged the creation of a
new organizational structure to correct existing inadequacies and to ensure
the proper development of the nation's military aeronautical program. Echoing criticisms voiced by the press, Kovan'ko decried the absence of planning
to be the "single obstacle to the natural development and broadening of
military aviation," and he blamed existing institutions for failing to provide the nation with the leadership and expertise it required to succeed in
this endeavor. Only through rationalizing the military's aeronautical sections and expanding the role of trained technicians and specialists would it
be possible to develop rapidly Russian military aviation. Failure to adopt
such measures, he warned, would have dire consequences as it would run
the risk of entrenching Russia "in last place among the European states in
the matter of aeronautical affairs."[23]

Similar to the letter that prefaced it, the Ministry's report drew attention
to the necessity of establishing a clear and orderly chain of command for

[22] *Vestnik vozdukhoplavaniia* 15 (1911): 3–5.
[23] RGVIA f. 2000, op. 7, d. 7 (Soobshcheniia po povodu planomernoi organizatsii voennogo
vozdukhoplavaniia v Rossii), l. 49. For a detailed examination of the politics and policies of
Imperial Russian military aviation, see Gregory Vitarbo, "The Power, Strength, and Future
of Russia: Aviation Culture and the Russian Imperial Officer Corps, 1908–1914" (Ph.D.
dissertation, University of Michigan, 1999).

the handling of all matters aeronautical. To this end, it outlined a series of institutional reforms that centered on the transfer of responsibility for the military aeronautical program from the Ministry of War's Central Engineering Administration [*Glavnoe inzhenernoe upravlenie*] to a newly created section attached to the General Staff. According to the report, the proposed changes would make possible the "hastening of tempos" regulating aeronautical development and would provide the state with its desired results at "a modest cost" and within a "short period." As if to bolster this claim, the report compared the task of establishing the Russian air fleet to the crash-course program of naval construction undertaken by Peter the Great at the beginning of the eighteenth century. As with Peter's navy, the report noted, it would be possible for the state to expand its air fleet quickly by obtaining the requisite planes and expertise from Western Europe while laying the foundations for future growth through investment in domestic aviation enterprises. Still, the report was quite clear that time was of the essence. Although it was realistic to expect that Russia would soon possess an air force "more powerful than any of its adversaries," the government could not waste time. The advance of aviation was moving too quickly for that. As such, the report warned by way of concluding, "the government that fails to establish a rational organization [*planomernost' organizatsii*] now will find it difficult to later reestablish lost status and time" as rival powers would press ahead in the race to control the skies.[24]

In addition to reorganizing the military's aviation departments, the state reached out to the public in an attempt to broaden the campaign to raise support for Russian aviation. Since revising its original mandate of building ships for the navy to include the task of constructing an air fleet, the Committee for the Establishment of the Fleet by Means of Voluntary Subscriptions had conducted its activities in a narrowly circumscribed fashion, directing its fund raising efforts largely toward the nation's richest and most well-established personages. Official publications boasted that by the middle of 1912 the Committee had succeeded in raising nearly 1.6 million rubles for the purchase of thirty-odd airplanes.[25] A closer examination suggests that the Committee's success was far less impressive. Of the money raised, the majority had come from preexisting funds transferred from the earlier naval campaign. By the Committee's own accounting, it had raised a mere 354,000 rubles from individual donations. Measured against the 3.6 million francs and 4 million marks generated by French and German aeronautical subscriptions, respectively, in 1912, Russian efforts were positively anemic.[26]

[24] RGVIA f. 2000, op. 7, d. 7, ll. 52–64.

[25] *Vozdushnyi flot–sila Rossii* (Moscow, 1913), 12.

[26] RGVIA f. 2000, op. 7, d. 59, l. 80; *Vozdushnyi flot–sila Rossii*, 16; and *Peterburgskii listok*, 14 August 1912.

Aware of the need to attract more support from the public, the Committee turned to the press, inviting the editorial boards of one dozen leading periodicals to meet with the Committee's governing body on 13 August 1912. As a prologue to the discussion, the Committee presented the assembled newsmen with a statement concerning its mission accompanied by newly printed brochures and an accounting of the funds it had thus far raised. Following its presentation, the Committee solicited advice from the journalists regarding the most favorable means of familiarizing the public with its activities and requested that the attending editors print stories pertaining to the Committee and the air fleet in forthcoming editions of their publications.[27]

The press's execution of the official request to publish stories about the Committee was decidedly mixed. Although most of the news agencies did oblige the government in the days following the conference, with articles and essays concerning the state subscription, their individual responses varied widely. The most impassioned implementation of the government's request came from the conservative newspaper *Svet* [*The World*], which published a week-long series of frenzied, patriotic front-page articles supporting the Committee and attempting to mobilize the nation's citizenry to "the great cause of the air fleet."[28] In contrast, *Birzhevyia vedomosti* [*Exchange Register*] and *Peterburgskii listok* [*Petersburg Leaflet*] saw fit to publish single, short notices reminding their readers that the State Committee existed and informing them of the Committee's future plans.[29] The left-leaning newspaper *Rech'* [*Speech*] declined to print anything.

The widely divergent responses to the Committee's request did not reflect disinterest on the part of the press. The nation's newspapers continued to devote considerable space to Russian aviation. They also continued to discuss aeronautical matters in decidedly patriotic terms. As demonstrated by the recurrent demand that Russia "not simply match the aeronautical capabilities of [its western competitors] but surpass them," public discussion of Russian aviation remained a highly emotional and intrinsically nationalistic affair.[30] To this extent, the published responses to the 13 August conference indicated a growing recognition by news publications that patriotic support for the defense of the nation was not necessarily synonymous with public support of state policies. Although all agreed on the fundamental importance of aviation to Russia's military preparedness and cultural standing, many disagreed with the government regarding the means by which policy

---

[27] RGVIA f. 2000, op. 7, d. 59, l. 69. Representatives of the following publications attended the meeting: *Birzhevyia vedomosti, Groza, Kolokol, Peterburgskii listok, Rech', Sankt Peterburgskiia vedomosti, Sel'skii vestnik, Svet, Tsarskosel'skoe delo, Vedomosty SPb., Gradnochal'stva,* and *Zemshchina*.

[28] See *Svet*, 14–20 August 1912. The quote appears in the article, "Vozdushnyi flot–sila Rossii," 14 August 1912.

[29] *Birzhevyia vedomosti*, 14 August 1912, and *Peterburgskii listok*, 14 August 1912.

[30] *Sankt Peterburgskiia vedomosti*, 14 August 1912.

had thus far been conducted. They signaled their dissatisfaction by largely ignoring the request of the state-sponsored Committee. In this way, the decision by some editorial boards to remain silent toward the Committee's call for support (and the relative silence of others) did not reflect disinterest in the issue of Russian military aviation. Rather, their responses were passive indictments of the government's capability to manage properly affairs of state. By effectively ignoring the Committee's appeal for support, these papers signaled their dissatisfaction with state policy while continuing to preach the importance of aviation to the nation's prosperity.

Although the outcome of the conference between state officials and public press representatives did not fundamentally alter the terms of Russia's aeronautical discourse, the meeting itself clearly indicated the government's growing recognition of the need to enlist society in a broad, state-directed campaign. Keenly aware of the importance of haste in developing aviation for national defense and mindful of the rapid successes being attained in Western Europe, the state accelerated its aeronautical program by embarking on a public-relations blitz. The press responded by continuing to publish calls for broader public participation in the aeronautical cause (as it had done since 1907) armed with the knowledge that, at least for the time being, the government was proving receptive to its proposals. Indeed, the state's interest in reinforcing its relationship with the press was further signified at the August meeting by the Committee's decision to appoint one of its members to act as a standing liaison between the Committee and the capital's press establishments.[31] Soon thereafter, the Committee improved press access to the nation's aeronautical fleet by helping to arrange flights for interested reporters.[32]

In the aftermath of the August meeting, the Committee redoubled efforts to popularize Russian military aviation by issuing a series of postcards, gold and silver commemorative badges, cheap tin buttons (emblazoned with the Committee's adopted slogan: "The air fleet is the strength of Russia"), and even a children's game called, "Air Battle: A Game of the Twentieth Century."[33] Together with these trinkets, the Committee attempted to broaden its appeal by producing a number of colorful, well-illustrated brochures aimed at educating readers of the importance of aviation and the efforts undertaken by the state to improve the nation's air fleet. Public involvement in the cause was further encouraged through writing competitions in which participants were asked to submit essays that would familiarize the Russian people with the cultural and military significance of aviation.[34]

[31] RGVIA f. 2000, op. 7, d. 59, l. 69.

[32] RGVIA f. 2000, op. 7, d. 16 (Pis'mo voennomu ministru o komandirovanii letchikov), ll. 46–7.

[33] RGVIA f. 2000, op. 7, d. 59, l. 67.

[34] Among the publications produced by the Committee were *Kratkii populiarnyi ocherk vozdukhoplavaniia i aviatsii* (Kazan', 1913); *Russkii morskoi i vozdushnyi flot sooruzhennyi na*

Accompanying the Committee's merchandising efforts and the military's reorganization of its aeronautical departments, the government signaled its renewed commitment by immediately increasing expenditures on the nation's air force. Following the transfer of the aeronautical command from the Central Engineering Administration to the General Staff on 12 September, the government approved the release of some 2.4 million rubles in accumulated credits, previously held by the Engineering Administration, for the purchase of new planes and equipment. In conjunction with this short-term measure, the General Staff undertook to devise a plan that would serve as the blueprint for the future. Completed by the late winter of 1912, the General Staff's project was both big and expensive, calling for the purchase of nearly 400 planes and the expenditure of 44 million rubles during the course of 1913–15.[35]

Notwithstanding the considerable sums spent by the Ministry of War, these efforts failed to resolve a number of fundamental dilemmas facing the nation's aeronautical program. The first of these was the problem of pilots. The rapid expansion of aviation detachments required a simultaneous expansion in the number of available fliers. Without pilots, Russia's air fleet would remain grounded; even as early as 1912, the military was faced with a shortage of qualified fliers.[36] To address this long-term need, the Ministry of War had decided in the spring of 1912 to expand its training program by expending 1.05 million rubles to relocate its flight school in Sevastopol' to the nearby village of Marmashai. The move, according to the Ministry, would provide the school with more room for growth, thus accommodating the increase in students expected to accompany the rapid expansion of the air fleet.[37] In the interim, the military attempted to meet the growing demand for qualified fliers by turning to Russia's private air clubs and circles.

Aware of the problem faced by the Ministry of War, IVAK had approached the government in the spring of 1912 with an offer to train military pilots free of charge at its facilities.[38] This apparent act of altruism was subsequently hailed by the press as an example of the ways in which the country's civilian organizations could work with the government for the betterment of the

---

dobrovol'nyia pozhertvovaniia (St. Petersburg, 1913); and the previously cited *Vozdushnyi flot–sila Rossii.* On the writing competitions, see *Avtomobil' i vozdukhoplavanie* 17 (1911): 484.

35 RGVIA f. 2000, op. 7, d. 231 (Doklad po zaprosam Dumy o snabzhenii aviatsionnym imushchestvom), ll. 12–14.

36 According to one estimate, in the summer of 1912 the Russian military possessed some 100 aircraft but only sixty pilots. See *Vozdukhoplavatel'* 6 (1912): 486.

37 RGVIA f. 2000, op. 7, d. 59, l. 81.

38 The Aero-Club's decision to train the military pilots is reported in *Imperatorskii Vserossiiskii Aero–Klub. Zhurnal. 101 otkrytago zasedaniia soveta IVAK, 11 iiulia 1912*: 122–3 (*Vozdukhoplavatel'* 9 [1912]).

national air fleet.[39] For its part, the state accepted the proposal and finalized similar arrangements with the private schools of the Moscow Society of Aeronautics and the Odessa Aero-Club. In exchange for training up to ten pilots a year, the Military Ministry agreed to compensate these organizations by providing them with a 500-ruble subsidy for each pilot they graduated.[40]

The problems inherent in this arrangement became apparent soon after the graduation of the first group of students. Despite the air clubs' assurances concerning the quality of their training regimens, the pilots they produced did not meet the military's qualifications. The extent to which the privately trained aviators fell short of military standards was made clear when one of the first graduates of the IVAK program crashed an army airplane on his maiden flight, ending the plane's career and with it his life.[41] The military was forced to retrain all of the officers it had enrolled in the air-club schools, thus forfeiting any benefits that it had hoped to gain from relying on the private organizations. Compounding these difficulties, IVAK reneged on its offer to train the military's fliers for free. The club submitted a petition to the government demanding 1,000 rubles for each military flier that it graduated, together with 500 rubles for each of its civilian students who agreed to enroll in the Russian air fleet reserves. Moreover, the IVAK leadership had the audacity to request 25,000 rubles for the equipment of a new aerodrome and an additional increase of more than 60,000 rubles to its *yearly* state subsidy to further the "fruitful activities" that it conducted on behalf of the nation.[42]

Aside from the problem of producing qualified pilots to man its planes, the Russian military was faced with additional misfortunes in the fall of 1912. These combined to cast further doubt on the capability of the state to cope with the tasks at hand. In an attempt to showcase Russian advances, the military organized a five-week competition, scheduled to run from late August to early September, that would coincide with similar competitions taking place in the West. In keeping with its goal of promoting Russia's nascent aeronautical industry, the military specified that only planes assembled in Russian factories were eligible to contend for the competition's 55,000 rubles in total prize money.[43] Much like the previous year's military maneuvers, however, the competition proved less than encouraging. Hampered by inclement weather and beset by numerous accidents, the competition dragged on until late October, ultimately losing the interest of the press. Of the three

[39] See, for example, the article entitled, "Ocherk deiatel'nosti aviatsionnoi shkoly IVAK," in *Vestnik vozdukhoplavaniia* 15 (1912): 2–5.

[40] RGVIA f. 1, op. 1, d. 76836 (Vozdukhoplavatel'noe delo), ll. 91–2.

[41] RGVIA f. 2000, op. 7, d. 59, l. 168.

[42] *Ibid.*, ll. 165–6.

[43] RGVIA f. 1, op. 1, d. 76836, l. 103. The Military Ministry's restrictions on the construction of the airplanes did not apply to their engines and components that could (and did) come from foreign manufacturers.

airplanes that were awarded prize money, only one, an S-6b biplane, might truly be called a "Russian" airplane. The remaining two craft, both produced by the Moscow Dux factory were nothing more than poor reproductions of outdated French Farman and Nieuport models.[44] During the course of the disappointing competition, the state experienced a further setback when a fire broke out at the yet to be completed training school in Marmashai, destroying a number of buildings and costing nearly 120,000 rubles in damages. Still more bad tidings followed. On 7 September the army's dirigible *Iastreb* [*Hawk*] sprang a leak and crashed, breaking its gondola in half and causing considerable damage to the inflatable airframe.[45] Miraculously, none of the militarily trained crewmen was seriously injured in the incident.

The press was quick to criticize the government for this most recent round of misadventures. Writing in regard to the Russian military competition, one leading aeronautical journal reported on the shoddy performance of the planes that took part in the event and posed the rhetorical question: "What did the competition do for Russian military aviation?" The journal's response: "Nothing. The planes were already well known and, to be blunt, not a one of them may truly be considered a military vehicle." The journal concluded that the only news to come out of the competition was that the military had wasted 75,000 rubles and received nothing in return.[46] Similar scorn was evidenced in press coverage concerning the fire at the training school. In an editorial devoted to "Our Air Fleet," the capital's leading newspaper, *Novoe vremia*, castigated the government for having "squandered over 1 million rubles" to rebuild the aeronautical school at the new location. As a result, the paper charged, the Russian training program had been forced "to start over from the beginning," at a desolate site whose "lack of water and poor access played a crucial role in the amount of destruction caused by the recent fire."[47]

The press's latest assault on the government's failures foretold serious inadequacies that were undermining Russia's attempt to build a modern air fleet. In this respect, the criticisms of the fall 1912 military competition suggested the systemic deficiency obstructing the nation's aeronautical program: the dearth of airplane factories. In the fall of 1912, the number of Russian factories capable of assembling aeronautical craft totaled a mere four, compared with nine in Germany and more than one dozen in France and the United States.[48] True, aviation had arrived late in Russia, but the continuing inability of the nation's industry to match the production capacity of western

---

44 *Vechernee vremia*, 1 October 1912.
45 *Sovremennoe slovo*, 8 September 1912, and *Rech'*, 8 September 1912.
46 "Po povodu russkago voennago konkursa," *Vestnik vozdukhoplavaniia* 14 (1912): 1–3. See also *Novoe vremia*, 6 October 1912.
47 "Nash vozdushnyi flot," *Novoe vremia*, 7 September 1912.
48 S. A. Adasinskii, "Proizvodstvo samoletov v Rossii," in G. S. Biushgens (ed.), *Aviatsiia v Rossii* (Moscow, 1988), 278–91 *et passim*; Morrow, *Great War*, 37; E. Chadeau, "L'industrie

competitors posed a serious threat to any hope of realizing its grandiose goals.

The crisis facing the Russian aviation industry did not escape the attention of journalists. As early as January 1910, *Vestnik vozdukhoplavaniia* had published an insightful article alerting its readers to the essential role that industry would play in the development of aviation.[49] However, amid the optimism and fanfare accompanying Russia's earliest airborne accomplishments, the warnings of the newly established journal failed to resonate among interested circles. Not so in 1912. Alarmed by the failures of the Russian military and keenly aware of the great strides being made in the West, the Russian press turned its attention to "the greatest obstacle (in addition to the lack of pilots) facing the air fleet: the absence of an established aviation industry."[50] Warning that the time of sporting aviation had given way to an era of military–industrial aviation, journalists again called on the government to take immediate steps, this time to dispel the "industrial indifference" [*promyshlennaia nezainteresovannost'*] that compelled the military to rely on foreign suppliers for aircraft.[51] In the wake of the disappointing military competition, one observer explicitly linked the poor performance of the participating planes to the state's policy of purchasing aircraft from the West:

We have obtained the majority of our aircraft from abroad. And we have obtained that which is cheap and readily available. The foreigners keep the more reliable and expensive equipment for themselves and ship us their inferior goods. It doesn't take a genius to realize that you get what you pay for.

As a result of the state's reliance on foreign manufacturers, this writer continued, the government had run the risk of irreparably damaging Russian aviation. In fact, the grim consequences of dependence on the West had already been seen in the 1912 military competition. Thus, the journalist concluded rather prosaically, "we find ourselves in the control of foreign factory owners and their managers from whose orders, as if from bewitched charms, emanate dark phenomena and infectious temptations driving us toward great mistakes."[52] The message was clear: Russia desperately needed to establish its own domestic aeronautical industry to provide the weapons required for its own defense. And during the current "era of vital transformations in aeronautics" it was essential that more be done by the state to realize this end.[53]

française d'aviation à la veille de la première guerre mondiale," *Revue historique des armeés* 2 (1981): 63–5; and Bilstein, *Flight in America*, 31.

[49] *Vestnik vozdukhoplavaniia* 3 (1910): 4–6.

[50] *Vechernee vremia*, 27 September 1912.

[51] *Aero i avtomobil'naia zhizn'* 20 (1912): 6, and *K sportu!* 17 (1912): 1.

[52] *Novoe vremia*, 6 October 1912.

[53] *Tiazhelee vozdukha* 7 (1912): 2.

To its credit, the Ministry of War *had* attempted to patronize the Russian aviation industry, beginning in 1910, by placing its initial orders with those few Russian factories capable of producing the planes and equipment that it needed. Hoping to hasten the development of domestic airplane construction, the Ministry even adopted the practice of purchasing foreign planes and patents for the purpose of providing Russian enterprises with models to copy.[54] Such efforts to jump-start aeronautical production, however, were bound to fail as they could not address the fundamental cause of the problem: the underdeveloped state of Russian industry in general. Lacking the machine tools, technicians, and skilled workers present in the West, Russian factories were hard-pressed to keep pace with the rapid advance of aviation technology. Even in those instances in which they were capable of reproducing an imported airplane chassis, Russian manufacturers were forced to equip their planes with motors and propellers imported from abroad.[55] Meanwhile, as the nation's factories continued to receive new models to reproduce, Western European manufacturers continued to hone their skills, precluding the possibility that Russia might overtake its more advanced rivals. Compounding this dilemma was the fact that, despite state assistance, Russian factories were incapable of producing their Blériot, Farman, and Nieuport copies at prices competitive with the western manufacturers' originals. Thus, as it endeavored to patronize national industry, the Ministry of War invariably paid higher prices for the older, inferior planes produced by domestic manufacturers.

Even with massive state intervention, Russia's aviation industry could not take flight without the active support of private business leaders and investors. As a critical source of start-up capital, private investment had proven the key element to the rapid growth of European and American airplane factories.[56] Unfortunately, such was not the case in Russia, where lack of investment capital and an uncertain demand for planes seriously threatened the success of Russian aeronautical firms. Although state purchases did provide some security amid the vagaries of conducting business in an emerging and weak market, lacking increased private investment (and more orders for new airplanes), the nation's aviation industry remained a highly risky enterprise.[57] The reasons behind the failure of the private sector to support airplane construction both concerned and confounded contemporary observers. In an attempt to draw attention to the plight of native industry, experts wrote of the "crisis" facing Russian aviation and endeavored

---

[54] See RGVIA f. 1, op. 1, d. 75771 (O zagotovlenii tabel'nogo imushchestva dlia aviatsionnykh otriadov), ll. 1–8, and RGVIA f. 802, op. 4, d. 2999 (Materialy o aviatsii v Rossii), ll. 66–7.

[55] RGVIA f. 1, op. 1, d. 75771, l. 1

[56] Bilstein, *Flight in America*, 29–30, and Morrow, *Great War*, 12–14.

[57] See the report issued by the director of the First Russian Association of Aeronautics in RGVIA f. 1, op. 1, d. 75771, ll. 11–12.

FIGURE 6. The Dux airplane factory in Moscow, circa 1915.

to mobilize support for Russia's fledgling factories through editorial exhortations. One commentator went so far as to attribute the lack of financial support to the proclivity of the Russian character against speculative ventures:

> The Russian individual is loath to approach an undertaking full of risk and adventure and as regards the [success of aeronautics] this is a real hindrance. The Russian individual (even one with means) is parsimonious with his donations. He may recklessly part with a ruble here or there but, all the same, he wants to see where his money is going . . . Having financed the first [aeronautical] competitions in Russia, society is now in a particularly sorry state. It doesn't want to part with its earnings.[58]

Although such musings obviously lacked empirical evidence, they did allude to a long-standing cultural trait that would adversely affect the nation's aviation industry for generations to come: the Russian public's deeply ingrained antipathy toward individual initiative and private enterprise in general.

Since the late seventeenth century, Russian state and society had struggled with the contradictions that accompanied the effort to rapidly modernize a tradition-bound and hierarchical nation. Faced with the formidable challenge of the West's growing military and economic might, Tsar Peter the Great propelled his country down the path to modernity by adopting a transcendent

---

[58] *Vestnik znaniia* 10 (1911): 902.

vision of development that sought to surmount the legacy of backwardness in a very short time. To secure the economic and industrial infrastructure essential for the establishment of a modern military, Peter looked to spur industrial growth by extending the scope and reach of state authority; borrowing technologies and expertise from the West, importing European institutions and habits, and enlisting the Empire's nobility into state service.[59] These policies rapidly transformed tsarist Russia from a medieval backwater into a modern Continental power. Still, the Petrine practices boded ill for the future as they imposed immense social and psychological burdens on Russia's inhabitants. Already conditioned to disdain those who pursued personal fortune by a popular culture in which individual initiative, private entrepreneurship, and profit-making enterprise suffered near-universal opprobrium, Russian citizens were further encouraged toward risk-averse behavior by a political culture in which the only certainty was the arbitrariness of state authorities.[60] Absent the firm protection of private property, legal institutions capable of evenly administering justice, and a tradition of contractual trust that could forge profitable social and economic partnerships, the western capitalist ethos and its attendant economic prosperity and industrial growth could not flourish in Russia.[61] In its place emerged a quasi-capitalistic, state-dominated economic culture that elevated the collective concerns of the nation over personal interests, cultivated the value of voluntary service at the expense of individual profit, and further ingrained dependence on higher authority in the routine administration of private affairs.

Although such cultural traits as collectivity and indifference toward financial gain would have an adverse effect on the development of Russia's aviation industry, when attributed to the nation's pilots these were seen as virtues. Unlike early European and American aviation heroes such as Blériot, Latham, and the Wright brothers, whose self-reliance, independence, and business acumen (as well as flying prowess) were integral components of their cultural iconography, Russian fliers were typically praised for their collective pursuit of the aeronautical cause and altruistic aversion to personal profit.[62] As discussed in Chapter 1, the death of Captain Lev Matsievich had occasioned an immense outpouring of commentary by the Russian press that focused on the selfless and ascetic nature of the pilot and his service to the nation. More than a simple flier motivated by a personal desire for fame and fortune, Matsievich was embraced as the embodiment of an idealized

---

[59] Vasili Klyuchevsky, *Peter the Great* (Boston: Beacon Press, 1958).

[60] James L. West, "Merchant Moscow in Historical Context," in James L. West and Iurii A. Petrov (eds.), *Merchant Moscow: Images of Russia's Vanished Bourgeoisie* (Princeton, NJ: Princeton University Press, 1998), 6.

[61] Tim McDaniel, *Autocracy, Capitalism, and Revolution in Russia* (Berkeley: University of California Press, 1988), 16–24.

[62] On the independence and entrepreneurial spirit of the Wright brothers, see Wohl, *Passion for Wings*, 11–15.

cultural type representing traditional Russian virtues such as collective service and asceticism. Such popular visions were regularly extended to the
nation's other aviators. Widely celebrated for their bravery, showmanship,
and derring-do, as were western pilots, Russia's fliers were also assigned
the attributes of selflessness and collectivism, highly regarded characteristics
that resonated with Russian citizens as archetypal cultural values.[63] Commenting in the wake of Mikhail Efimov's first flight in Russia, one contemporary observer noted how dissimilar the Russian "ideal flier" was from his
European peers. Whereas the typical European pilot was said to fly "only
for the sake of money," Russians, by contrast, were "distinguished by their
enormous presence of spirit, bravery, love of their vocation, and their complete absence of monetary considerations."[64] Efimov's subsequent decision
to abandon his lucrative career as an aeronautical performer to serve the
state as chief instructor at the Sevastopol' Aviation School seemed only to
confirm this sentiment.

Although the persistence of these cultural traits may have retarded the
development of Russian private aviation, by the spring of 1913 architects
of the state's policy of "buy now, build later" had managed at least the
appearance of success. Owing to a massive infusion of state expenditures,
the commander of the General Staff's Aeronautical Section could point to a
series of material accomplishments that suggested that Russia's military aviation program had finally gotten off the ground. The numbers were certainly
laudable. At the time of the transfer of responsibility for aeronautical matters to the General Staff in September 1912, the Russian army had possessed
eight aviation detachments that, for the most part, existed only on paper. Of
these eight detachments, only four were equipped with the full complement
of six airplanes, while three of the remaining detachments shared a collection
of eight machines. The final detachment could not boast a single aircraft. In
the early autumn of 1912 the Russian "air fleet" thus consisted of thirty-two
planes, with no special provisions having been made for ensuring their supply
or for furnishing them with spare parts.[65] By May 1913, however, the state
could claim substantial progress. In just under eight months, the number of
aviation detachments expanded to eighteen and the total number of planes
therein from 32 to 112. Aside from those aircraft already in the field, ninety
completed planes were awaiting deployment while an additional ninety-six,
scheduled for delivery in the next six weeks, were on order from various
factories. Thus, according to the estimates of the Ministry of War, Russian
military aviation had taken a gigantic step forward in the last half year. In
comparison with foreign air fleets, Russia now occupied second place (after

[63] Vitarbo, "Power," 132.
[64] Cited in E. V. Koroleva and V. A. Rudnik, *Soperniki orlov* (Odessa, 1976), 69–70.
[65] RGVIA f. 2000, op. 7, d. 231, l. 12. In addition to the thirty-two planes it already possessed,
the Ministry also noted that 155 airplanes were on order.

France) in the total number of military airplanes that it possessed.[66] Similarly, the military's lighter-than-air detachments boasted comparable advances. By May 1913, the number of dirigibles under military command had increased from ten to fifteen, nearly doubling Russia's standing in both categories by which European ministries measured their lighter-than-air forces: total cubic capacity and horsepower.[67]

THE RUSSIAN WARRIOR

While the state continued to expend considerable resources in its crash campaign to purchase a military air fleet, the nation's constructors struggled to match the engineering feats of their European counterparts. To this end, technicians like Ia. M. Gakkel', S. S. Shchetinin, and A. A. Antar endeavored to duplicate aircraft designs of the leading French manufacturers Nieuport, Blériot, and Voisin.[68] Of all Russian technicians, however, none demonstrated more skill in the field of original airplane design and construction than Igor Sikorsky.

The son of a prominent professor of psychology, Igor I. Sikorsky (1889–1972) would emerge as Imperial Russia's greatest aeronautical figure. As a child, Sikorsky's exposure to the futuristic fiction of Jules Verne inspired his interest in the possibilities of human flight. With the encouragement and support of his family, Sikorsky early on resolved to devote his energies to the science of aeronautics. Following his graduation from the St. Petersburg Naval Academy in 1906, Sikorsky traveled for a brief time in France before enrolling in the engineering department of Kiev's Polytechnic Institute. On the completion of his engineering studies, Sikorsky built his first flying machine in 1908, a rotary-powered craft patterned after the contraptions he had viewed as a child in the sketchbooks of Leonardo da Vinci. Sikorsky's earliest helicopters proved only partially successful. Owing to the limits of contemporary motors, these experimental aircraft were woefully underpowered and capable of only short "hops" in the air without passengers. In 1910, Sikorsky abandoned helicopters and turned his attention toward the construction of fixed-wing aircraft. Over the course of sixteen months (during which time he worked out of a barn on his father's estate outside Kiev) Sikorsky produced a series of monoplanes and biplanes, each more airworthy than its predecessor. In a succession of test flights personally

---

[66] *Ibid.* The Ministry included in its calculations those planes recently completed (but not yet delivered) as well as those scheduled to be built within the next month and a half. In doing so, it arrived at the optimistic figure of 298 Russian airplanes.

[67] *Ibid.*, l. 13.

[68] For a complete account of airplane constructors in Imperial Russia see V. B. Shavrov, *Istoriia konstruktsii samoletov v SSSR do 1938 g.* (Moscow, 1986), 38–174.

piloted by the inventor, Sikorsky's airplanes set Russian records for altitude and flight duration.[69]

The success of Sikorsky's earliest airplane series culminated in the late summer of 1912 with the first-place finish of the inventor's S-6b biplane at the Military Ministry's aeronautical competition.[70] The victory greatly enhanced Sikorsky's emerging reputation and drew public attention to the vital issue of domestic aircraft design and production. Sikorsky's strong showing at the competition was followed by another significant achievement, the 6 October 1912 debut of his S-5a airplane: a modified version of the S-6b capable of landing on water. The first functional hydroplane designed by a Russian, Sikorsky's aircraft was hailed by the press, and the constructor was lionized for his contributions to the development of the nation's aviation program.[71] Writing in the wake of the hydroplane's first successful flights, one paper emphasized Sikorsky's importance to the nation, calling attention to the fact that, "outside of the focus of public scrutiny, Sikorsky continues his great undertaking, attaining victory after victory and compelling us to be proud of him as the first Russian constructor mighty enough to compete with foreigners and even . . . to surpass them."[72] Although such imputations of innovative supremacy were certainly premature, Sikorsky's successes indicated that Russian inventors were indeed capable of approaching the standards set by western designers notwithstanding the underdeveloped state of the nation's industrial infrastructure. To this end, Sikorsky's earliest accomplishments were welcomed by the public as hopeful portents of the future.

Sikorsky's status as Russia's preeminent airplane designer was firmly entrenched in the spring of 1913 as the nation witnessed test flights of his latest creation: the world's first multiengine airplane. Manufactured by the Russo–Balt Carriage Factory, the four-engine aircraft (known for a time as the *Grand*) was of mammoth proportions. Surpassing sixty feet in length and graced with a wingspan approaching ninety feet, the *Grand* weighed in at close to two tons. Powered by four 100-horsepower Argus engines, the airplane could accommodate up to twelve passengers, inclusive of the two-man crew required to operate the behemoth. More impressive still, the *Grand* could lift in excess of 1,600 pounds and stay aloft for hours while maintaining a cruising speed of up to fifty-five miles an hour.[73] At that time the largest

[69] Dorothy Cochrane, Von Hardesty and Russell Lee, *The Aviation Careers of Igor Sikorsky* (Seattle, WA: University of Washington Press, 1989), 21–6, and K. N. Finne, *Igor Sikorsky: The Russian Years*. Edited by Carl J. Bobrow and Von Hardesty. Translated by Von Hardesty (Washington, D.C.: Smithsonian Institution Press, 1987), 28–9.

[70] See above, pp. 48–9.

[71] On Sikorsky's hydroplane see V. N. Bychkov, "Samolety v nachalom periode ikh razvitiia," in G. S. Biushgens (ed.), *Aviatsiia v Rossii*, 258, and Shavrov, *Istoriia konstruktsii*, 140–2.

[72] *Sankt Peterburgskiia vedomosti*, 9 October 1912. The ellipses appear in the original.

[73] *Tekhnika vozdukhoplavaniia* 9–10 (1913): 399–401.

airplane in the world, the *Grand* represented a major accomplishment for Russia's hard-pressed aviation industry.

Although Sikorsky's *Grand* was justifiably hailed by Russian contemporaries as a revolution in the history of world aeronautics, the "airplane-giant" symbolized the numerous contradictions that characterized Imperial aviation. A technical marvel incorporating design innovations that transformed the field of aeronautics, the *Grand* was an incongruous demonstration that Russia's underdeveloped and undistinguished industry was capable of inspired feats of genius. Sikorsky's resolve to construct a multiengine aircraft flew directly in the face of conventional wisdom. Aeronautical specialists had long believed that multiple-engine airplanes were inherently unstable. Supported by the mistaken theory that the failure of a single engine would produce asymmetrical propeller thrust, throwing the craft into a violent and uncontrollable spin, most experts dismissed the possibility of constructing multiple-engine airplanes. The detailed and careful experiments that Sikorsky conducted with the *Grand* convincingly proved skeptics wrong. Still, the Russian *Grand* earned only grudging respect from European observers, who derisively referred to Sikorsky's creation as the "Petersburg Duck."[74]

The perspicacity displayed by Sikorsky in the design and construction of the craft did not, however, extend to the more mundane consideration of the airplane's storage. Far surpassing the measurements of a typical aircraft, the *Grand* was so large that it could not fit into existing hangars. As a result, the 40,000-ruble airplane was initially stored outside, exposed to the elements and shielded from the eyes of curious onlookers by only a wooden fence.[75] Like the aviation industry itself, Sikorsky's airplane suffered from the inability of Russia's underdeveloped infrastructure to exploit the opportunities made possible by the nation's visionary technicians and inventors.

In contrast to the question of the *Grand*'s storage, considerable attention was devoted to the issue of the aircraft's name. Originally dubbed the *Big Baltic* [*Bolshoi Baltiiskii*] in deference to the factory where it was constructed, but popularly known as the *Grand*, Sikorsky's airplane received "a more appropriate" title in July when it was officially rechristened the *Russian Warrior* [*Russkii vitiaz'*].[76] August, noble, and (unlike the French moniker "Grand") authentically Russian, the new name juxtaposed the heroic image of a traditional Russian knight with the technological marvels of the modern world. Like the ancient *bogatyr'* who defended the nation from the eastern threat of the Mongol tribes, Sikorsky's aircraft promised to conquer the skies and advance Russia's interests against contemporary western challengers. With this in mind, journalists hailed the airborne victories of the

---

[74] Von Hardesty, "Introduction" to Finne, *Igor Sikorsky*, 18.

[75] *Tekhnika vozdukhoplavaniia* 4–5 (1913): 243, and G. I. Katyshev and V. P. Mikheev, *Kryl'ia Sikorskogo* (Moscow, 1992), 94. On the airplane's cost, see *Vechernee vremia*, 10 June 1913.

[76] *K sportu!* 21 (1913): 15.

FIGURE 7. Igor Sikorsky's *Russian Warrior*, 1913.

Russian Warrior, noting that the craft had "captured the attention of the entire civilized world" and that neighboring nations could only "watch with envy and dread" the flights undertaken by the largest airplane ever to be constructed.[77] Lost amid the fanfare of patriotic pronouncements that surrounded the appearance of the plane were unsettling facts concerning its airworthiness. Notwithstanding the aircraft's revolutionary design, two of the four engines used to power it were old and unreliable, a fact that seriously compromised the speed and safety of the airplane. Ironically, even though brand new, Imperial Russia's most advanced aircraft was threatened by obsolescence.[78]

THE MARASMUS OF IMPERIAL AVIATION

A product of Sikorsky's creative genius, the *Russian Warrior* was made possible by the generous financial support of Mikhail Shidlovskii. A member of the State Council and director of the Russo–Balt Carriage Factory, Shidlovskii had built a reputation as a visionary entrepreneur through his

---

[77] *Avtomobil'naia zhizn' i aviatsiia* 6 (1914): 19.

[78] *Tekhnika vozdukhoplavaniia* 9–10 (1913): 402. The *Russian Warrior* quickly fell victim to the nation's inexpert industry. Sikorsky's giant was destroyed at the 1913 military competition when the motor from a Russian-made biplane, flying overhead, came loose. The eighty-horsepower Dux engine fell to earth, hitting the *Russian Warrior* and demolishing the aircraft's port wing. See *Avtomobil'naia zhizn' i aviatsiia* 6 (1914): 21.

pioneering work in the nation's nascent automobile industry.[79] Combining sharp business acumen with a willingness to risk capital on speculative ventures, Shidlovskii was a rare commodity in Imperial Russia: a generous patron with money to spare. Like fellow businessman Dmitrii Riabushinskii, whose financial largess had made possible the creation of the world's first wind tunnel at a suburban estate outside of Moscow,[80] Shidlovskii spared no expense in transforming the nation's aeronautical visions into reality. His importance to the realization of Sikorsky's projects was not lost on contemporary observers. In reference to the instrumental role played by the factory director, one leading newspaper drew a stark comparison between Sikorsky's good fortune and the situation facing the designer's colleagues: "Sikorsky has succeeded in funding his projects. But Sikorsky did not work alone in this regard. Gakkel, Khioni and Porokhovshchikov also once constructed airplanes, but where are they now? They are with hundreds of others who studied in Russian aviation schools. They have left the field for lack of funding."[81]

The press's acknowledgment of Shidlovskii's role in supporting Sikorsky's projects was a veiled indication of continuing concerns about the future of the Russian aeronautical enterprise. Returning to a theme first addressed in 1912, newsmen again voiced frustration at the lack of private investment available for the development of Russian aviation. Measuring Russia's aeronautical successes against the public subscriptions and productive capacities of western rivals, the Russian press concluded that the nation's aviation program was undergoing a severe crisis.[82] In an impassioned letter to the newspaper *Birzhevoi den'* [*Exchange Day*], written in response to the ongoing debate over the poor state of the nation's aeronautical ventures, one perturbed pilot identified the absence of private funding as the key element in explaining the shortcomings of Russian aviation. In contrast to French and German fliers who flourished thanks to the donations of sponsors and benefactors, Russian fliers were denied opportunities owing to the paucity of patrons, like Shidlovskii, who were willing to support exhibitions and fund research. As such, whereas military programs were given opportunities to grow, private aviators were treated like "neglected stepsons," forced to endure second-class

---

[79] Shidlovskii's factory was the only manufacturer of Russian automobiles in the Imperial era. See Finne, *Igor Sikorsky*, 37.

[80] Joseph Bradley, "Merchant Moscow After Hours: Associations and Leisure," in West and Petrov (eds.), *Merchant Moscow*, 141–2.

[81] *Golos Rusi*, 9 February 1914. See also "Russkaia sportivnaia aviatsiia v 1914 g.," *Aero i avtomobil'naia zhizn'* 3 (1914): 5–8.

[82] See, for example, the articles titled "Nasha voennaia aviatsiia," *Vechernee vremia*, 15 June 1913; "Krizis russkoi aviatsii," *Ranee utro*, 12 July 1913; "Vozdushnaia opasnost'," *Golos Rusi*, 2 February 1914; and "My i sosedy," *Voskresenaia vechernaia gazeta*, 16 February 1914, among many others.

status at the expense of military expansion.[83] The dangerous consequences of this situation were pointed out by numerous commentators who diagnosed such symptoms as the poor quality of Russian-made aircraft, the underdevelopment of the nation's aviation industry and the questionable level of Russian military preparedness as emanating from the constraints facing private aviation.[84]

Ironically, the press concluded that the sorry state of private aviation and the uneasy, uncooperative relationship that existed between state agencies and public aeronautical establishments resulted from a lack of government initiative. In an attempt to explain the "marasmus of Russian aeronautics," one angry commentator drew explicit connections between the "death of private aeronautics in Russia" and the unimpressive performance of the autocracy's voluntary subscription campaign. In stark contrast to the success of French and German public drives that had, to date, raised some 6.5 million francs and 7.5 million marks, respectively, for both military and private aeronautical concerns, the Russian campaign had succeeded in squeezing only 2 million rubles from the public with "not a single kopeck of the money going to private aviation." As a result, this writer complained, "with each new day private aviation in Russia approaches its death. We do not possess a single world record and we cannot claim a single victory. . . . Where France and Germany each possess around 100 airplane factories, we have 5. And where Germany has almost 100 aeronautical societies with 100,000 members, France has 80 with 40,000 members. In Russia there are 10, with a membership of only 2,000."[85] Other commentators drew lessons from these figures and pointed to state failures as a means of explaining the "complete emasculation" of private aviation.[86] Unlike the military ministries in Germany and France, which recognized the fundamental importance of a reserve of private fliers to military preparedness (and therefore encouraged the growth of independent aeronautical societies), the Russian government lent no support to the nation's air clubs, thereby hindering the advancement of private aviation.[87] Compounding matters, one observer complained, the legal restrictions placed on private aviation remained so strict as to "kill even the idea of the possibility of the existence of aviation outside of state establishments."[88] Without state direction private aviation could not flourish. Nevertheless, the state had thus far proven unwilling to work with private aeronautical organizations to advance their mutual interest in developing Russian aviation.

[83] A. Agafonov, "Pasynki russkoi aviatsii," *Birzhevoi den'*, 29 January 1914.
[84] "Kustarnym sposobom," *Svet*, 4 July 1914.
[85] "Tam i zdes'," *Utro Rossii*, 22 March 1914.
[86] *Novoe vremia*, 9 February 1914.
[87] See also RGVIA f. 2000, d. 240 (Vyrezki iz gazet), l. 101.
[88] *Novoe vremia*, 9 February 1914.

Notwithstanding the indignation leveled against the state for its alleged failure to support private aviation, the activities of Russia's numerous aeronautical societies raised serious questions regarding their ability to work effectively with the government in preparing an air fleet for the nation's defense. In the spring of 1914, Russia's private aeronautical establishments convened in St. Petersburg for the Third Aeronautical Congress. Like previous Congresses held in 1911 and 1912, the Third Congress was intended to help coordinate the activities of the country's many circles, clubs, and societies, to assess the present condition of Russian aviation, and to provide a framework for the future development of aeronautics within the Russian Empire. The Third Congress fell far short of its goals. In light of the "deep crisis plaguing Russian aviation," aeronautical observers expected that the Third Congress would devote its attention to developing solutions to the problems besetting the industry. One observer even suggested the creation of "a central command establishment that would regulate the aeronautical life of the whole country and unite the activities of local aeronautical organizations"; a recommendation remarkably similar to plans for a still unrealized Aeronautical Union first proposed in 1911 and subsequently revived in 1912.[89] Unfortunately, the paltry results of the Third Aeronautical Congress made even the previous two gatherings appear productive. In a biting review of the Congress's activities, one disillusioned critic remarked that it "provided no possible means of familiarizing the public with the current status of Russian aeronautics, with all of its inadequacies and problems." Numerous other publications concurred, characterizing the activities of the Congress as evidence of the "complete bankruptcy of private aeronautics in Russia."[90]

The harsh criticism directed at the Third Aeronautical Congress was, in turn, a reflection of disillusionment with the capabilities of the Congress's individual institutional members. And this disillusionment was nowhere more apparent than in the growing vocal antipathy toward IVAK. Although the disaster of the 1911 St. Petersburg–Moscow Race dealt IVAK's reputation a serious blow, the club had never been immune from criticism. Despite its status as Russia's first and most prominent air club, IVAK had long come under sharp attacks for its bloated hierarchy, regal atmosphere, and lack of seriousness in serving the nation's aviation needs. As early as January 1910, one leading journal had openly derided IVAK, attacking it for attracting individuals who in no way contributed to the aeronautical cause. Claiming that "of the 700 members in the club, hardly two percent have any direct ties to aeronautics and can do anything in the field," the journal ridiculed IVAK for having obtained "the overwhelming majority of its members purely by

[89] *Moskovskiia vedomosti*, 9 April 1914.

[90] "Bankrotstvo," *Utro Rossii*, 16 April 1914. For similarly harsh reviews of the Congress, see *Novoe vremia* 10 & 11 April 1914; *Peterburgskaia gazeta*, 11 April 1914; *Peterburgskii kur'er'*, 11 April 1914; *Golos Rusi*, 12 April 1914; and *Rech'*, 15 April 1914.

chance and as a result of the fact that [aviation was] in fashion."[91] Similarly harsh criticisms were leveled by other observers. Characterizing IVAK's posh St. Petersburg headquarters (complete with fine chandeliers and tropical plants) as "a luxurious rout in which the Club's members and their guests could while away the hours," *Vestnik vozdukhoplavaniia* disparaged the dilettantish organization for having fostered the illusion that Russia possessed an establishment capable of advancing aviation when, in fact, IVAK had done nothing in this regard.[92] Three years later, and despite the club's best efforts, public opinion toward the organization had changed little. In a vicious 1913 exposé of the air club, a leading weekly castigated the club's members as "a group of typical bureaucratic servants who rally together under the flag of a beautiful sport but whose 'honorable' activity has done nothing for aviation in general or the nation's aviation in particular." Rather than advancing Russian aviation, the article alleged, "club members, in hot pursuit of tawdry badges and formal titles, profane this great sport and concern themselves, for the most part, with trying to enroll a few more ballerinas in the club. . . . The Chairman of the Aero-Club, Count Stenbok-Fermor, is a rabid ballet fan. Good for him. To each his own. But what does ballet have to do with aviation?"[93]

The animosity directed toward IVAK was a striking indication of the ongoing difficulties faced by the nation's aeronautical organizations. As the most prominent proponents of Russian aviation, organizations like IVAK had expected to play instrumental roles in fostering the air-mindedness of the nation's citizenry. In helping to coordinate the voluntary subscription, sponsoring exhibitions, organizing competitions, and training fliers, air clubs and societies had attempted to mobilize the nation, infusing ordinary citizens with a passion for flight and drawing on their financial support for the establishment of a Russian air fleet. Including in their ranks members of the most elite political, scientific, and cultural circles, aviation societies seemed destined to solve admirably the problems posed by the aeronautical age. Indeed, by the middle of 1914 the nation's aeronautical patrons could point to a series of real accomplishments: the creation of a nationwide network of aeronautical clubs, circles, and societies devoted to expanding air consciousness, the organization of countless competitions and public spectacles that had raised public awareness of flight, and, finally, the collection of funds that had helped to purchase a national air fleet, ranking second only to the French in its number of planes. Notwithstanding these gains, it was increasingly clear that aviation supporters had failed to solve a series of systemic problems that

[91] *Aero i avtomobil'naia zhizn'* 1 (1910): 8.
[92] *Vestnik vozdukhoplavaniia* 3 (1910): 6.
[93] Konstantin Makovskii, "'Deiateli' russkago vozdukhoplavaniia . . . ," *Sinii zhurnal* 35 (1913): 11. For yet another attack on the Aero-Club and its activities see M. N. Likharev, "A Vas'ka slushaet da kushaet ili nasha vozdukhoplavatel'," *Sinii zhurnal* 39 (1913): 7.

FIGURE 8. Igor Sikorsky's *Il'ia Muromets*, circa 1914. Photo courtesy Von Hardesty.

threatened to rob the nation of its airplane dreams. From the continuing conflicts between state and private enterprises to the indifference of private investors and from the difficulties of reproducing foreign airplane designs to the inability to establish an independent aviation industry, Imperial Russia had yet to overcome the formidable challenges posed by the modern age of flight.

FLIGHTS OF FANCY

As war clouds gathered on the nation's western horizon, Russian citizens were feted with a final, fleeting glimpse of the aeronautical glory they longed to attain. In the late spring and early summer of 1914, the public again turned its gaze skyward in tribute to the accomplishments of the country's greatest airplane constructor. Following the demolition of his prized *Russian Warrior*, Igor Sikorsky had rebounded with the creation of a second air giant, more stable, more airworthy, and more practical than his original. Named after Russia's most beloved folkloric hero, the *Il'ia Muromets* was unveiled to the public in a spectacular series of demonstration flights that sparked the imagination of the most obdurate skeptics and offered hope that Russia might yet transcend its condition and attain prominence in the battle for the skies.

Like its predecessor, the *Il'ia Muromets* was a stunning achievement in airplane construction. Possessing a wingspan some twenty percent greater than that of the *Russian Warrior* and capable of lifting more than 2,000 pounds, the *Il'ia Muromets* represented a significant improvement over Sikorsky's first multiple-engine airplane.[94] Of particular interest were the changes made by Sikorsky in the design of the aircraft's fuselage. Unlike the cabin of the *Russian Warrior*, which sat atop the plane's central frame, the passenger hold of the *Muromets* was incorporated into the fuselage, a design innovation streamlining the airplane that would serve as the model for all future military and civilian passenger craft.[95] More impressive still were the dimensions of the new passenger compartment. Over five feet wide and six feet high, it was capable of comfortably accommodating up to a dozen people (although, on one flight, Sikorsky was able to cram sixteen passengers and a dog into the plane). Specially equipped to meet passengers' needs on long-distance flights, the fuselage was divided into several compartments, complete with wicker chairs and small tables. The airplane also included a sleeping cabin and an observation platform that was mounted toward the rear of the craft. Additional features included a generator for producing electric light to illuminate the cabin, a heating system, and, in another aviation first, a toilet.[96]

The unveiling of the *Il'ia Muromets* was accompanied by delirious endorsements from the press. Completely forgetting the recent criticism they had leveled at the nation's aviation program, Russia's newsmen responded with a series of patriotic pronouncements that glorified Sikorsky and paid glowing tribute to his latest creation. Proclaiming the appearance of the new airplane as proof that the "light of creativity truly shines from the East," the press acknowledged the now-indisputable fact that Russian aviation could "soar so high and successfully."[97] Other awestruck observers used the occasion of the plane's unveiling to deride the accomplishments of the nation's competitors and to advance Sikorsky's flying giant as a herald of aviation's future.[98] The initial outburst of patriotic passion gave way to unrestrained nationalistic delirium in June of 1914 as Sikorsky undertook a round-trip flight between St. Petersburg and Kiev to demonstrate the capabilities of his airplane. Hailing the "brilliant flight of the glorious Russian flier" aboard his "miraculous *bogatyr'*," the press trumpeted the "colossal practical meaning" of the St. Petersburg–Kiev flight and proclaimed Sikorsky's latest creation incontrovertible proof that "Russian fliers, in their craftsmanship, experience, and endurance concede nothing to the so-called . . . German 'kings of the air.'"[99] With his "demonstration to the stunned world that Russia truly does possess dread military weapons for use against its enemies," Sikorsky

[94] For the technical specifications of the airplane see RGVIA f. 802, op. 4, d. 2113 (Perepiska s GUGSh o formirovanii eskadrili 'Il'ia Muromets'), l. 191.

[95] Shavrov, *Istoriia konstruktsii*, 222.

[96] Cochrane *et al.*, *Aviation Careers*, 37–8.

[97] *Nizhegorodskii listok*, 20 February 1914.

[98] See, for example, *Golos Rusi*, 23 February 1914. Alongside articles on the airplane the paper printed a cartoon that depicted a soaring *Il'ia Muromets* juxtaposed with an exploding zeppelin.

[99] *Moskovskiia vedomosti*, 19 June 1914, and *Golos Rusi*, 25 March 1914.

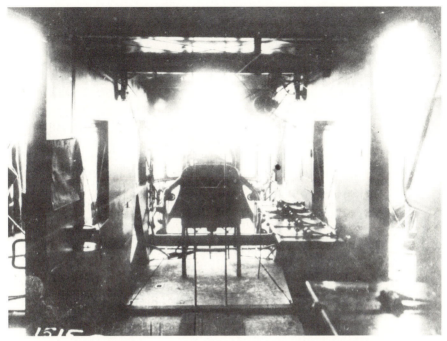

FIGURE 9. Inside the cabin of the *Il'ia Muromets*. Photo courtesy Von Hardesty.

had proven that "Russian military aviation [was] once again in the forefront of world aeronautics."[100]

The frenetic response to the presentation of the *Il'ia Muromets* took place at a time of growing European uncertainty and rising political tensions. Only the day before Sikorsky's air giant touched down at the Kiev aerodrome, the press had reported on the assassination of Habsburg Archduke Franz Ferdinand in Sarajevo, an event that shook the European community and that ultimately precipitated the First World War. In light of the tense atmosphere that hovered over Europe in the summer of 1914, the bombastic reception of the *Il'ia Muromets* is easily understood. For weeks preceding the St. Petersburg–Kiev flight, newspapers had been filled with reports documenting the strengths of the German air fleet and warning the public of increasingly frequent incursions by the German air force across the nation's western border.[101] For nervous Russians, anxious for reassurance of their personal safety, the successes of the *Il'ia Muromets* instilled the fanciful notion that the nation was prepared for the onset of war. And yet, like the

---

[100] *Avtomobil'naia zhizn' i aviatsiia* 7 (1914): 21, and *Russkoe znamia*, 22 June 1914.
[101] On the government's surveillance of the Austrian and German aviation programs, see RGVIA, f. 802, op. 4, d. 3001 (Raporty o razvitii vozdukhoplavaniia za granitsi).

fleeting wave of patriotic unity and national accord that would sweep over Russia in the first months of the conflict, the hope provided by the *Il'ia Muromets* could not transcend grim reality.

The outbreak of hostilities in August 1914 underscored the inherent contradictions that characterized Imperial Russia's quest for aeronautical pre-eminence. Although the Russian military boasted one of the world's largest aviation fleets in the summer of 1914, the potential impact of these resources was largely offset by the fact that the country's more than 260 aircraft were deployed along Europe's longest frontier. Stretching more than 700 miles from the Rumanian border to the shores of the Baltic Sea, Russia's two fronts against Austria–Hungary and Germany posed immense strategic and logistical problems. Efforts to coordinate aviation resources and strategy were further compounded by organizational disarray. In the early spring of 1914, the Imperial General Staff [*Stavka*] had approved a comprehensive plan for the reorganization and reequipment of the military's aviation sections. The five-year plan, which included the appropriation of some 300 new aircraft and the establishment of ten squadrons of Il'ia Muromtsy, had hardly been set into motion when the Great War began.[102] After years of preparation, the Russian air command was caught off guard. In addition to these factors, *Stavka* officials, like their counterparts in Western Europe, faced difficulties at first determining how best to incorporate their aeronautical detachments [*otriady*] with more traditional military units. In the absence of any uniform doctrine covering the application of aviation technology on the field of battle (and owing to the continuing limitations of the young technology itself), airplanes were initially restricted to undertaking reconnaissance and directing artillery bombardments.

Even so, from the outset of the war, Russian airplanes and pilots played important, if isolated, roles in the country's military campaigns. Significant in this regard were the heroism and the flying skill displayed in the opening weeks of combat by Captain Viacheslav Tkachev, commander of the 20th Air Corps *otriad* assigned to the Russian Fourth Army on the South-Western Front. On 25 August 1914, while undertaking a low-altitude reconnaissance mission near the town of Krasnik, Tkachev's airplane came under heavy ground fire from Austrian units. During the course of the attack, shrapnel punctured the fuel tank of his plane. While using his leg to stem the release of fuel, Tkachev made a forced landing between the opposing armies' front lines. Dragged to safety by Russian infantrymen, the pilot was able to report on the presence of a large concentration of enemy units shielded from ground observers owing to a nearby forest. Alerted to the threat of an impending

---

[102] RGVIA f. 802, op. 4, d. 3002 (Kratkii otchet deiatel'nosti glavnogo voenno-tekhnicheskogo upravleniia po vozdukhoplavatel'nomu otdeleniiu za 1914 g.), ll. 99–107.

FIGURE 10. "The War in the Air." Poster, 1915. Courtesy The Hoover Institution.

Austrian advance, Fourth Army commanders ordered a retreat that enabled more than 200,000 Russian soldiers to escape encirclement.[103]

If Tkachev's actions revealed the bravery of which Russian aviators were capable, credit for the most famous display of World War I aeronautical heroism belonged to Captain Petr Nesterov. Among the country's most esteemed prewar aviators, Nesterov had earlier cemented his flying celebrity on 9 September 1913 [n.s.] when he became the first person in history to complete a mid-air loop. One year later, the pilot demonstrated still greater courage. While on patrol over Russia's western military frontier, Nesterov spotted a two-seater Albatross biplane flying reconnaissance for the Austro–Hungarian army. The Russian pilot gave chase. After overtaking his slower opponent, Nesterov rammed the nose of his unarmed Moran-G monoplane into the tail section of the enemy aircraft. The force of the impact sent the two planes hurtling toward earth. The ensuing crashes claimed the lives of both Habsburg aviators as well as Nesterov.[104] For this heroic, first-ever feat of aerial ramming [*taran*], Nesterov earned the undying admiration of the Russian press and public. Invoking the rhetoric of self-sacrifice and collectivism earlier attributed to fliers such as Lev Matsievich and Mikhail Efimov, wartime publications bearing titles such as *Heroic Deeds of Russian Aviators* proclaimed Nesterov and his comrades patriotic models of Russian honor and bravery.[105] Tellingly, Nesterov's example would be repeated numerous times during the course of the First (and, later, the Second) World War, oftentimes with similarly fatal results.[106]

While pilots such as Tkachev and Nesterov exemplified the skill and bravery of Imperial Russian military aviators, the wartime exploits of Igor Sikorsky's Il'ia Muromtsy provided an incongruent demonstration of the extent to which Russia's beleaguered aviation program was capable of truly historic innovations. Following the first successful test flights of Sikorsky's air giant in the winter of 1913–14, the Military-Technical Administration [*Glavnoe voenno-tekhnicheskoe upravlenie*] had submitted an order to Mikhail Shidlovskii's Russo–Balt Factory for the delivery of ten aircraft (at a cost of 150,000 rubles apiece) by 12 March 1915. Characteristically, the requisition contract was not fulfilled by the agreed-on date. Owing to the factory's difficulties in securing the necessary engines from British and French sources, as late as 4 March 1915 only six of the expected ten Muromtsy had been delivered to the military.[107] In the meantime, army officials struggled to

---

[103] Timothy Wilson, "A Story Untold: The Imperial Russian Air Force, 1909–1917" (Ph.D. dissertation, Pennsylvania State University, 2001), 116–8.

[104] P. D. Duz', *Istoriia vozdukhoplavaniia i aviatsii v Rossii: iiul' 1914 g. – oktiabr' 1917 g.* (Moscow, Mashinostroenie, 1986), 288.

[105] Pavel Kritskii, *Podvigi Russkikh aviatorov* (Moscow, 1915).

[106] For accounts of *taran* involving Soviet pilots during the Second World War, see Chapter 9.

[107] RGVIA f. 802, op. 4, d. 2113, l. 73.

FIGURE 11. "The Heroic Exploit and Death of the Celebrated Flier Captain P. N. Nesterov." Poster, 1915. Courtesy The Hoover Institution.

find a suitable role for the aircraft. Their initial experiences did not bode well for the future of the Muromets. Following a series of minor accidents, and faced with the necessity of extended training for Muromsty aircrews as well as entrenched opposition to the airplane among high-ranking bureaucrats and rank-and-file pilots, the military decided to terminate its contract with the Russo–Balt Factory in early November 1914.[108]

With the fortunes of his company placed in jeopardy thanks to the impending cancellation of the military's 1.5-million-ruble order, Shidlovskii intervened with *Stavka* officials in an attempt to salvage the Il'ia Muromets program. In late November, he petitioned the Imperial General Staff to allow him to take personal command of the military's existing aircraft. Noting that his experience overseeing production of the planes as well as his status as a veteran naval officer qualified him for this important post, Shidlovskii argued that, with improved supervision (and the proper training of aircrews), the military potential of the airplane-behemoths would finally be realized.[109] Perhaps recognizing that it had nothing to lose from this unorthodox request, the *Stavka* agreed. On 14 December 1914 the General Staff ordered the formation of a unified "Squadron of Flying Ships" [*Eskadra vozdushnykh korablei*, or EVK] consisting of twelve Muromtsy, ten of which were assigned to active duty while the remaining two were reserved for training purposes.[110] Promoted to the rank of Major-General, Shidlovskii was placed in command of the squadron. To assist him with overseeing the training of flight crews, Shidlovskii enlisted the aid of the airplane's inventor, Igor Sikorsky.

In addition to marking a turn of fortune for the aerial giant, the organization of the EVK was followed by a series of practical innovations that would enable Russians to claim justifiably that, in at least one respect, their nation was at the forefront of world aeronautics. True to his promises, Shidlovskii proved to be an effective commander. Under his leadership, training of the Muromtsy aircrews quickly improved. So, too, did the manner in which the aircraft was deployed. A series of flights over German positions in the early spring of 1915 demonstrated the plane's utility not only as a reconnaissance instrument, but also its effectiveness as an offensive weapon. Owing to its comparatively massive range, size, and payload capacity, the Il'ia Muromets proved uniquely suited to its function as the world's first heavy bomber.[111] During an early mission over the Russian North-Western

[108] Ibid., ll. 150–1. See also Wilson, "Story Untold," 161–4. Despite an overly optimistic assessment of Imperial Russia's aeronautical fortunes resulting from only limited use of Russian archival and contemporary sources, Wilson's dissertation contains a very good summary of the wartime history of the Il'ia Muromtsy.

[109] Marat Khairulin, "Korablie eskadry v delakh protiv nepriatelia, iiul' 1914–dekabr' 1916 g.," *Mir aviatsii* (Ianvaria 1992): 6, cited in Wilson, "Story Untold," 164.

[110] RGVIA f. 802 op. 4, d. 2113, l. 11.

[111] The formation of the EVK predated the deployment of Italy's 21st Bomber Squadron by some eight months. See Lee Kennett, *The First Air War* (New York: The Free Press, 1991), 45–6.

FIGURE 12. Russian aviators demonstrate early bombardment techniques, 1915.

Front on 28 February 1915, for example, one Muromets aircrew released more than 600 pounds of bombs upon German ground forces. At a time when aerial assaults had previously been limited to an errant bomb or two being dropped from a single-engine airplane, the scale of bombardment made possible by Russia's aerial behemoth was truly historic.[112] Moreover, when equipped with its full compliment of six machine guns, the Il'ia Muromets proved almost impossible to bring down. Despite flying more than 400 sorties during the course of the war, only one of the seventy-three aircraft deployed between 1914 and 1918 was lost to enemy fire.[113] The significance of Russia's innovative bomber was underscored in mid-1916, when both the French and British governments finalized agreements to acquire design and production rights to the plane from the Russo–Balt Factory.

Unfortunately for the autocratic state, the successes of the Il'ia Muromets program could not reverse the tide of war. As early as the opening months of military hostilities, the inherent, systemic weaknesses of the Imperial

[112] Wilson, "Story Untold," 165. During the war, the twenty squadrons of Il'ia Muromtsy ultimately organized by the *Stavka* dropped a total of some sixty-five tons of bombs upon enemy positions. The activities of the EVK led to a series of other historic innovations related to aerial bombardment, including the first deployment of group bombing, the first nighttime bombing raids, and the first efforts at bomb damage assessment by use of photographic equipment.

[113] The lone Muromets lost in combat was brought down on 12 September 1916 [o.s] during an encounter with four German Albatross fighters. Only one of the German biplanes survived the aerial melee.

aviation program were fully revealed. In addition to the organizational chaos brought about by the ongoing administrative transition, the military's aviation detachments continued to suffer from the anemic growth of the aeronautical industry. In July 1914, the Russian Empire still possessed only four factories capable of producing airplane chassis and two factories that could produce motors.[114] Although the number of factories equipped to build airplanes and engines would expand to eight by the fall of 1915, Imperial Russia had entered the Great War woefully unprepared to challenge the colossal industrial capacity of its western foes.[115] Compounding the problem of production capacity, manufacturing problems bedeviled the nation's aviation factories, which undermined the airworthiness of Russian-made planes. Russian industry continued to demonstrate considerable ineptitude in reproducing the basic French models that served as the foundation of the military's air fleet. Only six weeks before the start of the war, *Novoe vremia* published an alarming article decrying the abilities of Russian manufacturers to duplicate widely used French Nieuport airplanes. Even with military fliers present to oversee the production of airplanes, the article revealed, domestic factories had proven incapable of producing reliable copies. Industrial incompetence had cost at least one military aviator his life.[116] As a result of the flimsy and slipshod production of Nieuport airplanes, one squadron commander issued an order forbidding his pilots from flying the aircraft.[117] In the two years since the disappointing military competition of 1912, Russian manufacturers had yet to perfect the process of reproducing already established airplane systems. This was a bad omen for a nation that had built its air fleet on the basis of imported aircraft and engines.

In addition to exacerbating the perennial problems plaguing the Russian aviation industry, the war created new obstacles. Within six weeks of the inauguration of hostilities, worried airplane factory owners began writing frantic letters to the General Staff warning of the persistent shortages they confronted in attempting to replenish the military's aircraft. Owing to a lack of motors and essential spare parts, Russian factories quickly encountered difficulties in constructing new planes. To alleviate this problem factories sent representatives abroad to France and Britain, hoping to secure a steady supply of parts and motors. When negotiations with the Western Allies failed to produce the requisite engines and components, agents were sent as far as Japan and the United States (and even to Denmark and Sweden) in a

---

[114] RGVIA f. 802, op. 4, d. 2998 (Doklady voennomu ministru i perepiska s GUGSh o rezultatakh sledstviia po delu germanskikh vozdukhoplavatelei), ll. 89–90. The military estimated that these factories could produce thirty new airplanes a month.

[115] RGVIA f. 802, op. 4, d. 3019 (Doklady o sostoianii i kachestva samoletov), l. 34.

[116] *Novoe vremia*, 14 June 1914.

[117] RGVIA f. 802, op. 4, d. 2846 (Perepiska s aviatsionnym obshchestvom 'Shchetinin' o nedostatakh konstruktsii samoletov 'N'iupor'), l. 32.

desperate attempt to sustain the military's aviation program.[118] Meanwhile, in one notorious case, more than fifty-six airplanes purchased from the American Curtiss Company arrived in such deplorable condition as to preclude their deployment to the field.[119] Russian factory owners were also forced to contend with the rising tide of worker unrest that grew in accordance with the dislocations of the war. Beginning in the summer of 1915 (and continuing until Russia's exit from the conflict), airplane manufacturing plants faced strikes and work stoppages that increasingly interrupted production and further undermined efforts to supply the army with the aircraft it needed.[120] Ironically, just as the nation was breaking ground in an innovative field of machine-powered flight, Russian aviation was breaking down for a lack of spare parts.

Imperial Russia's response to the arrival of the airplane revealed the complex web of social, cultural, and historical factors that would condition the nation's struggle to adapt to the modern age of flight. Enamored of the aerial feats accomplished by pilots and their flying machines, Russian citizens greeted the advent of aviation with excitement and enthusiasm. Like their contemporaries in Western Europe and the United States, they came to view their nation's achievements with patriotism and pride, projecting visions of national strength and vitality onto the men and machines that soared overhead and incorporating the airplane's image into the everyday discourses of popular culture. These seeming similarities with the West notwithstanding, Russian air-mindedness was conditioned as well by widespread concerns regarding the nation's ability to match the cultural and technical prowess of Europe. Against the backdrop of a disastrous war with Japan and amid growing social unrest in the Empire's major cities, citizens and statesmen of the tsarist order looked to the heavens for salvation from the present. More than a simple metaphor of strength and modernity, the airplane was also seen as a vehicle that would enable the nation to transcend its past. By fostering civic culture through the growth of voluntary organizations, contributing to the revitalization of the military, and demonstrating the autocracy's ability to adapt to changing circumstance, the airplane, it was believed, would facilitate a final break with those historical forces that had long plagued Russia's quest to join in full the nations of Europe. In this fashion, Russian culture endowed machine-powered flight with iconic significance, embracing the airplane as both a symbol and an agent of the country's modernization.

---

[118] RGVIA f. 802, op. 4, d. 2621 (Perepiska s GUGSh o predostavlenii voennymi agentami za granitsei).

[119] Timothy Wilson, "Broken Wings: The Curtiss Aeroplane Company, K-Boats, and the Russian Navy, 1914–1919," *The Journal of Military History* 66 (October 2002): 1061–83.

[120] RGVIA f. 802, op. 4, d. 3007 (Doklady voennomu ministru o roste zabastochnogo dvizheniia v aviatsionnykh fabrikakh).

The optimistic expectations and patriotic proclamations that gave shape to Russia's passion for wings obscured, however, the reality that the socially fractured and industrially underdeveloped nation was hard-pressed to meet the demands occasioned by the airplane. Dependent on European manufacturers for aircraft parts and motors, lacking an adequate number of skilled workers, factories, and technicians, and absent an entrepreneurial culture that encouraged individual initiative by rewarding personal risk, Russia could not match, let alone surpass, the scale and skill of its western rivals. Faced with these intractable problems, state officials turned to the past as a guide to the future. Modeling their aviation program on patterns first established during the reign of Peter the Great, Imperial leaders fell back on the oft-tested formula of borrowing from abroad to secure success at home. Relying on the machinery of the autocratic state to provide the direction, initiative, and resources necessary to purchase an air fleet, they sought to circumvent systemic inadequacies by imposing solutions from above. Their efforts were paralleled by civilian patrons as well, who, despite championing the interests of civic society, increasingly demanded that the state intervene to encourage and secure the nation's private aeronautical fortunes. In the end, this hierarchical, state-driven approach to forced development pursued by the autocracy and encouraged by the press served only to conceal the underlying challenges hampering the nation's long-term prospects.

Faced with the incongruous situation in which their air-minded dreams outpaced practical realities, citizens and statesmen alike invented past glories and embellished present successes a means of justifying faith in the their nation's greatness. They celebrated as their own the invention of the airplane and imparted historic significance to accomplishments of only relative importance while awaiting the transcendent event that, they believed, would finally propel Russia past its western rivals. Ironically, when genuine success did occur, it did so independently of official policies and programs. Theoretically advanced, pioneering, and practical, Igor Sikorsky's mammoth airplanes were colossal in both concept and scale. Accomplished through the creative efforts of a visionary individual, and supported by entrepreneurial patronage all too rare in Russia, the *Russian Warrior* and *Il'ia Muromets* aircraft bespoke the technical mastery of which Russians were capable. Still, these airplane-giants could not turn the tide of a faltering war effort, nor could they redress the fundamental problems plaguing the nation's aviation program. Their glory fleeting, they would serve only to inspire colossalist projects to come.

The near-complete destruction of the Russian air force and the collapse of industry that followed from tumultuous years of war, revolution, and civil war, meant that little would be left to those who followed in the wake of Imperial Russia's aeronautical patrons. Seizing power in October 1917, the country's new Soviet leaders would be compelled to begin anew the quest to develop a national aeronautical culture. Despite superficial differences that would distinguish "Red" aviation from its tsarist antecedent, Soviet political leaders and aeronautical officials faced issues and challenges nearly identical to those of their predecessors. The troublesome dilemma of state directive versus societal initiative, the continuing problem of a weak industrial and technical base, deep-seated opposition to private enterprise and the market together with a perceived need for rapid development in the face of European successes, all combined to influence profoundly Soviet Russia's response to aviation. Sharing their forebears' iconic vision of human flight, Soviet leaders would embrace, as well, the belief that the airplane was both a symbol and means of the nation's modernization. Pursued to new extremes by an ideologically driven state that promoted the utopian promise of a Communist kingdom to come, the Russian propensity to impel a sudden, transformative act would assume still greater importance in shaping the country's aeronautical culture.

The evolution and institutionalization of these national characteristics during the Soviet period are the subjects of the following chapters.

Part II

The Origins and Institutions of the Soviet Air Fleet, 1917–1929

The war taught us much, not only that people suffered, but also the fact that those who have the best technology, organization, discipline, and the best machines emerge on top; it is this that the war has taught us. It is essential to learn that without machines, without discipline, it is impossible to live in modern society. It is necessary to master the highest technology or be crushed.

– Vladimir Lenin (*Polnoe sobranie sochinenii*, 36: 116)

Aviation is the great instrument of the future. It joins the earth and the sea to the heavens, producing a great new arena for human creativity.

– Leon Trotsky (*Aviation: Instrument of the Future*, 1923)

3

Mandating Red Aviation

CONTINUITY AMID CHANGE IN THE HISTORY OF RUSSIA

The Imperial era of Russia's history came to an end on 2 March 1917. On that day, Tsar Nicholas II abdicated the throne aboard a railroad car stationed outside the provincial town of Pskov. The 300-year-old Romanov dynasty was replaced with a Provisional Government drawn from the ranks of the State Duma, the nation's parliamentary assembly. Dedicated to the principle of equality under the law and supportive of such basic civil liberties as freedom of the press, speech, and religion, Russia's new leadership aimed to establish a representative system modeled after the constitutional states of Western Europe. The experiment with western-styled governance did not last long. Lacking support outside of the nation's capital and wracked by administrative incompetence and political timidity, the Provisional Government could not withstand mounting public opposition to its policy of continuing the war. In late October, only eight months after its formation, the caretaker regime succumbed to an armed insurrection organized by the Bolshevik Party and its charismatic leader, Vladimir Lenin.

Adherents to the revolutionary socialist credo propagated by the nineteenth-century German theoretician Karl Marx, the Bolsheviks sought to transform backward, quasi-capitalistic Russia into the world's first Communist state. Through the nationalization of resources, state control of development, and unrelenting warfare against foreign and domestic "enemies of the working class," the leaders of the newly proclaimed Soviet Republic believed that they could impel industrial modernization, social equality, and material plenty for the benefit of the country's masses. They hoped to apply the tenets of Marxian socialism to realize the true ends of history: setting an example of measured and just development to oppressed peoples the world over that would in turn inspire the destruction of the international capitalist system and inaugurate a new, permanent era of freedom and equality. In the meantime, Russia plunged still deeper into violence and anarchy. A diverse coalition of forces engaged the country's self-ordained rulers in a ruthless and destructive Civil War. Surrounded by hostile enemies, unable to supply the cities under its control, and lacking the financial and material resources necessary to wage war, the Bolshevik regime faced immense challenges. In an effort to retain power, Party officials resorted to draconian measures, expropriating grain from the nation's peasants, conscripting urban citizens into service in "labor armies," and undertaking a widespread campaign of violence and terror aimed at eradicating dissent. In the end, these methods proved successful. The Bolsheviks emerged from the Russian Civil War secure in their role as the unrivaled leaders of a devastated and impoverished nation.

Historical assessments of the Bolsheviks' ascent to power are typically based on one of two interpretive approaches. The first emphasizes the extent to which the leaders, policies, institutions, and ideology of the Soviet regime represented radical departures from the Imperial era. Acknowledging the Bolsheviks' stated goal of effecting a revolutionary transformation of Russia (and, indeed, the entire world) and measuring change in terms of the novel strategies and tactics adopted to realize this end, supporters of this view conclude that the Revolution of October 1917, and the Revolution's subsequent institutionalization in the form of the Soviet state, represented a fundamental rupture in the history of the nation. The alternative approach underscores the degree to which the Soviet experience evolved from institutional, political, and cultural traditions deeply rooted in the nation's Imperial past. Although not dismissive of the more obvious distinctions separating Russia's prerevolutionary and postrevolutionary eras, those embracing this interpretation emphasize the persistence of broader historical continuities amid turbulence and upheaval during twentieth-century Russia's first two-and-a-half decades.[1]

Historians face similar issues in assessing the transition between Imperial and Soviet aeronautical culture. As was true of Russian society and politics, Russian aviation underwent seemingly profound changes resulting from years of revolution and civil war. In the decades that followed 1917, the airplane assumed increasing importance as the state undertook a relentless campaign to promote aeronautical development in order to assist in the realization of its social, economic, and military goals. Soviet authors encouraged the belief that the country's aeronautical culture, like the new socialist

---

[1] Perhaps the most emphatic argument for the differences between the Imperial and Soviet eras of Russia's history is made in Mikhail Heller and Aleksandr Nekrich, *Utopia in Power: The History of the Soviet Union from 1917 to the Present* (New York: Summit Books, 1986). Other works stressing historical "discontinuity" before and after October 1917 include Martin Malia, *The Soviet Tragedy: A History of Socialism in Russia, 1917–1991* (New York: The Free Press, 1994) and Stéphane Courtois *et al., Black Book of Communism: Crimes, Terror, Repression*, trans. Jonathan Murphy (Cambridge, MA: Harvard University Press, 1999). Among numerous recent works emphasizing continuities between the Imperial and Soviet periods are Peter Holquist, *Making War, Forging Revolution: Russia's Continuum of Crisis, 1914–1921* (Cambridge, MA: Harvard University Press, 2002) and Joshua A. Sanborn, *Drafting the Russian Nation: Military Conscription, Total War, and Mass Politics, 1905–1925* (DeKalb, IL: Northern Illinois University Press, 2003).

culture mandated by the state, was itself a product of the Revolution, created from whole cloth by the Party and its leaders in the absence of precedent from the discredited tsarist past.[2] The rapid growth of the aviation industry and the omnipresence of aeronautical themes in Soviet culture abetted historians' efforts to characterize Soviet aviation programs as a revolutionary departure from the failed policies of the Imperial era.

Belief in the unprecedented contributions of the Red Air Fleet and its pilots to the history of the Soviet Union owed much to contemporary accounts of Civil War aviation that underscored the importance of the airplane to the defense of the workers' and peasants' state. Beginning in the 1920s, observers trumpeted the accomplishments of Bolshevik aviators in defending the new regime from the forces of restoration. Like the soldiers who comprised the ranks of the Red Army, Soviet fliers were depicted as defenders of the Revolution, aerial guardians without whom the Bolsheviks' victory would not have been possible.[3]

Official rhetoric notwithstanding, aeronautics did not play a major role in determining the outcome of the Civil War. Limited by rapidly diminishing resources, an inability to field adequately trained pilots, and the constraints imposed by an as-yet relatively primitive technology, aviation cadres were reduced to transporting war matériel, providing reconnaissance, and dropping propaganda leaflets urging support for the Bolshevik Party. In terms of actual combat, airplanes appeared only sporadically and in relatively small numbers above Civil War battlefields.[4] The dearth of properly functioning aircraft (compounded by the scarcity of adequate repair facilities, reliable maintenance workers, and spare parts) made planes too valuable to risk losing by subjecting them to hostile fire. Despite efforts to preserve the remnants of the Imperial Air Fleet, even before the Civil War had drawn to a close in the spring of 1921, aviation, for all practical purposes, had ceased to exist in Russia.[5]

Even so, the dissolution of the Imperial Air Fleet and the subsequent phoenixlike emergence of its Soviet successor encouraged later historians to view the reinstitutionalization of aeronautical culture under the Bolshevik state as an enterprise wholly dissimilar to that of the preceding period. Employing rhetorical strategies reminiscent of those used by contemporary observers, later Soviet histories of the formation of the Red Air Force ignored

---

[2] For two works typical of this approach, see M. B. Liakhovetskii, *Aviatsiia v delakh i dumakh Il'icha* (Kiev, 1969) and S. I. Rudenko, *Lenin i aviatsiia* (Moscow, 1970).

[3] For specific examples of this practice in Soviet periodicals of the 1920s, see n. 16, this chapter.

[4] Robert A. Kilmarx, *A History of Soviet Air Power* (New York: Praeger, 1962), 49.

[5] RGVA f. 33987, op. 1, d. 127 (Perepiska o vozdushnom flote) and d. 179 (Perepiska s Glavvozdukhflotom o sostoianii vozdushnogo flota). For narrative accounts of Bolshevik aeronautical fortunes during the Civil War written by a contemporary participant, see GARF f. 7577, op. 1, d. 29 (Stat'i letchika Mozhaeva, A. V.).

or discounted the contributions of tsarist aviation patrons, establishing an official version of the past that would shape the views of generations to come.[6] The rapid rise to prominence of new personalities, policies, and institutions under the aegis of the Bolshevik Party would seem to confirm the claim that the Soviet state began its air-minded programs from scratch. In terms of equipment, cadres of pilots, and the fabrication of an industrial base capable of producing modern aircraft and parts, this was largely true. Given that so few material resources were bequeathed to the country's new rulers, it is impossible to ignore the argument that the Soviet aeronautical experience shared little in common with the Imperial legacy.

It would be a mistake, however, to give too much credence to this claim. Although Russia's aviation programs underwent wrenching alterations between the years 1917 and 1921, the fundamental economic and social issues that had structured earlier approaches to aeronautical development changed very little. Already significantly behind Western Europe in 1914, the ravages of war and revolution further retarded the country's progress, intensifying Russia's long-standing problems, without affecting or altering their essential nature. Like their Imperial predecessors, Russia's Soviet leaders were confronted with the challenge of introducing mechanized flight to an industrially backward agrarian nation. In the end, the symbolic and practical approaches that they adopted to resolve the dilemma of fostering airmindedness revealed the persistence of intrinsic cultural patterns that were first institutionalized by their autocratic antecedents. Notwithstanding the social and political convulsions that accompanied the Revolution in 1917, the airplane's assigned tasks in effecting the Soviet transition to modernity remained remarkably consistent with the modernizing roles previously envisioned by prewar Imperial patrons. Measured against the achievements and symbols of an earlier age, the material and thematic manifestations of Soviet aeronautical culture reveal continuity amid change in the history of Russia.

"FROM A DICTATORSHIP OF THE EARTH TO A DICTATORSHIP OF THE AIR"

Soviet leaders faced a difficult task in their quest to construct a modern, technologically proficient air force. Whatever benefits might have been derived from the buildup of the Imperial era were largely exhausted by the time the Bolsheviks finally solidified their hold on power. Although the mobilization of Russian industry in 1915 had increased productive capacities, the aviation

---

[6] This point is also noted in Von Hardesty, "Early Flight in Russia," in Robin Higham, John T. Greenwood, and Von Hardesty, eds., *Russian Aviation and Air Power in the Twentieth Century* (London: Cass, 1998). One account of the contributions made by Imperial Russia to Soviet aviation, written from the standpoint of official Soviet historical orthodoxy, is P. D. Duz', *Istoriia vozdukhoplavaniia i aviatsii v Rossii (period do 1914.)* (Moscow, 1979).

industry still could not meet the pressing needs imposed by total war, nor cope with the immense dislocations that took place during the final months of combat. Of the more than ninety-one aviation squadrons that ultimately saw duty during World War I, only thirty-three (comprising some 300 largely unserviceable and obsolete aircraft) remained operational by the spring of 1918.[7] The defection of air force personnel during the Civil War compounded the precipitous decline of the former Imperial Air Fleet as scores of officer–pilots deserted the Bolsheviks in the wake of October to take up arms with White guardist forces.[8]

The challenges posed by the destruction of the air force were greatly magnified as a result of widespread devastation. The routine and pervasive violence accompanying the Civil War fundamentally transformed the Russian landscape and imposed daunting new obstacles for those seeking to propel the nation into the modern age. By the end of 1921, Bolshevik leaders had witnessed the near-total collapse of Russia's industrial base. Factory output stood at less than twenty percent of its 1913 levels. Dizzying declines in the production of coal, steel, and pig iron meant that even those factories capable of operating were faced with continuous shortages of essential raw materials. The condition of the agricultural sector was equally bleak. In 1921 the nation harvested just over 37 million tons of grain, less than half of the amount collected in the last year before the war.[9]

The collapse of the Russian economy was accompanied by tremendous social dislocation that laid waste to Russia's major urban centers. In a desperate search for relief from the threats of famine and continuing unrest, urban residents fled the cities for the relative security of the countryside. By 1920, owing to the urban exodus, the population of Moscow had declined to half of its 1917 level. The former capital of St. Petersburg witnessed an even more catastrophic loss, plummeting from 2.5 million in 1917 to only 700,000 inhabitants in 1920.[10] The pressures caused by the mass flight from the cities were compounded by the demobilization of millions of Red Army men beginning in the winter of 1920–1. Returning to their native villages and towns, legions of former Soviet soldiers would ultimately prove instrumental in providing the personnel necessary for the administration of the new

---

7 V. S. Shumikhin, *Sovetskaia voennaia aviatsiia, 1917–1941* (Moscow, 1986), 19, and Alexander Boyd, *The Soviet Air Force Since 1918* (New York: Stein and Day, 1977), 6.

8 A. Akashev, "Kak sozdavalsia krasnyi vozdushnyi flot," *Samolet* 2(4) 1924: 3–5, and *Krasnyi vozdushnyi flot v grazhdanskoi voine v SSSR, 1918–1920 gg.: materialy voennu-istoricheskoi konferentsii provedennoi v TsDSA, 8 dekabria 1967 g.* (Moscow, 1968), 21.

9 Alec Nove, *An Economic History of the USSR, 1917–1991* (London: Penguin Books, 1992), 19.

10 Diane Koenker, "Urbanization and Deurbanization in the Russian Revolution and Civil War," in Diane Koenker, William Rosenberg, and Ronald G. Suny (eds.), *Party, State and Society in the Russian Civil War: Explorations in Social History* (Bloomington, IN: Indiana University Press, 1989), 81.

regime. But in the short term, with cities deserted and industrial production at a standstill, their return home only added to the chaos that prevailed in the Russian countryside.[11]

The destruction and dislocation occasioned by the Civil War proved problematic for the country's new leadership. Schooled in the deterministic maxims of nineteenth-century Marxism, members of the Bolshevik Party adhered to an eschatological vision predicated on a faith in the future triumph of industrial labor. Through the application of the "scientific" principles of dialectical materialism, Party theorists believed that they had reached an understanding of the past and that they would soon realize the ends of history in the establishment of the world's first socialist state. Guided by the principles of an urban ideology, they set out to recast the present in terms of a future modeled on the vision of a technically proficient and highly advanced industrial state. Notwithstanding such grandiloquent dreams, harsh economic and political realities in the wake of the Civil War compelled Bolshevik leaders to turn their immediate attention to the basic tasks of rebuilding social networks and political institutions as they attempted to modernize Europe's most backward major nation.

Faced with severe shortages of food and consumer goods and impatient to resolve a growing manpower crisis exacerbated by an ongoing military conflict with Poland, Soviet leaders resorted to the mass mobilization of the civilian population as a means of solving the country's critical domestic problems.[12] To this end, the decision of the Ninth Party Congress (29 March–4 April 1920) to approve a policy of compulsory labor and the subsequent creation of nationwide "labor armies" were important early attempts to mobilize and "militarize" Soviet society for the task of building socialism.[13] Although these policies were contested by some factions within the Party (and would be abolished with the introduction of the New Economic Policy [NEP] in 1921), their implementation in the spring of 1920 was a clear indication that the Party leadership was disposed to employing centrally

[11] Sheila Fitzpatrick, "The Legacy of the Civil War," in Koenker *et al.* (eds.), *Party, State, and Society*, 392, and Mark Von Hagen, *Soldiers in the Proletarian Dictatorship: The Red Army and the Soviet Socialist State, 1917–1930* (Ithaca, NY: Cornell University Press, 1990), 129.

[12] Robert V. Daniels, *The Conscience of the Revolution: Communist Opposition in Soviet Russia* (Cambridge, MA: Harvard University Press, 1960), 121–5, and Francesco Benvenuti, *The Bolsheviks and the Red Army, 1918–1922* (New York: Cambridge University Press, 1988), 162–8.

[13] James Bunyan, *The Origin of Forced Labor in the Soviet State, 1917–1921: Documents and Materials* (Baltimore: Johns Hopkins University Press, 1967), 117–50. For an analysis of the term "militarization" and its utility as a descriptor of Soviet political culture in the 1920s, see the introduction to Von Hagen, *Soldiers in the Proletarian Dictatorship*, 1–12. For a discussion of the Bolsheviks' mobilization of labor as a utopian experiment, see Richard Stites, *Revolutionary Dreams: Utopian Vision and Experimental Life in the Russian Revolution* (Oxford: Oxford University Press, 1989), 46–52.

controlled methods of mass mobilization to solve the problems they encountered in ruling the country. When the Civil War drew to a close, the Party would return to such strategies as the means for completing the socialist revolution launched in October 1917.

As the first wide-scale attempt to mobilize the public behind the revolutionary regime in the aftermath of the Civil War, the Bolshevik leadership's drive to raise public interest in aviation represented both the utopian propensities and political pragmatism of the country's new rulers. Committed to the task of overcoming Russia's backwardness and cognizant of the vital importance of technology to the establishment of a modern nation, leading Party figures embarked on a concerted campaign in the spring of 1923 to generate support for the establishment of a "Red" Air Fleet. Coordinating recruitment strategies first employed by Imperial aeronautical patrons with innovative approaches designed to foster air-mindedness, Bolshevik leaders purposely set out to create a uniquely Soviet aeronautical culture while establishing the institutional framework necessary for the development of the country's aviation programs.

At first glance, the Party's decision to invest scarce resources in aviation at a time of immense social dislocation and economic disarray might be judged an act of folly. The costs and demands associated with a large-scale aeronautical buildup would appear to have imposed unnecessary diversions from the essential tasks of stabilizing the economy, refashioning governing institutions, and fostering public support for the regime and its leaders. In the absence of an industrial infrastructure essential for the mass production of technically advanced airplane motors and chassis, and lacking the financial resources required for purchasing them from abroad, the country was woefully unprepared to succeed in this unlikely quest. Party leaders nevertheless viewed the air-minded effort as a logical and necessary step in guaranteeing the success of their revolutionary experiment. Convinced of the airplane's immense utility in facilitating rapid modernization and aware of the powerful symbolism associated with human flight, Bolshevik officials looked to aviation as an ideal instrument for resolving the key challenges that they faced in attempting to build the world's first socialist society. By demonstrating the Party's technical acuity and contributing to the military strength of the Soviet Republic, the aeronautical campaign, they believed, would legitimize the gains of October. At the same time, the airplane would foster a sense of solidarity among the populace, giving rise to new institutions, organizations, and networks that could be used to advance state interests relating to aeronautical and other matters.

FRIENDS OF THE AIR FLEET

The campaign to generate public support for a national air fleet began in earnest on 1 March 1923. On that date, thirty-three Soviet newspapers embarked on a coordinated effort to inform the public of the airplane's essential role in securing the workers' and peasants' revolution and to raise awareness of the state's commitment to aviation. For more than four months following 1 March, aeronautics dominated the Soviet press as countless stories on the "instrument of the future" commanded readers to turn their attention to the air fleet and endeavored to educate the Soviet public about the pressing need to conquer the air.[14] The Soviet press explored every facet of aviation, printing stories on such disparate subjects as the evolution of aeronautical warfare to the possible role of aviation in building the national economy. From the airplane's value as a "bearer of culture" to its potential applications in fighting forest fires and swarms of locusts, no topic touching on aviation was left unexplored. So complete was press coverage that every day, for eight consecutive weeks, the country's leading newspaper, *Izvestiia*, devoted the majority of its front page to aviation.[15]

The unrelenting attention to the issue of flight had appeared with little warning. Before 1 March the print media had shown only a passing concern for aviation. Although reports on the progress of European aviation had been published on an irregular basis and articles concerning the activities of Red aviators had appeared periodically during the course of the Civil War and the brief war with Poland, the press had given little indication that it was set to launch an extended public campaign.[16] More surprising still was the 9 March announcement that the first organizational meeting of a "Society of Friends of the Air Fleet" [*Obshchestvo druzei vozdushnogo flota*, or ODVF] had recently taken place on the grounds of a Moscow military school.[17] Committed to ensuring that Soviet Russia achieve a level of military preparedness comparable to that of the capitalist powers of Western Europe and aware of the vital role that aviation would play in attaining this goal, leading figures of the aeronautical industry had resolved to establish a "voluntary society" to support the development of Soviet air-mindedness. To this end, a group of aeronautical representatives gathered in Moscow on 8 March to lay the foundation for ODVF. Surprised to see "many unknown faces at the gathering," the representatives concluded that the one-week-old

---

[14] See "Orudie budushchego," *Pravda*, 3 June 1923; "Bol'she vnimanie vozdukhoplavaniiu," *Izvestiia KPSS*, 10 February 1923; "Vnimanie k vozdushnomu flotu," *Aero-sbornik* 1 (1923): 11–12; and "My dolzhny zavoevat' vozdukh!," *Pravda*, 25 May 1923, among countless others. The most complete coverage of aeronautical matters can be found in the newspaper *Izvestiia KPSS* (hereafter, *Izvestiia*), which led the press campaign.

[15] The coverage appeared from 1 March to 30 April. *Izvestiia* continued to run regular front-page articles on aviation well into the month of August.

[16] Examples of early Soviet reports on aviation include "Krasnye letchiki," *Izvestiia*, 4 July 1919; "Vozdushnyi flot," *Izvestiia*, 1 October 1920; "Eshche ob aviatsii," *Izvestiia*, 25 September 1920; and "Vozdukhoflot," *Izvestiia*, 28 January 1921. See also the regular coverage that appeared in the aeronautical journals *Vestnik vozdushnogo flota*, *Vozdukhoplavanie*, and *Vozdushnyi flot*.

[17] *Izvestiia*, 9 March 1923.

press campaign had proven immensely successful and that, in a spontaneous show of support for the Soviet cause, legions of ordinary citizens had flocked to the meeting to voice their approval of the establishment of the Red Air Fleet.[18]

The claims of public spontaneity made by the Party's press organs were highly disingenuous. The establishment of ODVF and the newspaper campaign that preceded it were, in fact, the products of a planned, systematic, and centralized strategy. Hardened by the experiences of the Civil War and alert to the continuing dangers posed by hostile foreign powers, Soviet Russia's political leadership had come to recognize the value of aviation in the conduct of modern warfare. As a reconnaissance instrument, method of transportation, and weapon of psychological terror, the airplane would play an increasingly important role in future battles.[19] Dedicated to ensuring the ultimate victory of the workers' and peasants' revolution against the forces of world imperialism, the Soviet leadership resolved to modernize the Red Army through organizational restructuring and by providing it with more technologically advanced weaponry.[20] Among Soviet Russia's technological concerns, Party leaders believed that aviation "occupied first place."[21]

In addition to facilitating efforts to mobilize support for Red aviation, the creation of ODVF promoted the larger imperative of modernizing the country by reconstructing political and social networks destroyed during the Civil War. As a Party-controlled agency designed to foment popular support for state policies, the "voluntary society" ODVF would function on the national and local levels as an institutional transmitter for the inculcation of social values deemed essential to the success of the Revolution. In this way, the establishment of ODVF demonstrated how the airplane would continue to serve an iconic role in new Soviet culture as both a symbol of the Bolshevik Party's technological acuity and as a means of facilitating the social, cultural, and military modernization of the nation.

Much like the Imperial campaign before it, the drive to construct the Soviet Air Fleet owed its origins to the influence and vision of a powerful state patron. In a series of memos circulated to the members of the Revolutionary Military Council of the Republic [*Revoliutsionnyi voennyi sovet*, or "Revvoensovet"] during the winter of 1922–3, Council Chairman Leon Trotsky drew attention to the state's pressing need for both military and civilian air fleets. He urged that the Council establish a "Society of Friends of the Red Air Fleets," institute an annual "Day of Aviation," and launch an

---

[18] "Obshchestvo druzei vozdushnogo flota," *Vestnik vozdushnogo flota* 2 (1923): 143.

[19] L. D. Trotskii, *Aviatsiia – orudie budushchego* (Ekaterinburg, 1923), 2.

[20] For background on the decision to reorganize the Red Army, see Von Hagen, *Soldiers in the Proletarian Dictatorship*, 183–205. The Soviet government's recognition of the importance of modernizing military technology is documented in RGASPI f. 5, op. 1, d. 2520 (Razvitiie voennoi tekhniki s 1914 g.), ll. 1–26.

[21] L. D. Trotskii, *Perspektivy i zadachi voennogo stroitel'stva* (Moscow, 1923), 17.

FIGURE 13. Yuri P. Annenkov, *Trotsky*, 1923. Oil on canvas. Location unkown. Photo: The David King Collection, London.

intensive media campaign to draw public attention to the endeavor.[22] The Revvoensovet responded by creating a governing Presidium to oversee the organization of the society and to monitor press content relating to aviation matters. On 6 February 1923, Council members met with representatives of eight Soviet newspapers to direct them on how best to implement the strategy. Following the new organization's inaugural meeting on 8 March, responsibility for the administration of the aeronautical campaign passed from the Revvoensovet to the new ODVF.[23]

According to the mandate handed down to the society, the purpose of ODVF was to ensure the establishment and growth of the Soviet Republic's military and civilian air fleets. To achieve this sweeping goal, ODVF numbered among its most important tasks the development of a stable and independent aviation industry, the promotion of scientific and technical research related to aviation, the mobilization of public attention toward the need for a national air fleet, the organization and development of sporting aviation, the regulation and maintenance of national aviation records, and, finally, the publication of aeronautical journals and books to popularize aeronautics.[24]

The diversity and difficulty of the obligations set before the organization required that ODVF possess a nationwide infrastructure in order for it properly to carry out its many responsibilities. Unlike the inaugural newspaper campaign, which was easily administered through the existing networks of the press industry, ODVF's other activities could not be realized without mobilizing local representatives to act on behalf of the society. Lacking individuals to collect donations, register new members, organize meetings, and distribute literature, ODVF could not operate, let alone accomplish the goals established by Party leaders.

The immediate need to recruit local supporters indicated the curiously inverted approach to organizational development pursued by the Party as it attempted to mandate an aeronautical program. Characterized by "the awkward circumstance [in which] five people, sitting in an office, suddenly proclaim themselves a society," the establishment of ODVF produced a public voluntary organization that included neither the public nor volunteers.[25]

---

[22] RGVA f. 33987, op. 1, d. 558 (Doklad ob organizatsii grazhdanskogo vozdushnogo flota), ll. 1–18.

[23] *Ibid.*, l. 55. Representatives from the following publications attended the meeting: *Bednota*, *Vestnik vozdushnogo flota*, *Voennyi vestnik*, *Izvestiia*, *Krasnaia niva*, *Rabochaia Moskva*, *Sovetskaia illiustratsiia*, and *Ekonomicheskaia zhizn'*. Among the members of the ODVF Presidium were such Party notables as Sergei Kamenev, Vladimir Antonov-Ovseenko, Anatolii Lunacharskii, Mikhail Frunze, and Feliks Dzerzhinskii. Soon thereafter Aleksei Rykov was appointed to chair the Presidium. The commission to draft the ODVF charter was chaired by Kamenev.

[24] GARF f. 7577, op. 1, d. 14 (Tsirkuliary ODVF vsem otdelam), l. 5.

[25] GARF f. 7577, op. 1, d. 40 (Stenogrammy i biulleteni 1-ogo vsesoiuznogo soveshaniia ODVF), ll. 171–2.

FIGURE 14. "Citizen! The Society of Friends of the Air Fleet calls you to its ranks! Come and enroll as a member of the Society!" Poster, 1923. Private collection. Photo: Scott W. Palmer.

In the weeks that followed the meeting of 8 March, ODVF leaders labored to conscript local personnel and to establish the institutional networks that were required if the society that they had preemptively founded were actually to function. To realize these ends more quickly, Party leaders assigned responsibility for fulfilling ODVF mandates to already existing political and social organizations. On factory shop floors, in trade union halls, and within Party cells and military units, individuals were enlisted to collect donations and to encourage their colleagues to join the society. Typically, entire factories and associations were enrolled in ODVF on the basis of "collective membership."[26] In these instances, ODVF recruited ready-made chapters of dues-paying members as well as new administrators (drawn from the existing ranks of factory or trade union officials) who simply added ODVF matters to their already long lists of duties.[27]

As a result of these methods ODVF expanded quickly. Between 8 March and the beginning of August the organization's central presidium boasted that no fewer than 106,000 citizens had enrolled in the organization.[28] In financial terms, that support produced millions of rubles. The press, in turn, trumpeted these successes as part of its ongoing campaign both to demonstrate and to generate nationwide support for building the air fleet, publishing notices concerning donations and the establishment of new ODVF chapters on a daily basis for more than six months. In this way, the aeronautical drive moved forward under the curious momentum initiated by the Party's announcement that spontaneous popular support had produced ODVF. The Party, meanwhile, continued its impatient efforts to manufacture that same "spontaneity." Although the efficacy of the Party's methods in concocting and controlling the aeronautical crash campaign would ultimately be called into question, the fact remained that ODVF had been mandated into existence.

After creating ODVF to serve the general task of popularizing and propagandizing the idea of Soviet aeronautics, the Revvoensovet established a second organization to oversee the development of a civil aviation program. Directed by Aleksandr Krasnoshchekov, chairman of the nation's Industrial Bank (PromBank), the "Voluntary Air Fleet" [*Dobrovol'nyi vozdushnyi flot,* or "Dobrolet"] was founded on 17 March to act as a self-financing commercial enterprise that would assist industry, trade, and business interests regarding the construction of a national air fleet.[29] The State Bank (GosBank)

[26] GARF f. 7577, op. 1, d. 21(Biulleteni nn. 4, 6–10 agitsektsii ODVF za 1923), ll. 209–10.

[27] GARF f. 9404, op. 1, d. 14, ll. 3–5. On enrolling in ODVF new members paid a fee of one gold ruble. For an example of the typical workload imposed on a local Party functionary (and ODVF member), see Peter Kenez, *The Birth of the Propaganda State: Soviet Methods of Mass Mobilization, 1917–1929* (Cambridge: Cambridge University Press, 1985), 140–1.

[28] GARF f. 7577, op. 1, d. 40, l. 71. The ODVF leadership noted that it was awaiting the completion of an additional 460,000 membership applications.

[29] GARF f. 7577, op. 1, d. 1 (Izveshchenie ob organizovanim sobraniem Dobroleta), l. 3.

provided start-up capital for the commercial venture, setting aside nearly 2 million rubles to fund Dobrolet's early projects.[30] Subsequent funding was to come from the issuance of stock shares, 1 million of which, beginning in late March, were offered for sale to Soviet enterprises and trusts at the cost of one gold ruble apiece. Two months later, the organization began selling shares to private citizens. To encourage sales, Dobrolet announced that any organization purchasing 25,000 shares would earn the right to use one of the venture's airplanes once they had been acquired.[31]

With the funds supplied from GosBank and those raised through stock sales, Dobrolet was expected to fulfill a host of functions. Among its more important tasks, the commercial venture was to develop a network of air communications, regulate airline routes, manage commercial relations with foreign airlines, and oversee the purchase of airplanes from foreign suppliers.[32] In short, Dobrolet was to act as a commercial airline syndicate, managing all aspects of civilian air transport and overseeing the activities of affiliate organizations throughout the country. Dobrolet's early efforts were made somewhat easier as sales of the syndicate's stock quickly exceeded expectations. By late April, *Izvestiia* reported that 800,000 of the initial offering of 1 million shares had been purchased by Soviet enterprises. This unexpected success led to the announcement that a second offering of 1 million shares would be made available to corporate investors.[33]

The auspicious debut of the Dobrolet stock offering was followed in May by the opening of the first regular commercial air route between the Soviet Republic and a foreign state. Undertaken with Germany through the joint venture aviation firm *Deruluft*, the Königsberg–Moscow air route was an early product of the Treaty of Friendship and Cooperation signed by Soviet and German representatives at Rapallo in April 1922.[34] Forced to disband its aviation squadrons and prevented from producing military aircraft by the Treaty of Versailles, Germany's Weimar government secretly negotiated with the Bolsheviks the establishment of a clandestine aviation production facility on Soviet soil. As part of the agreement, the German firm Junkers was given permission in late 1922 to construct airplanes at a Soviet plant located in Fili. In exchange for this concession, the Soviets received access to techniques involved in the design and production of all-metal aircraft.

[30] RGVA f. 33987, op. 1, d. 558, ll. 19–21.

[31] *Pravda*, 22 March 1923.

[32] GARF f. 7577, op. 1, d. 2 (Ustava Dobroleta), ll. 1–18.

[33] *Izvestiia*, 26 April 1923.

[34] Yale University Russian Archives Project. Materials on Soviet–German Military Cooperation. Document 13. "RVA Order No. 1286 with instructions concerning the arranging of regular flights by the German–Russian society for air communication between Moscow and Königsberg." For an overview of the Rapallo treaty and the resulting military cooperation between the Soviet Union and Germany, see John Erickson, *The Soviet High Command: A Military–Political History, 1918–1941* (London: St. Martin's, 1962), 144–63.

Although Junkers would quit the Fili facility in 1926 under a grow-ing cloud of mutual recriminations and suspicion between the firm and its host government, the information and expertise obtained from the Germans played an influential role in shaping Soviet aviation fortunes between 1925 and 1939.[35] One beneficiary of the secret agreement was Andrei Tupolev, a rising star in the young field of Soviet airplane design. A former student of Nikolai Zhukovskii, Imperial and Soviet Russia's premier expert in aerody-namics, Tupolev had helped to construct Russia's first wind tunnels before co-founding with his mentor, in 1918, the Central Aero-Hydrodynamic Institute [*Tsentral'nyi aero-gidrodynamicheskii institut*, or "TsAGI"], an autonomous institution that housed an array of departments, testing facilities, and labo-ratories devoted to aspects of experimental airplane design.[36] In September 1922, Tupolev was appointed to chair a new TsAGI commission charged with designing and constructing all-metal aircraft for the Red Air Fleet. The Fili connection proved crucial to these efforts, as the information gleaned from German technicians enabled Tupolev's design team to develop the coun-try's first all-metal combat airplane, the ANT-3, a reconnaissance plane that debuted in the summer of 1925.[37] Thus, following the example of their Impe-rial predecessors, Soviet officials sought to realize their air-minded goals by acquiring training and expertise from abroad while laying the foundations of an aviation industry at home. In the meantime, German-produced Junkers and later Dutch Fokker aircraft were sold in substantial numbers to the Soviet government. These planes would form the backbone of the Red Air Fleet throughout the 1920s.[38]

No less important than the commercial and technical benefits that cooper-ation with Germany afforded the country, the air corridor to Königsberg was a symbolic repudiation of the Soviet state's political isolation from Western Europe. Shortly after the first flights had taken place between the two cities, one Soviet newspaper noted that the "threads of friendship" represented by the individual airplanes would "soon weave a strong and useful fabric" that would "serve to bridge the two nations."[39] In testament to the air route's sym-bolic significance, the most prominent propagandist of Soviet power, the poet Vladimir Mayakovsky penned a short poem titled, "Moscow–Königsberg,"

[35] Yale University Russian Archives Project. Document 116. "Report from K. Ye. Voroshilov to the Politburo on the speeding up of the abrogation of the contract for the delivery of bombers with the German firm Junkers, in connection with the systematic non-fulfillment of their contractual obligations."

[36] Zhukovskii won the active patronage of Lenin after siding with the Bolsheviks in 1918. Party leaders would later bestow on him the honorary title "Father of Soviet Aviation."

[37] John T. Greenwood, "The Designers: Their Design Bureaux and Aircraft" in Higham *et al.* (eds.), *Russian Aviation*, 167.

[38] Lennart Andersson, *Soviet Aircraft and Aviation, 1917–1941* (Annapolis, MD: Naval Insti-tute Press, 1994), 37 and 47–50.

[39] "Moskva-Keningsberg," *Izvestiia* 15 October 1922.

which trumpeted the wonders of modern air travel and the labor of those who had made it possible.[40] Based on the impressions formed during a recent flight to Germany, Mayakovsky's verse described the sensations that he experienced while in the air and offered his thoughts concerning the future of Soviet aviation. After ruminating on the generations of dreamers and heroes who had worked to make human flight a reality, Mayakovsky concluded his poem with a tribute to the recent accomplishments of the Soviet government. The poem communicated Mayakovsky's belief that the "air-river to Königsberg" was both a meaningful achievement and a propitious symbol of the new heights that the country would yet attain.

Soviet aviation, it appeared, had "taken off." Through the establishment of Dobrolet and ODVF and illicit cooperation with Germany, the Party leadership had laid the foundations for what it hoped would be the rapid and successful development of a modern air fleet. Nevertheless, Party leaders did not clearly spell out the exact relationship between the "commercial venture" and the "voluntary society," leaving open to question the mechanics of their interaction. Lingering concerns regarding the organizations' respective roles would trouble the country's aeronautical supporters for some time to come.

The creation of ODVF and Dobrolet and the inauguration of the all-union newspaper campaign were not the only methods undertaken to win public support and raise money for the conquest of the air. As the spring of 1923 turned to summer, the Party moved quickly to expand the scope of the aeronautical mobilization drive. Designed to "encourage all party, soviet, and professional organizations as well as the entire population of workers and peasants to assist in the construction of a national air fleet," ODVF organized a nationwide "Week of the Air Fleet" (held from 24 June to 1 July) to increase membership in the society and to collect donations for the Red Air Force. Similar to strategies first employed during the Imperial era, the approach of ODVF relied on aeronautical spectacles as a central element in winning public support for aviation. Accompanying celebrations in Moscow and Petrograd, a series of regional ODVF "aviation weeks" were held in urban centers throughout the Republic. In cities such as Vladimir, Orel, Riazan', Tula, Tambov, and Kaluga, festivities were arranged to celebrate Soviet airborne efforts and to unite provincial residents behind the cause of socialist aviation.[41]

Organized and administered by the local ODVF chapters that had mushroomed in the months following the Party's February summons, aviation weeks showcased Soviet aeronautical prowess. Offering such standard fare as flight demonstrations, educational exhibits, and recruitment pavilions for those interested in ODVF, these Soviet spectacles followed the well-tested

[40] V. V. Maiakovskii, *Polnoe sobranie sochinenii*, 13 vols. (Moscow, 1955), Vol. 5, 90–3.
[41] GARF f. 7577, op. 1, d. 14, l. 3, and *Izvestiia*, 23 June 1923.

FIGURE 15. An early air-minded display sponsored by the Society of Friends of the Air-Fleet, 1923.

patterns earlier established by Imperial air shows. At the same time, citizens were encouraged to participate actively in the campaign through essay competitions, poetry readings, and poster contests devoted to the topic of the Red Air Fleet. Postcards, pamphlets, and well-illustrated journals were offered for sale to the general public as part of the Society's efforts to raise aeronautical consciousness and to generate revenues for the construction of an air force, while mass-produced buttons, depicting airplanes with names such as *Il'ich, Red October,* and *Red Army Soldier,* suggested a direct correlation between the power of modern flight technology and the political power exercised by Soviet authorities.[42]

In many respects, these approaches to mobilizing public support closely mirrored the methods earlier employed by the Imperial Committee for the Establishment of the Air Fleet. Eager to reach as broad an audience as possible, ODVF, like its Imperial predecessor, relied on the print media and organized spectacles as basic resources in informing the public of aviation's importance. Combining aeronautical encounters with educational demonstrations and flag-waving slogans, both the Imperial and the Soviet aeronautical

---

[42] *Izvestiia,* 9 May 1923. For a sampling of the literary creations produced during one local competition (sponsored by the ODVF chapter in Perm) see *Rasskazy, stikhi, chastushki* (Perm: Perm ODVF, 1925) and GARF f. 7577, op. 1, d. 12 (Protokol zasedaniia agitsektsii ODVF ot 5 maia 1923), l. 1.

FIGURE 16. Cover illustration of the publication *Flier: Tales and Poems*, one of the many air-minded literary collections sponsored by ODVF to raise citizens' awareness of the importance of aviation. Photo: The David King Collection, London.

campaigns aimed to increase popular awareness of aviation while inciting citizens to contribute time and money to the cause of air readiness. In contrast to the Imperial campaign, however, ODVF benefited from a close relationship with the institutions of state power. Unlike Imperial organizations, which recruited their members and conducted their business independently of the tsarist government, ODVF pursued activities and issues that were intimately linked with Party policies and goals. Whereas, for example, the Imperial State Committee's appeals to the Russian press had been dependent on the willingness of individual editors to implement committee requests, Bolshevik Party control over the Soviet press industry accorded the Military Council an opportunity to mandate press content, enabling the Revvoensovet to enlist the country's leading publications in the fight to establish a Soviet "dictatorship of the air."[43] In stark contrast, the freedoms granted the Imperial press meant that editorial boards could (and oftentimes did) ignore official appeals to serve as heralds of the state's aviation campaign. As a result, the Soviet Air Fleet campaign was characterized by a degree of thematic cohesion and unity of purpose never achieved in the Imperial era. Moreover, the hierarchical structure of the voluntary society afforded ODVF leaders an opportunity to produce uniform messages and to coordinate recruitment strategies on a broad front throughout the country. Constructed from the top down and administered from the center, ODVF did not suffer from the organizational diversity that had weakened the various independent Imperial air clubs. Created by the Party to serve the Party's interests, ODVF enjoyed a base of official support that could ensure a level of sustained institutional activity eclipsing anything accomplished by IVAK and its rival organizations.

The approach chosen by Party leaders to propagate interest in aviation demonstrated their commitment to a comprehensive program of forced modernization directed exclusively from above. Aware of the numerous problems posed by Russia's technological and cultural backwardness, Soviet leaders throughout the 1920s utilized mass-mobilization campaigns in the belief that such measures would allow them to efficiently direct social forces in rapid fulfillment of the Party's perceived political needs.[44] From the standpoint of Soviet aeronautical concerns, this approach provided dual benefits to those in power. It created institutions to channel popular involvement in the construction of the air fleet while creating ready symbols that reinforced the Party's

---

43 RGVA f. 33987, op. 2, d. 209 (Tsirkuliary i svodki soveta ODVF), l. 27. On Soviet press politics, see Jeffrey Brooks, "Public and Private Values in the Soviet Press, 1921–1928," *Slavic Review* 1 (1989): 19.

44 For a discussion of the influence of Bolshevik perceptions of cultural backwardness in shaping Soviet social mobilization policies during the 1920s, see William E. Odom, *The Soviet Volunteers: Modernization and Bureaucracy in a Public Mass Organization* (Princeton, NJ: Princeton University Press, 1973), 33–9. Among the numerous Party-led mass mobilization efforts carried out during the 1920s were campaigns to increase literacy rates, encourage atheism, develop a civil defense system, and discourage drunkenness.

authority. The enthusiastic popular response to the campaign heralded in the state-controlled press allowed Soviet leaders to justify their costly program of aeronautical expansion as the fulfillment of popular sentiment. As the campaign came to be framed by the rhetoric of national defense, ideological purity, and revolutionary vigilance, its successes would be further construed as proof of popular support for the regime. In the wake of such recent internal challenges to Party authority as the Tambov peasants' uprising (1920–1), the Kronstadt mutiny (1921), and the ongoing Basmachi rebellion in Central Asia (1918–24), the political capital imparted to Soviet leaders by widespread "voluntary" participation in a Party-directed campaign bolstered their claim to speak on behalf of the country's masses. No less important, the state-centered approach to aeronautical construction allowed the Party to control debate over an issue of vital military, economic, and cultural significance. The manner in which ODVF was established and the terms under which the air fleet campaign was conducted reveal the Party's iconic understanding of the airplane as both an instrument and symbol of modernization. The Party enlisted large segments of the population behind the cause of aviation while exploiting the symbolic dividend of the accompanying supportive displays of mass "volunteerism."

"AVIATION: INSTRUMENT OF THE FUTURE"

Aviation's iconic significance within early Soviet culture was clearly displayed in the wake of the Twelfth Party Congress, which convened in Moscow from 17 to 25 April 1923. Following the conclusion of the Congress, participants were treated to a "ceremonial assembly" on 26 April designed to celebrate the recent establishment of ODVF and to chart a course for the organization's continuing efforts. Attracting a capacity crowd to the Hall of Columns (which had been decorated with red bunting and rows of model airplanes), the assembly functioned as an official pep rally intended to increase members' excitement and to heighten recruitment tempos as the air fleet campaign entered into the late spring and summer of the year. Before a large audience of friends and workers of the air fleet, the Party's leading representatives spoke about the accomplishments thus far attained by ODVF, pondered its current standing, and reiterated the basic themes that the Party had chosen to popularize the aeronautical cause.[45]

In his introductory speech before the assembly, the architect of the voluntary society, Leon Trotsky, clarified the Party's reasoning for pursuing aeronautical development at a time of economic and social disarray. Summarizing the concerns that had inspired the formation of the ODVF and the inauguration of the drive to build an air fleet, his comments revealed the

---

[45] *Torzhestvennoe zasedanie ODVF, 26 aprelia 1923 g.* (Moscow, 1923).

peculiar conception of flight that structured the Party's approach to aeronautical modernization. The speech was a curious amalgam of dialectical
reasoning and patriotic rhetoric that proclaimed the need to conquer "vast
space" [*prostranstvo*] as the "fundamental task" facing Soviet Russia. Both
the country's "greatest ally and most terrible adversary," *prostranstvo* had
played a vital role in shielding the Revolution from foreign armies and White
guardist insurgents during the years of the Civil War.[46] Capable of seizing
control of isolated cities and regions, but unable to subdue the entire countryside, the forces hostile to Bolshevik power had succumbed to the seemingly
infinite expanses of the Russian hinterlands. In this way, Trotsky reasoned,
unlike tiny Hungary (where a Communist revolution had failed in 1919),
Russia's tremendous size had proven a great asset in securing the Bolshevik
victory and saving the Revolution. Thanks to "swamps, lakes, dense forests,
and immense space," Soviet power had resisted the reactionary opponents
of October, and, when necessary, it would do so again, notwithstanding the
"hundreds of thousands and millions of tons of poisonous gas, explosives
and dynamite . . . directed toward the Soviet Republic" by the "rabid" forces
of the western, capitalist powers.[47]

Despite the defensive benefits bequeathed by natural resources and geographical expanse, *prostranstvo* had also contributed to the prevailing backwardness of the country relative to the advanced states of Western Europe. In
this sense, Trotsky credited the physical separation effected by *prostranstvo*
for having created the cultural and economic "distance" that divided the
nation internally and distinguished it from its European neighbors. Isolated
from the progressive influences of the twentieth century, Russia's hinterlands
had not achieved the level of economic, cultural, and social development
present in its more advanced urban centers. The enormous size of the Russian
Empire had made possible a condition in which a "barbarous, nomadic economy functioned alongside the most modern, American-style factories." Even
in the contemporary, progressive Soviet Republic, Trotsky noted, the effects
of *prostranstvo* were visible in the lives of its numerous "backward tribes
who live much like cavemen."[48] The geographical space that separated rural
Russia from the nation's urban centers contributed to lingering backwardness and threatened to impede the progressive vision promised by the Bolshevik Revolution. *Prostranstvo*, Trotsky suggested, was to be understood
both in real and symbolic terms. Just as it had shielded the Revolution from
the forces of reaction, so too had it isolated rural Russia from the advent of
the modern age. The question facing the country was how to overcome the
barriers imposed by *prostranstvo* in forging a united, modern, and technologically proficient order.

[46] RGVA f. 33987, op. 1, d. 558, l. 143.
[47] *Ibid.*, ll. 143–4.
[48] *Ibid.*, l. 145.

Trotsky's extended discussion of the perils of *prostranstvo* was a clear indication of the Party's continuing concern with the difficulties imposed by the country's legacy of backwardness. Having overseen an urban revolution in Europe's most rural nation, Soviet leaders were faced with the troublesome task of attempting to reconcile Russia's agrarian realities to the industrial visions implicit in their Marxist ideology. The method through which the Party might achieve the modernization of Soviet Russia was the subject addressed by Trotsky in a series of essays and speeches published in 1923 under the title *Problems of Everyday Life*.[49] Alerting his audience to the importance of organizational and educational work in solidifying the achievements of October, Trotsky announced that the country was now compelled to turn its attention to "practical everyday work in the fields of Soviet cultural and economic construction."[50] Through a long and patient struggle with the tyranny of habit and custom, aided by the application of important new technologies such as cinema and radio, Soviet Russia would improve the educational level of its citizens and facilitate the modernization of the economy and culture.[51]

One important factor in the struggle to overcome the backwardness and inertia produced by *prostranstvo* involved the coordinated efforts of the Party and Soviet citizens in developing an aeronautical program that would raise the country's economic, military, and cultural standing. As a "weapon in the battle with the malevolent qualities of *prostranstvo*," the airplane could defend the nation, facilitate communication, and help supply rural regions by delivering goods and services. Moreover, unlike automobiles or locomotives (whose range of service was dependent on costly networks of roads and railbeds), the airplane could fly anywhere so long as it had room to land (a prerequisite easily met in Russia). In fulfilling these functions, aviation would provide the additional benefit of reducing the temporal distance that separated rural from urban Russia. As a visible, functioning herald of Soviet power, the airplane would overcome symbolic *prostranstvo* by "tearing the countryside away from its rural isolation, backwardness, cultural alienation, and intellectual poverty."[52]

The modernizing capabilities promised by aviation could not, however, be realized without the direction and leadership of the Party. As the "vanguard and medium of the proletariat's historical aims" and the "principal lever

[49] L. D. Trotskii, *Voprosy byta* (Moscow, 1923). Subsequent citations are drawn from the translated compilation of Trotsky's speeches and essays, *Problems of Everyday Life and Other Writings on Culture and Science* (New York: Monad Press, 1973).

[50] Trotsky, "Not by Politics Alone," in *Problems of Everyday Life*, 16–17.

[51] Trotsky, "Vodka, the Church, and the Cinema" and "Radio, Science, Technology and Society," in *Problems of Everyday Life*, 31–5 and 250–63. The impact of Trotsky's discussion of cultural and economic modernization on intra-Party politics is briefly summarized in Von Hagen, *Soldiers in the Proletarian Dictatorship*, 185–8.

[52] RGVA f. 33987, op. 1, d. 558, l. 145.

of every conscious forward movement," the Party was the motivating force behind the development of the Soviet nation and the inauguration of "new forms of life."[53] The material expression of these new forms of life, Trotsky proclaimed, would be realized through Party efforts to raise cultural standards by encouraging public initiative and the activities of the masses. To this end, Trotsky singled out voluntary societies as the "organizing instruments" of the socialist order to come. Working in conjunction with the state, local soviets, trade unions, and cooperative units, voluntary societies like ODVF would serve as the "new social structures" that would give shape to Soviet society as a whole.[54] Nevertheless, the establishment and direction of these associations would be regulated by the Party, for it was only "within the framework of the dictatorship of the proletariat" that the "socialist content" of daily life could be ensured and successful modernization could be achieved. Ultimately, in the view of the Party's leadership, "socialist construction [was] planned construction on the largest scale."[55] Societies such as ODVF were to serve as the basic building blocks in fulfilling the Party's plan.

Trotsky's commentary on the airplane's role in overcoming Russian *prostransvto* revealed the continuity of vision that linked emerging Soviet aviation culture with the air-minded assumptions of the Imperial past. Eager to bridge the historical divide that separated Russia from the advanced states of Western Europe, prewar patrons had embraced aeronautical success as demonstrable proof of their belonging to the modern world. Contrasting the "philistinism and savagery" of Russia's rural countryside with the mechanical marvels of machine-powered flight, Imperial observers saw aviation achievements as evidence that their nation could rapidly conquer both history and the present. The airplane vindicated their deeply held convictions regarding Russia's inherent greatness, and it avouched the nation's ability to realize, tangibly, dreams of future glory. Similar visions structured the approach of Soviet leaders. Believing that the development of a national air fleet was an essential catalyst in the quest to realize socialism, Party leaders advanced the airplane and aeronautical associations as both symbols of modernity and as means of implementing their modernist visions. They embraced the dualistic notion that the airplane was an "instrument of the future": a transportation technology ubiquitous throughout the industrially advanced world and a convenient contrivance capable of transporting the country into the future.

The Party leadership's underlying assumptions concerning the airplane's contributions to the advent of socialism shaped their approach to generating

---

[53] Trotsky, "From the Old Family to the New," in *Problems of Everyday Life*, 37; "Habit and Custom," *ibid.*, 26, and "How to Begin," *ibid.*, 70.

[54] Trotsky, "How to Begin," *ibid.*, 70–1.

[55] Trotsky, "Not by Politics Alone," *ibid.*, 17.

and institutionalizing support for aviation. Faced with the chaotic social and political conditions bequeathed by the Revolution and Civil War and beholden to an eschatological vision of economic and industrial progress, Party officials turned to the airplane to accomplish their own transcendent act. They looked to circumvent present reality through a comprehensive program of forced aeronautical modernization directed exclusively from above. In creating the centrally controlled, mass-based "voluntary" society ODVF, the Soviet leadership endeavored to radically reconstruct civic and social networks while achieving the doctrinal objective of a technologically proficient, industrially advanced, and class-conscious Russia.[56] By uniting the Party's ideological vision with the social "volunteerism" of the masses, ODVF contributed to the country's unification. The organization realized the necessity of constructing and maintaining a modern air fleet while serving as a ready-made symbol of the Soviet leadership's authority and power. To these ends, aeronautical instruments like the Society of Friends of the Air Fleet functioned in iconic fashion. They symbolized the new, modern world made possible by the October Revolution, while providing the institutional structures necessary for the material realization of the regime's revolutionary dreams.

[56] Kenez, *Birth of the Propaganda State*, 254.

4

The Images and Institutions
of Soviet Air-Mindedness

"SOVIETIZING" THE HEAVENS

ODVF's symbolic significance in advancing the Party's multiple agendas was evident in published reports of the excitement that surrounded activities to win popular support for Soviet aviation. In the innumerable speeches, essays, and articles that appeared in the wake of the 1 March 1923 announcement, ODVF spokesmen repeatedly referred to the initiative and enthusiasm demonstrated by the masses rallying to the ever-expanding campaign as an example of emerging socialist civic consciousness.[1] Having recognized the "essential need" of the aeronautical enterprise, Soviet workers, Party representatives claimed, "expressed their collective desire to construct an air fleet" through active participation in official programs designed to support Red aviation.[2] In cities and towns across the country, concerned citizens allegedly rallied to realize the Party's aeronautical goals.

Central to the Party's mobilization strategy was an attempt to establish the historical credentials of Soviet aviation and to call attention to its continuing importance as the "flying catalyst of the world revolution."[3] ODVF publications routinely exaggerated the role played by the Red Air Fleet in defending the October Revolution and securing the Bolsheviks' victory during the Civil War. Essays trumpeting the training regimen and martial skills of Soviet pilots were published by leading newspapers to popularize a positive image of the country's airborne cadres.[4] Airmen were immortalized in such poems as "Red Fliers" and "To the Gladiators of the Air," which celebrated Soviet pilots as "daredevil defenders" and heralded their role in

---

[1] See, for example, "Puti vozrozhdeniia Krasnogo vozdushnogo flota," *Aero* 4 (1923): 53; "Rabochaia podderzhka," *Pravda*, 26 April 1923; and "Puti sozdaniia vozdushnogo flota," *Izvestiia*, 23 May 1923, among others.

[2] GARF f. 7577, op. 1, d. 30 (Stat'i Podvoiskogo i drugikh avtorov o razvitii aviatsii), l. 13.

[3] *Aviatsiia i vozdukhoplavanie* 1 (1923): 1.

[4] Some of these included "Krasnye zavoevateli vozdukha," *Izvestiia*, 23 February 1923; "Akademii Krasnogo vozdushnogo flota (Budushchim nashim kryl'iam)," *Izvestiia*, 1 March 1923; "Ocherki krasnoi aviatsii: letchiki," *Izvestiia*, 17 March 1923; "V akademii vozdushnogo flota," *Pravda* 22 May 1923; "U krasnykh letunov," *Pravda*, 31 May 1923; and "Shkola i vozdushnyi flot," *Pravda* 7 June 1923.

securing peace and stability for the country's earthbound citizens by "Sovi-
etizing the heavens."[5] Together with the hagiographic articles that appeared
in the press, narrative collections recounted the heroic wartime exploits of
"Red Eagle" fliers who had fought to vanquish the forces of restoration.[6]
Although not dissimilar from the glowing treatment accorded native pilots
by the contemporary European media, these publications routinely over-
stated the actual significance of both airmen and airplanes in the conduct of
Civil War military operations in order to heighten the profile of aviation and
to raise public support for the state's aeronautical campaign. Ultimately, the
compensatory rhetoric employed by ODVF revealed less about the reality of
Soviet aviation in the period leading up to 1923 than it did about the Party's
aspirations for the Red Air Fleet in the years that followed.

This conscious glorification of Soviet pilots conformed with similar efforts
to instill public respect and admiration for the soldiers of the Red Army.
Throughout the 1920s the Party's efforts to legitimate its political authority
involved wide-ranging attempts to raise public esteem for the accomplishments of the armed forces. On posters, in the press, and through mass-
produced pamphlets, the figure of the Red Army soldier was idealized as
an example of revolutionary vigilance, ideological purity, and heroic sacrifice.[7] Lavish reenactments of revolutionary "pseudo-events" (such as the
storming of the Winter Palace), mass spectacles, and theatrical performances
were often undertaken by Red Army units, creating a basic mythology surrounding the Revolution and the soldiers that had made revolution possible.[8] Together with annual festivities organized to celebrate the anniversary
of the Red Army's establishment, these politically inspired cultural productions helped to enshrine the Soviet military as the most respected of the young
state's new institutions. The adulation simultaneously accorded to the pilots
of the Red Air Fleet had the additional benefit of informing those elements of
the population unfamiliar with the importance of aviation that airmen, too,

[5] K. Martin, "Krasnye letchiki," *Izvestiia*, 9 March 1923, and A. Zharov, "Gladiatoram vozdukha," *Izvestiia*, 4 April 1923.

[6] Among the many ODVF publications celebrating Civil War aviators are P. Adamovich, *Krasnye orly* (Moscow, 1923); *Krasnyi vozdushnyi flot na sluzhbe revoliutsii: boevye epizody*
(Moscow, 1923); A. N. Lapchinskii, ed., *Krasnyi vozdushnyi flot: iubileinyi sbornik, 1918–
1923* (Moscow, 1923); A. V. Sergeev, *Piat' let stroitel'stva i bor'by vozdushnogo flota, 1917–
1922*, 2 vols. (Moscow, 1926); and N. S. Bobrov, ed., *Kryl'ia sovetov: sbornik rasskazov i
vospominanii* (Moscow, 1928).

[7] For depictions of the Red Army soldier in Soviet propaganda posters see Stephen White, *The
Bolshevik Poster* (New Haven, CT: Yale University Press, 1988), *et passim*.

[8] Peter Kenez, *The Birth of the Propaganda State: Soviet Methods of Mass Mobilization, 1917–
1929* (Cambridge: Cambridge University Press, 1985), 211–15. On the Red Army's participation in the staging of urban mass spectacles, see James von Geldern, *Bolshevik Festivals,
1917–1920* (Berkeley, CA: University of California Press, 1993), 132–3, and Richard Stites,
Revolutionary Dreams: Utopian Vision and Experimental Life in the Russian Revolution
(Oxford: Oxford University Press, 1989), 94–7.

played a vital role in defending the nation from foreign aggressors. Thus the pilots of the Red Air Fleet (or, at least, the characterizations of these pilots) were upheld by the Party and ODVF as animate icons of the Soviet age: daring young men willing to risk their lives in defense of the Revolution.

Accompanying early efforts to document the revolutionary vigilance of Red airmen, ODVF officials downplayed the historical accomplishments of the Imperial air force. Unwilling to acknowledge that the Imperial military had achieved some success in the years preceding the October Revolution, the Soviet press and ODVF publications dismissed the tsarist air fleet as a "laughingstock," largely ignoring it and its history.[9] In those instances when Imperial efforts were discussed in detail, Soviet commentators stressed the hierarchical and pedigreed nature of the air service, disparaging its "elitist" and "aristocratic" atmosphere in which members of the nobility dominated the officer corps.[10] In contrast to its autocratic predecessor, the new Red Air Fleet was hailed as a model of proletarian equality. Even before the inauguration of the air fleet campaign, *Izvestiia* trumpeted the fact that, under Bolshevik rule, workers and peasants already comprised sixty percent of the flying corps' personnel.[11] In citing such figures, the newspaper gave evidence of the social advances achieved by the working class as a result of October.[12]

ODVF efforts to generate interest in aviation also relied on frequent newspaper articles and mass-produced pamphlets that described the danger posed to the Soviet public by their western bourgeois enemies. In countless speeches and essays, ODVF spokesmen warned citizens "not to forget for a moment that the Republic [was] surrounded by capitalist countries" and that "foreign capitalist sharks" were "arming themselves at a rabid pace" in order to "destroy Soviet factories, industries, cities and villages."[13] Accompanying these frenzied declarations, brochures with titles such as *The War in the Air* and *The Air-Fleets of Our Enemies* were produced by local ODVF chapters to foster fears of war among the population.[14] Depicting the threat posed by

9 "Ocherki Krasnoi aviatsii," *Izvestiia*, 9 March 1923. For two rare exceptions in the early Soviet era see, N. A. Iatsuk, *Aviatsiia i ee kul'turnoe znachenie* (Moscow, 1923) and A. E. Raevskii, *Zolotye gody avio-sport* (Moscow, 1924), both of which contain brief references to pre-Revolutionary Russian events. Interestingly, Iatsuk and Raevskii were former Imperial aviators who sided with the Bolsheviks in 1917.

10 *Izvestiia*, 3 March 1923, and *Krasnyi*, 33.

11 *Izvestiia*, 18 February 1923. See also, "Uchoba letnomu delu," *Izvestiia*, 4 April 1923.

12 "Pervyi vypusk komanidrov Krasnogo vozdukhflota," *Izvestiia*, 6 February 1923; "Ocherki krasnoi aviatsii: letchiki," *Izvestiia*, 17 March 1923; and "Aviatsionnaia zhizn' v Petrograde," *Pravda*, 3 April 1923.

13 GARF f. 7577, op. 1, d. 30, l. 19; *Aero-sbornik* 1 (1923): 31; *Vestnik vozdushnogo flota* 2 (1925): 47; and *Aviadrug* 1 (1924): 15. Dozens of similarly vitriolic pamphlets produced and distributed by local ODVF chapters during the early 1920s can be found in GARF f. r-9550 (Kollektsiia listovok sovetskogo perioda).

14 A. Anoshchenko, *Voina v vozdukhe* (Moscow, 1923) and F. Mikhailov, *Vozdushnye sily nashikh vragov* (Ural ODVF, 1924).

the West in graphically uncompromising terms, these propagandistic tracts warned citizens of the dangers posed by European air fleets and urged them to contribute to ODVF as a way of preparing for the "fratricidal wars" that would be launched by the "salivating, imperialist curs."[15] Such vituperative publications were designed to increase support for the air fleet by raising public anxieties concerning the possibility of a future war. More important, in conditioning citizens to fear the ever-present reality of "bourgeois encirclement," ODVF publications helped to cultivate unity by rallying citizens to support the Party's aeronautical campaign through heightened awareness of the danger posed by western governments.

Alongside xenophobic pamphlets, the Party printed parables and tales that addressed the threat posed by airborne foreign enemies. Typical was the short story "Squadrons of the World Commune," which depicted the danger of foreign intervention in similarly consequential (if, perhaps, less immediate) terms. In the wake of a Soviet victory in the "World Civil War," the isolated remnants of the international bourgeoisie have retreated to the island of Madagascar. There, under the dictatorship of Field Marshal Fokht (a reference to French General Ferdinand Foch), they plot a world counter-revolution. Through experimentation with the deadly tsetse fly, bourgeois scientists attempt to produce a poison gas that will be used to kill millions of innocent people. Alerted to the counterrevolutionaries' nefarious plot by an African emissary, Soviet pilots mobilize a multinational squadron of fighter planes, bombers, and dirigibles that dispatches the evil Fokht and saves the world from the bourgeois threat.[16]

Soviet fears of an impending airborne chemical attack from the West received institutional expression in the spring of 1924 with the formation of the "Society of Friends of the Chemical Industry" [Dobrokhim]. Organized in response to the "feverish buildup of chemical weapons taking place in the West," Dobrokhim was to assist the Red Army in preparing for war by raising public support for the chemical industry, encouraging donations to finance chemical research and schooling the entire population in the elements of basic chemical defense.[17] Modeled directly after ODVF, Dobrokhim had the mission of working alongside the aeronautical organization in developing the nation's chemical warfare capabilities.[18] Although Dobrokhim would never attain the size or scope of ODVF, its establishment, as part of a broader campaign to ensure the "chemicalization" [*khimizatsiia*] of both the Red Army and the civilian population, underscored the Party leadership's abiding concern with the military threat posed by western technical

[15] Mikhailov, *Vozdushnye*, 13–15.
[16] Sergei Budantsev, "Eskadril'ia vsemirnoi kommuny," *Krasnaia niva* 18 (1923): 5–7.
[17] *Izvestiia*, 20 May 1924, and "Dobrokhim," *Pravda*, 18 May 1924.
[18] William Odom, *The Soviet Volunteers: Modernization and Bureaucracy in a Public Mass Organization* (Princeton, NJ: Princeton University Press, 1973), 71–5.

proficiency and its reliance on state-centered mass-mobilization campaigns to meet that threat.

ODVF spokesmen and Party representatives continued, in the meantime, to lay the foundations for airborne defenses by educating the public about the need to participate in the construction of Soviet aviation. Far behind other European nations in the number and quality of planes that it possessed, Soviet Russia could ill afford to ignore the danger posed by its lack of production capacity. In a direct reference to the failed policies of the Imperial era, the chairman of ODVF and the vice-chairman of the Council of People's Commissars [*Sovet narodnykh komissarov*, or "Sovnarkom"], Aleksei Rykov, publicly warned that Russia, "could not depend upon the technology, factories, and creative genius of Western Europe" to provide the nation with an air force.[19] Only with the construction of its own airplanes through the establishment of an independent aviation industry could the Soviet Union achieve "aeronautical emancipation from Europe," thereby placing Soviet aeronautics on the "proper path" toward modernization.[20] To achieve these goals, however, it was essential that citizens play an active role in helping to "build an air fleet in *Russia*, by *Russian* workers, with *Russian* materials from the plans of *Russian* engineers."[21]

The Party's repeated public calls for the establishment of an independent Russian aviation industry echoed the similarly pressing appeals articulated by Imperial newsmen in the years that preceded the First World War. Many Soviet commentators cited the "do-nothing" and "destructive" policies of the Imperial era as examples that the state should not follow if it was to avoid a fate similar to that of the defunct tsarist empire.[22] The need to build Soviet aviation was all the more urgent in light of the rapid progress being made by the major powers of Western Europe. Following Sergei Kamenev's hyperbolized proclamation that "every month and every day new reports reach us regarding the accomplishments of our likely enemies," Soviet representatives repeatedly expressed concern that the advances made by British and French airplane manufacturers would prove the decisive edge in securing western victory over the Republic's armies in the war to come.[23] Soviet officials likewise cited the British employment of aviation squadrons to suppress armed uprisings by Afghani and Somali rebels in 1919–20 as demonstrations

---

[19] *Torzhestvennoe zasedanie ODVF, 26 aprelia 1923 g.* (Moscow, 1923), 13.

[20] *Ibid.*, 14, and A. Porokhovshchikov, "Na pravil'nyi put'," *Izvestiia*, 23 March 1923.

[21] A. Blazhkova, "Vozdushnyi flot–sila Rossii," *Tekhnika i snabzhenie krasnoi armii* 1 (1923): 38. The italics appear in the original.

[22] "Obshchestvo druzei vozdushnogo flota," *Izvestiia*, 7 March 1923, and "Nasha pobeda," *Daesh Sibiri krasnye kryl'ia* 2 (1924): 5, among others.

[23] *Torzhestvennoe*, 15, in addition to the following articles: A. Lapchinksii, "Vnimanie k vozdushnomu flotu," *Izvestiia*, 20 February 1923; N. Anoshchenko, "Pomni o Zapade!," *Izvestiia*, 23 March 1923; and Iu. Steklov, "Udvoim, utroim, udesiaterim usiliia!," *Izvestiia*, 16 May 1923.

of the technical proficiency commanded by the imperialist West as well as "lessons" regarding the decisive role played by airplanes in determining battlefield fortunes.[24] Like the warnings sounded by the Imperial press during the 1911–12 Italian–Turkish War, such examples were employed by Soviet spokesmen to prove the importance of aviation in modern warfare and to encourage public support of a national aeronautical program.

Similarities between Soviet and Imperial pronouncements notwithstanding, the fact remained that aeronautical technology had undergone significant advances during the decade 1912–23. In contrast to the limited roles of artillery spotting and reconnaissance played by aircraft during the First World War, steady improvements in engine design and lift capacity, coupled with the proliferation of chemical weapons, indicated that aviation would assume an increasingly consequential position in future combat. Alert to the dangers these innovations posed, Soviet leaders pointed to the inevitable application of the airplane in waging "total war" against the Soviet Union's civilian population. In nightmarish scenarios, Party spokesmen warned that European air fleets would launch surprise assaults that would bring death and destruction to millions of Soviet innocents huddled behind the battlefield lines.[25] Escadrilles of airplanes, possessing great range and carrying capacities, would travel deep into the Soviet interior, destroying the concept of the front and eradicating the difference between the military and the civilian population as well.[26] Owing to the speed and reach of European aircraft, the future war would be won in only a matter of hours as resistance collapsed, industry was destroyed, and the whole population confronted the chaos, anarchy, and horror of modern aerial warfare.[27]

The Party hierarchy's fears of the expanding role played by aviation in modern warfare mirrored similar concerns voiced by West European public officials and private citizens. Even before the start of the First World War, popular journals and magazines in Western Europe and the United States had published sensationalist fiction warning of the impending disaster that would be wrought by the airplane. The most famous of these was H. G. Well's *The War in the Air* (1908), which derived much of its literary impact from the author's keen insight, subsequently echoed in official Soviet pronouncements, that aeronautical advances would eradicate the distinction between combatants and citizens.[28] Not surprisingly then, throughout the 1920s, observers in England, France, Germany, and the United States warned

---

[24] *Vestnik vozdushnogo flota* 1 (1920): 13, and Ia. D. Bliumkin, "Vnimanie k vozdushnomu flotu!," *Aero-sbornik* 1 (1923): 11–12.

[25] *Torzhestvennoe*, 15–16.

[26] L. D. Trotskii, *Zadachi Dobrokhima* (Khar'kov, 1924), 10.

[27] "Sovetskoi Rossii nuzhen vozdushnyi flot," *Izvestiia*, 25 August 1922.

[28] Robert Wohl, *A Passion for Wings: Aviation and the Western Imagination, 1908–1918* (New Haven, CT: Yale University Press, 1994), 74.

of the growing importance of the airplane as a vital component in building a system of national defense. To this extent, the Party leaders' expressed interest in aviation reflected broader European concerns over how best to incorporate the new technology into existing military doctrine.

Such shared sentiments notwithstanding, the Soviet approach to aeronautical modernization was more heavily influenced by ongoing intra-Party debates regarding the proper functions to be assumed by military and civilian institutions in the future socialist state. From the closing years of the Civil War until Trotsky's *de facto* removal as head of the Red Army by the spring of 1924, members of the Soviet High Command debated fundamental issues of military doctrine and entertained a variety of proposals concerning the restructuring of the nation's armed forces.[29] Best expressed in Mikhail Frunze's 1925 essay "Front and Rear in Future War," which crystallized Bolshevik thinking regarding the necessity of integrating the military into the country's economic life, these debates revealed the extent to which Party leaders intended to militarize the entire civilian apparatus of their new state.[30] Although differences would emerge over issues such as offensive strategy, organizational structure, and the wisdom of incorporating former Imperial officers into the Red Army, all of the major players within the military leadership agreed that the evolution of total war required an institutionalized total response in which civilian and military duties should be fully coordinated to serve the needs of the state.[31] The Soviet response to the challenge of aeronautical modernization reflected this general consensus and helped to further the leadership's drive toward integrating a modern military establishment into the new society they were attempting to build.[32] As Party and ODVF pronouncements made clear, it was "essential to secure the union of civilian and military aviation and to achieve maximum coordination among all flying organizations" in order to develop an advanced air force.[33]

A SOVIET ULTIMATUM

Efforts to win public support for the Party's aeronautical program were abetted, in part, by the diplomatic maneuvers of the country's European adversaries. On 8 May 1923, following a fervid anti-Soviet propaganda campaign in the British press, the British Foreign Office delivered a diplomatic note to the Bolshevik government that demanded redress of a host of grievances

[29] David R. Stone, *Hammer and Rifle: The Militarization of the Soviet Union, 1926–1933* (Lawrence, KS: University Press of Kansas, 2000).

[30] Stone, *Hammer and Rifle*, 16.

[31] Mark Von Hagen, *Soldiers in the Proletarian Dictatorship: The Red Army and the Soviet Socialist State, 1917–1930* (Ithaca, NY: Cornell University Press, 1990), 243–52.

[32] Odom, *Soviet Volunteers*, 32.

[33] Trotskii, *Perspektivy i zadachi*, 17.

concerning Soviet policy toward Great Britain. In the event that the Soviet government did not meet the conditions stipulated in the memorandum, the British warned, the Anglo–Soviet trade agreement of March 1921 would be revoked and the British chargé d'affaires would be recalled from Moscow. Coinciding with the widely publicized visits of French Marshal Foch and the British Chief of the General Staff to Poland and the 10 May assassination of Vatslav Vorovskii, the Soviet envoy to the Lausanne Conference, the "Curzon ultimatum" (as the note came to be called) shocked the Soviet government and heightened fears of an impending war.[34] The ultimatum also provided ODVF with additional material for waging its aeronautical campaign.

In response to the memorandum, the Party leadership launched a massive propaganda offensive intended to illustrate the solidarity of Soviet citizens in the face of the "villainous and predatory ultimatum."[35] On 12 May, a mammoth demonstration was orchestrated outside Moscow's Bolshoi Theater to protest the assassination of Vorovskii and the demands set forth in the diplomatic note. Leading officials meanwhile mounted an impassioned attack on the British government. Accompanying the array of articles, essays, and editorials that appeared over the following weeks, numerous cartoons and poems that depicted Curzon and his diplomatic communiqué in sharply satirical terms were published by the Soviet press.[36] Among the more noteworthy contributions to this collection was a poem by Mayakovsky titled "It Means This!" ["*Eto znachit vot chto!*"], which used the occasion of the diplomatic ultimatum to urge support for the air fleet. Recounting the recent series of western actions threatening Soviet security, Mayakovsky asserted that the country's defense would be guaranteed only after it had "spent its last ruble on airplanes." Once "red fliers herald [Soviet] strength in the heavens," he concluded, the populace might take solace in the knowledge that their safety was ensured.[37] This explicit association of Curzon's ultimatum with the air fleet signaled the Party's intention to use the diplomatic note as a vehicle to bolster public interest in the ongoing aeronautical campaign.

Following Mayakovsky's poetic admonition, ODVF announced the inauguration of a special campaign designed to further focus citizens' attention on the air fleet. The defiant symbol for the new campaign, a winged clenched fist emblazoned with the initials "O. D. V. F.," was widely circulated on posters and in the press while satirical postcards depicting Lord Curzon were produced for sale to the nation's public.[38] More important, ODVF established a special collection to raise money for the construction of a squadron of

[34] E. H. Carr, *The Interregnum, 1923–1924* (New York: Macmillian, 1954), 173–81.

[35] GARF f. 7577, op. 1, d. 21, l. 212.

[36] These appeared on the front pages of both *Izvestiia* and *Pravda* between 16 May and 13 June.

[37] The poem was published in *Izvestiia*, 23 May 1923.

[38] GARF f. 7577, op. 1, d. 21, l. 216 and "Ul'timatum ODVF SSSR," *Samolet* 2 (1923): 37.

military airplanes. Observing that the recent ultimatum delivered by the English bourgeoisie compelled the Soviet state to quickly build an air fleet, the ODVF leadership proclaimed that it would meet Curzon's preposterous demands with an ultimatum of its own, to be delivered in the form of a new squadron of military aircraft.[39] Collections for the new squadron, which would bear the moniker "Our Ultimatum!" [*Nash ul'timatum!*], were to be raised throughout the country as a demonstration of Soviet citizens' unified opposition to the threats of the western bourgeois powers. Working together with regional newspapers, factories, and Party organizations, local ODVF chapters sponsored special collections to raise the capital needed to purchase individual planes. Between May and November 1923 the Ultimatum Campaign collected millions of rubles, providing funds for the construction of a squadron of eleven airplanes that was presented to Party officials on 11 November at the Trotsky Airfield outside Moscow.[40]

The appropriation of the Curzon ultimatum as a foil to win support for the Red Air Fleet signaled a shift in the Party's strategy to popularize aviation. Before the delivery of the diplomatic note, the program devised by the Revvoensovet had called for press and ODVF publications to devote the majority of their attention to the airplane's nonmilitary applications in developing the Soviet economy and modernizing culture. In those particular instances in which official organs addressed martial themes, they were to do so in only the most general terms, speculating on the possibility of a second world war or a renewed intervention on Russian soil.[41] The Curzon note, however, provided ODVF officials with an opportunity to link the Soviet Air Fleet to a concrete and visible (albeit exaggerated) military threat. In focusing so much attention on the diplomatic skirmish, ODVF officials endeavored to foster public fears of war in order to sustain high levels of interest in the aeronautical campaign. Exaggerated rhetoric and the integration of foreign events in the conduct of the mobilization drive would become henceforth constant features of Soviet aviation culture.

THE RHETORIC AND REALITY OF COMPULSORY VOLUNTEERISM

The well-publicized presentation of the "Ultimatum squadron" and the continuing feverish pace of the aeronautical drive obscured numerous organizational problems encountered by the voluntary society as it mobilized the

---

[39] GARF f. 7577, op. 1, d. 30, l. 22.

[40] RGVA f. 29, op. 1, d. 25 (Svedeniia o sostoianii ODVF na 15 ianvaria 1925 g.), l. 280, and *Izvestiia*, 13 November 1923. The success of the campaign spawned other fund raisers including one for the construction of a squadron titled, "Far Eastern Ultimatum"; see *Izvestiia*, 18 September 1923.

[41] RGVA f. 33987, op. 1, d. 558, ll. 73–7.

country to establish the Red Air Fleet. As the campaign to answer Curzon reached its apogee in the early fall of 1923, the society's governing presidium convened a union-wide meeting of ODVF representatives to coordinate strategies between the center and periphery and to address the problems faced by the organization's rank-and-file members. Held in Moscow from 15 to 18 September, the First All-Union Conference of ODVF revealed that behind official claims of order and competence both the voluntary society and its campaign had suffered through serious bouts of confusion and disorganization.

In a series of reports delivered to the gathered representatives, ODVF's central administration acknowledged that the rapid pace of the mobilization campaign inaugurated on 1 March had resulted in organizational chaos. Despite enrolling more than 100,000 members in the voluntary society, Moscow found itself "horribly behind" in its efforts to marshal the resources collected in the provinces. Lack of communication among national, regional, and local organizations had produced numerous instances in which the Society's different associations and chapters had worked at cross purposes collecting dues, distributing literature, and delivering monetary donations to the central administration. In other cases, poor coordination between the central administration and local chapters meant that recruitment efforts had overlapped and agitational work had been unnecessarily repeated. This "parallelism," officials noted, wasted considerable time and undermined efforts to run an efficient and systematic campaign.[42]

To address these organizational problems, the ODVF central leadership announced that a bold leap forward would be undertaken to restructure the administrative hierarchy that had "chaotically and spontaneously" developed during the aeronautical campaign. Noting that in many cases local chapters had been functioning without sufficient guidance from the center, the Society's national leadership called for strengthening ODVF's central governing apparatus by uniting existing township [*volost'*] and regional [*okrug*] units into new districts [*raiony*]. This process, they argued, would bolster the organization by bringing all chapters under the aegis of the central Moscow authorities. This would enable Moscow to coordinate activities better throughout the country and to assume full responsibility for administering the campaign.[43] According to the central leadership, the process would also assist in developing social consciousness among ODVF members. In the absence of uniform institutions and initiatives, ODVF had thus far failed to exploit fully the human resources that it had assembled through the inaugural campaign. On joining the voluntary society, each ODVF recruit received a membership card in exchange for a five-ruble donation. Aside from the membership card, however, "no substantive programs existed to unite

---

[42] GARF f. 7577, op. 1, d. 40, l. 38.
[43] *Ibid.*, l. 12.

ODVF activists as one mass."[44] Concerned with the organizational diversity
that had manifested itself during the mobilization campaign, and believing
that they needed to establish closer ties between individual members, Party
leaders moved to bolster their administrative control over regional and local
chapters by tying the voluntary society more tightly to the Party and imposing conformity on the society as a whole.

To facilitate unification, ODVF officials announced that air circles, air
clubs, and air corners would be created within military units, factories, and
Party cells. These would serve as social networks for ODVF members, supplying them with recent aeronautical literature, ODVF directives, and agitational materials. They would also serve as bases from which members could
expand the Society through "concrete deeds and work." Moscow leaders
hoped that these institutions would provide the dual benefits of "furthering agitational–enlightenment work while serving as a catalyst for the unification of [the] membership into one mass."[45] To hasten the growth of
the Society, ODVF's leadership also announced that new emphasis would
be placed on "collective membership," the process by which entire factories, military units, and enterprises joined the voluntary society as individual
units. Through the expansion of collective membership, the ODVF presidium expected to increase the Society's total membership from some 100,000
to no fewer than 1 million citizens by the end of 1924. Finally, Moscow
announced that the voluntary society would extend its publication ventures
by inaugurating the new journal *Samolet*, which would be devoted exclusively to the air fleet and the activities of ODVF.

The "unification drive" announced at the All-Union Conference represented more than just an attempt to bring local ODVF chapters into line
with Moscow. The new policy also reflected the Party's growing insistence
that individual members assume active and responsible roles in the growth of
the Society and the success of Soviet aviation. Through participation in aviation corners, air clubs, and circles, ODVF members would be encouraged
to work toward expanding the aeronautical campaign throughout the country. They would also help contribute a growing sense of unity and purpose
among the Society's widening membership. The "personal connections" fostered through participation in local circles and clubs were part of the continuing effort by Party officials to instill a sense of collective civic responsibility
among the masses.

For all of the painstaking efforts undertaken by the Society, the policies
announced by the leadership were an odd approach to developing the country's aeronautical capabilities. In light of the widespread and endemic organizational problems acknowledged by the governing presidium, the proclaimed
objective of increasing ODVF membership by a factor of ten in little more

44 *Ibid.*, l. 85.
45 *Ibid.*

than twelve months' time was, at best, an impetuous proposition. Although the introduction of so many new members would certainly increase the financial resources available for the construction of airplanes, experience thus far had demonstrated that in the absence of adequate administrative oversight most of the money raised would never reach Moscow. Such a rapid proliferation of members, moreover, would make exceedingly difficult any efforts to reorganize ODVF's nationwide administration. In similar fashion, the proclaimed intention of strengthening individuals' personal ties with ODVF was contradicted by the leadership's actions to bring the Society's far-flung chapters closer in line with Moscow. At the same time that individual members were celebrated as the central components of the Society's success, the ODVF presidium suppressed spontaneous, individual expressions of air-mindedness by subordinating the activities of all local and regional organizations to a centrally mandated Party line.

Accompanying efforts to expand membership and to strengthen Party control over the organization, ODVF leaders announced that, henceforth, the Society would direct more of its resources toward recruiting members from among the country's rural inhabitants. To date, ODVF's accomplishments had been achieved solely in major urban centers as aeronautical spectacles and recruitment campaigns were organized to entertain and enlighten municipal residents. In the meantime, peasant attitudes toward ODVF membership had remained "passive" and "uninspired." To ensure that the entire country participate in the campaign, it was essential to "directly and forcibly pound [*zarubit'*] into the heads of the peasants" the vital need for an air fleet.[46] ODVF's leadership announced that it would begin coordinating activities with provincial mutual-aid societies, utilizing those institutions (as it had urban trade union and Party cells) to provide the organizational framework necessary to propagate the Society's interests at local levels throughout the country's rural regions.

Local representatives to the All-Union Conference expressed general support for the decision to turn attention toward the peasantry. Although individual members voiced differing opinions regarding the wisdom of utilizing the mutual-aid societies, all agreed that the village was fascinated with aviation and that attempts to agitate in the countryside would meet with an enthusiastic response. This agreement did not, however, extend to Moscow's plans for further centralizing the ODVF bureaucracy. Concerned that centralization would put the brakes on local efforts, numerous representatives rose to proclaim their opposition to the leadership's restructuring plans. Citing the shortcomings evidenced in Moscow's early administration of the campaign, local representatives to the conference implored the ODVF leadership to grant more independence to provincial organizations. One perturbed

[46] GARF f. 7577, op. 1, d. 40, l. 31.

member went so far as to remind the presidium that those in the provinces also had experience and noted that "Moscow should not be the only one dictating how to run things." Nevertheless, the ODVF leadership concluded that "sufficient agreement" existed to proceed with Moscow's new program.[47]

MILITARIZATION, CENTRALIZATION, AND THE COLOSSALIST IMPULSE

The reorganization of ODVF in the fall of 1923 was only the first in what would become a series of major administrative overhauls intended to impose order and efficiency on the aeronautical society. In May 1925 ODVF merged with Dobrokhim to form a new "voluntary" society that would function under the name "Society of Friends of the Aviation and Chemical Industries" (or "Aviakhim"). Its mission differed very little from those previously undertaken by the two independent organizations. Aviakhim continued efforts to raise chemical consciousness, to generate public support for state policies, and to promote air-mindedness through the orchestration of aeronautical spectacles, air shows, and agit-flights. More significantly, the creation of Aviakhim pointed to an ongoing transition in Soviet aviation culture. Although aeronautical development would remain the society's most important function, the pairing of aviation and chemical interests indicated the Party leadership's growing concern with exploiting the military potential of flight technology.[48]

The immediate result of the ODVF–Dobrokhim union was confusion and disarray. By officials' own admissions, neither of the two public mass societies was adequately prepared to tackle the numerous tasks assigned to them by the Party. Both suffered from a host of institutional problems, including poor coordination with Party organizations, weak administrative authority, lack of direction, and an apathetic membership. The union only aggravated these difficulties. Indeed, the extent to which ODVF and Dobrokhim were unprepared to handle major organizational challenges was clearly revealed during the course of the administrative transition. The liquidation committee established to oversee the ODVF–Dobrokhim merger proceeded in a slow, inefficient, and haphazard fashion, requiring almost one full year to complete the union following its perfunctory announcement in March 1925.[49] Despite the apparent congruence of aeronautical and chemical interests, the union of ODVF and Dobrokhim proved to be an administrative nightmare.

The difficulties associated with the societies' merger were compounded by the simultaneous efforts of Aviakhim officials to implement a new Party directive on "socialist civic consciousness" [*sotsialisticheskaia*

---

[47] *Ibid., et passim.*
[48] GARF f. r-9404, op. 1, d. 23, l. 7.
[49] *Ibid.,* l. 4.

obshchestvennost'] first discussed at the Thirteenth Party Congress and sub-sequently heralded in the press.[50] The latest in a series of efforts to increase the efficiency of voluntary societies and to generate public activism in sup-port of the regime's policies, the campaign for socialist civic consciousness attempted to instill collectivist sentiments among the nation's populace and to incite active participation in public life by an otherwise passive citizenry through the development of "real workers' democracy" within civic orga-nizations.[51] In practical terms, this meant an end to the custom of enrolling new "volunteers" through collective membership.[52] In contrast to the sup-port for collective memberships articulated at the outset of the aeronautical campaign in 1923, the conscription of entire factories and organizations now came under attack. Collective membership was denounced for having "crushed the initiative and spirit of individual cells" and for having produced a listless organization that failed to capture the interest of those coerced into "voluntary" service.[53]

In keeping with the new goal of reconstituting society "on the basis of genuine [voluntary] civic consciousness" (and in the hope of redressing the innumerable problems besetting ODVF and Dobrokhim), Aviakhim's gov-erning administration initiated a nationwide campaign to "reregister" all of the society's members. The reregistration campaign effectively purged the society's ranks, as many less than enthusiastic ODVF and Dobrokhim mem-bers seized on the opportunity to "disenroll" from the organization into which they had been previously "volunteered." The society's loss of sup-port was startling. One concerned official from the Donbass lamented that reregistration had proven "catastrophic" as "workers left [Aviakhim] by the thousands." Before the union, the combined enrollment of the region's ODVF and Dobrokhim chapters had totaled over 19,000. After the conclu-sion of the reregistration period, the number of members had plummeted to under 11,000, a decline of more than forty-three percent.[54] Similar dire results accompanied the merger in the Saratov region [*oblast'*], where local Aviakhim officials were forced to contend with a calamitous eighty-percent decline in revenues as members, "having lost interest in the work of the soci-ety," bolted from the organization in droves.[55] Losses throughout the country as a whole, although not quite as precipitous, were still significant. Before the

[50] See the Congress's resolution "Ob ocherednykh zadachakh partiinogo stroitel'stva" in *Trinadtsatyi s"ezd RKP(b): stenograficheskii otchet* (Moscow, 1924), 604–17, and "O formakh massovykh organizatsii," *Pravda*, 25 February 1925.

[51] *Trinadtsatyi s"ezd*, 608–9.

[52] A. F. Glagolev, compiler, *Avia-agit doklad: konspekt* (Moscow: ODVF, 1925), 34.

[53] GARF f. r-9404, op. 1, d. 14 (Protokoly sovmestnykh zasedanii biuro prezidiumov Avi-akhima), l. 4.

[54] *Ibid.*, ll. 15–16.

[55] TsDNISO, f. 2639, op. 1, d. 1 (Materialy i svodki ob Aviakhime), l. 19, and TsDNISO f. 2639, op.1, d. 3 (Otchet o rabote fraktsii Aviakhima), ll. 3–6.

administrative union, ODVF and Dobrokhim claimed membership figures of 1.5 million and 1.3 million, respectively. Following the conclusion of the reregistration campaign in mid-1926, Aviakhim's membership had fallen to 1,986,000 or just 77.2% of the preunion total.[56]

The administrative bumbling of the ODVF–Dobrokhim union and the voluntary exodus of dues-paying members produced by the reregistration campaign pointed to a continuing pattern of mismanagement and bureaucratic interference that directly contradicted the stated goals of Party officials. In language very similar to that used at the 1923 ODVF conference, Aviakhim officials acknowledged that the transition to the new organization had produced initial chaos, but claimed that, by the spring of 1926, these problems had been solved and that newly achieved administrative efficiency and competency had transformed Aviakhim into a genuine civic association.[57] In no time, they assured, the voluntary society would be functioning smoothly and energetically. On a broader note, Aviakhim representatives pointed to the significance of the societies' merger in contributing to the ongoing process of socialist construction. In a characteristic example of Soviet bureaucratic jargon, officials dismissed the "apparent crisis" brought about by the union as nothing more than "the maturation of the social organism," a necessary component in the development of the new society and proof that the joint ODVF–Dobrokhim enterprise was "actively contributing to the growth of Soviet civic consciousness."[58]

The reorganization, amalgamation, and reshuffling of bureaucratic organizations exemplified by the ODVF–Dobrokhim merger revealed the contradictory nature of Soviet political culture in which Party officials endeavored to inspire local enthusiasm and individual initiative by mandating administrative changes from above. Dissatisfied with the level of energy demonstrated by their conscripted volunteers, Soviet officials sought to bolster members' commitment by reforming the organizational structures that governed their activities.[59] In direct contradiction of official instructions to encourage citizens' personal initiative and social activism, Aviakhim officials moved immediately to suppress the possibility of spontaneity on the part of the rank-and-file membership. Following the administrative union, the society's presidium disbanded local and regional aeronautical journals in favor of expanding the distribution of the central journal *Aviatsiia i khimiia* [*Aviation and Chemistry*]. The center also imposed rigid new guidelines concerning the proper organization of the nation's aeronautical circles, "avia-corners," and

---

[56] GARF f. r-9404, op. 1, d. 23, ll. 3–5.
[57] GARF f. r-9404, op. 1, d. 14, l. 2.
[58] GARF f. r-9404, op. 1, d. 23, l. 3.
[59] For similar patterns of institutional behavior in relation to another contemporary voluntary society, see Daniel Peris, *Storming the Heavens: The Soviet League of the Militant Godless* (Ithaca, NY: Cornell University Press, 1998).

cells. To assist in these efforts, the society mass produced brochures and guidebooks that clearly detailed the precise components (from books and magazines to posters, charts, and instructional graphs) that should be present in each local organization.[60] In their haste to strengthen Party control over the society's individual cells, Aviakhim officials thus revisited the mistakes made by ODVF officials during 1923. They sacrificed the possibility of genuine local initiative for heightened central authority and organizational uniformity while continuing to demand that individual members play a more active and responsible role in the day-to-day administration of local chapters. These efforts again revealed the paradox of Soviet political culture in which leading officials endeavored to encourage spontaneous social commitments by exhorting citizens to take active roles in voluntary societies while constantly narrowing the parameters in which citizens could act. Such measures all but ensured that Aviakhim would require still further "restructuring" in the not-too-distant future as the society's understandably dispassionate membership failed to respond to the administration's prodding. Still more disconcerting, Aviakhim officials would fall back on the well-established formula of measuring success not in nebulous qualitative terms but rather by the more easily quantifiable yardstick of the organization's size. To this end, they made clear their objective of rapidly expanding the society's membership, albeit on a "voluntary" individual basis.

Less than one year following the conclusion of the ODVF–Dobrokhim union, Soviet aeronautical culture witnessed another major institutional transformation. In January 1927, Aviakhim merged with the Society for Assistance to Defense [*Obshchestvo sodeistviia oborony*, or OSO] to form Osoaviakhim, a "mega-society" devoted to civil defense and the military education of the country's populace. The creation of Osoaviakhim represented a fundamental shift in both the direction and the content of Soviet aviation. Although Osoaviakhim continued to promote the development of civil aviation, the society now undertook efforts to train citizens in rifle marksmanship, chemical defense, and partisan warfare tactics as well. The society's new civil defense mission meant that Soviet aviation culture would take on an increasingly militaristic character.

The creation of Osoaviakhim represented the administrative culmination of the Party leadership's long-standing effort to strengthen military preparedness through the militarization of the Soviet Union's civilian population. Although the incorporation of civilian organizations into the military command structure had been proposed as early as 1923 by Leon Trotsky, the first real progress toward institutionalizing this goal was not achieved until 1926.

---

[60] See the following instructional guides published by Aviakhim: *Avia-agitatsiia i propaganda: metody i formy raboty* (Moscow, 1925); A. F. Glagolev, compiler, *Aviakul'tury v rabochii klub: material po aviarabote v rabochikh klubakh* (Moscow, 1925); *Avia-ugolok: materialy* (Moscow, 1925); and the previously cited Glagolev, *Avia-agit-doklad*.

In July of that year the OSO was founded through the administrative transformation of the preexisting Military Scientific Society [*Voennoe nauchnoe obshchestvo*, or VNO]. Established in 1920 by the military academy of the Red Army General Staff in Moscow, the VNO was a professional military organization dedicated to the study of the World War and the Russian Civil War, the development of military doctrine, and the education of Red Army officers. The OSO's new charter ended the "parochial intra-army character" of VNO activities by creating a broader mass voluntary organization devoted to state defense that included civilian as well as military members.[61] As such, the creation of the OSO was an important step in the Party's efforts to militarize Soviet society in preparation for what leaders believed was an impending conflict with the capitalist powers of Western Europe.[62]

In his introductory speech before the First (and only) All-Union Conference of Aviakhim in January 1927, Commissar of Defense Klim Voroshilov explained the underlying military and political concerns that had motivated the decision to create Osoaviakhim. According to Voroshilov, the current configuration of independent voluntary organizations had prevented Party officials from properly coordinating the nation's defenses. Although Aviakhim had undertaken effective cultural work, its members were not prepared to address, nor had they addressed, issues pertaining to the state's defense. This lack of attention toward civil defense by an association possessing such clear relevance to military preparedness could be eradicated only by the administrative union. Once Aviakhim was joined to the OSO, Voroshilov informed the gathered representatives, the Society's members would be able "to address the question of militarization and the education of the broad mass of workers and peasants in preparing state defenses."[63]

The creation of Osoaviakhim would also assist the Party in "broadening" public participation in state military concerns by greatly increasing the number of citizens enrolled in the civil defense society. According to Voroshilov, civil defense was a concern in which "every citizen wanted to participate." More accurately, of course, civil defense was a concern in which the *Party* wanted every citizen to participate, just as it had wanted citizens to participate in its previous campaigns to build the air fleet, increase literacy, stamp out religion, and popularize the radio. Like these earlier initiatives, the creation of Osoaviakhim reflected the underlying assumption of Soviet political culture that forced association, when coupled with the mindful and

---

[61] In keeping with Soviet practice, the transformation of the VNO from an exclusively military to a military–civilian society was carried out by Party directive and over the objections of the VNO membership. See Odom, *Soviet Volunteers*, 75–7.

[62] Von Hagen, *Soldiers in the Proletarian Dictatorship*, 246–7. For specific policies and programs relating to the militarization of Soviet society undertaken by Osoaviakhim, see RGVA f. 33988, op. 1, d. 628 (Soobrazheniia o voennoi podgotovke trudiashchikhsia) and d. 633 (Piatiletnyi plan razvitiia Osoaviakhima).

[63] GARF f. r-9404, op. 1, d. 37, l. 60.

omnipresent tutelage of the Communist Party, could inspire the popular civic-mindedness and provide the institutional networks necessary for the proper functioning of "socialist society."

By way of justifying the expansion of the OSO, Voroshilov pointed to the relative weakness of Soviet defense organizations in comparison with those in neighboring states. Although the country boasted 2 million citizens in defense-related societies, measured in terms of per capita membership, this number was significantly lower than that of Finland, Poland, Rumania, and Latvia. In light of these realities, Voroshilov called the current Soviet civil defense network "an insignificant and amorphous mass" that could attain success only through the amalgamation of OSO–Aviakhim and the subsequent "active participation" of Osoaviakhim members in the unified work of the society. What this would mean on a practical day-to-day basis, however, was unclear. Voroshilov's speech was weak on particulars. He presented no evidence that an administrative union of OSO–Aviakhim would prove the best way to achieve the Party's military goals. Instead, he underscored his convictions through rhetorical paroxysms, warning the assembled representatives that "there is not one single government in the world, not one single government on the whole planet, that has been so careless and lukewarm about the defense of its own borders as the Soviet Union." The unification of OSO–Aviakhim, however, would rectify this problem. Unification would create a society "comprising the militarized members of the [two] organizations," who would take it upon themselves "to militarize the whole country" through participation in Osoaviakhim.[64]

Voroshilov concluded by noting that the current international situation compelled the Party to act quickly and decisively in rectifying the shoddy state of its defensive networks. Recent diplomatic setbacks in China and Józef Piłsudski's May 1926 military coup in Poland had been viewed with alarm by the Party hierarchy. Accompanying these developments, continuing sour relations with Great Britain, France, and the United States compounded latent fears of an impending military confrontation. The country now found itself subject to intense pressure by "the watchdogs of capitalism" who were actively preparing for the inevitable moment when they would attack the Soviet Union.[65] As such, the OSO–Aviakhim union was a pressing necessity.

Although foreign events played an important role in raising awareness of the bourgeois threat, the fundamental factor feeding Party leaders' continuing fear of foreign intervention remained their ideologically driven worldview. As we have seen, Party spokesmen had put to good use popular fears of renewed warfare during the years 1923–4 to engender support for ODVF and the campaign to build the Red Air Fleet. Although Soviet rhetoric concerning the impending approach of the world revolution had cooled somewhat

[64] *Ibid.*, 64–7.
[65] *Ibid.*, 64.

from the frenzied, high-pitched proclamations that had been issued during (and immediately after) the Civil War years, the leadership remained convinced that a military confrontation with the forces of capital would prove the inevitable (and, ultimately, desirable) result of the Russian workers' and peasants' revolution. In 1927, the leadership again invoked the specter of war to justify its course of action and to mobilize public support for its policies. As Voroshilov made clear in his closing remarks to the All-Union Conference, the impending conflict with capital remained an ever-present threat in the minds of Soviet officials:

I can tell you on the full authority of Vladimir Il'ich Lenin that war for our Union is unavoidable and that war will come, if not today, then tomorrow; if not tomorrow, then within a year; if not within a year, than within five to ten years. Lenin was very clear about this. He wrote and spoke about it often. Now, we too, say and write the same in our official and unofficial promulgations.[66]

If the Party's reversion to war-mongering scare tactics signaled a return to already established patterns of institutional behavior, so, too, did the manner in which it implemented the OSO–Aviakhim union. Voroshilov's acknowledgment before the Conference that the creation of Osoaviakhim was undertaken despite the disagreement voiced by members of both societies and his subsequent admonition that "patriotism" for the individual societies be eradicated and replaced with patriotism for the united Osoaviakhim, were clear indications that rank-and-file opposition to the administrative merger had existed.[67] In this regard, the creation of Osoaviakhim proceeded along lines similar to those that had accompanied the initial formation of ODVF and the subsequent creation of Aviakhim. In each instance the Party acted not in response to the genuine initiative of ordinary citizens but through administrative fiat; mandating bureaucratic changes from above in order to serve its own perceived political and social goals. The only difference between the OSO–Aviakhim union and the previous campaigns initiated by Party officials was the enormous scope of the new enterprise. Osoaviakhim was a mammoth undertaking producing a truly all-Union organizational network of citizens that would boast more than 12 million members within five years of its formation.[68] To this end, the OSO–Aviakhim union signaled the onset of the "colossalist" mindset that would become a hallmark of 1930s Soviet culture. Similar to Gosplan (and, increasingly, the Party itself), Osoaviakhim was a massive, bureaucratic expression of Soviet leaders' conviction that they could engineer society through rationalized planning and

---

[66] *Ibid.*, 69.

[67] *Ibid.*, l. 58. See also Odom, *Soviet Volunteers*, 84–5.

[68] Odom, *Soviet Volunteers*, 173. Odom correctly notes that the society's official membership figures were very misleading, perhaps overstating the effective membership by as much as fifty to sixty percent. Even so, Osoaviakhim remained, by far, the largest social organization in the Soviet Union.

centralized control. The "institutional collectivization" of the nation's two most prominent social organizations, in turn, revealed the totalistic (if not totalitarian) impulses of Soviet political culture as Party leaders endeavored to create a comprehensive civil defense network that would bind all citizens to the state through militarized local institutions under strict Party control.

The recurrent permutations of public aeronautical organizations during the 1920s revealed the underlying tensions at play as the Party hierarchy endeavored to encourage popular enthusiasm for aviation and the construction of the Red Air Fleet. Through the fabrication of a bureaucratic network that would foster mass "volunteerism," Party officials sought to modernize the country's aviation capabilities while creating institutions and symbols intended to augment their political authority. Their actions, however, indicated the inherently contradictory purposes that the voluntary society was designed to pursue. Eager to bring increasing numbers of citizens under the control of a centralized hierarchy, the Party leadership subordinated effective administration to the chimerical goal of rapidly increasing the society's numbers. Through the adoption of "collective membership," which created new local chapters by administrative fiat, the Party impelled the exponential expansion of aeronautical institutions in a headlong rush to forge a modern air force and to realize their designs of social engineering. Although these methods would lead to impressive growth on paper, they undermined long-term efforts to institutionalize air-mindedness throughout the country by exacerbating the constant administrative problems facing local organizations. Ultimately, Party leaders' approaches to mobilizing aeronautical support created little more than "pseudo-organizations," state-mandated substitutes for private associations that suppressed local initiative and circumvented individual spontaneity while conscripting millions of citizens into state service on behalf of Party-dictated goals.[69]

The nature of the early Soviet aeronautical campaign and the manner in which it was executed differed only in degree from the earlier efforts undertaken by tsarist state officials. Influenced by a shared tradition that equated modernity with industrial development, Bolshevik leaders, like their Imperial predecessors, attempted Russia's rapid transformation from a backward and aeronautically challenged nation into a modern, proficient, and air-minded state. Conjoining the Russian predilection for a sudden transcendent act with the totalizing impulses of Marxist ideology, they sought to demonstrate mastery over the present by imposing from above a state-driven approach to modernization. They believed that they could telescope development, upstaging the more technically proficient states of Western Europe on the way to creating the world's most advanced and powerful air force. To this end, they looked to purchase technology and expertise from abroad while attempting to lay the foundations of future greatness at home, revisiting patterns of institutional behavior first intimated by their tsarist antecedents.

Soviet officials also followed established Imperial precedent in attaching excessive significance to events and accomplishments of only relative importance. Seeking to generate nationwide support for the construction of an air fleet during a period of economic hardship, and eager to legitimate their ideological vision through demonstrations of technological acuity and social solidarity, Soviet leaders resorted to the rhetoric of compensatory symbolism as a means of winning converts to the aeronautical cause. They exaggerated the contributions of Civil War aviators in order to distinguish "Red" aviation from its Imperial variant, and they issued bombastic "ultimatums" in response to inflated foreign threats to bolster support for the regime and its policies. Compensatory symbolism played a role, as well, in shaping those organizations mandated to serve the Party's aeronautical agenda. Attuned to the political utility of public displays of mass "volunteerism," Party leaders repeatedly expanded the scale and scope of aeronautical societies to broaden their control over the drive to "Sovietize" the heavens. Measuring their efforts not on the basis of actual technical innovations but, rather, through the innovative custom of equating size with success, Party leaders found a convenient way of responding to the institutional challenges posed by the airplane. They portrayed organizational aggrandizement and the imposition of hierarchical uniformity as "progress," despite the deleterious results these imposed on the country's long-term development.

Like other state-mandated pseudo-organizations designed to promote socialist construction, ODVF (and its successors) reflected the peculiar proclivity of Bolshevik political culture to value uniform bureaucratic development at the expense of gainful activity. Subordinating practical considerations to the theoretical dictates of Marxist ideology, state officials embraced the mass organization as a transcendent agent, expecting it to rapidly propel the country toward its glorious socialist future while accomplishing the air-minded mandates of a modern nation.

In one critical respect, however, ODVF, Aviakhim, and Osoaviakhim were unique. Unlike other contemporary societies that promoted atheism, literacy, sobriety, or the use of the radio, the activities undertaken by aeronautical organizations possessed enormous potential in winning over international converts to the socialist crusade. A highly visible symbol of technological acuity and industrial modernity, the airplane was a ready-made beacon of progress and power that might effectively be put to use proselytizing the accomplishments of the socialist system. A quintessential example of the state's ability to master technique, the airplane could herald the success of Soviet planning. It could demonstrate to the world the ingenuity of the Party's leaders and attest to the rectitude of their developmental vision.

Before aviation successes could be showcased abroad, however, Soviet officials first had to complete their domestic campaign to forge a "dictatorship of the air." Faced with the challenge of convincing Russia's "numerous backward tribes" to support the Party and its cause, Bolshevik leaders exploited the cultural resonance of flight in an attempt to impose modernity on the country's vast hinterlands. They employed the symbolic and material benefits of the airplane to bind rural residents to their urban counterparts in the construction of the world's first socialist society. In addition to revealing Party leaders' inherent disdain for the peasant milieu, the aviation campaign in the villages produced innovative strategies and techniques that would be later put to use in elevating the country's international standing. In the broader context, it disclosed the persistent influence of inherited structures and forms in shaping the content of Soviet aviation culture.

We will examine the nature and impact of the Party's efforts to inculcate rural air-mindedness in Chapter 5.

5

Aeronautical Iconography
and Political Legitimacy

THE "TURN TO THE VILLAGE"

From its very inception in the spring of 1923, the campaign to construct the Red Air Fleet was designed to achieve the multiple goals of fostering air-mindedness, building an air force, and reconstituting the social and political networks that had been destroyed by the Revolution and the Civil War. In support of these tasks, high-ranking Party officials exploited the airplane, using its image to raise public awareness of the possibility of foreign attack, to educate citizens of Party efforts to prevent this possibility, and to reinforce the impression of their power and authority throughout regions only recently brought under their control. Like the policies undertaken before 1917, Bolshevik efforts were rooted in an iconic vision of flight that sought to link political officials to a recognized symbol of modernization while harnessing the airplane as a means of realizing the state's larger designs. Initial postrevolutionary efforts to promote aviation had, however, focused almost entirely on Soviet Russia's largest metropolitan centers. Concentrating activity in major cities such as Petrograd and Moscow, officials quickly developed a network of urban organizations by recruiting new members from factories, Party cells, trade unions, and the military. The stated objective that air-mindedness permeate the entire Soviet Republic, however, meant that, beginning in the winter of 1923–4, aeronautical propaganda would increasingly be applied to winning over rural residents to the cause of Red aviation.

The ensuing attempt to raise the aeronautical consciousness of the peasantry was an extension of Party leaders' ongoing efforts to facilitate a "union" [*smychka*] between their urban constituents and the country's peasant masses. Formally ratified by the Thirteenth Party Congress in May 1924, the policy of *smychka* had been underway, in earnest, since the end of War Communism in 1921.[1] Adopted in part as a response to the exigencies of the Civil War and in part out of an ideologically driven exuberance to destroy

---

[1] *Trinadtsatyi s"ezd RKP(b): stenograficheskii otchet* (Moscow, 1924), 633–46. For a narrative overview of the policy, see N. N. Saburov, *Bor'ba partii za ustanovlenie ekonomicheskoi smychki rabochego klassa s trudiashchimsia krest'ianstvom, 1921–1925 gg.* (Leningrad: Izdatel'stvo Leningradskogo universiteta, 1975), 66–76.

the remnants of capitalism, War Communism had entailed the nationalization of industry, the abolition of private manufacturing and trade, and the
forced requisitioning of the peasantry's grain stocks. Not surprisingly, the
policy earned the Soviet government the enmity of the peasants. An integral
part of the emerging New Economic Policy, *smychka* attempted to salvage
the Party's image by rectifying the disastrous economic dislocation caused
by War Communism.[2] Keeping with the Party's broader legitimating claim
of embodying the interests of workers and peasants, *smychka* also sought
to generate provincial support for Soviet power by encouraging political
cooperation and cultural exchange between urban and rural inhabitants.

The bureaucratic foundation for an aeronautical "turn to the village" (as
smychka euphemistically came to be known) was established at the All-Union
Conference of ODVF in September 1923. In addition to addressing much-
needed administrative reform, conference delegates spent considerable time
developing strategies for enticing rural residents to become friends of the air
fleet. Although pleased with the campaign's success in enrolling well over
100,000 members by the end of 1923, Party officials voiced concern about
the lack of activity outside major urban centers. They therefore launched an
All-Union Campaign in the Villages on 15 December 1923 that was intended
to "explain to the peasantry, in simple and clear words, the nature of aviation
and aeronautics and their importance in defending the country and assisting
in its economic development." Through direct appeals tailored to peasant
audiences, they hoped to encourage rural residents' cooperation and fraternal assistance in the construction of Red aviation. The turn to the village
would liquidate "aeronautical illiteracy" among the peasantry, thus paving
the way for a truly "all-union" effort to build the air fleet.[3] The incorporation of rural residents in the aeronautical campaign would produce the
added benefit of hastening urbanization by bringing peasants into contact
with new technologies and agricultural methods. In this way, the airplane
would play both a symbolic and functional role in supporting the political
and cultural goals of the worker–peasant *smychka* by drawing the village
closer to the city.[4]

The effort to inculcate air-mindedness among rural residents produced
literature different from that disseminated to urban audiences. The pamphlets, short stories, poems, and tales intended for peasant consumption
were designed to communicate specific messages regarding the economic
prosperity of the peasantry, the budding friendship of city and village, and the
Party's dedicated efforts to employ aviation in realizing these ends. A closer
examination reveals the considerable extent to which state propagandists

[2] Alec Nove, *An Economic History of the USSR, 1917–1991* (London: Penguin Books, 1992),
88–91.
[3] "Aviatsionnaia kampaniia v derevne," *Samolet* 2 (1923): 30.
[4] GARF f. 7577, op. 1, d. 30, ll. 18–19.

relied on styles and motifs inherited from the Imperial past to communicate their vision of the Soviet Union's socialist future. It also reveals that even during the brief period of 1921–5, when Party officials were actively working to court the peasantry, they simultaneously communicated an underlying condescension toward and disdain for their rural charges. This antipathetic subtext of aeronautical propaganda indicated the inimical, antirural sentiments that lay at the heart of the Party's ideological visions. Its presence calls into question the possibility that the peasantry could ever be granted equal status within the worker–peasant state.

"OUR RELIGION IS THE AIRPLANE"

The collection titled *The Aeronautical Adventures of Egor Poddevkin* was characteristic of the literary strategies devised to raise peasants' consciousness of aviation and *smychka*.[5] The publication comprised three short tales that related the encounters of an air-minded Red Army veteran as he traveled by plane through the remote Russian countryside. In the collection's first story, "The Enchanted Sled," Poddevkin journeys to the isolated and listless settlement of Dremotovo. Located forty *versty* from the nearest market town, the "sleepy" village is cut off from the outside world by the onset of winter.[6] Unable to travel through the deep snowdrifts that cover the landscape, the misfortunate residents of Dremotovo "languish in a sea of snow, their energy sapped, unable to act." The village is dying in its isolation. It "needs a tie to the city, especially now at a time when the urban proletariat is forging bonds of friendship with the peasantry."[7]

Dremotovo's winter slumber is stirred by the unexpected arrival of Egor Poddevkin. Late at night, in the middle of a howling blizzard, the leather-clad hero suddenly appears at the door of a local residence. The drowsy villagers are surprised to hear that he has traveled the 600 *versty* from Moscow in only one evening. They are still more astonished to learn that he has traveled by air. Poddevkin introduces the local inhabitants to his ski-equipped airplane. They are frightened by the "winged monster" and are convinced that the city slicker's story and his metallic contraption are simply parts of an elaborate ruse. Their doubts are dispelled the following morning, however, when Poddevkin takes several into the air aboard his "flying sled." The demonstration convinces even the most skeptical that humans can, indeed, fly. They all acknowledge that had they not seen it with their own eyes they never would have believed such a thing possible. The peasants' worldview is profoundly

---

[5] N. Riazanov, *Prikliucheniia Egora Poddevkina na samolete* (Khar'kov: Ukrvozdukhput', 1924).

[6] The name of the village is derived from the Russian word *dremota* or "slumber." One *versta* equals approximately 0.63 miles.

[7] *Ibid.*, 4.

transformed by their aeronautical encounter. Thanks to Poddevkin's visit, the residents of Dremotovo come to recognize the value of the airplane and its practical applications in their daily lives. No longer will they need horses, sleds, river barges, and the like to travel through the forests and ravines. The airplane will do this for them. It will make their lives easier and more productive. As Poddevkin prepares to depart from Dremotovo, he reminds the villagers that this will all prove possible only if they work together to build the air fleet:

Above everything else, I tell you that you must become members of the Society of Friends of the Air Fleet in order to strengthen your ties to the air. You must turn all of your energy toward this task and pool your resources so that you can purchase such a wondrous machine![8]

Having thus awakened the sleepy village to the realities of the aeronautical age, the pilot departs for his next destination.

Poddevkin's subsequent adventures follow the basic pattern established in "The Enchanted Sled." In "The Miraculous Smoke," the Red Army veteran travels hundreds of miles over dense forests and swamps to reach the isolated settlement of Goriuchino ["Flameville"]. There, legions of insects plague the village's inhabitants. The foul vermin have invaded the locals' homes where they "survive like kulaks" by sucking the blood of their impoverished hosts. The villagers' misery is compounded by the ever-present threat of forest fires. Goriuchino's residents live in constant fear of the annual conflagrations that consume the forests and rye fields that "would otherwise help to rebuild the entire Soviet Republic." Poddevkin's arrival offers the peasants salvation. The intrepid pilot dispatches the insect menace with his crop-dusting plane and then utilizes the craft to douse a fire. Having thus relieved the peasants and saved the forests, Poddevkin instructs, "villagers, build airplanes! For they will deliver you from all misfortune."[9] A similar message is imparted by the collection's final installment, "Devil in a Straw Hat," in which Poddevkin employs his cloud-seeding airplane to bring much-needed rain to a parched village. Thanks to the timely intervention of the air-minded veteran, the harvest is saved and the villagers are kept from starvation.

The message of the airplane's practicality was repeated in innumerable short stories and tales. In "How Uncle Vlas Became an ODVF Member," the aged peasant Vlas is initially suspicious of the "flying aeroplane–bird."[10] He is incredulous at the thought that humans can fly. Even if it is true, he sees no value in the enterprise. The return of his son from the Civil War signals the beginning of Vlas's aeronautical conversion. Through a series of discussions with the young Red Army veteran, Vlas learns of the airplane's

[8] *Ibid.*, 10.
[9] *Ibid.*, 11 and 18.
[10] "Kak diadia Vlas vstupil v chleny ODVF," *Aviadrug* 1 (April 1924): 19–22.

ability to battle both imperialists and insects, to assist with the harvest, and to provide the village with goods from the city. Thus convinced that aviation will bring prosperity and security to the nation, Uncle Vlas sells a bag of flour to pay for his ODVF membership and, from then on, contributes money on a regular basis to the air fleet. The short story triptych "How It Will Be" told rural audiences of still more ways in which airplanes would benefit the countryside.[11] In the collection's initial tale, an airplane proves instrumental in delivering medical assistance. The peasant Marina's daughter is desperately sick, but her remote village is located more than fifty *versty* from the nearest hospital. Thanks to the presence of an ODVF airplane, a doctor arrives in the nick of time to save the dying girl. "With tears of joy, Marina ran outside and lovingly looked up at the plane, gleaming like the sun. After all, had it not been for the plane, her daughter would have died."[12] The two other tales of "How It Will Be" related (with somewhat less pathos) the airplane's usefulness in battling locusts and bringing crops more efficiently to market.

Publications such as these reveal the thematic strategies that would come to dominate all literary, cinematic, and graphic productions aimed at the peasantry. Concerned that rural Russians would be confused by and disinterested in detailed technical descriptions, Party leaders instructed propagandists to keep their messages simple and clear.[13] Rather than befuddling audiences with complicated scientific discussions, aeronautical representatives were directed to focus on the practical benefits that provincial citizens would realize once the country had established its air fleet. Soviet aviation literature portrayed the airplane as a transcendent instrument capable of radically transforming the peasant and his environs. Offering rural residents salvation from cultural despair and economic hardship by assisting agricultural production, supplying goods and services, and protecting households from predatory capitalists, kulaks, and foreigners, the airplane promised to fundamentally alter the everyday realities of village life. It would raise the peasantry to never-before-realized levels of material plenty, bringing a new life of prosperity and happiness to those who submitted to the Party's authority and supported its program of industrial modernization.

The themes chosen by Party officials were abetted by the exploitation of time-honored literary styles and illustrative materials tailored to suit peasants' perceived tastes. As we shall shortly see, the use of traditional rhymed

[11] "Kak budet," *Daesh Sibiri krasnye kryl'ia* 4 (1925): 15–19.

[12] *Ibid.*, 17.

[13] See, for example, Aleksei Rykov's admonition to Aviakhim members in GARF f. r-9404, op. 1, d. 23 (Otchet o rabote sovetov, prezidiumov, biuro prezidiumov, sekretariatov i sektsii Soiuza Aviakhim SSSR i Aviakhim RSFSR), l. 2, and discussions concerning the inauguration of the journal *Daesh motor* in RGVA f. 29, op. 1, d. 52 (Protokoly zasedaniia redaktsionogo soveta ODVF), l. 34.

meter [*skazka*] and the visual depiction of air-minded subjects after the fashion of the illustrative woodcut [*lubok*] were but two obvious examples of the
Party's effort to communicate in forms more readily familiar and thus, perhaps, more readily acceptable to the peasantry. Somewhat less obvious, but
far more pervasive, was the Party's co-opting of images and narrative structures rooted in the traditions of the Russian Orthodox Church. Undertaken
in conjunction with state efforts to promote atheism, the use of religious
themes to advance the aeronautical agenda revealed both the utilitarianism
and utopianism of Bolshevik leaders who hoped to undermine and denigrate the Church by employing established religious forms to serve their
own political ends.

One example of the manner in which Soviet aviation propaganda
employed religious tropes was witnessed in the depiction of soldiers and
military veterans. An important focal point employed by the Bolsheviks to
inculcate socialist ideas among the populace in the wake of the Civil War, the
Red Army veteran emerged as well as a central image in the Party's efforts
to inculcate popular air-mindedness.[14] Significantly, in both the Poddevkin
series and the tale of Uncle Vlas, it is a Red Army veteran who introduces
aviation to the countryside, winning over skeptical peasants through aerial
demonstrations and reasoned arguments.[15] These examples were typical as
state propagandists routinely utilized the figure of the returning soldier as
the structuring element of their aeronautical narratives. Cast in the archetypal role of the prophet, the soldier was depicted as a teacher and guide, an
individual who, having partaken in the foreordained kingdom of progress
through his service to the state, returns to his people as a witness and oracle
of the technological glories to come.

The decision of authorities to link the image of the veteran to airplane construction can be attributed, in part, to the Party's broader policy of employing Red Army soldiers to help build socialist culture. Throughout the early
1920s, the Soviet political leadership looked to experienced soldiers "to fill
the burgeoning bureaucracies and, most significantly, to reform, if not over-
turn, the established political order in the countryside."[16] A graduate of the
"school of socialism," the peasant–soldier was considered a vital component
in bridging the cultural and political divide that separated rural Russians
from their urbanist leaders. Tied to the village from which he came and
shaped by the state that he had served, the Red Army veteran was believed
to be well suited to facilitating *smychka* between city and village. In the

---

[14] Roger R. Reese, *Stalin's Reluctant Soldiers: A Social History of the Red Army, 1925–1941*
(Lawrence, KS: University Press of Kansas, 1996), 3.

[15] The Red Army veteran was portrayed in an identical fashion in the 1920's cinematic productions *Contact!*, *Toward Aerial Victory*, *On Wings, Higher* and *Aero NT-54*.

[16] Mark Von Hagen, *Soldiers in the Proletarian Dictatorship: The Red Army and the Soviet
Socialist State, 1917–1930* (Ithaca, NY: Cornell University Press, 1990), 8.

symbolic world of Soviet propaganda, the depiction of the empty-headed peasant turned politically conscious soldier was a transparent metaphor of the revolutionary transformation of Russia from a backward agrarian nation to a modern industrial power that would take place under the leadership of the Communist Party.

The portrayal of the Red Army veteran as a prophet of enlightenment and technological acuity was juxtaposed by the frequent appearance of the politically obscurant, scientifically skeptical, and typically inebriated Orthodox priest. Negative portrayals of the Russian clergy were directly related to the campaign to denigrate religion and promote atheism that had led to the institutionalization of the "League of the Militant Godless" in the summer of 1924.[17] Aviation officials served the interests of the "Godless" by incorporating strong anticlerical images in their air-minded publications. These caricatures drew a sharp distinction between the progress made possible by contemporary Soviet science and the backwardness of traditional Russian faith.

The cultural nexus between aviation and religion appeared most strikingly in a lengthy *skazka* titled *Concerning Priestly Angst and Pains, of Locusts and of Aeroplanes*.[18] The story concerned the efforts of the residents of the isolated village Odintsovka to eradicate the recurrent threat of locusts. When the insects first appear and threaten the harvest, the village's overweight and gluttonous priest, Ivan, admonishes the residents to pray for deliverance. Father Ivan claims that the locusts have been sent by God to punish the peasants for their sinful ways. For a fee, the priest offers to conduct a series of prayer services that will appease the Lord and save the crops. The naive and trusting villagers gratefully accept the offer. They allow the priest to "harvest the kopecks from their pockets" in the hope that his prayers will rid them of the locusts. Despite the peasants' obedience to their priest, the insect menace does not disappear. The locusts destroy the grain and bring hardship to the village.

The situation for Odintsovka's peasants worsens the following summer. The locusts return for a second year in a row, threatening to consume the crop and bring economic misery to the village. The panic-stricken and fearful peasants return to their priest. They implore him to perform more prayer

---

[17] Recently, three monographs devoted to various institutional and social aspects of the antireligious campaign have appeared. See William Husband, *"Godless Communists:" Atheism and Society in Soviet Russia, 1917–1932* (DeKalb, IL: Northern Illinois University Press, 2000); Glennys Young, *Power and the Sacred in Revolutionary Russia: Religious Activists in the Village* (University Park, PA: Pennsylvania State University Press, 1997); and Daniel Peris, *Storming the Heavens: The Soviet League of the Militant Godless* (Ithaca, NY: Cornell University Press, 1998). None, however, addresses the links between the creed of "the Godless" and state efforts to promote air-mindedness.

[18] R. Berezov and A. Glagolev, *O popovskoi zabote, o saranche i o samolete* (Moscow: ODVF, 1925).

Да здравствует большевистская безбожная печать!

FIGURE 17. "Long live the Bolshevik atheist press!" Throughout the 1920s airplanes were used as symbols and instruments in promoting the Communist Party's "Godless" propaganda. Courtesy The Hoover Institution.

services. Father Ivan agrees, enriching himself by exacting an even greater amount of tribute from the impoverished villagers. He again performs his prayers, and, again, the locusts destroy the harvest.

The peasants return to the fields the next spring to sow the very last remnants of their seed grain. There is trepidation and fear in their hearts. Will the locusts return? As the villagers nervously await their fate, Odintsovka is stirred by the arrival of a group of seasonal workers. Every summer, as harvest time nears, scores of laborers return from their urban factories to help bring in the crops. This year, they are accompanied by a Red Army veteran.

The Red Army man soon learns of the villagers' plight. He hears tales of their annual battle with the insatiable locusts and the ongoing efforts to combat the insects with religion. The veteran summons the residents of Odintsovka together to inform them that he has an answer to their predicament. Miraculous machines have been invented that fly through the air. The Soviet Union possesses many of these "aeroplanes" that are often used to fight locusts by spraying fields with a special gas. Odintsovka's peasants listen with rapt attention as the Red Army veteran intones in the rhymed meter of the *skazka*:

There is no place throughout this land	*Nu, a gde selo ne smozhet –*
Where Soviet power can't lend a hand	*Vlast' Sovetskaia pomozhet*
They will send without delay	*I na pomoshch' k nam prishlet*
An aeroplane to save the day.	*S etoi tsel'iu samolet.*[19]

With these words of encouragement, the Red Army man sets out for Moscow. He will soon return with a crop-dusting aeroplane that will rid the village once and for all of its insect menace.

As the villagers eagerly await the veteran's return, they are chastised by Father Ivan for putting faith in the soldier. The priest is angry with his parishioners for abandoning God, and he warns that more dire consequences await if the villagers do not repent. Days turn into weeks and still the Red Army man does not arrive with the airplane. Odintsovka's residents grow more concerned with each passing day. Almost three weeks following the veteran's departure, the villagers are horrified to discover that the locusts have returned. As Father Ivan beseeches them to again petition God, the peasants are plunged into despair. Should the locusts devour this year's harvest, a great many people will die. Just then, when all hope appears lost, a "strange noise" is heard in the sky. It grows louder and louder as it approaches from afar. Anxious and fearful, Odintsovka's residents look to the heavens. There, they see a wondrous sight: the airplane promised by the Red Army soldier! True to his word, the Red Army man has returned, bringing with him the

---

[19] *Ibid.*, 21.

most advanced technology the Soviet Union has to offer. He dusts the village's crops, killing the locusts, guaranteeing the success of the harvest, and chasing the priest from the village.

Such derogatory depictions of Orthodox clergy were repeated routinely in Soviet aeronautical propaganda productions. The lengthy poem–story *Friends of the Air Fleet, or the Airplane "Stepanida,"* likewise portrayed a rural clergyman and his faithful parishioners as obscurant opponents of Soviet aviation.[20] In the 1925 film *Aero NT-54*, a drunken priest works in close association with local moonshiners and criminals to thwart the aeronautical goals of a Red Army veteran.[21] Similar efforts to promote aviation at the expense of religious faith appeared on a regular basis in printed publications. The satirical journal *Krokodil* was particularly adept at blending air-minded propaganda with antireligious images. In July 1923, at the height of the inaugural air fleet campaign, the periodical published a special issue devoted almost entirely to aviation. The issue contained many humorous tales, cartoons, and *skazki* that promoted the aeronautical cause and attacked the church. On the cover, a particularly militant cartoon depicted a squadron of Soviet airplanes chasing Christ, the Mother of God, and the Heavenly Host from the skies (Figure 18). The illustration was accompanied by this refrain:

In the heavens a wild affray	*Na nebesakh perepolokh:*
God's been shot down by a plane.	*Pogib ot samoleta bog.*
And on the ground another one	*I na zemle nash samolet*
Has the capitalists on the run.	*Razrushit kapitala gnet.*[22]

The contemporary short poem "Aero-verses" attacked religion as well, acknowledging directly the desire of Party officials to replace popular faith in the traditions of the Church with a secular faith in the power of Soviet technology:

No longer will we consider ourselves worthless dust.	*Dovol'no shchitat' sebe nikchemnoiu pyliu.*
Who instructed us in the narcotic of faith?	*Chemu nauchil nas religii durman?*
Into the heavens we launch the aviation squadron	*V nebo zapustim aero-eskadril'iu*
Our religion is the airplane.	*Nasha religiia–aeroplan.*[23]

The routine and pervasive association of aviation and atheism that dominated official propaganda aimed at the peasantry points to the unique process

---

[20] R. Akul'shin, *Druz'ia vozdushnogo flota ili samolet "Stepanida"* (Moscow, 1925).
[21] *Aero NT-54.* (Sevzapkino, 1925).
[22] *Krokodil,* 15 July 1923.
[23] V. Sudnev, "Aero-stikhi," *Daesh motor* 5 (1925): 30.

FIGURE 18. Mikhail Cheremnykh, "*Krokodil* for the Air Fleet!" *Krokodil*, 15 July 1923.

by which long-standing forms and symbols of the Imperial era would be incorporated into the fabric of a newly emerging Soviet culture. As Party leaders labored to complete their revolutionary assault on the vestiges of the old order, they co-opted established genres and semantic markers, divested them of their inherited meanings by inverting the hierarchical relationships on which they were based, and infused them with a new values system that accorded with the mandates of Bolshevik ideology.[24] Attuned to the spiritual and religious significance of flight, and convinced of the material benefits that aeronautical development would ensure, Soviet authorities embraced the airplane as the principle iconic emblem of their modernizing vision. Although official representations of flight would undergo gradual shifts in response to changing political and social circumstances, the iconic function of the airplane, firmly entrenched from the beginning of the Party's aeronautical campaign, would remain a constant and omnipresent feature of Soviet culture for generations to come.

AERONAUTICAL ICONS

The transmutation of "old" religious archetypes into the "new" archetypes of the air-minded state was not limited to newspaper editorials and propaganda pamphlets. The mobilization of the press and publishing industries was accompanied by stunning visual productions that were intended to capture viewers' imaginations by instilling in them an appreciation of modernistic aeronautical forms. Many of these novel images were created by leading avant-garde artists. In 1923, the constructivist Aleksandr Rodchenko was commissioned to design a series of logos for ODVF and Dobrolet that were later attached to newspapers and journals, stationery, lapel pins, and membership badges. Other artists, including the suprematists Kazimir Malevich and Il'ia Chashnik, incorporated aeronautical themes into their artistic productions and architectural designs, while airplane-inspired patterns were used to decorate textiles, teapots, and china. From an aesthetic standpoint, the use of aeronautical shapes and images in artistic creations reflected the desire to capture the modern perspectives and sensations revealed by the development of a new technology. In more practical terms, these artistic productions helped to raise popular consciousness by linking aviation to otherwise familiar and everyday objects.

The experimental efforts of artists and graphic designers notwithstanding, the most ubiquitous example of the exploitation of aviation imagery involved the Party's use of political posters. In a country that remained largely illiterate at the beginning of the twentieth century, visual images were

---

[24] Iu. M. Lotman and B. A. Uspenskii, "Binary Models in the Dynamics of Russian Culture," in Iu. M. Lotman, B. A. Uspenskii, and L. Ia. Ginzburg (eds.), *The Semiotics of Russian Cultural History* (Ithaca, NY: Cornell University Press, 1985), 33.

FIGURE 19. "Telephone, telegraph, postal, and radio workers! Build airplanes to further the people's ties!" Poster, ca. 1924. Private collection. Photo: Scott W. Palmer.

an important medium for communicating otherwise complex and difficult ideas. In times past, this function had been served by the traditional peasant illustrated woodcut [*lubok*], Russian Orthodox iconography, and the newsprint graphics of the Imperial era. Following the Revolution, the political poster became Soviet officials' graphic of choice. During the course of the 1920s, Party leaders, cognizant of the ability of visual images to communicate ideological messages to diverse and oftentimes uneducated audiences, diverted considerable resources to ensure that their ideas and policies would be represented graphically throughout the country.[25]

Soviet aviation posters incorporated a wide variety of images and motifs consciously designed to communicate those messages deemed most essential by the Party hierarchy.[26] In the earliest years of the aeronautical drive, these messages focused on familiarizing citizens with the airplane and educating them of the economic, military, and cultural benefits that would be realized following the construction of a national air fleet. Nearly all of these posters adhered to the Party dictum that propaganda materials be simple and direct, "accessible and understandable to the broad masses of workers and peasants."[27] As such, although a few aviation posters drew their artistic

[25] Stephen White, *The Bolshevik Poster* (New Haven, CT: Yale University Press, 1988), 1–7.
[26] GARF f. 7577, op. 1, d. 21, l. 212.
[27] RGVA f. 29, op. 1, d. 52, l. 31.

inspiration from the avant-garde experiments of Rodchenko and the constructivists (Figure 19), the vast majority were indebted to the less abstract and more readily comprehensible art of the realist tradition.

One widely distributed poster attempted to cajole citizens into joining ODVF by linking participation in the voluntary society to patriotic duty. A clear imitation of Englishman Alfred Leete's famous recruitment poster from the First World War that depicted Lord Kitchener's stern face admonishing young Britons "Your country needs YOU," the ODVF variant (complete with glaring pilot and accusatory index finger) asked the pressing question, "What have you done for the Air Fleet?"[28] (Figure 20). A similar message (albeit accompanied by a more original illustration) was communicated by a 1923 Rodchenko poster that portrayed a Soviet airplane distributing the association's shares as it circled the globe. The poster's reproachful caption proclaimed, "Shame on your name if it does not appear on the Dobrolet roster" and warned citizens that "the whole country keeps watch on this roster." An admonitory approach appeared as well in another 1923 Rodchenko production that announced, "Only a shareholder of Dobrolet is a citizen of the USSR."[29] By associating the individual's sense of community and personal responsibility with ongoing efforts to support the Red Air Fleet, these posters reflected the society's underlying mission to serve as one of the "new social structures" that would contribute to the construction of the coming socialist order.[30]

Soviet leaders faced real challenges, however, in attempting to appeal to the patriotism and political loyalty of the peasant population. The Party's relationship with the peasants had never been very good. Recurrent outbursts of rural unrest, including a particularly violent revolt in Tambov province during 1920–1, had demonstrated that the Bolshevik government might, at best, expect only tenuous support from its provincial constituents. Compounding these difficulties was the latent mistrust of the village that shaped the urbanist perspectives of nearly all Communist Party leaders. These factors dictated that the Party's strategy for raising rural air-mindedness would proceed along a path different from that chosen for metropolitan audiences. In place of appeals to patriotism and Party loyalty, rural aeronautical propaganda endeavored to convince peasant audiences that the Soviet state was cognizant of their needs and was willing to work with them to achieve the shared goals of economic prosperity and national security. As with the literary productions previously discussed, peasant-directed posters

---

[28] For a discussion and reproduction of the Leete poster see, respectively, White, *Bolshevik Poster*, 46–8, and Igor Golomstock, *Totalitarian Art in the Soviet Union, the Third Reich, Fascist Italy and the People's Republic of China* (London: Collins Harvill, 1990), 25.

[29] Selim Khan-Magomedov, *Rodchenko: The Complete Work*. Edited by Vieri Quilici. (London: Thames and Hudson, 1986), 146.

[30] See above, Chapter 3, p. 101.

FIGURE 20. "What have you done for the air fleet?" Poster, 1923. Private collection. Photo: Scott W. Palmer.

FIGURE 21. Aleksandr Apsit, "Year of the Proletarian Dictatorship." Poster, 1919. Courtesy The Hoover Institution.

co-opted recognized forms to raise awareness of the airplane and to generate enthusiasm for airplane construction. In addition to furthering the *smychka* of city and countryside, these posters worked to legitimate Soviet authority by transforming established archetypes associated with the backward "old" order, into modern "new" variants inextricably linked to the state and its policies.

Aleksandr Apsit's famous poster "Year of the Proletarian Dictatorship" (1918) was one of the first works of Soviet political art to exploit familiar iconic forms in an effort to communicate the theme of worker–peasant unity[31] (Figure 21). At the dawn of the new socialist order a worker and peasant, arms in hand, stand vigil over the broken chains and oppressive symbols of the Imperial past. Together they guard the gateway to industrial development and agricultural prosperity opened up by the Bolshevik Party. Indebted to the iconographic tradition of Russian Orthodoxy in its calculated use of colors and framing, "The Year of the Proletarian Dictatorship" served as both a stylistic and substantive model for subsequent propagandists.[32] The poster appealed to the eye while its heroic and uncomplicated imagery was readily understandable to Soviet audiences. Such symbolism was used throughout the early 1920s as the Party's campaign to bolster its standing among the peasantry progressed. Not surprisingly, authorities employed similar strategies in their campaign to generate peasant support for the Red Air Fleet.

One typical poster depicted two separate columns of workers and peasants resolutely advancing toward the viewer as a squadron of Soviet airplanes circles above (Figure 22). At the head of both columns, representatives from each of the two groups encourage their comrades to follow their lead while holding high overhead a banner emblazoned with the initials M. O. D. V. F. (the acronym for the Moscow branch of the Friends of the Air Fleet). Beneath the illustration an inscription proclaims that the "revolutionary energy and iron will" of workers and peasants will ensure the construction of the new aviation squadron "Red Moscow." The cooperation of the two social groups in building the squadron is underscored by the framing of the poster. A centrally located obelisk draws the viewer's gaze inwards and up, toward the gleaming planes that circle over the heads of the converging citizens. Such imagery communicated the Party's abiding expectation that aviation would play a crucial role in bridging the cultural, economic, and technological rifts that separated the city from the village.

The unity of workers and peasants in the task of building Soviet aviation was also the theme of a poster sponsored by Ural ODVF (Figure 23). In this piece, a worker and a peasant stand before an anvil laboring to turn a

---

[31] Victoria Bonnell, *Iconography of Power: Soviet Political Posters Under Lenin and Stalin* (Berkeley, CA: University of California Press, 1997), 22–3.
[32] White, *Bolshevik Poster*, 26.

FIGURE 22. "Workers and peasants have built MODVF with their revolutionary energy and iron will." Poster, 1925. Private collection. Photo: Scott W. Palmer.

FIGURE 23. A. Laramonov, "The 250,000 members of Ural ODVF will build the steel bulwark of the Red Air Fleet!" Poster, ca. 1924. Private collection. Photo: Scott W. Palmer.

piece of heated metal into a usable tool. As the worker strikes the iron with his hammer, the resulting sparks fly into the air and are transformed into a squadron of airplanes. The poster's caption makes the transparent imagery complete, "the 250,000 members of Ural ODVF will build the steel bulwark of the air fleet." The Ural ODVF poster was not terribly original from the standpoint of its artistic and thematic content. The blacksmith was a metaphor for socialist construction that appeared with considerable regularity in contemporary propaganda.[33] Nevertheless, the poster was significant for communicating the importance of urban–rural unity to the establishment of a modern air fleet. Only once workers labored together with peasants, the poster suggested, would the country prove capable of achieving its aeronautical goals. In communicating this message, the Ural ODVF poster underscored the campaign's concern not only with building airplanes, but with forging the social, political, and institutional networks that would help to shape the socialist order.

In addition to those aimed at furthering *smychka*, a number of posters sought to appeal to peasant audiences in more immediate, material terms. The themes and motifs that dominated these productions advanced the simple message that the airplane was an important tool that would bring tangible benefits to the nation's peasant masses. One such poster, emblazoned with the slogan, "The Red Air Fleet is the defense of laborers," depicted a troika of airplanes soaring over a large field of grain while, in the foreground, a peasant portrayed in silhouette points to the sky (Figure 24). Such a seemingly incongruous combination of modern airplanes and the vast Russian countryside drew its inspiration from Trotsky's oft-repeated admonition that the air fleet would play a crucial role in modernizing the nation by bridging the vast space [*prostranstvo*] that separated the village from the city.[34]

In yet another poster produced for rural audiences, a peasant family stands at the edge of a ripening field (Figure 25). There, they greet the arrival of an approaching airplane. Strewn about on the earth beneath their feet are the chitinous shells of dead locusts. The caption reads: "Peasants! Dobrolet protects your field from predators!" Posters such as this, like the propaganda pamphlets, poems, and short stories that accompanied them, communicated in clear and unambiguous terms the Party's abiding message that the airplane would directly benefit the economic interests of the countryside. It also suggested that the air fleet would protect citizens from predators both real (locusts) and symbolic (kulaks and foreign agents).

The composition and framing of this particular poster were also significant as they revealed the extent to which Soviet authorities relied on the incorporation and inversion of inherited forms to advance their vision of the aeronautical future. Clearly inspired by Aleksandr Ivanov's monumental

---

[33] Bonnell, *Iconography of Power*, 24–28.
[34] See above, Chapter 3, pp. 99–101.

FIGURE 24. "The Red Air Fleet is the defense of laborers." Poster, 1925. Private collection. Photo: Scott W. Palmer.

FIGURE 25. Mikhail Maliutin, "Peasants!! Dobrolet protects your fields from predators." Poster, 1925. Private collection. Photo: Scott W. Palmer.

FIGURE 26. Aleksandr A. Ivanov, *The Appearance of Christ Before the People (Return of the Messiah)*, 1837–58. Oil on canvas, 540 × 750 cm (213 × 295 in). Tretyakov Gallery, Moscow.

painting *The Appearance of Christ Before the People (Return of the Messiah)* (Figure 26), the Dobrolet production invited viewers to transpose their traditional belief system by accepting the airplane as a modern instrument and symbol of material salvation. Other posters reflected the persistence of Orthodox motifs through the placement of subjects within golden-hued halos (Figure 27). In a similar fashion, stars were employed as modern-age mandorlas, underscoring the christological function of aviators and airplanes as transcendent bearers of progress and salvation (Figures 28 and 29).

Overt associations of Christianity with machine-powered flight were not, of course, unique to Soviet culture. American observers had articulated their air-minded aspirations in decidedly religious fashion from the very beginning of the airplane's rise to prominence.[35] Western Europeans expressed similar sentiments years later when, following Charles Lindbergh's triumphal descent before enraptured crowds outside of Paris, they greeted the American flier as the "New Christ."[36] Even so, the decision by propagandists of the world's first avowedly atheistic state to visualize Soviet pilots and airplanes

---

[35] Joseph J. Corn, *The Winged Gospel: America's Romance with Aviation, 1900–1950* (New York: Oxford University Press, 1983).

[36] Modris Eksteins, *Rites of Spring: The Great War and the Birth of the Modern Age* (New York: Doubleday, 1989), 242–7.

FIGURE 27. "Let's have motors!" Poster, 1924. Private collection. Photo: Scott W. Palmer.

FIGURE 28. "Red wings are the reliable defense of the USSR." Poster, 1925. Private collection. Photo: Scott W. Palmer.

FIGURE 29. "Join the ranks of ODVF." Poster, 1925. Private collection. Photo: Scott W. Palmer.

FIGURE 30. An "avia-corner," 1925.

in christological fashion should not obscure the essential dissimilarity that distinguished these separate archetypal images. Whereas, in the West, the airplane was recognized as a triumphant symbol of modern technology and personal liberation, in Russia, it assumed iconic significance. It was seen as the mark of and the means by which the technological transformation of a backward nation into its modern prototype would be collectively realized.

Party leaders' intentional effort to co-opt and invert traditional Russian forms with modern Soviet variants was underscored as well by posters' placement and usage. Appropriating the Orthodox practice of displaying devotional images and other sacred items in the "Holy Corner" of the home, ODVF officials promoted the institution of "avia-corners" for the public display of aviation posters and propaganda materials. Organized throughout the country in workers' clubs, factories, and peasant reading rooms, avia-corners were intended "to serve as the organizational centers of aviation life" for all Soviet citizens.[37] They were new secular sites of worship for the air-minded faithful. To ensure their orthodox composition and emplacement, ODVF produced pamphlets and brochures that explained in precise detail the nature of the items and the hierarchical arrangement that should

---

[37] A. F. Glagolev, compiler, *Aviakul'tury v rabochii klub: material po aviarabote v rabochikh klubakh* (Moscow: ODVF, 1925), 11.

be incorporated into authorized corners.[38] According to officials, "properly decorated" and "placed in the most conspicuous location," the avia-corner would serve as a "living illustration" [*zhivaia kartina*] of the wonders of aviation, reminding ODVF members of their responsibilities to the nation while encouraging the aeronautically uninitiated to participate in the cause of building the air fleet.[39]

AIR-MINDED RITUALS

Whatever benefits Party authorities realized from the orchestration of avia-corners or the dissemination of propaganda pamphlets, political posters, and films, the use of scripted images could not compare to the effect produced by the arrival of an actual plane at an isolated rural outpost. The overwhelming impression that aeronautical craft could make on uninitiated peasant audiences had been recognized as early as the Imperial era. In the years following the First World War, foreign military units had used airplanes to similar effect in terrifying and demoralizing indigenous tribesmen as they undertook campaigns of imperial conquest.[40] Party authorities were aware of these precedents, and they were eager to take advantage of the impact that aircraft might have in furthering their campaign to raise peasant awareness. During the first "Soviet Week of the Air Fleet" (24 June–1 July 1923), officials dispatched several airplanes to villages and towns in the districts that surrounded Moscow and Petrograd. On landing in their designated locations, the airplanes' pilots delivered speeches about the benefits of aviation, distributed aeronautical literature and membership applications, and invited those willing to join the society to board the craft for short excursions into the air.

This direct approach to swaying popular opinion was also used with great effect during the fall of 1924. In the village of Undol, located in Vladimir province, a production crew gathered to shoot a short propaganda film about a peasant's encounter with mechanized flight. To assist in production, Dobrolet loaned the film crew a Junkers airplane that was used as a prop in several scenes. The plane also proved to be a useful promotional gimmick in publicizing the forthcoming film as Dobrolet officials organized free demonstration flights for the hundreds of local peasants and workers who served as extras in the movie. As word spread of the flights, interested residents from all over the region flocked to observe the airplane. The crowds grew larger each day of filming, with some peasants journeying from as far away as twenty miles in the hope of flying aboard the craft. Many of those

---

[38] *Aviaugolok: materialy* (Moscow: ODVF, 1925) and A. F. Glagolev, compiler, *Avia-agit-doklad: konspekt* (Moscow: ODVF, 1925).

[39] Glagolev, *Aviakul'tury*, 12–13.

[40] See, for example, *Aero-sbornik*, 1 (1923): 12.

who came to Undol camped outdoors near the plane for several nights "in expectation of more flights."[41]

The overwhelmingly positive receptions accorded these early flights confirmed Party officials' suspicions that direct contact between peasants and airplanes was a certain means of quickly expanding provincial enthusiasm for Red aviation. In response, ODVF embarked on a special drive to ensure that increasing numbers of rural inhabitants would "go to aeronautical events, view airplanes close up, look them over, ask questions and (when possible) fly aboard them."[42] The result was a dramatic increase in the number of airplanes sent out from Moscow and other major urban areas to villages and settlements in the Soviet hinterlands. Although staged spectacles, similar to those first organized during the Imperial era, continued to play an important role in mobilizing urban audiences for the aeronautical cause, the possibility of reproducing "aviation weeks" and elaborate exhibits was more problematic the farther one traveled from the center. The advent of the "agitational flight" or agit-flight [*agit-polet*], as these expeditions came to be known, resolved these difficulties by bringing the airplane to the countryside, thereby introducing aviation to millions of citizens who would otherwise never have the opportunity to experience first-hand the wonders of aeronautical technology.

The agit-flight involved much more than simply dispatching a plane or two to a remote village. The undertaking was a complex affair that required a considerable amount of planning and foresight (not to mention a degree of showmanship on the part of the aircrews, who were expected to enact a ritualized performance at each stop along the agit-plane's designated route). To maximize the efficiency and effectiveness of the few aircraft at their disposal, officials grouped their planes into separate "agit-squadrons" that were assigned to patrol geographical regions stretching from far-northern reaches near the Arctic Circle to as far south and east as the Caucasus and Central Asia. Although they eventually expanded to include as many as eight airplanes each as resources increased during the late 1920s and early 1930s, each agit-squadron initially comprised a single aircraft. These individual planes were dispatched along circuitous routes that oftentimes stretched for thousands of miles over sparsely populated territory. Mechanical failures, inclement weather, communication problems, and chronic shortages of fuel and spare parts were common occurrences.[43]

Agitational squadrons quickly developed a standardized routine that was performed at each of the rural stops along their flight paths. In the days

---

[41] "Fil'm Obshchestva Dobroleta," *Kino-nedelia* 14 (37) (October 1924): 16. See also, "Fil'ma Dobroleta," *Novyi zritel'*, 16 September 1924.

[42] *Chto takoe aeroplan i kakaia ot nikh pol'za* (Moscow, n.d.), 7.

[43] See GARF f. r-9404, op. 1, d. 24 (Perepiska s ekipazhami samoletov po podgotovke agit-obletov i doklady upolnomochennykh samoletov o rabote prodelannoi v period agitobletov, 2 ianvaria–30 marta 1926 g.), *et passim*.

FIGURE 31. Peasants disembark from an airplane following an aerial baptism, ca. 1925.

leading up to the scheduled arrival of an airplane, local Party organizations, military units, and aeronautical agencies advertised the upcoming event while local newspapers aided preparations by printing stories and essays (typically wired from Moscow) about Red aviation and its importance to the country. These measures were intended to inspire the interest of local residents and to ensure an adequate turnout once the agit-plane arrived. On setting down at their destination, the crew of the agit-plane would disembark from the craft, deliver speeches on the benefits of aviation, distribute literature, and recruit new members into the society's ranks by bringing locals on board for a tour of the airplane. The agit-visit would invariably conclude with a series of demonstration flights in which local residents were brought aboard the airplane for short excursions into the air. These flights were particularly noteworthy as they combined efforts to raise aeronautical consciousness with the Party's ongoing campaign to promote atheism. In an effort to eradicate peasant "superstition," rural believers were taken into the air by pilots in order to prove that there was no God, angels, or other celestial spirits in the heavens. Antireligious flights proved so successful that they quickly became standard practice for all agit-squadrons. In their reports to Party authorities, pilots routinely detailed the number of "air baptisms" [*vozdushnoe kreshchenie*] that they performed on their routes.[44] Once again, state authorities co-opted and inverted inherited forms to further their cause of constructing

---

[44] GARF f. r-9404, op. 1, d. 10 (Doklady upolnomochennykh samoletov o rabote prodelannoi v period agitobleta, 7 dekabria–29 dekabria 1925 g.), *et passim*.

a new culture. In this instance, they employed the airplane as the central element of a new social ritual; a technological conversion by air created by the Party to counteract the spiritual conversion by water performed by the Church.

Agitational flights met with considerable success despite the many environmental, human, and mechanical problems that they routinely encountered. Between the spring of 1925 and the fall of 1926, Soviet aircrews crisscrossed the nation, introducing the technologically uninitiated to the wonder of machine-powered flight and winning over tens of thousands to the cause of Red aviation. During the summer of 1925 alone, the agit-planes assigned to the principal "northern" and "southern" air routes covered more than 16,000 miles in an effort to bring aviation to rural Russians. Along the way, they visited 133 individual settlements, undertook 909 demonstration flights, carried 3,047 passengers aloft, and distributed almost four tons of literature and printed materials to the citizens they encountered. Two other agit-planes, flying shorter routes, between Moscow–Kursk–Penza–Vladimir and Moscow–Briansk–Tver', recorded comparable successes.[45]

The official accounts left by aircrews indicate that agit-flights were both a popular and an effective way of introducing the peasantry to the air age. In reports to their superiors, agit-flight crews repeatedly noted the "enthusiasm," "interest," and "deep concern" for aviation invariably expressed by rural audiences.[46] One such account, recorded on a mission to Kaluga province during the winter of 1924–5, offered convincing testimony to the genuine excitement with which peasants embraced aviation. According to this report, the crew of the agit-plane was, "as always," greeted by scores of local residents. Despite the fact that the airplane's arrival was accompanied by subzero temperatures, the area's inhabitants had gathered in a nearby field hours in advance in expectation of the aircraft. Following the plane's landing, the locals remained outside in the freezing air for several more hours listening to the speeches delivered by the aircrew, inspecting the aircraft, and inundating the fliers with questions about aviation and the air fleet campaign. Those fortunate enough to fly aboard the agit-plane during the scheduled demonstration flights were "choked with happiness" for having been taken into the skies, and they tirelessly recounted the experience to any and all willing to listen.[47]

Strikingly similar reactions were reported by the journalist, author, and literary critic Viktor Shklovskii who accompanied the crew of the agit-plane

---

[45] *Ibid.*, l. 4. The "northern route" originated in Nizhnii Novgorod and included among its major stops the cities of Chistopol', Perm, Kotlas, Arkhangel'sk, Kargopol', and Tver'. The agit-plane on the longer "southern route" departed from Voronezh and visited Stalingrad, Astrakhan, Orenburg, Samara, Saratov, and Lipetsk as well as dozens of smaller villages and settlements.

[46] GARF f. r-9404, op. 1, d. 24, ll. 37 and 204–5.

[47] *Ibid.*, ll. 88–9.

Turn to the Village [*Litsom k derevne*] during the spring and summer of 1925 as it traveled throughout the Don River basin along the southern air route.[48] Shklovskii's experiences aboard the airplane (and its encounters with local inhabitants) were recorded in a series of articles published by leading periodicals. An essay written for the magazine *Zhurnalist* [*Journalist*] described the reception of the aircraft by the residents of the remote town of Boguchar, a settlement in Voronezh *oblast'*. According to Shklovskii, the appearance of the agit-plane was a cause of celebration for the inhabitants of the Russian backwater. Young and old alike rushed to meet the aircraft following its landing, "running toward it," Shklovskii observed, "as if they expected the occupants to pass out money." The peasants' enthusiastic greeting was accompanied by innumerable questions concerning the plane, its capabilities, and "what lay beyond the clouds above." So great was the villagers' fascination with this "scout of the heavens," Shklovskii noted, that many spent the night in the open field at the side of the aircraft.[49]

Although it is difficult to measure the veracity of such accounts, there is little reason to believe that they did not accurately reflect the thoughts and feelings with which most rural Soviet citizens greeted the arrival of the aeronautical age. In remote regions where isolated inhabitants still used oxen-driven plows to till the soil, the sight of a soaring airplane was certainly an awe-inspiring and momentous event capable of generating profound emotions among most every audience. The striking similarities that may be found in contemporary accounts of peasant–airplane encounters, however, suggest that much more than coincidence must be credited in explaining their shared features. To be certain, conscientious flight crews and air-minded journalists had a vested interest in accurately reporting the particulars of their individual encounters with the peasantry. Factual descriptions of these meetings provided Party officials with important information that could be used to modify and direct the ongoing "turn to the village." Nevertheless, as with short stories, *skazki*, posters, and poems, the aeronautical "conversion narrative" was also a useful propaganda genre for communicating ideas about the Party, its programs, and political authority.

The political utility of the conversion narrative was clearly revealed in Shklovskii's short essay, "Aboard the Agit-Plane *Turn to the Village*," which described the excitement, wonder, and bewilderment with which a group of peasants greet the arrival of an agit-plane. The "isolated" and "unwashed"

---

[48] Shklovskii's presence was part of a broader initiative to raise the profile of the aeronautical campaign by recruiting respected literary figures to participate in agit-flights. They published their onboard experiences in the form of newspaper editorials and short stories. Other famous writers enjoined to accompany agit-squadrons during the summer of 1925 included Boris Pil'niak, Vera Inber, and Vsevolod Ivanov. See "Samolety sredi rabochikh i krest'ian, *Izvestiia*, 23 July 1925.

[49] V. Shklovskii, "Derevnia skuchaet po gorodu," *Zhurnalist* 8–9 (1925): 193–5.

masses are awestruck by the flying machine and are eager to absorb the instruction offered by the aerial propagandists. The agit-crew's presentation on the applications of modern aviation technology in assisting the rural economy contrasts sharply with the reality faced by the villagers. The poor peasants suffer greatly in their efforts to bring in the harvest. Threatened by insufficient and irregular rainfall and compelled to farm fields "gutted with ravines as if with syphilis," they are condemned to a lifetime of backbreaking and unproductive labor.[50] The airplane, Shklovskii proclaims, will change all of this. It will ensure the prosperity of these impoverished farmers and raise the economic status of the nation as a whole by supplying the village and bringing the benefits of modern technology to the backward steppe. The article served as a platform for extolling the importance of aviation technology in modernizing the countryside, facilitating the *smychka* of urban and rural Russians, and celebrating the Party as the agent of enlightenment and modernization.

More important than the airplane's ability to ensure economic prosperity was its power to transform the consciousness of Soviet Russia's rural citizens. In an essay titled, "What Lies beyond the Darkened Clouds?" Shklovskii used the conversion narrative to express an abiding faith in the civilizing role of aviation technology. The essay recounts the reaction of a village elder who travels aboard an agit-plane for the first time. Following the completion of the demonstration flight, the old peasant is inundated with questions by his rural neighbors. Afraid of the unknown and unseen forces of nature, the peasants demand an answer to the pressing question, "What is beyond the darkened clouds?" [*Chto za khmaroi?*]. Having experienced the reality of mechanized flight, the village elder lays aside the villagers' fears by instructing them that, "beyond the clouds there is only space." Shklovskii concludes that this programmed encounter demonstrated the vital importance of aviation in liberating the village from backwardness and ignorance. By laying aside peasants' irrational fear of the unknown, the airplane proved an essential instrument in educating the village. Thus armed with the tools of modern technology, Shklovskii proclaimed, the Soviet Union would prove capable of overcoming the "darkness" [*khmara*] of rural Russia.[51]

Shklovskii's ruminations on the modernizing role of aviation technology highlight the problematic relationship between city and country that characterized Soviet political culture from the onset of the Civil War. In much the same way that mid-nineteenth-century proponents of European colonialism "fixed upon railroads as the key symbol of the superiority, material as well as moral, that Western societies had attained over all others," twentieth-century spokesmen for Soviet power focused on the airplane as a central token in demarcating the superiority of their urban, industrial ideology over

[50] V. Shklovskii, "Na samolete 'Litsom k derevne'," *Ogonek* 30 (1925): 12.
[51] V. Shklovskii, "Chto za khmaroi?," *Ogonek* 32 (1925): 14.

the traditions and practices of the rural village community.[52] Time and again in their propaganda tracts, periodicals, and posters, aeronautical spokesmen depicted the peasantry as naive, fearful, and superstitious; more willing to trust the avaricious and inebriated clergy than they were to trust the educated representatives of Soviet power. Notwithstanding the implicit claim of equality suggested by the Party's political–cultural "union" between city and village, state propaganda belied the belief that the peasantry could ever emerge as a coequal partner in the proletarian dictatorship. As contemporary visual and written sources made clear, the peasantry was not understood to be the rural counterpart of the urban working class. It was perceived, rather, as a backward and retrograde social caste that required the leadership and tutelage of the technologically proficient proletariat in order to rise above its native state of ignorance. The village was the antithesis of the modern and urbane city. It was an uncultured and churlish repository of antiquated tradition that, if left on its own, would continue to impede the development and prosperity of the nation as a whole.

The airplane's arrival bridged cultural and geographic divides, it disrupted long-held views of time and space, and it challenged faith in God and nature while offering impoverished peasant audiences the hope of improving their economic standing. Aviation produced wonder and amazement in the minds of even sophisticated viewers, and it testified to the clear material superiority of the city over the countryside. As the masters of this new technological marvel, Party officials consciously endeavored to benefit from the Promethian impulses associated with flight. Similar to British colonial administrators and missionaries who were "convinced that only a large influx of Western technology could shake India from its lethargy and alleviate the poverty and backwardness of its masses," Soviet officials looked to the airplane as a civilizing element that would "quickly overcome the ancient darkness and superstition of village life" and thus "tear the countryside away from its rural isolation, backwardness, cultural alienation and intellectual poverty."[53] They manipulated aeronautical images to win rural support for the construction of socialist culture while employing agit-planes and agit-flights to project their authority across the vast spaces of the Russian countryside.

Although it is impossible to measure the effectiveness of Party efforts to associate aviation with its political authority, anecdotal evidence suggests that the aerial turn to the village met with no mean success. As one scholar has discovered, the link between aviation and the Party was firmly entrenched in the popular consciousness by the late 1920s. During the agricultural collectivization campaign of 1929–30, for example, peasants in the Duminichii

---

[52] Michael Adas, *Machines as the Measure of Men: Science, Technology, and Ideologies of Western Dominance* (Ithaca, NY: Cornell University Press, 1989), 223.

[53] Adas, *Machines*, 225; M. Shel', "Aviatsiia v dele khoziastva," *Daesh Sibiri krasnye kryl'ia* 3 (1924): 27; and RGVA f. 33987, op. 1, d. 558, l. 145.

district of Zapadnoi *oblast'* speculated that airplanes were being employed by state authorities to gather information on agricultural productivity. This aerial intelligence, the villagers believed, was then used by Moscow officials to set higher procurement quotas that enabled them to squeeze more grain from the village.[54] As a result of these rumors, local peasants came to further mistrust Party officials and they greeted the appearance of airplanes with growing suspicion. Such incidents suggest that ongoing efforts to raise rural awareness of the airplane's utility were far more successful than originally had been planned. They produced a reciprocity of perception in which some citizens viewed both aviation and the state in terms unintended by Party authorities. While officials labored to create a symbol system in which airplanes served as iconographic representations of the Communist Party's power, authority, and modernity, at least some citizens transposed these official images, visualizing the Party as little more than an arbitrary authority that had augmented its power through modern technology.

[54] Sheila Fitzpatrick, *Stalin's Peasants: Resistance and Survival in the Russian Village After Collectivization* (Oxford: Oxford University Press, 1994), 46–7.

6

Aviation in Service to the State

COMPENSATORY SYMBOLISM AND THE POLITICS OF LEGITIMATION

Buoyed by their apparent success in promoting air-mindedness among urban and rural residents, Party officials rapidly moved to expand the scope and intensity of aeronautical activities across the entire Soviet Union. Even amid the confusion and disarray occasioned by the May 1925 administrative merger of ODVF and Dobrokhim, by early 1926 the number of operational agit-squadrons had increased from three to five as "avia-chemical expeditions" were launched to such far-flung locations as Nizhegorodskaia *oblast'* and the isolated steppe of Dagestan. Meanwhile, the inauguration of "Aviakhim Day" (14 July 1926) gave citizens annual cause to celebrate the accomplishments of the volunteer society. Publishing efforts also continued apace as the new enterprise printed increasing amounts of educational materials, short stories, poems, and propaganda tracts. Within eighteen months of the administrative union, officials pointed to the appearance of no fewer than twenty new books and eleven informational brochures (comprising a total circulation of some 884,000 copies) as quantitative signs of their organization's success. Aviakhim also made considerable progress in terms of local networks, organizations, and cells. By the end of 1926, the society sponsored 37 clubs, 923 circles, 2,006 libraries, and 6,506 avia-corners throughout the country.[1]

Accompanying the well-publicized expansion of the civil aviation program, Soviet military aviation had also made progress by 1926 thanks to ongoing secret collaboration with Weimar Germany. On 15 April 1925, Soviet and German agents finalized an agreement to open a joint flight-training program in the city of Lipetsk, some 200 miles south of Moscow.[2] Using a preexisting aerodrome as the base, state officials ordered the construction of a hangar, workshop, fuel and ammunition stores, and an

---

[1] GARF f. r-9404, op. 1, d. 23, ll. 1–8.
[2] Yale University Russian Archives Project. Materials on Soviet–German Military Cooperation. Document 67. "Protocol of the Soviet-German Agreement on Organizing an Aviation School at Lipetsk."

administration building to support the staff and trainees. The Weimar government, for its part, provided the aircraft and technicians. By the end of 1926 sixty-five planes comprising seven different models were already stationed at the facility. Before the school was officially closed in October 1933, a total of 120 pilots and 100 observers would complete the program.[3]

Of all the steps taken by state officials, however, none was more revealing than the decision to establish a special "Committee on Big Flights" in early 1925.[4] Inspired by the success of earlier flights between locations such as Baku and Tehran and Termez and Kabul, the Committee on Big Flights was charged with organizing a series of high-profile prestige flights intended to raise the international profile of the Soviet Union and its aviation programs. As its first major undertaking, the Committee dispatched a squadron of six airplanes to the Chinese capital, Peking, on 10 June. A response to contemporary long-distance flights being undertaken by European and American pilots, the Moscow–Peking expedition was a conscious attempt by Party officials to secure the Soviet Union a place among the ranks of the world's leading aeronautical powers.[5] The flight was also endowed with political symbolism, as it coincided with the increasingly active opposition of the Chinese Communist Party to the British colonial presence in East Asia. Officials intended that the flight, in addition to revealing the capabilities of the Red Air Fleet, would serve as a tacit demonstration of the Soviet Union's "sympathy and friendship for the Chinese people."[6] In this regard, at least, the enterprise was truly innovative. Undertaken three years before American Charles Lindbergh's 1928 diplomatic tour of Latin America, the flight to Peking was history's first premeditated attempt to promote international goodwill through the use of aviation.[7]

By contemporary Soviet standards the "Great Flight," as the Moscow–Peking expedition came to be known, was an ambitious enterprise. The flight path stretched along a southeasterly axis covering more than 4,000 miles of isolated and frequently inhospitable terrain from Moscow to Sarapul' to

[3] Lennart Andersson, *Soviet Aircraft and Aviation, 1917–1941* (Annapolis, MD: Naval Institute Press, 1994), 28–30.

[4] Robert A. Kilmarx, *A History of Soviet Air Power* (New York: Praeger, 1962), 14.

[5] The most spectacular long-distance flight of the period had occurred between April and September 1924 when two United States Army Douglas biplanes completed the first around-the-world flight, covering 27,500 miles in just over fifteen days of flying time. For a narrative description of the event, see Lowell Thomas and Lowell Thomas, Jr., *Famous First Flights That Changed History* (Garden City, NY: Doubleday and Company, 1968), 61–87.

[6] "Perelet Moskva–Mongoliia–Kitai," *Izvestiia*, 10 June 1925.

[7] Roger E. Bilstein, *Flight in America: From the Wrights to the Astronauts* (Baltimore: Johns Hopkins University Press, 1984), 77. The circumstances surrounding Lindbergh's flight are described in Roger E. Bilstein, *Flight Patterns: Trends of Aeronautical Development in the United States, 1918–1929* (Athens, GA: University of Georgia Press, 1983), 167–70.

FIGURE 32. Airplanes of the Great Flight squadron prepare to depart Moscow for Peking on the morning of 10 June 1925.

Sverdlovsk to Krasnoiarsk to Irkutsk, and ultimately to Peking. Along the route, landing sites were established at one dozen urban centers to service the squadron's airplanes and to allow aircrews time to rest from their strenuous encounters with mountains, desert, and steppe. Despite these precautions, inclement weather and mechanical difficulties forced the crews of the six participating aircraft to make numerous unscheduled landings. One unfortunate crew was compelled to withdraw from the expedition fewer than 300 miles from Peking when their aircraft's landing gear was destroyed during an otherwise routine descent.[8] Yet, by the time the Great Flight concluded on 13 July, five weeks after the squadron's departure from Moscow, four of the six airplanes had arrived safely in China. Considering the vast distance involved, the harsh and varied terrain over which the pilots flew, and the primitive technical support available to the participating crews, the completion of the Moscow–Peking expedition was a noteworthy accomplishment.

Aside from demonstrating the remarkable feats of bravery and endurance of which the country's pilots were capable, the Great Flight underscored the central role played by political symbolism in shaping Soviet aviation culture. Accompanying the crews of the six participating airplanes, officials dispatched military spokesmen, journalists from the newspapers *Pravda*, *Izvestiia*, and *Leningradskaia pravda*, as well as a representative from the State Telegraph Agency [*Rosta*] to monitor the progress of the Great Flight and to compose the feature stories that appeared daily in the country's press.[9]

[8] *Izvestiia*, 18 July 1925.
[9] See, *Izvestiia*, 10 June–18 July 1925.

Two *Proletkino* cameramen also flew aboard the aircraft to provide a visual record of the expedition.[10] At each designated landing site, these representatives helped organize rallies, deliver speeches, orchestrate tours of the airplanes, and disseminate the copious amount of propaganda material carried aboard the aircraft. More than an "expedition" organized to test the abilities of Soviet aircrews and airplanes, the Great Flight was, in fact, an international agit-flight through which Party leaders intended to communicate their political messages to foreign as well as domestic audiences.

The centrality of political considerations in defining the aerial expedition was further underscored on 5 June when, five days before the departure of the squadron from Moscow, officials in the People's Commissariat of Foreign Affairs (NKID) responded to an invitation from the Japanese government by deciding that the squadron would continue on to Tokyo following its arrival in Peking. Intent on counterbalancing the recent "machinations" of British diplomats in the Far East, NKID officials believed that an aerial demonstration of Soviet–Japanese friendship would prove an "important step in [their] continuing efforts to bring about England's political isolation."[11] They subsequently made the flight to Tokyo a reality: securing Chinese approval for overflight rights across the eastern portion of the country, dispatching aviation specialists to service and reequip the planes following their arrival in Peking, and making arrangements for a grandiose state reception in honor of the Soviet flight crews who were expected to arrive in Tokyo on 25 July.[12] NKID representatives also prepared to host two Japanese military pilots who, earlier, had been granted permission by the Politburo to fly over the USSR en route from Tokyo to Moscow.[13] As a means of underscoring the cooperative relationship between the two governments, the departure of the Japanese pilots was planned to coincide with the Soviet expedition's 25 July arrival in Tokyo.

In the meantime, state officials utilized the Great Flight to draw domestic attention to the great strides made by the Soviet Union under the leadership of the Communist Party. Press coverage of the expedition pointed to the advances made in the aviation industry, repeatedly noting that four of the six planes participating in the flight had been manufactured either in whole or

---

[10] *Izvestiia*, 10 June 1925. For copies of the films produced during the flight see RGAKFD "Aviakinozhurnal, No. 3" (O-11598-II), "Moguchie kryl'ia" (O-17651 I), "Velikii perelet" (O-2721-I-VI), and "Vostochnyi perelet" (1-12935).

[11] RGAE f. 9527, op. 1, d. 13 (Perepiska s RVS, NKID SSSR, i Sovetom po grazhdanskoi aviatsii po organizatsii pereleta Peking–Tokio), ll. 4–5.

[12] RGAE f. 9527, op. 1, d. 12 (Perepiska s RVS, NKID SSSR, i Sovetom po grazhdanskoi aviatsii po organizatsii pereleta Moskva–Peking), l. 23. See also RGAE f. 9257, op. 1, d. 11 (Perepiska s RVS, NKID SSSR, i Sovetom po grazhdanskoi aviatsii po organizatsii pereleta Moskva–Peking–Tokio).

[13] RGASPI f. 17, op. 1, d. 502 (Zasedanie Politburo ot 7 maia 1925 g.).

FIGURE 33. Muscovites view a map depicting the route of the Great Flight from Moscow to Peking, 1925.

in part by Soviet factories.[14] Although the Soviet aviation program had been in existence only two short years, the Party's ability to inspire the "Bolshevik audacity and persistence of Soviet workers" had enabled the country to make swift strides in the design and construction of modern aircraft.[15] As a result of the Party's leadership, the "victorious working class, tempered in the forge of revolution" had quickly overcome the "principal difficulties and obstacles

[14] The squadron was composed of two Junkers models purchased from Germany, an AK-1 wooden monoplane, one Polikarpov R-2 biplane, and two Polikarpov R-1 biplanes. The Polikarpov R-1 was noteworthy for being the Soviet Union's first mass-produced airplane. It was based on the World War I-era British DeHavilland DH-4 (which had been selected for license production in Moscow just prior to the Revolution) and supplemented by technical improvements derived from DH-9 and DH-9a aircraft captured by Bolshevik forces during the Civil War. The R-1 that participated in the Great Flight was powered by a 400-horsepower American "Liberty" engine built at Soviet State Aviation Factory No. 1. Designated as the M-5, the engine was the first to be serially produced by the Soviet aviation industry. See Alexander Boyd, *The Soviet Air Force Since 1918* (New York: Stein and Day, 1977), 7, and V. B. Shavrov, *Istoriia konstruktsii samoletov v SSSR do 1938 g.* (Moscow, 1986), 332–6.

[15] *Izvestiia*, 10 June 1925.

that lay in the way of conquering the aerial elements."[16] "New, incontrovertible proof of the immense and rapid development of the Soviet Union's technical and productive strengths," the Great Flight allegedly demonstrated "the colossal technical, organizational, and political accomplishments of the revolutionary proletariat."[17]

Official accounts also went to considerable lengths to distinguish the Moscow–Peking expedition from similar events undertaken in the West. Whereas the appearance of European air squadrons in Asia, Africa, and the Middle East had long been associated with "imperialist conquest, exploitation, and oppression," the flight to Peking demonstrated "the atmosphere of sympathy and trust" that allegedly characterized the relationship between the Soviet Union and the people of China.[18] One commentator noted that, "although the Chinese people have seen many foreign airplanes appear in their territory," the arrival of the Soviet expedition was the first time that airplanes had come from abroad "not to oppress, but to deliver fraternal greetings and sympathy."[19] Typical of the bombastic language that characterized Soviet political discourse, state publications contrasted the beneficence of the mission with the militarism and duplicity of western governments:

We do not fly to Mongolia and China armed with machine guns and threats in the manner that has accompanied the appearance of bourgeois technology in these regions. We fly to the East toward our friends. Our mighty flight is singular proof of the strength of our friendship and the friendship of our strength [*sila druzhby i druzhba sily*].[20]

Even more important than the moral imperatives motivating the flight to Peking were the organizational differences said to distinguish Soviet aviation from its western counterparts. According to official accounts, both the origin of the Great Flight as well as the expedition's format had resulted from the unique social and political structures that had given rise to Soviet aviation culture. "Soviet civic consciousness," in particular, was credited with having made possible the flight's successful completion.[21] As a means of highlighting the political and moral superiority of Soviet socialism over American and European capitalism, press accounts emphasized the cooperative nature of the aeronautical enterprise. Whereas, in the West, aviation advances resulted from the self-interest and greed of individual fliers, Soviet accomplishments such as the Great Flight were made possible by the collective effort of the

---

[16] I. Fel'dman, "Uspekhi Krasnoi aviatsii–delo ruk trudiashchikhsia," *Biulleten' Aviakhima posviashchennyi pereletu Moskva–Mongoliia–Kitai i uchastiiu sovetskikh planeristov v Ronskikh planernykh sostiazaniiakh v Germanii* (Moscow, 1925), 5.

[17] *Izvestiia*, 18 July 1925.

[18] *Izvestiia*, 11 June 1925.

[19] L. M. Karakhan, "Znachenie pereleta Moskva–Kitai," *Biulleten'*, 3.

[20] A. Lapchinskii, "K pereletu Moskva–Kitai," *Aviatsiia i khimiia* 6 (1925): 11.

[21] *Izvestiia*, 10 June 1925.

entire country. The flight was described as "a comprehensive test in which not only our fliers, our factories, our Soviet made airplanes and motors take part, but in which the entire terrestrial organization [*zemnaia organizatsiia*] and labor of the Air Fleet participates on a Union-wide scale."[22] The alleged superiority of Red aviation even extended to the selection of airplanes. Contemporary accounts were particularly critical of American pilots who took precautions to arrange special motors and equipment for their record-setting flights. In contrast to the self-promoting Americans, Soviet flight crews were expected to fly aboard standard unmodified aircraft even on undertakings as demanding as the Great Flight:

We do not select special machines for our flights as the Americans do, for example, in their attempts to circle the globe. We do not make special orders for long distance flights nor do we advertise sponsors in order to purchase special planes. We use that which we already have. That is to say, we endeavor not to set records, but to verify the capabilities of the aircraft in our Air Fleet. As such, we naturally view our fliers not as racer–individualists [*gonshchiki–individualisty*], but as a worker collective that fulfills practical tasks without inflating the value of our resources.[23]

Given the country's complete dependence on foreign manufacturers for the chassis and engines that it endeavored to reproduce, comments of this sort were highly disingenuous. Intended to detract attention from the limited capabilities of the Soviet aviation industry, they reflected the propensity of Russian spokesmen to adopt the rhetoric of compensatory symbolism when measuring their progress against western standards.

More important, the claims were patently false. In contradistinction to state officials' proclamations, special modifications were, in fact, made to the aircraft that participated in the Great Flight. Faced with a host of potential problems arising from the country's inadequate production facilities and lack of a service infrastructure, the Main Inspectorate of the Civilian Air Fleet subjected the planes to a number of adjustments in advance of their departure. Two additional gas tanks were attached to the undercarriage of each aircraft in order to extend their range of operation. Modifications to the airplanes' cabins (including the installation of new gauges and reinforced cockpit seats) were also completed in an attempt to reduce the amount of fatigue that the fliers were expected to encounter. Much more important, however, was an order to equip the airplanes with engines personally chosen by participating pilots in consultation with their mechanics.[24] In addition to demonstrating the disingenuousness of official proclamations regarding the reputed moral superiority of the Red Air Fleet, this decision revealed the presence of a serious obstacle to Soviet dreams of aeronautical glory: the

[22] Lapchinskii, "K pereletu Moskva–Kitai," 11.
[23] *Ibid.*
[24] RGVA f. 29, op. 74, d. 1 (Materialy o podgotovke pereleta Moskva–Peking), ll. 1–2.

lack of reliable, domestically produced engines and spare parts. As we have already seen, the production of airplane engines had proven the chief impediment to the Imperial state's efforts to maintain an effective air force during the First World War.[25] Nearly a decade later, little had changed. Indeed, the problem was so acute that it would become the focus of a special campaign in 1925–6 to raise money for the purchase of foreign engines and parts that could be copied and then converted into domestic serial production. Under the slogan "Let's have motors!" state officials aimed to raise citizens' consciousness of the centrality of engine assembly to the country's future aviation successes. Repeated efforts to convince the public that "Red motors should be built in Soviet factories" notwithstanding, the problems surrounding engine development and production would bedevil state officials for years to come.

More immediately, the issue threatened to wreck officials' plans for extending the Great Flight to Tokyo. Although four of the six aircraft successfully arrived in Peking by 13 July, they did so only in spite of recurrent mechanical difficulties. None was in any condition to fly on to Japan. Fearing that the cancellation of the Tokyo flight would prove a diplomatic embarrassment, NKID officials pressured the Main Inspectorate of the Civilian Air Fleet to quickly resolve the problem. When efforts to repair the planes proved futile, three new engines were ordered from Moscow.[26] Typical of the endemic acquisition problems that plagued the Soviet aviation industry, however, the replacement motors could not be made ready for shipment before 8 August. On that day, more than three weeks after the initial request for the expeditious delivery of the engines had been received by NKID officials, the motors were placed aboard a train to Peking. Three more weeks would pass before they reached their destination. In the meantime, the costs associated with the expedition continued to mount. Having originally earmarked just under 75,000 rubles for the project, Soviet officials were forced to appropriate an additional 15,000 rubles (and 26,000 Chinese dollars) to support the flight crews stranded in China. Added to the 85,000 rubles spent obtaining and transporting the new engines from Moscow and the estimated 46,000 rubles that were required for extending the journey to Tokyo, the enterprise would cost the state more than 221,000 rubles by the time it was completed.[27]

The denouement of the Great Flight seems to have hardly justified the expenditure of such substantial sums. Following the arrival of the new engines at the end of August, the two Soviet-constructed R-1 aircraft,

---

[25] See Chapter 2, pp. 72–3.

[26] No effort was made to replace the engine in the fourth plane. Deemed beyond repair in the field, it was returned to Moscow aboard a rail car. RGAE f. 9257, op. 1, d. 11, l. 23.

[27] RGAE f. 9527, op. 1, d. 11, *et passim*. These figures do not include the unknown costs associated with transporting the unrepairable aircraft back to Moscow.

piloted by Mikhail Volkovoinov and Mikhail Gromov, departed for Tokyo. The aircrews faced terrible weather conditions as their flights coincided with the start of the typhoon season. Although the airplane piloted by Gromov successfully landed at the Tokyo aerodrome on 2 September, engine failure forced Volkovoinov to make an emergency landing near the city of Shiminoseki southwest of the capital. Unable to repair the aircraft, Volkovoinov and his copilot were subsequently escorted to Tokyo aboard a railcar by Japanese officials.[28] Despite the less-than-august end to the enterprise, state propagandists heralded the Moscow–Peking–Tokyo flight as "a world victory for Soviet aviation."[29] The triumphant claim appears much less convincing given the concurrent accomplishment of the two Japanese military aviators who had departed Tokyo for Moscow on 25 July. They arrived on 28 August, completing the nearly 6,000-mile journey in twenty-nine days.[30] The reverse trip had taken the Soviet fliers almost three months.

   The problems encountered in carrying out the expedition to Peking and Tokyo did not dissuade Party officials from attempting further prestige flights the following summer. On 16 July 1926 a Khioni V aircraft dubbed *Moscow Aviakhim* [*Moskovskii aviakhim*] departed on a trans-European aerial tour scheduled to take Nikolai Shibanov and a copilot from Moscow to Paris and back. From the start the trip was plagued by mechanical difficulties that brought the aircraft down on ten separate occasions before the crew had cleared German airspace. The tour ended abruptly on 21 July when engine failure forced an emergency landing during which Shibanov crashed into a telephone pole, irreparably damaging the plane.[31] To the chagrin of the country's officials, Shibanov's public failure was compounded by foreign success over Soviet airspace when, one week later, the French military aviator André Girier piloted a Breguet-19 airplane on a nonstop flight between Paris and Omsk.[32]

   The mechanical problems that scuttled the Moscow–Paris flight were not the only challenges with which officials were forced to contend. The entire enterprise was characterized by confusion and disarray. These circumstances were detailed in a scathing secret report written by the Soviet representative assigned to greet the crew on their arrival in Paris. Noting that he had not received essential background information regarding the fliers and their itinerary before the Moscow departure and that he had been left completely uninformed about their progress once underway, the representative decried the "idiotic situation" that had arisen when he was unable to answer

[28] RGAE f. 9527, op. 1, d. 12, l. 53.
[29] *Izvestiia*, 3 September 1925.
[30] *Izvestiia*, 28 August 1925.
[31] RGAE f. 9527, op. 1, d. 9 (Materialy o mezhdunarodnykh poletakh sovetskikh letchikov), ll. 332–3.
[32] *L'Aerophile*, 1–15 July 1926, 195–7.

FIGURE 34. The ANT-3 *Proletariat.*

questions put to him by French governmental officials, industrial spokesmen, and local journalists concerning the plane's status and its expected date of arrival. What little information he did have at his disposal came from dispatches appearing in "hostile" [*vrazhdebnye*] newspapers such as *L'Echo*, which had sarcastically reported that "Shibanov appears to be completing the flight in 100 kilometer hops, studying German territory quite closely. If everything proceeds normally, as it has so far, we can expect that the Soviet fliers will visit us around Christmas." The state's inability to provide the fliers with a reliable aircraft and its lax organization in advance of the flight led the representative to the conclusion that the Soviet Union's aviation program had "failed its first test in front of the Europeans":

While the French have no problems flying from Paris to Omsk, we cannot even make it from Moscow to Paris. It's offensive. Really offensive. It's offensive because we don't have the aircraft or the motors. And, it's thanks to attempts like this one, undertaken with inadequate resources, that brave lads and excellent flies like Kolia Shibanov are forced to suffer.[33]

As a result of the affair, the Soviet Union was now forced "to repair its ruined reputation." The opportunity to do so came at the end of August when Mikhail Gromov and copilot E. V. Rodzevich successfully completed the round-trip flight from Moscow to Paris aboard the *Proletariat*, an ANT-3 airplane equipped with a French-built Napier-Lion Series V engine. Once

---

[33] RGAE f. 9527, op. 1, d. 9, ll. 295–303.

back in Moscow, the airmen were treated to a heroes' welcome. Party officials heralded the flight with typical hyperbole, proclaiming it "one of the greatest accomplishments of world aviation."[34]

Although the arrival of Gromov and Rodzevich in Moscow provided Soviet citizens with cause for celebration, it did nothing to address the systemic deficiencies hampering state efforts to match western successes. Insofar as it encouraged the execution of similar spectacles (notwithstanding the continuing inadequacy of available resources), the flight to Paris may have proven counterproductive. Attuned to the airplane's powerful symbolic value and impatient to demonstrate material progress through displays of aeronautical mastery, Soviet leaders would increasingly turn toward high-profile prestige flights in order to legitimate their authority before audiences at home and abroad. Convinced that their vision of socialist development would quickly enable them to surpass the technological and industrial accomplishments of the capitalist world, they celebrated organization, discipline, and collectivity as Soviet-inspired predicates to the achievement of progress. In the meantime, they relied on foreign manufacturers to provide the engines and equipment necessary to effect their air-minded schemes. Like their Imperial predecessors, who inflated contemporary exploits in forecasting Russia's future success, Soviet spokesmen employed the rhetorical strategy of compensatory symbolism in an effort to demonstrate socialism's inevitable victory in the war versus capitalism. Measuring success against standards set by Western Europe and America, but unable to match those standards without help from the same, they exaggerated the accomplishments of native airmen and aircraft while expecting the Soviet Union's sudden transformation into the world's preeminent aviation power.

THE YEAR OF BIG FLIGHTS

The following year, 1927, witnessed a subtle shift in Soviet aviation culture as the state significantly expanded efforts to project images of competence and accomplishment. During the years leading up to the formation of Osoaviakhim, the organization's predecessors, ODVF and Aviakhim, had focused on inculcating public air-mindedness and developing domestic support for the construction of the Red Air Fleet. Although similar efforts would continue throughout the late 1920s and 1930s, from 1927 onward Soviet aviation endeavors were increasingly linked to celebrating industrial achievements and promoting civil defense.

The change in aviation symbolism and rhetoric may be explained in part by the Party's evolving response to the challenges of economic development and industrial modernization. These, in turn, served as important catalysts

[34] *Ibid.*, l. 512.

in shaping the direction of Soviet political culture as Party officials struggled to comprehend and control contemporary circumstances that did not conform to their blueprint for constructing a socialist utopia. When they proclaimed victory in October 1917, Bolshevik leaders did so expecting that their example would spark a worldwide revolution that would sweep from power the bourgeoisie and install proletarian governments throughout the industrially advanced states of Western Europe. These governments, they believed, would then assist Russia in developing the industrial infrastructure considered a prerequisite to socialism. By the early 1920s, however, it was apparent that, in the near term at least, prospects for revolution in Europe were exceedingly dim. Contrary to the expectations of Party ideology, economically impoverished and industrially backward Soviet Russia was on its own. From this reality emerged the theoretical novelty "socialism in one country," which argued that, through the creation of an industrial base and the realization of a new proletarian culture, Russia could achieve socialism on its own without waiting for international revolution. First articulated by Nikolai Bukharin and Josef Stalin in early 1924, "socialism in one country" came to dominate Party politics as supporters waged a successful battle to discredit and depose those opposing their vision.[35] By mid-1927, "socialism in one country" supplied the theoretical foundation for pursuing a program of rapid industrial expansion under the guidance of the Party's new leader, Stalin.

In addition to radically altering the Soviet Union's political and economic landscape, the new line on socialist development produced subtle, but important, changes in official representations of aviation. As the ultimate victory of the world revolution was now understood to depend on Soviet success in building the model socialist economy, it became all the more important that Party officials possess a symbolic rhetoric capable of advancing their claim of historical mastery. As the quintessential image of modernization and technical acuity, the airplane became the central component of a symbol–system that equated progress with industrial, scientific, and technological advances. No longer viewed primarily as an instrument for mobilizing citizens behind the Party and its programs, aviation was increasingly enlisted as a testament to the implementation of the socialist ideal. Demonstrations of socialism's superiority over the capitalist economies of Western Europe and the United States, Soviet airplanes and their pilots were advanced as concrete examples of the successful transformation of a country and its people through a system of planned economic development.

From a material standpoint, as the Party moved toward rapidly implementing its industrial designs it had much less need to lobby citizens' economic

---

[35] Chief among these was the architect of the Red Air Fleet, Leon Trotsky. His expulsion from the Central Committee in September 1927 marked the entrenchment of the new theoretical model as the prevailing orthodoxy of the Communist Party leadership.

support through the artifice of voluntary subscription campaigns. The decision to invest almost all available resources in heavy industry and to increase substantially the country's military budget ensured that enterprises crucial to aviation would be funded at significantly higher levels. Thus the focus of official aeronautical iconology shifted from the airplane itself to the industrial, technical, and political realities that made possible the mass production of airplanes. Whereas in the spring of 1923, Party leaders had worked to cultivate popular air-mindedness and to create public enthusiasm for the airplane as a symbol of power and progress, by 1927 they increasingly employed that symbol to support the broader interests of industrial and technological development. Airplanes and prestige flights emerged as important vehicles for convincing audiences that new production policies, keyed toward heavy industry and the military, were producing propitious results.

No less important a factor in contributing to the shift in rhetoric was the Party's increasing concern with demonstrating the technical competence and military preparedness of its armed forces to potential foreign adversaries. This aspect of the state's promotional strategy unfolded in 1927 against the backdrop of diplomatic and foreign policy crises that severely undermined the Soviet Union's international standing and prestige. In the early spring of the year, the Soviet espionage service suffered a series of debilitating blows when its spies were uncovered and arrested in Czechoslovakia, Poland, Turkey, Switzerland, and Lithuania. In April, Chinese police raided the office of the Soviet military attaché in Peking, where they discovered incriminating documents indicating that Soviet agents had been interfering in Chinese internal affairs. One week later, General Chiang Kai-Shek began a systematic purge of the Kuomintang's Communist membership, effectively destroying the Soviet Union's China policy. Still worse news followed. Escalating diplomatic tensions with Great Britain came to a head in May when the British government raided the extraterritorial office of the Soviet trade representative in London. In the aftermath, the British revoked their 1921 trade agreement with the Soviet Union and severed diplomatic relations. As if to add injury to mounting insults, in early June, the Soviet ambassador to Poland was assassinated by a Russian émigré.

Party leaders responded to this rapid succession of foreign policy disasters by ratcheting up public rhetoric concerning the dangers emanating from the capitalist West. Throughout the spring and summer of 1927, newspapers were filled with sensationalist stories warning citizens of anti-Soviet military preparations underway in Great Britain, France, and China. Satirical poems and cartoons depicting the fiendish plans of foreign statesmen like Neville Chamberlain and Johnson Hicks raised public anxiety that the West was plotting an attack. By early summer, press coverage had reached such excessive heights that general panic began to spread among the population. Rumors of an impending invasion led to the hoarding of grain and basic

FIGURE 35. An air-minded display on Moscow's Red Square, ca. 1925.

foodstuffs as citizens braced themselves for the inevitable conflict with the forces of European capitalism.[36]

As if to assuage the public anxiety initiated and fed by the press, both the frequency and scope of aeronautical events increased as the "war scare" intensified. Hoping to raise domestic confidence in (and foreign concern for) Soviet military aviation, Osoaviakhim officials organized a year-long campaign of high-profile "big flights" [*bol'shie perelety*] to demonstrate the technical competence and aeronautical skills of Soviet airplanes and air-crews. Continuing the tradition established by the 1925 Great Flight, Soviet airmen embarked on lengthy excursions between such locations as Tblisi and Moscow, Moscow and Wrangel Island, and Tashkent and Kabul. In mid-August, the ANT-3 *Proletariat* was again dispatched to Western Europe, this time on a 4,000-mile tour that included stops at Stockholm, Paris, Prague, and Berlin. As was true of each of the year's "big flights," the *Proletariat*'s journey was undertaken to "underscore the high quality of Soviet airplanes and the endurance of Soviet fliers" to audiences at home and abroad.[37] To ensure that Continental spectators grasped this message, less than one month following the successful completion of the flight, the *Proletariat* repeated its performance with a second 4,500-mile tour of other European capitals.[38]

[36] Alfred G. Meyer, "The War Scare of 1927," *Soviet Union/Union Soviétique* 5 (1978): 7–9.

[37] "Polet vokrug Evropy," *Izvestiia*, 14 August 1927, and "Tri dnia vokrug Evropy," *Krasnaia niva* 38 (1927): 10.

[38] *Izvestiia*, 9 September 1927.

FIGURE 36. A squadron of Soviet airplanes forms the name "Lenin," date unknown.

Prestige flights were not the only aviation spectacles undertaken in 1927. Throughout the year, newly constructed squadrons were unveiled with much fanfare at aerodromes across the country.[39] Meanwhile, airplanes named in

[39] See, for example, "Prazdnik v vozdukhe," *Izvestiia* 26 July 1927.

honor of such Communist luminaries as Frunze, Dzerzhinskii, Stalin, and, of course, Lenin, appeared with increasing frequency at official Party functions and festivals.[40] As the number of these demonstrations increased, so too did their scope. In early November festivities held in conjunction with the celebration of the Revolution's tenth anniversary were accompanied by an aerial parade in which more than three-dozen aircraft, flying in formation, spelled out the names of Party luminaries. It was the largest aviation spectacle organized to date in the Soviet Union.[41]

One of the year's more unusual efforts to demonstrate Soviet mastery of the skies was the "star flight" competition held on 19 June. Unlike typical exhibitions, which were intended primarily to demonstrate the speed of the aircraft and the endurance of pilots, the star flight was designed to test the teamwork and precision of the Red Air Fleet's cadres. Twelve flight crews were positioned at ten different cities located 300 to 700 miles from Moscow. Each was instructed to proceed to the Soviet capital along a precise route and at a constant speed while maintaining a specific altitude for at least one-third of their journey. Ideally, if each of the crews followed its flight plan to the letter, all twelve would arrive at the air base at the same time.[42] The star flight was heralded as definitive proof that "high levels of readiness, training, discipline, and precision" were the characteristic features of the Red Air Fleet's pilots and airplanes.[43] The demonstration was also trumpeted as evidence that the Soviet Union had mastered technique. Of the dozen planes that took part in the star flight, ten had been constructed domestically, a clear indication, according to official sources, that the Soviet aviation industry had attained a high level of technical competence. According to one official, the Soviet-made aircraft had performed their missions quickly, efficiently, and with "clocklike precision," demonstrating the country's ability to conquer space and time through the application of modern science and technology.[44]

The orchestration of the star flight also pointed to the prominence increasingly attached to discipline and collective action within contemporary Soviet political culture. The race had been designed to test the ability of the participating aircrews to coordinate their efforts and to achieve a designated objective by acting in unison. Although a single aircrew was acknowledged as the star flight's "victor," the subsequent assembly held to celebrate the

---

[40] The naming of airplanes in honor of esteemed comrades extended to revolutionary martyrs as well. In the course of the year, airplanes bearing the names of P. L. Voikov as well as the condemned American anarchists Nicola Sacco and Bartolomeo Vanzetti were unveiled before the Soviet public.

[41] V. S. Shumikhin, *Sovetskaia voennaia aviatsiia, 1917–1941* (Moscow, 1986), 133–4.

[42] A second "star flight" involving two fewer aircraft but covering much greater distances was held on 15 September. See "Vtoroi zvezdnyi perelet nachalsia," *Izvestiia*, 16 September 1927.

[43] "Itogi zvezdnogo pereleta," *Pravda*, 22 June 1927.

[44] I. Fel'dman, "Na boevom poste," *Krasnaia niva* 29 (1927): 8.

race focused on the achievements of all the participating fliers. Press coverage appearing after the race similarly emphasized the collective nature of the
flight while downplaying the significance of the individual pilots' successes.
One article drew an explicit contrast between the star flight and the achievements of western airmen. Citing Charles Lindbergh's recent solo flight across
the Atlantic Ocean as an example of "bourgeois individualism," this piece
proclaimed that "our Soviet cadres demonstrated their superiority [to western pilots] by acting not as individuals, but in unison, that is, as a mass." This
collectivity, the article continued, was particularly important to the future
success of Soviet aviation owing to the fact that *aviation, both in peace and
war, is only useful when it is employed on the principle of the mass.*[45] Such
sentiments, while trumpeting Soviet achievements and downplaying western
success, pointed to the growing social and political significance that would
be attached to the collective throughout the 1930s.

The "year of big flights" reached its apogee in late summer with the return
of pilot Semyon Shestakov and flight engineer Dmitrii Fufaev from a 12,000-
mile round-trip journey between Moscow and Tokyo aboard the ANT-3 *Our
Answer* [*Nash otvet*]. Like all of the demonstrations organized during the
course of the year, the Moscow–Tokyo–Moscow flight was undertaken to
allay citizens' fears of an impending invasion.[46] The flight sought to confirm
that the Soviet Union's industrial capabilities and technical acuity were no
less than those possessed by the West. In the keynote speech delivered at the
ceremony held in honor of the fliers, the vice chairman of the Revvoensovet,
Iosif Unshlikht, addressed this very issue:

This brilliant flight has proven to us that mass-produced Soviet aircraft completely
satisfy the most rigorous tests that are applied to aviation technology. Recent years
have been noteworthy for the series of accomplishments that we have achieved in
general industrial production and our aviation industry in particular. During the
past year the intensification of the USSR's industrialization program has produced
outstanding achievements.[47]

Unshlikht's direct association of the Tokyo flight with the country's improving productive capacity underscored the growing importance of aviation
as a symbolic marker of the state's economic policies. As the Five-Year
Plan unfolded from 1928 to 1932, officials increasingly tied aeronautics to
the ongoing industrialization drive, thus ensuring that the airplane would
become a still more prominent icon of Soviet power and authority.

---

[45] A. Rozanov, "Zvezdnyi perelet 1927 g.," *Aviatsiia i khimiia* 8 (13) (1927): 23–4. All italics
    appear in the original.
[46] "Znachenie pereleta Moskva–Tokio," *Izvestiia*, 2 September 1927. For an account of the
    flight from the perspective of the airplane's pilot see S. Shestakov, "Nad taigoi," *Krasnaia
    niva* 8 (February 1928): 16.
[47] "Perelet Moskva–Tokio–Moskva zakonchen," *Izvestiia*, 23 September 1927.

FIGURE 37. Airmen Semyon Shestakov and Dmitrii Fufaev in Japan following their successful flight from Moscow to Tokyo, September 1927.

At first glance, the Party's appropriation of aviation spectacles to allay public concerns during the protracted crisis of 1927 appears to have been a reasoned response to unexpected adversity. Anxious to calm a worried populace and to halt a run on grain and basic goods, Party officials responded with a series of grandiose displays intended to bolster citizens' morale and their sense of security. A closer examination of the circumstances surrounding the "war scare," however, reveals that the year's aviation productions (and the scare itself) were less spontaneous reactions to unforeseen and unfavorable events than the essential components of a consciously crafted strategy to legitimate the Party and its policy objectives.

Declassified documents from military intelligence archives indicate that, contrary to the vocal public posturing of officials, the Party's highest-ranking leaders did not believe that war with the West was imminent, or even likely, in 1927. Threat assessments conducted by the Red Army intelligence service in late 1926 and again in early 1927 had concluded that no immediate danger of hostilities between the Soviet Union and its capitalist neighbors existed. Even as late as July 1927, following the resolution of the crises in London and Peking, Mikhail Tukhachevskii reported that the Red Army's military planners were proceeding on the assumption that an outbreak of war remained an unlikely occurrence during the next five years.

Still further indication of Party officials' true mindset was the fact that the cornerstone of their comprehensive strategy for national industrialization, the Five-Year Plan, was set to commence only in 1928, somewhat too late to affect the outcome of a war expected to erupt in the preceding year. Nevertheless, throughout the summer and fall of 1927 Soviet officials continued to raise the specter of an impending attack in their public speeches and in the press. Their actions appear to justify the conclusion that the "war scare" of 1927 was "almost certainly a deliberate fabrication fully supported if not actually invented" by the highest-ranking officials of the Soviet government.[48]

The mobilization of public opinion through fear-mongering tactics had been a constant feature of Soviet political culture since the early 1920s.[49] In terms of its international context, careful staging, and highly visible incorporation of aeronautical demonstrations and symbolism, the "war scare" of 1927 was little different from the "Ultimatum Campaign" that had unfolded in the spring of 1923. At that time, Soviet officials had used the pretext of a threatening British diplomatic note to foster public fears of the possibility of war in order to raise donations for the construction of the Red Air Fleet.[50] Just four short years after Party officials had answered the Curzon note with an "ultimatum" of their own, they again mobilized Soviet citizens with threats of an impending war in order to generate a national "answer to Chamberlain." The consonance of these two episodes was openly acknowledged in the press. Throughout 1927 newspaper stories, editorials, and political cartoons made direct reference to the earlier Ultimatum Campaign as an example of how the public should respond to the most recent foreign "threat."[51] Differences between the two war scares were slight. Whereas, in 1923, public participation in aeronautical construction had been the object of officials' desires, in 1927 aeronautical symbolism was employed to augment a campaign intended to generate confidence in and support for a program of rapid industrial expansion. In both cases, however, the means undertaken to achieve these results was the same. The inherent consonance of 1927 and 1923 was directly addressed by the General Inspector of the Civilian Air

---

[48] Raymond W. Leonard, "The Kremlin's Secret Soldiers: The Story of Military Intelligence, 1918–1933" (Ph.D. dissertation, University of Kansas, 1997), 182–4. David Stone has likewise reached the conclusion that the "War Scare" was orchestrated by Party leaders to assist their plans for hastening the militarization of civilian organizations and to generate support for higher military procurement levels. See David R. Stone, *Hammer and Rifle: The Militarization of the Soviet Union, 1926–1933* (Lawrence, KS: University Press of Kansas, 2000), 43–63.

[49] A. K. Sokolov (ed.), *Golos naroda: pis'ma i otkliki riadovykh sovetskikh grazhdan o sobitiakh, 1918–1932.* (Moscow: ROSSPEN, 1997), 195.

[50] See Chapter 3, pp. 109–11.

[51] See *Izvestiia* and *Pravda*, August–December 1927.

Fleet and Osoaviakhim spokesman Valentin Zarzar in an article published by the newspaper *Izvestiia*. Titled "From the 'Ultimatum' to the 'Answer to Chamberlain,'" the article evaluated the progress of Soviet aeronautical culture between the two war scares, favorably concluding that in both cases citizens had responded properly to the Party's exhortations by rallying to the country's defense through support of aviation.[52]

AN AERIAL EMBASSY TO EUROPE

As the 1920s drew to a close, and as the state's forced industrialization campaign rapidly intensified, officials expanded efforts to influence public opinion through the staging of high-profile prestige flights. Increasingly, foreign audiences were the objects of aviation displays as Party propagandists, intent on validating the achievements of planned development, sent airplanes and aircrews abroad to demonstrate the Soviet Union's parity with the West. The 10 July 1929 dispatch of the newly constructed ANT-9 monoplane *Wings of the Soviets [Kryl'ia sovetov]* on a 5,600 mile European tour typified these efforts. An attempt to attain political legitimacy through the exploitation of aviation, the undertaking mirrored the 1925 Great Flight to Peking and Tokyo. Mikhail Gromov, the veteran pilot decorated for his participation in the expedition to the Far East, headed the three-man aircrew. As earlier, the fliers were accompanied by a bevy of state officials and journalists who were charged with representing the Soviet government abroad and documenting the journey for audiences at home. Like the earlier expedition, the flight of the *Wings of the Soviets* was not intended to realize any specific aviation goals or to set any particular international flight records.[53] Rather, it was undertaken "to demonstrate the new airplane's performance under the normal conditions of a typical European air route." Soviet officials hoped that such a flight would enable them to "assess the capabilities of the ANT-9 and to compare its performance with similar, three-engine European craft."[54] The positive results, they hoped, would provide evidence of the rapid advances recently made by Soviet industry.

According to the periodical press, the performance of the *Wings of the Soviets* exceeded all expectations. On each leg of its journey, the plane met the challenge of at least matching rival foreign aircraft. More promisingly, the ANT-9 had managed to best the standards set by a Rohrbach aircraft on its flight between Berlin and Travemünde, shaving more than ten minutes from the time established by the German-made plane. Following the completion

---

[52] V. Zarzar, "Ot 'Ul'timatuma' k 'Otvetu Chemberlenu,'" *Izvetsiia*, 6–7 November 1927.

[53] S. Kamenev, "Posle pereleta 'Strany sovetov,'" *Vestnik vozdushnogo flota* 12 (December 1929): 2.

[54] V. Zarzar, "Kryl'ia sovetov nad Evropoi," *Aviatsiia i khimiia* 9 (38) (September 1929): 3–4.

of the European circuit, Osoaviakhim officials proclaimed that the flight had "illustrated the substantial growth of our aviation industry, thereby raising the prestige of Soviet aviation as a whole in the eyes of the USSR's laboring masses and in the eyes of our class enemies abroad."[55] For their inspirational value, the accomplishments of the *Wings of the Soviets* were likened to "fireworks which, in their bright and concentrated form, demonstrate to all laborers of the proletarian state, the levels of success that can be attained in the course of socialist competition and through the comradely collective work of the laboring masses."[56]

As usual, the reality underlying official rhetoric was somewhat different. Rushed to completion in time for its public unveiling during Moscow's May Day celebration, the ANT-9 was assembled in only seventeen weeks, approximately half the time required for building comparable aircraft in the West. Although state officials proudly trumpeted this fact as evidence of high-production tempos unique to Soviet industry, the plane, not surprisingly, showed obvious signs of poor workmanship. Major Emer Yeager, an American military attaché in Poland who had an opportunity to inspect the *Wings of the Soviets* during the final leg of its tour, addressed the issue of build-quality in his report to U.S. intelligence officials. He noted that none of the seams of the aircraft's corrugated aluminum skin were welded together, nor were the nailheads soldered, a common practice used to maintain structural integrity under the stress induced from takeoffs and landings. Moreover, the improper installation of the plane's three propellers had required emergency repairs to the engine bushings following its arrival in Paris. By the time the *Wings of the Soviets* arrived in Warsaw on 7 August, Yeager reported, "the whole plane showed more signs of wear than its tour through Europe should warrant on a well-constructed plane. In fact, the impression made on me and the employees of the commercial airfield was that the workmanship was extremely crude." These circumstances, the American concluded, supported local opinions that "this has not been the great triumphant flight that the Soviets hoped it would be."[57]

Although the ANT-9 may have proven an imperfect platform for showcasing Soviet technical accomplishments to European audiences, the air tour did generate new grist for the Party's domestic propaganda mill as the onboard journalists transformed their experience into narratives highly critical of the

[55] RGVA f. 33989, op. 1, d. 65 (General'nyi sekretariat Osoaviakhima o rabote Osoaviakhima), l. 140, and V. Zarzar, "Itogi bol'shogo evropeiskogo pereleta samoleta 'Kryl'ia sovetov,'" *Vestnik vozdushnogo flota* 9 (September 1929): 7.

[56] V. Zarzar, "Itogi bol'shogo evropeiskogo pereleta samoleta 'Kryl'ia sovetov,'" 7.

[57] "Report from Maj. Emer Yeager, military attaché, Warsaw, Poland, 12 August 1929;" MID 2090, roll 20, frame 121; Correspondence of the Military Intelligence Division Relating to General, Political, Economic, and Military Conditions in Russia and the Soviet Union, 1918–1941 (National Archives Microfilm Publication M14430); National Archives, Washington, D.C., and RGVA f. 33989, op. 1, d. 65, l. 139.

countries which they had visited.[58] Most noteworthy were the travelogues *On 'Wings' Across Europe* and *Europe Underfoot* that recounted the impressions formed by expedition members as they traversed the Continent by air, stopping to meet and interact with official dignitaries and regular citizens. Combining detailed descriptions of takeoffs, landings, and the sensation of flying with sketches of the sights and sounds of Berlin, Paris, Rome, and London, the books offered Soviet readers a glimpse at the novelty of aerial tourism. No less important, they endeavored to convince citizens of their homeland's inherent superiority, extolling the virtues of Soviet society while condemning the corrupt and decadent bourgeois West.

The accounts were quite fulsome. In between narrative descriptions of their visits to the Roman Coliseum, the Tower of London, and the Champs Elysée, the authors penned diatribes decrying European militarism, inequality, and hypocrisy. The depths of the capitalist world's decadence were revealed during the delegation's stopover in Paris where members visited the "Palais des Nations," an imposing eight-story building situated near the city's center. Housing nearly 600 women gathered from around the globe, the Palais de Nations ranked among the world's largest brothels. It was clear evidence of the debauchery and exploitation characteristic of capitalism. Overcoming their aversion, the delegates paid thirty francs for a tour of the facility. They learned that each room of the "palace" was decorated in accordance with the nationality or ethnicity of its occupant. A special salon equipped with whips, chains, and rods was available for patrons inclined to sadomasochistic tendencies.[59]

In contrast to the morass of despair produce by the capitalist system, the Soviet-built airplane shone like a beacon. It was a ray of hope for all Soviet citizens and for those in the West sympathetic to the socialist cause. Describing the atmosphere of pride and fraternity that he and his comrades felt aboard the airplane, and mixing metaphors like compost, one author noted that, inside the familiar and comfortable cabin,

one feels at home, as if one is in an old, well-known apartment. Our "aerial apartment" is all the more dear to us as it is an unsullied piece of Soviet land, rushing across the borders of the capitalist states like the fabled flying carpet; a carpet woven from Soviet "threads," by Soviet hands, on a Soviet "loom."[60]

According to this writer, Soviet citizens living abroad welcomed the airplane as proof of the revolution's impending victory: "Surrounded on all sides by white guardists and counterrevolutionaries," and compelled to witness daily

[58] Cf. I. Bobryshev, *Na 'kryl'iakh' po Evrope: pis'ma s puti* (Moscow, Molodaia gvardiia, 1930); A. N. Garri, *Evropa pod nogami: ocherki* (Moscow: Izd. Federatsiia, 1930); and M. E. Kol'tsov, *Khochu letat'* (Moscow, 1931).

[59] Boris Efimov, *Desiat' desiatiletii: o tom, chto videl, perezhil, zapomnil* (Moscow: Vagrius, 2000), 163–4, and Garri, *Evropa pod nogami*, 118–21.

[60] Bobryshev, *Na kryl'iakh*, 27–8.

the injustices of the bourgeois world, embassy officials, workers, and other Soviet "colonists" greeted the airplane and its occupants with red flags and renditions of the "Internationale" before watching with "unconcealed envy" as the ANT-9 departed for its Soviet homeland.[61]

Although it is impossible to measure the success of this propagandistic doggerel in shaping readers' opinions, such fairy-tale accounts were certainly useful in obscuring the unspoken objective of the European tour: identifying foreign solutions to the systemic problems hindering domestic aeronautical development. Despite the relatively rapid growth of the Red Air Fleet since the spring of 1923, Soviet aviation successes remained overwhelmingly dependent on the importation of foreign engines and airframes. Nearly all of the aircraft designated for Soviet serial production, including the Polikarpov R-1 and U-2 planes that formed the backbone of the country's air fleet in the late twenties, were built with foreign parts or were mock-ups of foreign models. Even the *Wings of the Soviets*, ostensibly the most advanced Soviet airplane constructed to date, was clearly derivative of Junkers designs and came equipped with Titan engines imported from France.[62] Far from the glorious achievement heralded in official accounts, the *Wings of the Soviets* was something of a Potemkin production. It was a technological showpiece whose principal value was to mask the abiding problems of the Soviet aircraft industry.

These problems were the subject of a detailed investigation undertaken during the winter of 1928–9, coterminous with the construction of the ANT-9. Chaired by Sergei Kamenev, the top-secret Special Commission on Experimental Motors and Aircraft Construction revealed the distressing circumstances surrounding Soviet efforts to master serial aircraft production. According to the testimony gathered by the Commission, the country's aviation industry suffered from a host of systemic defects, not the least of which were inadequate metallurgical production, a lack of machine tools, and substandard construction materials.[63] The Commission's findings were neither isolated nor unique. Subsequent investigations conducted at the end of 1930 identified the continuing existence of widespread and elementary deficiencies, including an insufficient number of quality machine tools, an inability to manufacture basic parts (evidenced by the production of cracked cylinder heads, stripped or improperly threaded bolts, and warped engine cowlings), as well as woefully inept construction practices that produced airplanes with loose bolts, leaking oil pans, and improperly attached propellers.[64] To solve

[61] *Ibid.*, 40–6.
[62] Boyd, *Soviet Air Force*, 28–33, and Andersson, *Soviet Aircraft*, 228–9.
[63] RGVA f. 33989, op. 1, d. 75 (Komissiia tov. Kameneva po voprosu ob opytnakh motorakh i samoletstroenii) and RGVA f. 29, op. 74, d. 2 (Doklad nachal'nika VVS SSSR po opytnomu stroitel'stvu UVVS RKKA).
[64] RGVA f. 33989, op. 1, d. 92 (Dokladnye zapiski VAO o samoletakh i motorstroenii) and d. 94 (Spravki Ostekhbiuro), *et passim*.

these problems, the Commission called for expanding the number of bureaus and institutions responsible for engine and airframe assembly, improving the quality and scope of Soviet metallurgy, heightening the tempo of production, and dramatically increasing the amount of money available to aviation concerns. Above all, however, it was "essential to arrange for highly qualified foreign specialists to assist in the construction of experimental airplanes and motors."[65]

The *Wings of the Soviets* expedition directly served these interests by facilitating the types of contacts called for in the Commission's report. Not unlike Tsar Peter the Great's famous seventeenth-century European embassy, the ANT-9 tour provided Soviet authorities with valuable opportunities to assess western techniques first-hand and to identify potential sources of expertise and matériel. At each stop, expedition members met with foreign aviation officials, toured aerodromes and aviation factories, and queried their hosts on the latest advances in manufacturing, transport, and design. Their stay in Germany, cohosted by the leading aeronautical firms, *Deruluft* and Lufthansa, included a side trip to the coastal airport in Travemünde where they inspected the world's largest aircraft, the Dornier DO-X, a twelve-engine seaplane capable of seating over 160 passengers. Disparaging comments that an airplane of such size could only be intended "to advance German colonial interests" aside, the multiengine behemoth doubtless influenced Soviet authorities' subsequent decision to construct an air-giant of their own.[66] Stopovers in France and Great Britain were marked by similar events. In Italy, expedition members met with the Fascist government's *Il Duce*, Benito Mussolini, and Air Minister Italo Balbo, the latter of whom, not coincidentally, had only recently returned from an aerial expedition of his own to the Soviet Black Sea port of Odessa. Accompanied by a squadron of forty Savioa Marchetti S-55 seaplanes, Balbo's visit to Odessa had been hosted by his Soviet counterpart Pavel Baranov, Chief of the Military Air Force [*Voenno-vozdushnye sily*, or VVS]. The aerial diplomacy conducted between Moscow and Rome laid the foundation for the Soviet purchase of thirty S-55s.[67]

LAND OF THE SOVIETS

The drive to acquire foreign technology inevitably led Soviet officials to pursue new contacts abroad. As the Party embarked on its crash campaign of

---

[65] RGVA f. 33989, op. 1, d. 75, l. 3.
[66] Bobryshev, *Na 'kryl'iakh,'* 17. On the initial Soviet reaction to the DO-X, see Yale University Russian Archives Project. Documents on Soviet–German Military Cooperation. Document 165. "Letter No. 126/g from V. K. Putna to K. Ye. Voroshilov on the invention by Professor Dornier of the hydroplane DO-X."
[67] On the Soviet visit to Rome, see Garri, *Evropa*, 76–7 and 95–7 and Efimov, *Desiat'*, 159–60. Balbo's visit to Odessa is discussed in Robert Wohl, *The Spectacle of Flight: Aviation and the Western Imagination, 1920–1950* (New Haven, CT: Yale University Press, 2005), 69–71.

forced industrialization, officials spared no effort identifying and cultivating potential sources of expertise and advice. The achievement of autarky rested on the ability to secure and exploit the most recent advances in a wide range of scientific and technological fields. Increasingly, the most important source of those advances was the United States of America.

From the outset of the Bolshevik regime, the United States had occupied a special place in Soviet popular and political culture.[68] Although highly critical of the injustice and inequality that they perceived in American society, leading Party figures recognized the United States as the quintessential example of a modern, industrialized nation. They openly admired America's mechanized factories, its innovative technologies, and its unrivaled productive capacity. Many believed that America could contribute to the realization of Russia's socialist future by functioning as a model for economic development. By merging American mechanization and efficiency with Soviet organization and social justice, the Bolshevik Revolution would achieve its goal of a productive, modern, and just social order.

Given America's prominence in the development of aviation, it is not surprising that the United States would come to play an integral role in Soviet aeronautical fortunes. Party authorities well understood that they had much to gain from fostering contacts with the country that had pioneered machine-powered flight. Largely overshadowed by European advances in the years surrounding the First World War, by the end of the 1920s, the United States had responded with a series of organizational and technological innovations that would secure for generations to come its position as the the world's preeminent aviation superpower. Combining free-enterprise practices with timely federal subsidies and incentives, America's commercial aviation industry oversaw the development of the first transcontinental air system by 1927.[69] The illuminated runways, expanded airframes, and more powerful and efficient engines that had made this feat possible keenly interested Soviet officials. So, too, did America's territorial expanse, diverse climate, and topography. Already predisposed to view the United States as a model of Russia's industrial future, Soviet aviation officials saw clear parallels between the American experience and the geographic and environmental challenges that they faced in their quest to establish a union-wide air network.

Cultivating contacts with U.S. enterprises in the 1920s required special maneuvering, however, as the Soviet Union had yet to be formally recognized by the American government. To facilitate this process, Soviet officials opened the New York-based American Trading Company (Amtorg) in

---

[68] Alan Ball, *Imagining America: Influence and Images in Twentieth-Century Russia* (New York: Rowman and Littlefield, 2003).

[69] F. Robert van der Linden, *Airlines and Air Mail: The Post Office and the Birth of the Commercial Aviation Industry* (Lexington, KY: University of Kentucky Press, 2002).

1924. Ostensibly intended to promote commercial exchange between the two countries, Amtorg organized the purchase of U.S. products for export to the Soviet Union. Accounting for almost $40 million in orders during its first two years of operation, it quickly became the largest single buyer of American agricultural and industrial equipment for shipment overseas.[70] More important, as a research bureau and a recruitment center, the company provided legitimate cover for the conduct of wide-scale industrial and technical intelligence operations. It identified leading enterprises in industrial sectors deemed essential to Soviet interests, and it nurtured relationships with key personnel who might facilitate the acquisition of advanced technologies. The company proved its worth almost immediately, assisting in the covert shipment of a large number of Liberty airplane motors to Moscow in 1925.[71] This early success notwithstanding, the establishment of business contacts, the pilfering of production secrets, and the recruitment of spies could be abetted through the careful manipulation of the Soviet Union's image abroad. To this end, Amtorg functioned as a public-relations firm as well, promoting Soviet socialism as a peaceful, productive, and legitimate alternative to western capitalism. And in the 1920s no device was more important to establishing Soviet legitimacy than the airplane.

On the morning of 23 August 1929, an ANT-4 airplane dubbed *Land of the Soviets* [*Strana sovetov*] lifted off from Shchelkovo airfield outside of Moscow on a four-week 13,000-mile flight to the United States of America. The route chosen for the four-man crew would carry the airplane over the vast expanse of the Siberian tundra, across the Bering Straits, and down though the Pacific Northwest to the coast of northern California. From there, the *Land of the Soviets* would cross the United States along the transcontinental airmail route, which followed a rough line from Salt Lake City to Chicago to Detroit before reaching its final destination, New York City. The aeronautical journey would prove the decade's last major undertaking for Soviet aviation. Coming only four months after the Party's formal acceptance of the first Five-Year Plan in April 1929, the Moscow–New York flight was yet another attempt to demonstrate the advances made by Soviet industry under the guidance of the Communist Party. The enterprise also signaled the state's growing interest in cultivating contacts and gathering intelligence relating to American aviation. Intent on capitalizing on the publicity generated by the flight, the Soviet government dispatched its first high-level aviation delegation to the United States in time to arrive for the New York touchdown of the *Land of the Soviets*. Headed by VVS chief Pavel Baranov

---

[70] Katherine Siegel, *Loans and Legitimacy: The Evolution of Soviet–American Relations, 1919–1933* (Lexington, KY: University of Kentucky Press, 1996), 84–5.
[71] Katherine A. S. Sibley, "Soviet Industrial Espionage Against American Military Technology and the US Response, 1930–1945," *Intelligence and National Security* 14:2 (Summer 1999): 99.

and including prominent engineers such as ANT-4 designer Andrei Tupolev, the delegation was on hand to welcome the hero–fliers and to debrief them on their journey. Afterward, with Amtorg representatives in tow, they embarked on a journey of their own, visiting an array of American companies. Before leaving the United States, they concluded a deal with the Curtiss Company for the acquisition of several 600-horsepower Conqueror motors.[72]

The compensatory rhetoric that had accompanied earlier prestige flights resounded throughout the fall as the *Land of the Soviets* progressed toward the western coast of the United States. The nation's newspapers and journals closely tracked the progress of the aircrew, extolling the completion of each leg of the journey as yet another victory of Soviet aviation. Patriotic newsreels documented every aspect of the flight, visually testifying to the success of Soviet industry.[73] When the plane finally landed at Curtiss airfield in New York, the newspaper *Izvestiia* characteristically proclaimed the flight to be "the greatest accomplishment in the history of world aviation."[74]

A closer examination casts doubt on such grandiose claims. Although the ANT-4 flew farther on a single mission than any Soviet aircraft to date, the plane took far longer to complete its heroic journey than observers expected. Even discounting the fact that the mission was set back more than two weeks when the original ANT-4 (which departed Moscow on 8 August) crashed in Siberia, the *Land of the Soviets* required two-and-a-half months to complete a flight that American experts had believed would be accomplished in only four weeks.[75] Once the second plane was underway, the aircraft's limited range, inclement weather, and all-too-frequent mechanical problems compelled the flight crew to make nearly two dozen stops between Moscow and New York. At one point, in early October, mechanical failure forced an unscheduled landing in Waterfall, Alaska, where the crew waited nine days for the arrival and installment of a new engine.[76] Yet another new engine was installed two days later after the plane landed in Seattle, Washington. By the time the aircraft arrived in New York on 1 November, ten weeks had passed since the Moscow departure. Although the flight did demonstrate the impressive fortitude and perseverance of Soviet airmen, from a technological standpoint, the journey was not a breakthrough. The airplane

[72] Boyd, *Soviet Air Force*, 38.

[73] See, RGAKFD "Kryl'ia Oktiabria" (k/t O-20437-I); "Sovkinozhurnal No. 49/228, 1929" (O-2070); "Sovkinozhurnal No. 81/260, 1929" (O-2100-k/t) and "Sovkinozhurnal No. 84/263, 1929" (O-2103).

[74] *Izvestiia*, 5 November 1929. See also I. Groza, "Ot pobedy k pobede," *Aviatsiia i khimiia* 12 (41) (December 1929): 2.

[75] "Memorandum of Details in Connection with the Proposed Flight over the United States of a Soviet Airplane in the Latter Part of July, 1929," MID 2090, roll 20, frame 927. (National Archives Microfilm Publication M14430).

[76] *Seattle Post-Intelligencer*, 14 October 1929. For the complete itinerary of the Moscow–New York flight, see *Aircraft Year Book* (New York, 1930), Vol. 12, 134–5.

was too slow, its range too limited, and its engines far too unreliable to be considered a serious advance in design or construction. These realities did not, however, dissuade propagandists from heralding the *Land of the Soviets* and its Moscow–New York flight as a "miracle in the air."[77] In numerous articles and editorials devoted to the journey, Soviet newsmen celebrated the completion of the flight as a triumph of Soviet industry and as proof that Soviet science and technology were rapidly overtaking that of the West.[78]

Technical questions aside, the ANT-4 retained considerable political value. The flight was a diplomatic overture intended to foster better relations with the United States and the beneficial trade agreements that might follow. In the same way that airplanes had earlier been used to transcend the vast economic and cultural expanses that divided Soviet Russia's far-flung citizens, one was now employed to bridge the ideological chasm that separated the Soviet Union from an important source of much-needed technology and expertise. The centrality of diplomacy was underscored by Osoaviakhim officials in an express telegram forwarded to the ANT-4 fliers on the day before they entered U.S. airspace. Warning the crewmen that they would be "at the center of attention of all those around them," Soviet officials took pains to remind them "of the necessity of utmost amicability and absolutely proper conduct, discretion, and courtesy in [their] public appearances" as their "socialist fatherland" would be judged in accordance with their actions.[79]

From the outset political considerations shaped every aspect of the mission. After securing U.S. approval for the flight, Osoaviakhim officials began working with Amtorg to make certain that the airplane would be properly received by the American public. The Communist front organization "Friends of Soviet Russia" was enlisted to ensure that adequately numerous and vocally pro-Soviet crowds would be on hand to greet the airplane at each of its major stops. In the weeks leading up to the ANT-4's American arrival, Amtorg collected background materials on the plane to support a broad information campaign among the American press undertaken by pro-Soviet periodicals. For fear of inciting anti-Soviet sentiments among the American public, officials censored references to the pilots' service in the Red Army and their membership in the Communist Party.[80] Judging by the receptions that greeted the airplane's arrival, the campaign was not without success. American newspaper reports indicate that sizable audiences were on hand

[77] *Izvestiia*, 2 November 1929.

[78] K. Genger, "Bol'shie sovetskie perelety," *Vestnik vozdushnogo flota* 10–11 (October–November 1929): 31; M. Beliakov, "Moskva–N'iu-Iork," *Krasnaia niva* 48 (November 1929): 8–9; and Groza, "Ot pobedy," among others.

[79] RGAE f. 9527, op. 1, d. 89 (Materialy o perelete "Strany Sovetov" Moskva–N'iu-Iork, chast' 1), l. 110.

[80] RGAE f. 9527, op. 1, d, 88 (Materialy o perelete "Strany Sovetov" Moskva–N'iu-Iork, chast' 2), ll. 182–183 and 264.

FIGURE 38. "The fliers of the *Land of the Soviets*." Postcard, 1929.

to welcome the *Land of the Soviets* and its flight crew at several of the aircraft's stops. In Seattle and San Francisco "visibly excited" and "enthusiastic" crowds were reported, while in New York, a crowd "of approximately 8,000 Russian–Americans and Friends of the Soviet Union" turned out to welcome the airborne visitors. The convivial atmosphere of the aeronautical tour was disturbed only in San Francisco, where anti-Soviet demonstrations cast a slight shadow on an otherwise bright reception.[81]

The reactions of American citizens proved no less useful to Soviet officials than did the agit-flight itself. In glowing articles ecstatic newsmen cited Americans' response to the airplane as proof of the flight's international significance and as a demonstration of the politically persuasive power that accompanied aeronautical modernization. The periodical *Aviatsiia i khimiia* [*Aviation and Chemistry*] captured the exultant mood of state officials in a lengthy story on the "Greeting of the *Land of the Soviets* in New York." According to the Osoaviakhim journal, as word of the airplane's arrival reached the metropolis, "workers left their jobs to gather at the office of the Friends of the Soviet Union." From there, they boarded buses, cars, and trains in order to reach Curtiss airfield where the plane was scheduled to land. As the plane descended toward the earth, the crowd (which, according to the journal, consisted almost exclusively of workers and numbered in the thousands) let out "joyous exclamations, like peals of thunder"

---

[81] *Seattle Post-Intelligencer*, 14 October 1929; *San Francisco Chronicle*, 20 October 1929; and *New York Sun*, 2 November 1929.

in fraternal greeting to the Soviet pilots. Waving red flags and singing the "Internationale," the onlookers, "as if one mass, broke through the cordon of dark-blue policemen and rushed toward the taxiing airplane."[82] Only the unexpected appearance of Charles Lindbergh's well-known blue and yellow airplane prevented grave injury from befalling excited spectators and pilots alike. Arriving to greet the international visitors, Lindbergh detracted attention from the Soviet aircraft, giving the crewmen ample time to park their plane safely in a nearby hangar.[83] In response to the boisterous New York greeting, Soviet officials concluded that the appearance of the *Land of the Soviets* had successfully drawn together American citizens and workers of the Soviet Union as a unifying symbol of the victory that would be attained when humanity was freed from the imperialist yoke.

A similarly transparent attempt to extract political capital from the flight was revealed in two celebratory letters ostensibly submitted to the journal *Ogonek* by "Stepan," a Russian worker on hand to greet the *Land of the Soviets'* earlier arrival in Seattle. Despite difficult economic circumstances that frequently forced him to forego eating, the patriotic laborer traveled from his home in San Francisco to the Pacific Northwest in order to welcome the Soviet airplane and its crew.[84] There, along with the "tens of thousands" of workers and Soviet patriots, Stepan joined in singing the "Internationale" as testament to the great technical achievement of proletarian production. In light of his experience, Stepan expressed certainty "that Soviet airplanes are good and sound, and that our fliers are much better than any others anywhere else in the world." He concluded by noting that "we, here, are proud of the Soviet state and we are using all of our strength to help it grow for it is our only salvation from the evil capitalists."

As a symbol of salvation from foreign oppression and a resource for relieving the heavy burdens of history, the airplane came to occupy a prominent position in Soviet political culture of the 1920s. Beholden to the realization of an industrial utopia that demanded the modernization of Russia's agrarian economy, Soviet officials exploited aviation images to generate support for their regime and its policies. Facing obdurate resistance from the country's

---

[82] Petr Apriianskii, "Vstrecha samoleta 'Strana Sovetov' v N'iu-Iork," *Aviatsiia i khimiia* 12 (41) (December 1929): 22–3.

[83] *New York Times*, 2 November 1929.

[84] "Sovetskii grazhdanin za rubezhom," *Ogonek* 49 (349) (15 December 1929): 5. Apparently, "Stepan" did not know that the *Land of the Soviets* would appear in the San Francisco Bay Area three days later. Whether this was a result of poor publicity by Amtorg and the "Friends of the Soviet Union" or a factual oversight by *Ogonek* ghostwriters is unknown. Whatever the explanation for Stepan's confusion, American newspaper accounts of the Seattle visit (and the photograph that accompanied *Ogonek*'s publication of his letters) indicate that the "Soviet citizen" grossly overestimated the size of crowd that greeted the airplane. See *Seattle Post-Intelligencer*, 14–16 October 1929.

tradition-bound peasantry, they appropriated styles and motifs from the Imperial past to communicate their vision of the socialist future. *Chastushki, skazki,* and other long-standing genres were suffused with modern meanings through the incorporation of aeronautical themes. Airplanes were portrayed as heavenly messengers bringing with them glad tidings of progress and prosperity, while pilots played the role of prophets announcing the approach of the Marxist kingdom to come. Intent on destroying the Russian Orthodox Church, propagandists endeavored to replace established religion with the secular rituals of their new air-minded faith. Aviation posters consciously adopted the conventions of religious iconography. Conspicuously located in "avia-corners" throughout the country, they were intended to supplant the "Holy Corners" central to the lives of Orthodox believers. In a similar fashion, "aerial baptisms" were advanced as substitutes for the spiritual baptisms of the church, while new conversion narratives were written as testaments to the verity of Party visions.

Efforts to proselytize their mastery of the air quickly extended to the international arena as Soviet officials utilized aviation as a means of legitimating their industrial designs. Beginning in the summer of 1925 and continuing throughout the decade, the state orchestrated a series of high-profile "expeditions" that saw airplanes dispatched to the Far East and Europe. Intended to demonstrate the achievements of the socialist system and to enhance the reputation of the country's airplanes and aircrews, these prestige flights revealed the fundamental role played by politics and propaganda in defining the contours of Soviet flight culture. As a means of underscoring the superiority of their system, state agencies extolled the unique virtues of "socialist" aviation. No less skilled than their western counterparts, Soviet airmen were said to be morally superior to other nations' fliers. For, in marked distinction from the "bourgeois individualists" of Europe and the United States, Soviet fliers were characterized by their altruism and self-sacrifice. No less was true of Soviet airplanes (those "symbols of salvation") that, as the productive expressions of the worker-collective, bespoke the progress and unity allegedly achieved under socialism. The appearance of each new plane was celebrated as a victory in the struggle to match (and ultimately surpass) the capitalist West. Meanwhile, each new flight was heralded as the world's greatest aeronautical accomplishment.

Such rhetoric did not reflect reality. Lacking an adequate industrial base and beholden to European manufacturers for airframes, engines, and parts, Soviet aviation relied heavily on foreign assistance throughout the 1920s. Although the country's engineers made strides in duplicating imported models, their aircraft remained derivative of and dependent on those designed in the West. To a certain extent, official bombast successfully masked inferiority as Party spokesmen exploited grandiose aeronautical displays in order to impress domestic and foreign audiences. Enlisting the support of state-controlled media and publishing houses and coordinating activities with "fellow-traveler" organizations abroad, carefully orchestrated aviation events seemed to suggest that rapid progress was being made by the "Land of the Soviets." No less important, prestige flights facilitated that progress as the state revisited long-standing patterns in the history of Russia by utilizing foreign tours to gather information and to cultivate contacts in Western Europe and the United States. Tying the arrival of their airplanes abroad with factory tours and meetings with foreign industrial and political leaders, Soviet representatives simultaneously worked to improve their country's international image while gathering the intelligence and expertise that, they believed, would enable them to complete their conquest of the West.

By the end of the decade, the airplane had emerged as the Soviet Union's most prominent icon of progress and modernity. Employed at home as a means of winning converts to the Party's modernizing crusade and dispatched abroad to proselytize the accomplishments of the socialist faith, aviation revealed the extent to which the Bolshevik embrace of technology was shaped by cultural traditions inherited from Russia's long past. As Party officials seized on the West's most advanced technological marvel as a symbol and means of effecting modernization, they simultaneously reverted to the customary practices of appropriating inherited forms to legitimate current policies, exaggerating native accomplishments in response to foreign successes, and borrowing from abroad to facilitate development at home. In the decade to come, these tendencies would become still more pronounced as, driven by the fantastic expectations and frenetic excesses of the 1930s, Soviet flight culture would reach new heights of propagandistic exuberance before descending into chaos amid politically motivated terror and military catastrophe.

Part III

Soviet Aviation in the Age of Stalin, 1929–1945

We were born to make fairy tales come true,
To overcome vast distances and space,
Our reason has formed steel wings for our hands,
And throbbing engines our hearts have replaced.
– "Ever Higher (Aviation March)"

In the terrible spring of 1933 I saw people dying from hunger. I saw women and children with distended bellies, turning blue, still breathing but with vacant lifeless eyes. And corpses – corpses in ragged sheepskin coats and cheap felt boots; corpses in peasant huts, in the melting snow of old Vologda, under the bridges of Kharkov. . . . I saw all of this and did not go out of my mind or commit suicide. Nor did I curse those who had sent me out to take away the peasants' grain in the winter, and in the spring to persuade the barely walking, skeleton-thin or sickly-swollen people to go into the fields in order to "fulfill the Bolshevik sowing plan in shock-worker style."

Nor did I lose my faith. As before, I believed because I wanted to believe.
– Lev Kopelev (*Education of a True Believer*)

7

Soviet Aviation and Stalinist Culture

THE GREAT BREAK

Irrespective of the airplane's lack of technical merits, the *Land of the Soviets'* American tour appeared to augur a shift in fortune for Soviet aviation and the country as a whole. By the time the ANT-4 arrived in New York on 1 November 1929, the Soviet Union's official program of rapid industrial development was well underway. Drafted by the State Planning Commission (GosPlan) in August 1928 (and augmented the following spring), the Five Year Plan for the Development of the National Economy (FYP) represented the utopian culmination of Soviet leaders' modernizing visions. Committed to the creation of the world's most industrially advanced society and impatient to realize their dreams of productivity and prosperity, Soviet leaders embarked on a breakneck campaign between the years 1928 and 1932 to "catch and surpass" the technical and manufacturing levels of their bourgeois enemies. Believing that their interests were inimical to those of the capitalist West and driven by fear of foreign encirclement, Soviet officials aimed, simultaneously, to buttress their military preparedness and to lay the foundations for industrial autarky. To achieve these goals, state agents established production targets for planned development that focused on expanding heavy industry and the production of raw materials. At first merely unrealistic, official quotas were quickly revised upward to absurdly fantastic levels. Fixated on large-scale enterprises, the mass production of standardized goods, and absolute, centralized control, Soviet officials undertook to make the country conform to their machine-age vision of modernity. In short order, their plans for "socialist" development quickly became parody, "reduced to the proposition: build as many factories as possible, as quickly as possible, all exclusively under state control."[1]

Measured against concurrent developments in the West, however, the Soviet industrialization drive appeared, to many contemporaries, immensely successful. While Party leaders reveled in the expansion of their country's manufacturing output and optimistically forecasted the imminent arrival of

---

[1] Stephen Kotkin, *Magnetic Mountain: Stalinism as a Civilization* (Berkeley, CA: University of California Press, 1995), 32.

Communism, "bourgeois" governments struggled to cope with the dislocations occasioned by the deepening Depression. In the United States and Europe, fortunes evaporated with the collapse of the stock market in October 1929. Industrial production ground to a halt. Millions of workers found themselves living hand to mouth. Mired in crisis, "world capital," it seemed, teetered on the edge of the abyss. Meanwhile, Soviet citizens worked at a feverish pace to realize the Party's plan for constructing the bright future. Through their labor and the guidance of Soviet officials they were advancing, Josef Stalin proclaimed, "full steam ahead along the path of industrialization." "Leaving behind the age-old 'Russian' backwardness," the USSR was becoming "a country of metal, a country of automobiles, a country of tractors" as the emergence of new industries and the expansion of manufacturing bespoke the productive prowess of the world's first "socialist state."[2]

The achievements of 1928–32 were a source of immense pride for state propagandists who tirelessly proclaimed that, owing to the wisdom of Stalin and the iron will of the Communist Party, the country was quickly closing the developmental gap separating it from the bourgeois West. Colossal construction projects such as the Dneprostroi Dam, the White Sea Canal, and the mines of Magnitogorsk seemed to vouchsafe such grandiose claims. As did the statistics published by GosPlan. According to officials, the annual rate of growth in industrial production was an astounding 19.2 percent during the first FYP.[3] Between 1928 and 1932 the volume of retail trade increased 175 percent. The number of workers employed in industry more than doubled. By 1932, industrial output stood at 219 percent of its 1928 totals.[4] Such fantastic numbers appeared to lend material proof to Stalin's famous slogan: "There are no fortresses that Bolsheviks cannot storm." According to contemporary rhetoric the country was at war, scaling heights, advancing along "fronts," and conquering the legacies imposed by history. It was marching forward toward an inevitable victory that would depose once and for all the despotism of inequality and want. No obstacles could withstand the Party's headlong rush to vanquish the constraints of time and space. In one great break with the past the country would mobilize its collective will, marshal all available resources, and engage the enemy. It would accomplish in one final battle with backwardness the transcendent act that would transform the Soviet Union into the world's most modern nation.

Warfare or not, the industrialization campaign did produce legions of victims. What official sources did not acknowledge, of course, was that the country's unprecedented industrial and technological gains were matched

---

[2] Iosif Stalin, "God velikogo pereloma," *Pravda*, 7 November 1929.
[3] Peter Kenez, *A History of the Soviet Union from Beginning to End* (Cambridge: Cambridge University Press, 1999), 91.
[4] *Pravda*, 10 January 1933.

by unprecedented upheaval, inefficiency, and waste. As forests were razed, rivers dammed, and resources consumed for the cause of development, so too were ordinary men, women, and their children. In the villages, the onset of the FYP was accompanied by deportations and death. The Party's latent hostility toward the countryside turned to open violence in the fall of 1929 as it launched a campaign to collectivize agricultural production. Convinced that only large-scale enterprises could produce the grain surpluses believed necessary for industrialization, the state seized lands and livestock across the USSR, forcing the peasantry to join collective farms. Those who resisted (and a great many did) were shot or exiled to Siberia, Central Asia, and the far North. The long-term repercussions would prove devastating. In the cities, the onset of the FYP brought with it a culture of repression. Denunciation, arrest, and murder became daily routine as ideologues and opportunists targeted wreckers, saboteurs, and other "enemies of the people" said to oppose the Party's totalistic vision. To be certain, some citizens eagerly embraced the path proffered them by state propagandists. They willingly, even enthusiastically, joined the crusade, committing themselves bodily and spiritually to the realization of Communism. Still, the zealots' ardor does not excuse their excess. The Soviet quest produced misery and destruction on a scale never before imagined.

TECHNOLOGY TRANSFER, TEMPOS, AND TERROR

Against the backdrop of famine and terror, the "aerofication" of the Soviet Union proceeded apace as officials undertook the rapid expansion of civilian aviation routes in a furious effort to copy America's transcontinental air system. Among its more noteworthy accomplishments, the FYP for civilian aviation officially witnessed a fourfold increase in the existing air network, a tenfold increase in passenger traffic, and exponential growth in the number of miles flown and the delivery of airmail and freight.[5] The country's aviation industrial base saw impressive gains as well. Between 1928 and 1932, the number of enterprises devoted to airplane construction increased from twelve to thirty-one as major new plants were brought on line in locations including Leningrad, Kazan, Irkutsk, and Komsomol'sk-na-Amure. Proportional increases in the number of employed workers during the same period (from 8,695 to 24,497) were accompanied by the development of fifty-six experimental aircraft and seventeen experimental motors of which eleven and five, respectively, were converted to serial production. Overall, the country's annual output of airplanes jumped from 608 to 2,509, prompting Stalin to

---

[5] RGAE f. 4372, op. 30, d. 695 (Svedeniia i spravka ob itogakh vypolneniia plana aerofikatsii za pervomu piatiletku), 10.

announce, in January 1933, that earlier "We had no aviation industry. Now we have one."[6]

The aviation successes achieved by the FYP owed as much to foreign assistance as they did to the "iron will" of Party leaders, the enthusiasm of their followers, or the sacrifice of the rest. Efficient organizational models, innovative technical designs, and advanced equipment were essential prerequisites to building a modern industry. The Soviet Union did not have them. As in the past, the country's leaders looked abroad for assistance. They increasingly relied on their growing industrial intelligence network to provide access to the technical and material resources necessary to promote development. The opening of New York City's Amtorg Trading Company in 1924 was essential in this regard. Through Amtorg (and a number of smaller enterprises located across the United States), the Soviet government secured access to American industry long before it achieved full diplomatic recognition. During the thirties and forties Soviet intelligence officials also exploited American corporations' eagerness to do business, the country's lax export controls, and its ample supply of leftist sympathizers to acquire cutting-edge technology and industrial secrets in wide-ranging fields of economic and military significance. Although a complete account of Soviet espionage in the United States will never be possible, existing evidence clearly reveals that, in the years preceding the Second World War, foreign and domestic agents in service to the Soviet state undertook a campaign of covert and open intelligence unprecedented in modern history.[7] This campaign was largely abetted by the American business community. Hoping to forge durable business relationships and ensure steady sales during a period of immense economic hardship, American firms eagerly extended every courtesy to Soviet guests, acquainting them with the layout of their factories and familiarizing them with construction techniques in order to secure sales of equipment and profitable licensing agreements.

The events surrounding the dispatch of a four-man commission from Moscow to the United States in the fall of 1931 were an early indication of America's gregarious embrace of Soviet trade overtures. From early December 1931 to mid-April 1932, the commission crisscrossed the country by airplane and automobile, gathering first-hand information on the operation of American airways, the organization of airfields, and the methods and materials employed in the production of aircraft. Commission members began their work in Washington, D.C., where they spent several days interviewing officials in the Aeronautics Division of the U.S. Department

---

[6] John T. Greenwood, "The Aviation Industry," in Robin Higham, John T. Greenwood, and Von Hardesty (eds.), *Russian Aviation and Air Power in the Twentieth Century* (London: Cass, 1998), 134–5.

[7] Harvey Klehr and John Earl Haynes, *Venona: Decoding Soviet Espionage in America* (New Haven, CT: Yale University Press, 1999).

of Commerce. From there, they departed on a nationwide journey, stopping in more than a dozen cities to visit Boeing, Ford, Curtiss-Wright, and other major aviation firms. Before departing for home, commission members returned to the Department of Commerce where, for three full days, the head of the Aeronautics Division answered detailed queries concerning America's aerial communications network and infrastructure, aviation production, and engine development. The extent of the commission members' questions intimated the sizable gap separating Soviet and American aviation capabilities. The response that they received revealed the willingness of American representatives to assist in closing that gap.[8]

The number of Soviet aviation delegations to the United States increased dramatically following the commission's return to Moscow. So, too, did the scope and duration of their visits. Initially confined to short tours of workshops and production plants, Soviet officials exploited America's liberal free-trade policies and few controls over technology transfer to gain increasing access to specific construction techniques and to familiarize themselves with engine systems licensed for production abroad. By 1933, Soviet delegations were regular fixtures in U.S. airplane factories as leading firms including Curtiss-Wright, Boeing, Pratt & Whitney, and Douglas (to name just a few) allowed scores of Soviet construction engineers, trade representatives, graduate students, pilots, and state officials to ensconce themselves in their facilities for periods of up to six months.

The growing presence of Soviet personnel was a source of consternation for those monitoring the situation for the American government. Alarmed by the volume of visitors and the lengths of their stays, officials in the U.S. Navy's Bureau of Aeronautics and the Office of Naval Intelligence (ONI) questioned the wisdom of allowing so many foreign representatives into the nation's airplane engine and accessory plants. Noting that the expanding number of these individuals would make it increasingly difficult to safeguard experimental work and detailed information as to the state and technical characteristics of American military procurement contracts, they recommended reconsideration of the practice. C. S. Fliedner, a civilian engineer working for the ONI, was particularly vocal. He urged that immediate steps be taken to place limits on both the number of Soviets allowed into U.S. aircraft factories and the duration of their stays. After all, he observed, "I do not believe that the Soviet government would allow an American civilian engineer or naval officer into a Soviet factory manufacturing material for their army or navy. So why should we be so generous?"[9]

---

[8] RGAE f. 9527, op. 1, d. 270 (Pis'ma rukovoditelia delegatsii VOGVF v SShA t. Silina s kratkim otchetom o rezul'tatakh poezdki po SShA) and d. 272 (Zapis' besed chlenov komissii VOGVF v Departamente Kommertsii SShA).

[9] NARA Record Group 72 ("Bureau of Aeronautics – General Correspondence, 1925–42"), Box 1188, Folder EF 61/A2-14, vol. 1.

Unfortunately, Fliedner and his associates had virtually no control over the situation. Although American factories working on government contract were required to obtain ONI clearance in advance of inviting foreign delegations to tour their facilities, the process was entirely pro forma. In the midst of America's economic depression, aviation firms were desperate to secure sales in order to remain in business. They did so by peddling access to their most recent technical innovations and manufacturing processes. Eager to promote commerce and to prevent the bankruptcy of enterprises critical to the nation's military interests, the federal government did little to intervene. As long as corporate officials followed the federal policy of not permitting their guests into factory areas where work was underway on U.S. military contracts, ONI officials had no choice but to acquiesce to company requests. The result was that growing numbers of Soviet technicians and engineers acquired a growing amount of information relating to cutting-edge advances in aviation. Most of this was gathered legally, as even ONI representatives were forced to admit:

The presence of these foreigners at our plants is a matter of national policy. As long as American industry considers it good business to sell all of our manufacturing processes and equipment as fast as they develop them, there is little that we can do about this except to prevent direct access to our restricted work. It's a lousy situation, but it is one of the characteristics, apparently, of our democracy.[10]

Of course, extended operations in American factories also provided Soviet agents with ample opportunities for clandestine espionage, as evidenced by Messrs. Konal'kov and Rasianov who were caught, in April 1931, taking photographs in restricted departments of the Lukens Steel Company by using a concealed, miniaturized motion-picture camera.[11] American companies invariably abetted such covert operations by requesting unusually long stays for their Soviet guests or by seeking to extend visitors' tenure beyond their originally sanctioned time frame. In other cases, the Soviets maintained a continual presence at key factories by simply dispatching new "delegates" to replace those whose tenure was about to expire.[12] ONI officials were not blind to these activities, but they were unable to challenge them. Commenting on a November 1937 request from the Wright Aviation Corporation to approve a Soviet technician's six-month stay at the company's Patterson, New Jersey, headquarters, an exasperated ONI agent posed the rhetorical question: "Why should a competent test engineer require a six-month visit instead of six days to thoroughly go into all testing procedures?

---

[10] NARA Record Group 72, Box 1187, Folder EF 61/A2-14, vol. 2.

[11] NARA Record Group 38 ("Office of the Chief of Naval Operations, Division of Naval Intelligence – General Correspondence, 1929–42"), Entry 81, Box 53, Folder 1.

[12] *Ibid.*, Boxes 53–55, *et passim.*

Actually, three days should be sufficient to cover everything *if* he is a test engineer."[13]

The acquisition of American technology and production techniques was indispensable to the modernization and expansion of Soviet aviation. By itself, however, it was not enough to overcome the considerable advantage enjoyed by the United States and Europe's leading air powers. Hoping to more effectively direct and control the development of Soviet aviation programs, state authorities undertook a series of sweeping organizational changes as the FYP unfolded. Similar to the consolidation of voluntary associations devoted to aviation, chemistry, and civil defense that had culminated in the January 1927 establishment of Osoaviakhim, these maneuvers aimed to centralize all enterprises associated with the aviation industry into a single bureaucratic entity.[14] The result was the formation, in December 1931, of the Central Administration of the Aviation Industry [*Glavnoe upravlenie aviatsionnoi promyshlennosti*, or GUAP]. Glavaviaprom (as the organization was also known) oversaw all aspects of civil and military serial aviation construction. Responsibility for technical innovations and scientific research fell principally to TsAGI, as the previously autonomous experimental design institution was now subordinated to GUAP. The third major component of the Soviet aviation–industrial complex comprised the experimental design bureaus [*opytnye konstruktorskie biura*, or OKBs]. These emerged in the mid-1930s to expedite the development of new airplane prototypes and their conversion to serial production. Attached to specific industrial facilities and associated with individual designers, OKBs quickly proliferated (from eight in 1935 to thirty in 1939) as Soviet technicians grew increasingly adept at assimilating the techniques and materials obtained from the West.[15]

The strategy of centralizing the design and manufacture of aircraft based on foreign models paid early dividends. During the course of the FYP the number of new domestic planes increased considerably. One was the TB-1 (a military variant of the ANT-4), which entered serial production as the country's first heavy bomber in 1930. The Polikarpov R-5, a two-seat reconnaissance-bomber biplane, and the fighter models I-3 and U-2 were also first mass produced between 1929 and 1932. These became the principal attack aircraft of the 1930s air fleet. More promising, the country's constructors broke new ground with the development of the Tupolev TB-3, the world's first four-engine cantilever monoplane bomber. By 1932, 150 had been delivered to the VVS. Work also began on the next generation of aircraft as prototypes of the I-15 and I-16 fighters and the high-speed Stal'-6 monoplane appeared. Progress in airframe design was not, however, duplicated

[13] NARA Record Group 72, Box 1188, Folder EF 61/A2-14, vol. 3. Emphasis in original.
[14] For a detailed account of this process, see Greenwood, "The Aviation Industry," *op cit*.
[15] John T. Greenwood, "The Designers: Their Design Bureaux and Aircraft," in Higham *et al.* (eds.), *Russian Aviation*, 162–90.

with motors. Soviet engine production remained inadequate despite considerable assistance from abroad. By the time that production quantity was finally achieved in 1929 on the industry mainstay M-17 (a license-built BMW VI), the motor was obsolescent. To make up the difference, aviation officials returned abroad, supplementing their stock of M-17s with the purchase of 480-horsepower Gnôme-Rhône 9ASB radial engines that were licensed for production under the Soviet designation M-22.[16] Meanwhile, they struggled to produce a working prototype of the M-34, an adaptation of the M-17 intended to serve as the principal power plant for aircraft manufactured in the last half of the decade.

In certain key respects, the strategies adopted during the FYP proved successful. Although not yet comparable in size or scope to the American system after which it was patterned, the "aerofication" campaign did result in considerable improvement to the country's aviation network and industrial base. The breakneck approach contributed to the rapid development of a pool of skilled technicians and designers capable of reproducing foreign aircraft components and, at times, improving them through "add-on engineering."[17] It also constructed an industrial base capable of producing new airplanes in quantities never before possible. It did not, however, free the Soviet Union from dependence on the West. Autarky in aviation was not achieved during the 1930s. Nor would it ever be. As with almost every other industrial and technical endeavor, the Soviet Union continued to depend on critical infusions of technology from the West in order to fuel its own development.[18] Although this did not preclude the production of some quality aircraft and occasional technical innovations, it also did not realize the Party leaders' professed goal. The benefits believed to derive from a position of relative backwardness proved illusory.[19] The Soviet Union was incapable of attaining autochthonous growth.

Institutionalized dependence on the West was further abetted by Soviet political culture. The Party's perpetual demand for speed and its emphasis on colossal scale contributed directly to the perseverance of aeronautical design and production problems long since solved in the United States and Europe.

[16] Alexander Boyd, *The Soviet Air Force Since 1918* (New York: Stein and Day, 1977), 30–4, and Lennart Andersson, *Soviet Aircraft and Aviation, 1917–1941* (Annapolis, MD: Naval Institute Press, 1994), *et passim*.

[17] Ulrich Albrecht, *The Soviet Armaments Industry* (Chur, Switzerland: Harwood Academic, 1993), 13.

[18] George D. Holliday, *Technology Transfer to the USSR, 1928–1937 and 1966–1975: The Role of Western Technology in Soviet Economic Development* (Boulder, CO: Westview, 1979); Antony C. Sutton, *Western Technology and Soviet Economic Development, 1917–1965*. 3 vols. (Stanford, CA: Hoover Institution Press, 1968–73); and Albrecht, *Soviet Armaments Industry*.

[19] Alexander Gerschenkron, *Economic Backwardness in Historical Perspective* (Cambridge, MA: Harvard University Press, 1962).

The hyperactive political atmosphere consciously cultivated by Party leaders placed strains on engineers and constructors to exceed already absurdly exaggerated quotas and tempos. Whereas, in the United States, for example, it was typical for a new aircraft to require from two years to thirty months to move from initial design to production, in the land of socialist tempos the state demanded that planes be developed and flown in one year and that production in quantity be attained within eighteen months.[20] The forced production tempos and the rapid expansion of industry inevitably had a deleterious impact on quality control. Soviet engineers and constructors continued to struggle with build-quality issues throughout the decade.[21]

As in other areas of industry, Party leaders looked to scapegoat technical specialists [*spetsy*] for the chronic waste, chaos, and inefficiency induced by their own foolish policies. The first blow had been struck in late 1927 when a group of engineers was arrested in the North Caucasian town of Shakty. Accused of conspiring with agents abroad to sabotage the nation's mines, they were placed on trial in May 1928. Forty-four men were sent to prison. Five were sentenced to death. The Shakty trial marked the beginning of a protracted campaign to root out "enemies," "saboteurs," and "foreign agents." As the industrialization drive picked up steam, so too did the pace of perfunctory justice. In late 1930 former employees of GosPlan and the Supreme Council of the Economy (VSNKh), together with a group of engineers, were accused of plotting to facilitate a French attack on the Soviet Union. These eight "Industrial Party" ringleaders were found guilty and sentenced to lengthy prison terms. In September, four dozen officials from the People's Commissariat of Trade were charged with sabotaging food deliveries. All were executed for their alleged crimes. By the spring of 1931, as many as 7,000 engineers had been arrested by the state police.[22]

Aviation designers numbered among the first victims of the state's war against the *spetsy*. On 1 September 1928, OGPU agents arrested the floatplane specialist Dmitrii Grigorovich along with several members of the experimental department he headed. In October 1929, Nikolai Polikarpov was apprehended and jailed by the secret police. A skilled engineer responsible for the design of the highly successful U-2 and R-5 biplanes, he was accused of attempting to sabotage the aviation industry following crashes of his I-6 and DI-2 prototype aircraft. Although the waves of arrests ebbed and flowed in accordance with the arbitrary political tides, by the end of the decade

---

[20] See the testimony of visiting engineer N. A. Sokolov to officials of the Douglas Company in NARA Record Group 72, Box 187, Folder EF 61/A14-2, vol. 2.

[21] See RGAE f. 9527, op. 1, d. 665 (Materialy o razvitii grazhdanskogo vozdushnogo flota v 1935 – 1937 gg.) and d. 802 (Perepiska s SNK i STO SSSR i drugimi organizatsiiami ob opytnom stroitel'stve samoletov dlia nuzhd GVF) and below, pp. 205 and 209–12.

[22] Ronald Grigor Suny, *The Soviet Experiment: Russia, the USSR, and the Successor States* (New York: Oxford University Press, 1998), 235–7.

few of the country's top aviation engineers had escaped the attention of the security organs. Only the state's desperate need for these highly skilled technicians spared their lives. To ensure that they continued to contribute to the construction of socialism, they were transferred to special penal workshops [*sharagy*] overseen by the OGPU. There, political prisoners labored alongside free employees designing the next generation of Soviet aircraft.[23]

THE AIRPLANE-COLOSSUS

Institutionalized dependence on the West, inefficiency, and the incarceration of innocents were not the only characteristics of Soviet aviation culture. Another was a marked propensity to produce oversized aircraft. The ANT-9 and ANT-4 that flew to Europe and the United States in 1929 were but the first in a series of increasingly large planes to emerge from Stalin's Soviet Union. Spearheaded by the country's leading constructor Andrei Tupolev, design bureaus rapidly expanded the size and cargo capacity of their airframes during the 1930s. Most incorporated major features clearly derived from German Junkers' models. In this respect the new airplanes demonstrated the developing skill of Soviet specialists in adapting foreign models to meet native requirements through add-on engineering, albeit without breaking new technological ground.

Even before the first ANT-4 had flown, plans were drawn up to begin work on the next big airplane, the ANT-6 (TB-3). A larger, four-engine version of the ANT-4, the ANT-6 typified the contemporary Soviet practice of simply enlarging the wing, chassis, tail section, cockpit, and engine-propeller units from a previously manufactured plane to produce a "new" model.[24] A similar process was used to develop the five-engine ANT-14 and the six-engine ANT-16 (TB-4). The design of these two aerial giants called for increasing the size of the earlier ANT-6 by around fifty percent and attaching additional motors to compensate for the added weight.[25] The progressive growth in the dimensions of these aircraft demonstrated not only the Soviet fetish with size, but with tempos as well. Under intense pressure from Party officials, the prototype ANT-14 was rushed to completion two-and-a-half months ahead of schedule. State officials heralded its appearance on 14 August 1931 as a "deeply symbolic victory" indicative of the speed and skill with which the Soviet Union had mastered aviation. According to Valentin Zarzar, the plane "demonstrates that we lead the world in airplane construction and have conquered technique in one of the most decisive arenas of aerofication.

---

[23] L. L. Kerber, *Stalin's Aviation Gulag: A Memoir of Andrei Tupolev and the Purge Era*. Edited by Von Hardesty (Washington, D.C.: Smithsonian Institution Press, 1996).

[24] *Ibid.*, 82.

[25] A. M. Shabota, "Vospominaniia o Sigizmunde Aleksandroviche Levanevskom," 26. (Unpublished manuscript in possession of author.)

FIGURE 39. The ANT-14 *Pravda*.

It demonstrates that the technical revolution realized in our air fleet is based on *our* accomplishments."[26] The symbolism was tempered only by reality. The hastily finished ANT-14 still lacked an intercom system enabling the pilot to communicate with the crew, and the absence of requisite wiring prevented the illumination of the plane's interior. Meanwhile, the aircraft's central engine was lost to malfunction during its maiden flight. As late as mid-September the overworked engineers at TsAGI had "done nothing to ensure that these defects would be quickly repaired in order that the aircraft could begin to operate not only in principle, but also in fact [*ne tol'ko na slovakh, no na dele*]."[27]

The colossalist impulse in aviation mirrored broader trends in Stalinist culture. Like large-scale construction projects that marshaled the forces of nature by damming rivers or forging new waterways, huge airplanes bespoke the Party's ability to conquer the heavens and the earth through the application of technology. Grandiose icons of dawning socialist modernity, they legitimated both the Party's vision and the methods chosen to effect its realization. Intended to overshadow similar aircraft constructed abroad, the "airplane-giants" [*samolety-giganty*] suggested that the Soviet Union was already surpassing its capitalist enemies. The planes provided striking evidence of the country's ability to exceed, literally, standards

[26] V. Zarzar, "ANT-14," *Krasnaia niva* 24 (30 August 1931): 5–6. Emphasis in the original.
[27] RGAE f. 9527, op. 1, d. 266 (Perepiska s SNK i STO SSSR o khode kapital'nogo stroitel'stva i raport o dosrochnoi postroike samoleta ANT-14), l. 190.

established by western aeronautical powers. What the airplanes lacked in technical refinement they made up for in sheer mass. Intended to impress, yet crude and derivative, they were quintessential exemplars of compensatory symbolism.

The Party's vested interest in producing prestige aircraft was not the only factor that influenced the direction of airplane design. The construction of aerial giants also accorded with contemporary Soviet military doctrine. Even more than their counterparts in the West, Soviet leaders were keenly interested in the arguments advanced by Giulio Douhet's 1921 treatise, *The Command of the Air*. The officer in charge of the first aerial bombardment in history and, later, head of Fascist Italy's aviation program, Douhet postulated that the airplane would play the decisive role in future international conflicts. By using aircraft to strike targets deep behind enemy lines, a combatant nation could visit immense devastation on the industrial and military infrastructures of its enemies, disrupting the daily lives of citizens, and destroying their morale en route to a rapid victory.[28] To achieve these ends Douhet advocated the construction of huge fleets of long-range bombers, capable of commanding the air and delivering explosive, incendiary, and chemical weapons in enormous quantities. These ideas exerted considerable influence in shaping the Soviet military's approach to aviation. Throughout the late 1920s and 1930s, prominent Soviet officials echoed Douhet in forecasting the important role of strategic bombing in future campaigns. Perhaps none was more influential than Vasilii Khripin. A Red Air Fleet commander during the Civil War and author of the introduction to the Russian translation of *The Command of the Air*, Khripin was an early and vocal advocate of the importance of heavy bombers. As head of the Operational Section of the GU VVS during the mid-1920s and, later, as deputy director of the VVS under Iakov Alksnis, he put his theories into practice, overseeing the construction of the Special Purpose Aviation Army, the world's first strategic bomber force. By 1936 Khripin could boast that bombers comprised upward of sixty percent of the expanding Red Air Force.[29]

The Soviet military's infatuation with Douhet's theories and the Party's abiding interest in exploiting aviation to obtain political legitimacy explain the propensity of Soviet design bureaus to pursue the development and production of oversized aircraft. As both symbols of state authority and as means of exerting that authority through the rhetorical and real conduct of war, the airplane-giants fulfilled mutually compatible missions. The large, heavy bombers believed capable of delivering payloads deep behind enemy

---

[28] Giulio Douhet, *The Command of the Air*. Translated by Dino Ferrari (New York: Coward-McCann, 1942), 57–8.

[29] Reina Pennington, "From Chaos to the Eve of the Great Patriotic War, 1922–41," in Higham *et al.* (eds.), *Russian Aviation*, 43–4, and Boyd, *Soviet Air Force*, 57–8.

lines were also seen as ideal instruments for waging ideological warfare on the international stage. Magnified by the Stalinist propensity toward excess, the size of Soviet aircraft would quickly reach colossal proportions.

On 17 September 1932, more than 100 delegates representing thirty-nine periodicals gathered in Moscow to commemorate the fortieth anniversary of the writer and social activist Maxim Gorky. One after another, speakers rose to honor the accomplishments of the well-known writer and to praise his ability to raise social consciousness through his literary works. Encouraged by editors from the popular journal *Ogonek*, the delegates proposed to honor Gorky by constructing a giant new aircraft that would bear the writer's name. Following the unanimous ratification of a resolution calling for the aeronautical monument, the attendees concluded their meeting by forming a "Special Committee" to oversee a voluntary donation drive that would raise funds for the plane's construction.[30] The committee was immediately successful. Within three days of its formation it had collected more than 400,000 rubles in support of the project.[31]

The airplane envisioned by the delegates at the Moscow meeting was intended to serve the dual functions expected of all *agit-samolety*: It would be both bearer and symbol of Party-mandated enlightenment. To assist in fulfilling its mission, the *Maxim Gorky* would be equipped with an array of the Soviet Union's "most recent technological achievements," including a typography, telephone switchboard, photographic laboratory, and a radio transmitting station capable of beaming broadcasts along the air routes it would fly. In addition, the *Maxim Gorky* would include a motion-picture projector to enable Party activists to screen propaganda films for the largely illiterate peasant audiences they routinely encountered. On the underside of its wings, rows of built-in lights would allow the aircrew to transmit electronic text messages to the earthbound citizens over whom the plane flew.[32] As the ultimate propaganda weapon, the *Maxim Gorky* would serve as the flagship of a new agit-squadron once it emerged from the assembly line on 1 May 1934. Continuing in the tradition of the 1920s, the new squadron would travel throughout the Soviet Union bearing news of the advances made by

---

[30] The Special Committee was composed of sixty-nine luminaries from Soviet political, cultural, and technical fields and included such prominent figures as Nikolai Bukharin, Karl Radek, Mikhail Tomskii, Aleksei Tolstoi, and Andrei Tupolev. RGAE f. 9527, op. 1, d. 370 (Resoliutsiia obshchego sobraniia redaktsionnykh i literaturnykh rabotnikov 39 zhurnalov i gazet Zhurnal'no-Gazetnogo Ob"edineniia sostoiashchegosia 17 IX 1932 g.), ll. 2–3 and RGAE f. 9527, op. 1, d. 385 (Resoliutsiia obshchego sobraniia redaktsionnykh i literaturnykh rabotnikov 39 zhurnalov i gazet Zhurnal'no-Gazetnogo Ob"edineniia sostoiashchegosia 17 IX 1932 g.).

[31] "Gigant-samolet 'Maksim Gor'kii,'" *Ogonek* 28 (20 September 1932): 1.

[32] RGAE, f. 9527, op. 1, d. 517 (O eskadrilia "M. Gor'kogo"; vyrezki iz gazet; besedy nachal'nika GUGVF s predstaviteliami sovetskoi pechati), l. 1.

the Party and rallying the populace to support the construction of socialism. In the interim, the "Maxim Gorky Agitational Squadron," consisting of five airplanes and a dirigible, began work in earnest to raise public donations for the ANT-20.[33]

Aside from providing the Party with an additional tool with which to enlighten its citizenry, the *Maxim Gorky* was supposed to symbolize the tremendous strides made by Soviet science and technology. Although airplanes had served for two decades as markers of modernity and national strength, proponents of the *Maxim Gorky* made clear their intention that this craft would be much more than just another airplane. The world's largest and most politically advanced state demanded the world's largest and most technologically advanced airplane: a flying monument to the skill of the country's workers and the enlightened leadership of party officials. In short, "the plane would not only be of gigantic size and possess tremendous lift capacity, but it would also be of high enough quality to reflect all of our recent accomplishments in aviation technology. In all of its flying specifications and internal equipment, it would be the best built plane to date."[34]

The design and construction of so large a plane presented a host of challenges to the TsAGI engineers and technicians charged with fulfilling the order. Initial estimates indicated that the fifty-nine-ton, 112-foot-long, eight-engine behemoth would cost more than 5 million rubles and require some 750,000 hours of labor to complete.[35] As the nation lacked appropriate facilities to accommodate such an enormous aircraft, the *Maxim Gorky* was constructed at the TsAGI workshops and then partially dismantled for transportation to the Moscow aerodrome for reassembly. Time was also a factor. In keeping with the Soviet propensity of forcing the tempo of industrial projects, the resolution calling for the construction of the *Maxim Gorky* demanded that the plane be built in the shortest time possible.[36] In the end, TsAGI was given just over eighteen months to deliver the aircraft to Party officials.

The *Maxim Gorky* was unveiled to the public on 19 June 1934. It appeared over Red Square as part of the festivities celebrating the return of the *Cheliuskin* expedition whose members had been rescued from an ice floe after several months of arctic isolation.[37] The airplane-giant provided an

---

[33] RGAE, f. 9527, op. 1, d. 517, ll. 106–107. The squadron included the ANT-14 (by now christened *Pravda*), an ANT-9, Stal'-2, U-2, and G-1 aircraft. A V-3 dirigible was scheduled to join the squadron at a later date, following its construction.

[34] *Ibid.*, l. 3.

[35] RGAE, f. 9527, op. 1, d. 371 (Protokol zasedaniia Vsesoiuznogo Komiteta po postroike agit-samoleta "Maksim Gor'kii"), l. 6.

[36] RGAE, f. 9527, op. 1, d. 370 (Materialy o sozdanii fonda dlia sooruzheniia agitatsionnogo samolete "Maksim Gor'kii"), l. 3.

[37] For details on the *Cheliuskin* rescue, see the subsequent discussion on p. 221.

FIGURE 40. The ANT-20 *Maxim Gorky* under construction, 1933.

awesome spectacle for the tens of thousands of citizens who gathered to observe the celebration. The decorated flier Mikhail Gromov piloted the craft on its maiden flight. He waxed rhapsodic in fulsome praise of the airplane. "Seized by an unforgettable feeling of peace and pride in [the Soviet] victory over the earth, the ice, and the air," Gromov proclaimed his experience at the helm "the happiest day of my life" and noted that the quality and workmanship of the nation's new plane testified to the tremendous advances recently accomplished by proletarian industry.[38] Not surprisingly, the plane's debut also met with a rapturous response from the nation's press. For weeks on end leading publications printed articles enumerating the plane's technical specifications and capabilities and retelling the story of its construction. The journal *Ogonek* went so far as to devote its entire 5 July issue to the *Maxim Gorky* and its meaning to Soviet culture.

Foreign observers were not as smitten with the plane. First Lieutenant Thomas D. White, assistant military attaché for the U.S. Army present in Moscow in the summer of 1934, was particularly critical. In a report to American military authorities he cast aspersions on Soviet claims of having constructed the world's most modern and technically advanced airplane,

[38] M. Gromov, "Izumitel'naia mashina!," *Pravda*, 21 June 1934.

FIGURE 41. The *Maxim Gorky* on display over Red Square, 1934.

noting that the all-metal cantilever wing monoplane was merely an over-sized edition of prior ANT-type aircraft. As it appeared to have simply been assembled on the basis of blueprints from previously existing aircraft, the plane represented no great engineering advance. This fact, White noted, was of considerable importance for it explained the short period required for planning and constructing the airplane. More disconcerting than the short-cuts taken in designing the *Maxim Gorky* were many indications of poor workmanship and shoddy construction techniques. The plane was "unbelievably ponderous in construction. Even the tail wheel is made of steel filled with cement."[39]

The problems apparent with the *Maxim Gorky* project did not end with the design and construction of the airplane-giant. The new aeronautical squadron organized to provide the ANT-20 with an operational base was proving chronically inept. Despite the Party's claims of having triumphed over technique, the enterprise was plagued by appalling disorder. In the months preceding the debut of the *Maxim Gorky*, reports from the agit-squadron's field commander complained that routine mechanical

[39] NARA, "Correspondence of the Military Intelligence Division Relating to General, Political, Economic, and Military Conditions in Russia and the Soviet Union, 1918–1941" (Microfilm Publication M1443), MID 2090, roll 20, frame 188.

FIGURE 42. Pilot Ivan Mikheev at the helm of the *Maxim Gorky* during one of the airplane's demonstration flights. Photo: The David King Collection, London.

breakdowns, slapdash organization, inadequate repair facilities, and constant shortages of fuel and essential spare parts seriously interfered with the squadron's activities. The circumstances surrounding operations were so poor that, owing to an absence of hangars, all of the squadron's airplanes were stored out in the open.[40] The lack of properly trained personnel and all-too-infrequent maintenance contributed to a growing number of accidents. The most serious occurred on 5 September 1933, claiming the lives of Abram Gol'tsman, head of GUGVF, GosPlan's Valentin Zarzar, and Glavaviaprom chief Pavel Baranov. The following spring, the squadron suffered through a particularly serious bout of incompetence that saw five airplanes crash in fewer than four months. Although the number of aircraft assigned to the Maxim Gorky Squadron expanded to twenty-three by the winter of 1934–5, owing to continuing accidents and mechanical failures only half of these were typically available for use.[41] Given these persistent problems it is easy to question the wisdom of devoting such an inordinate amount of labor and resources to the production a single aircraft. Perhaps the most telling indication of misplaced priorities surfaced on 22 June 1934. On that date, three days after the public debut of the *Maxim Gorky*, *Pravda* announced the inauguration of a new voluntary subscription campaign to raise funds for the construction of a hangar large enough to house the airplane-giant.[42]

Criticism of Soviet leaders' short-sightedness should not, however, overlook the broader social and political considerations that motivated the construction of the ANT-20. The *Maxim Gorky* concerned much more than merely affirming the capabilities of Soviet aviation technology. The campaign was intended to unite the country's citizenry behind a collective cause while legitimating the authority and policies of Party leaders. As was true of every aeronautical project undertaken since the early 1920s, the *Maxim Gorky* provided a façade of popular legitimacy for the Soviet regime by demonstrating the scientific basis of the Party's political hegemony.[43] From the inauguration of the campaign in September 1932 to the debut of the aircraft in June 1934 (and beyond), Party officials and press organs heralded the ANT-20 as proof of the Soviet leadership's technical prowess. The construction of the airplane validated the industrial policies pursued under Stalin. It demonstrated the extent to which the country had developed "under the glorious banner of socialism."[44] As the largest, "most technically advanced" airplane in the world, the *Maxim Gorky* provided material evidence that the Soviet Union was overtaking its capitalist rivals. Its appearance intimated that the attainment of the Communist kingdom was soon to follow.

[40] RGAE, f. 9527, op. 1, d. 654 (Doklady nachal'nika glavnoi inspektsii o rabote agiteskadril'ia), l. 37.

[41] The agit-squadron's woes are chronicled in RGAE f. 9576, op. 1, d. 5 (Materialy o rabote eskadril'ia, 1933–1936).

[42] "Postroim bazu dlia 'Maksima Gor'kogo,'" *Pravda*, 22 June 1934.

[43] Kendall Bailes, *Technology and Society Under Lenin and Stalin: Origins of the Soviet Technical Intelligentsia, 1917–1941* (Princeton, NJ: Princeton University Press, 1978), 383–4.

[44] "Rozhdenie giganta," *Pravda*, 21 June 1934.

FIGURE 43. An informational and fund-raising kiosk sponsored by the Special Committee for the Construction of the Airplane-Giant *Maxim Gorky* located on Pushkin Square in Moscow, 1932.

Still, the *Maxim Gorky* was more than a technical triumph. The aircraft was also meant to demonstrate the unique and unrivaled cohesion said to characterize Soviet society. A "great victory of the Soviet community [*obshchestvennost'*]," the plane was an "expression of the collective will of the people and the Party."[45] United behind a common cause under the guidance of the Party, the Soviet people had acted as one – contributing to the construction of the airplane-giant through participation in the union-wide voluntary subscription campaign. The unity allegedly fostered by the *Maxim Gorky* was the subject of a revealing article written by the well-known journalist Mikhail Kol'tsov. Published by *Pravda* in the wake of the airplane's debut and subsequently reprinted in other periodicals, the piece celebrated the airplane as the collective embodiment of the Party and the people. Noting that the construction of the airplane-giant was possible only in the proletarian state where "labor is a deed of honor, a deed of glory, a deed of valor and heroism," Kol'tsov paid homage to the plane's advanced technical features, the wisdom of the Party, and the policy of central planning. Still, he noted, the construction of the airplane was possible only because of the effort

---

[45] "'Maksim Gor'kii' letaet!," *Komsomol'skaia pravda*, 21 June 1934 and "Sovetskaia obshchestvennost' stroit Maksim Gor'kii," *Ogonek* 29 (20 October 1932): 11.

that "we" had undertaken. But "who," he asked rhetorically, "is we?" The answer to this question took the form of a two-page litany:

We – this is Andrei Nikolaevich Tupolev, one of the brightest and most talented minds of Soviet technology . . . We – this is Komsomol member Petia from Syzranskii *raion* who sent in eight rubles [for the construction of the plane] . . . We – this is the constructors of TsAGI who labored with Tupolev . . . We – this is the party, Soviet military and writers collective that helped to build the plane . . . We – this is the many millions of the best reading, writing, thinking and working Soviet people who endeavored to build the agit-plane-giant . . . We – this is Klim Voroshilov, blacksmith of our military might and Sergo Ordzhonikidze, the builder of the greatest industry in the world – Soviet industry . . . We – this is great Stalin, the constructor and engineer of classless, socialist society, the leader of the Leninist party, the bold and solicitous teacher of our country's narod, who instructs us to move ever forward.[46]

Parroting the liturgical tone often adopted by Stalin in his speeches before Party gatherings, Kol'tsov's article used the repetitive, rhetorical style of the Orthodox litany to convey in personal, quasi-spiritual terms, the significance of the *Maxim Gorky* to Soviet society.[47] The language underscored the campaign's intent to cultivate a shared sense of community through the creation of a common point of reference.[48]

Like the medieval cathedrals that were believed by contemporaries to unite heaven and earth in glorifying God, the *Maxim Gorky* was intended to be a glorious expression of the Party's grandeur and its unity with the people. It was to serve as a secular site of worship, providing the Soviet Union's militantly atheistic, materialist leaders with a focal point around which might be organized new social rituals. A grandiose, new link in the great chain of Communist becoming, the airship behemoth functioned, both symbolically and materially, in a manner identical to the sacred buildings of the Orthodox faith. Like a Christian church, whose architecture (in consciously recalling an ark or ship) revealed its emblematic function of spiritually transporting the faithful to heaven, the *Maxim Gorky* promised to transport the nation into the utopian Other World. It was an example of the faith made flesh (or, in any event, steel, glass, and rubber); a physical manifestation of the Party's spirit of industry whose creation would advance believers closer to their socialist paradise.

---

[46] "Kak my eto delaem," *Pravda* 21 June 1934. The same article also appeared in *Ogonek* 15 (20 August 1934): 5–7. The introduction of each component of the national collective was followed by a two- to three-sentence description of the contributions made to the plane by the named individual or group.

[47] Lev Kopelev, *Education of a True Believer*. Translated by Gart Kern (New York: Harper & Row, 1980), 262, and Robert Conquest, *Stalin: Breaker of Nations* (New York: Penguin, 1991), 109.

[48] Jeffrey Brooks, *Thank You, Comrade Stalin!: Soviet Popular Culture from Revolution to Cold War* (Princeton, NJ: Princeton University Press, 2001), 147.

FIGURE 44. "The readers and workers of the Party-Soviet press have given six million rubles for the construction of the airplane-giant *Maxim Gorky*." Postcard, 1934.

The communal, quasi-spiritual sentiments associated with the ANT-20 by writers like Kol'tsov were subsequently echoed in letters and telegrams sent by private citizens to the country's leaders and leading periodicals. Proclaiming their pride in having contributed to the construction of the "miraculous [*chudesnoi*] peaceful giant," writers acknowledged their personal attachment to "our dear Maxim" and pledged to support Party efforts to build still more steel birds that would "rule over our land."[49] Whether such messages reflected individuals' honest responses or were merely ritualistic expressions calculated to appease authorities remains, of course, open to debate. Given the importance of collectivist visions in Russians' everyday efforts to construct a sense of self, it would seem that citizens' correspondence regarding the *Maxim Gorky* reflected the sincere desire of ordinary men and women to derive personal meaning through participation in an extraordinary common cause.[50] Such considerations certainly influenced Party leaders' attempts

---

[49] RGAE, f. 9527, op. 1, d. 804 (Kopii pisem i telegram o sobleznovanii v sviazi gibel'iu samoleta im. M. Gor'kogo), *et passim*.

[50] Mark D. Steinberg, "The Injured and Insurgent Self: The Moral Imagination of Russia's Lower-Class Writers," in Reginald Zelnik (ed.), *Workers and Intelligentsia in Late Imperial Russia* (Berkeley, CA: University of California Press, 1999), 309–29.

to derive legitimacy from the project by framing it within the rhetoric of community.

If the *Maxim Gorky* served to legitimate the Party by fostering a sense of self and community, it also worked to detract attention from the underlying failures of the Soviet system. As citizens sacrificed their rubles and kopecks to support the construction of the aerial giant, millions of peasants paid a far dearer price. The campaign to build the ANT-20 coincided with the outbreak of a murderous famine. Academic debates regarding their intent aside, Party officials were directly responsible for the events that transpired between 1932 and 1933.[51] Amid falling agricultural prices on the international market and declining domestic output occasioned by collectivization, Soviet leaders embarked on a rapacious campaign to squeeze the countryside in order to fund their increasingly grandiose industrial projects. As the state dumped grain on a glutted world market, Soviet cities began rationing and peasants began to starve. The famine reached its brutal heights in early 1933. Even as men and women resorted to eating dogs and rats, bark and grass, mortality rates continued to rise. Disease and epidemic soon followed. So too did madness, suicide, and cannibalism.[52] By the end of the year, upward of 7 million had fallen victim. Tragically and ironically, airplanes abetted these deaths. Advertised in the mid-1920s as bearers of cultural enlightenment and economic prosperity to the provinces, they facilitated the murder and immiseration of millions as officials eagerly dispatched agit-crews to rural areas in order to promote the hastening of grain procurement tempos. In 1933, thirteen of the Maxim Gorky Squadron's twenty propaganda tours took place in the Ukraine, the Northern Caucasus, and the lower Volga, precisely those regions hardest hit by the famine.[53]

Still, even death could be turned to the state's political advantage, as demonstrated when disaster struck the *Maxim Gorky*. On 18 May 1935 the airplane participated in a public flyover at the Moscow aerodrome. As usual for exhibitions involving the ANT-20, two Polikarpov biplanes flew on either side of the *Maxim Gorky* to provide symmetry and scale for the

---

[51] The standard account of the 1932–3 famine is Robert Conquest, *Harvest of Sorrow: Soviet Collectivization and the Terror-Famine* (New York: Oxford University Press, 1986). Conquest argues that the famine in Ukraine was intentionally orchestrated by the Soviet regime in order to suppress nationalism in the region. More recently, "revisionist" historians have sought to absolve Stalin and the Soviet government from charges of intentional genocide by arguing that the famine resulted from an unavoidable confluence of factors including poor weather and the unintended chaos resulting from the state's disastrous agricultural policies. For this viewpoint, see Mark Tauger, "The 1932 Harvest and the Famine of 1933," *Slavic Review* 50:1 (Spring 1990), 70–89 and, more recently, R. W. Davies and Stephen G. Wheatcroft, *The Years of Hunger: Soviet Agriculture, 1931–1933* (New York: Palgrave Macmillan, 2004).

[52] Catherine Merridale, *Night of Stone: Death and Memory in Twentieth-Century Russia* (New York: Penguin, 2000), 170.

[53] RGAE, f. 9576, op. 1, d. 5, l. 27.

FIGURE 45. Moments before disaster. Pilot Ivan Blagin attempts to complete an unauthorized aerial loop in proximity to the ANT-20 *Maxim Gorky*. 18 May 1935. Photo: The David King Collection, London.

citizens and Party officials gathered below. Despite express orders prohibiting stunt maneuvers near the vicinity of the aerial giant, Ivan Blagin, the pilot at the helm of one of the escort planes, endeavored to complete a loop around the ANT-20. As Blagin exited from the loop, his plane slammed into the *Maxim Gorky*, lodging in its port wing. The giant airplane shuddered and then spun out of control. The behemoth plunged to earth, breaking up into several pieces before crashing in the suburb of Sokol, not far from the aerodrome. The plane was completely destroyed. Compounding the disaster was the fact that in addition to its regular eleven-man crew, the *Maxim Gorky* had carried aloft thirty-six shock workers from TsAGI. The death toll stood at forty-eight (including Blagin). The victims of the crash were honored with a public funeral on 20 May. Their cremated remains lay in state in Moscow's Hall of Columns from 11:00 A.M. until 4:00 P.M. while a crowd of more than 100,000 citizens paid their last respects to the "fallen heroes."[54] Following the visitation, the forty-seven urns containing the ashes of the deceased (accompanied by leading Soviet officials and an honor guard of 5,000 aviation workers) were transported to the cemetery located on the grounds of the city's Novodeivichyi Monastery. There they were laid to rest

[54] "Poslednee proshchanie," *Krest'ianskaia gazeta*, 21 May 1935.

ДА ЗДРАВСТВУЕТ НАША СЧАСТЛИВАЯ СОЦИАЛИСТИЧЕСКАЯ РОДИНА. ДА ЗДРАВСТВУЕТ НАШ ЛЮБИМЫЙ ВЕЛИКИЙ СТАЛИН!

FIGURE 46. Gustav Klutsis, "Long live our happy socialist motherland and long live our beloved and great STALIN!" In this poster from the mid-1930s, a squadron of ANT-20s emblazoned with the names of Party leaders flies over Red Square. Photo: The David King Collection, London.

beneath a tremendous granite relief of the airplane. A large plate attached to the monastery wall commemorated the accident and condemned the man who caused it.

Characteristically, the concerns of political utility and social unity that had prompted the creation of the *Maxim Gorky* did not diminish with the airplane's crash. In the immediate aftermath of the accident, the Party launched a campaign to raise citizens' awareness of the need for "iron discipline" and to urge them to fight against the "hooliganism" and "anarchism" displayed by the disgraced Blagin.[55] In addition, it quickly began a new subscription drive to replace the lost aircraft by raising funds for the construction of three new ANT-20s (to be named the *Vladimir Lenin, Josef Stalin*, and *Maxim Gorky II*).[56] Within days, workers passed resolutions and sent in donations calling for the creation of "an entire squadron of airplane-giants" that would include aircraft dedicated to Sergo Ordzhonikidze, Klim Voroshilov, Mikhail Kalinin, and other Party luminaries.[57] In the end, however, the sum of this effort proved unequal to its parts. Although a second ANT-20 would finally appear in 1939, it did so without the celebratory fanfare accorded the original. The slow-moving ponderous aircraft was limited to service as a civilian transport plane, ferrying passengers and cargo between Moscow and the Northern Caucasus. Transferred to Tashkent following the German invasion in June 1941, the *Maxim Gorky* twin met an ironic fate. On 14 December 1942, the aircraft crashed as a result of pilot error, claiming the lives of twenty-six passengers and ten crewmen.[58]

STALIN'S ROUTE

The creation, display, and destruction of the *Maxim Gorky* took place against the backdrop of a paradigmatic shift in Soviet culture that would profoundly influence official representations of aviation for the remainder of the decade. Between the spring of 1932 and the summer of 1934, the Party embarked on a series of measures designed to mobilize the country's writers, painters, sculptors, and musicians to assist in the tasks of socialist construction. Administratively, the mobilization drive led to the formation of new professional unions, one of which was created for each branch of the arts. The new unions

---

[55] "Chernaia molniia," *Izvestiia*, 20 May 1935; "Korabliu i liudiam," *Izvestiia*, 20 May 1935; and "Za ditsiplinu i bezavariinost'," *Krest'ianskaia gazeta*, 21 May 1935, among many others.

[56] RGAE f. 9527, op. 1, d. 804, l. 4.

[57] See, "'Vladimir Lenin,' 'Iosif Stalin,' 'Maksim Gor'kii' postroim v kratchaishii srok – takov otvet millionov" *Pravda*, 21 May 1935; "Prizyv millionov," *Krest'ianskaia gazeta*, 24 May 1935; "Postroim eskadril'iu gigantov," *Samolet* 100 (June 1935): 2–3; and "Pust' podymutsia nad sovetskoi zemlei novye moshchnye samolety podobnye 'Maksimu Gor'komu,'" *Sovetskii Sibir'*, 23 May 1935, among others.

[58] Dmitrii Sobolev, "Tragediia 'Maksima Gor'kogo'," *Rodina* 8 (August 2004): 54.

were designed to provide Party leaders with bureaucratic mechanisms for controlling artistic production across the entirety of the Soviet Union. As membership in the appropriate union was mandatory for those who sought official recognition as "cultural workers" (and the accompanying stipends that subsidized "cultural work"), Party officials were able to ensure creative uniformity and enforce ideological purity by expelling those who did not adhere to politically correct fashions and form.

Artistically, the new line on culture also meant the imposition of "socialist realism," an official style of representation first applied to literature but quickly extended to include all creative genres. According to official spokesmen, socialist realism demanded that art portray daily life "in its revolutionary development." Combining the "truthfulness and historical concreteness of artistic depiction" with "the task of ideological transformation," socialist realist productions embodied a "revolutionary romanticism" that sought to remodel and reeducate the working masses in the spirit of socialism.[59] In other words, socialist realist art depicted reality not as it really was but as it *would be*, following the attainment of socialism. Incorporating elements of realism and romanticism with folkloric tropes and religious motifs, socialist realism produced dogmatically determined art that eschewed experimentation with content or form. What this meant in practice was that a new artistic orthodoxy emerged in which "everyone behaved as he was supposed to according to Stalinist ideology: the workers were enthusiastic about their tasks, the enemy vicious, cowardly and ever-present; and the Party always emerged victorious in every contest." Irony, contradiction, and unscripted conflict all were eradicated in favor of a grand "master narrative" that accorded with the Party's prevailing worldview.[60]

More immediately, socialist realism served Party interests by creating "positive heroes" who could serve as models for the country's ordinary citizens. Exemplars of socialist rectitude and forbearance, positive heroes were paradigmatic expressions of the "New Soviet Person," individuals whose exploits advanced the collective cause of socialism by contributing to the well-being of the country as a whole. The emergence of positive heroes under the rubric of socialist realism stood in sharp contrast to the cult of the machine that had dominated Soviet culture during the period of the first FYP. Whereas earlier, technological creations such as blast furnaces, tractors, and airplane-giants had been treated more heroically than the humans who operated them, from 1932 onward technology was subordinated to its human masters as the state sought to motivate citizens by providing them iconic figures to emulate.

The institutionalization of positive heroism was given material impetus during the winter of 1933–4 as Soviet citizens watched with rapt attention

---

[59] Andrei Zhdanov cited in Suny, *Soviet Experiment*, 270.

[60] Kenez, *History of the Soviet Union*, 124, and Katerina Clark, *The Soviet Novel: History as Ritual* (Chicago: University of Chicago Press, 1981).

the events surrounding the icebreaker *Cheliuskin*. Dispatched beyond the Arctic Circle with a contingent of scientists for the ostensible purpose of identifying a navigable northern sea route, the ship became trapped in ice following the onset of winter. Abandoning the vessel as its hull collapsed, the expedition's members were forced to bivouac on an ice floe for two months. The crisis was finally resolved in early April 1934 when seven pilots, led by Mikhail Vodopianov and Sigizmund Levanevskii, completed a series of daring airlifts that rescued the stranded "Cheliuskintsy" from their encampment. In recognition of the fliers' contribution, the "seven bold ones" were named the first "Heroes of the Soviet Union" in a Kremlin ceremony on 16 April.[61]

The further cultivation of positive heroes required more than mere slogans. If the country's industry could overcome temporal constraints through the rapid manufacture of airplane-giants, then Soviet aviators would be required to conquer both time and space through daring exploits designed to showcase the discipline, heroism, and endurance of which Soviet citizens were uniquely capable. In the aftermath of the *Maxim Gorky* catastrophe Party leaders set out to match deeds to rhetoric by orchestrating a series of record-setting flights intended not only to highlight the technical acuity of the Soviet aviation industry but, more important, to draw attention to the Soviet Union's flying cadres. These prestige displays would bring the Soviet Union's aviation program international renown and would elevate aviators ever higher within the pantheon of positive socialist heroes.

Unfortunately, the new campaign to raise the profile of the country's flying cadres got off to an inauspicious start. On 3 August 1935, a three-man crew consisting of Sigizmund Levanevskii (pilot), Georgii Baidukov (copilot), and Vasilii Levchenko (navigator) departed Moscow in an attempt to establish a new-world distance record. Flying aboard an ANT-25 monoplane, the crew endeavored to complete an 11,000-mile nonstop flight between the Soviet capital and San Francisco, California. The choice of the American destination was significant as it underscored Soviet leaders' continuing efforts to cultivate ties with the United States and its aviation manufacturers. As if to reinforce these sentiments, American Ambassador William C. Bullitt was invited to accompany Klimet Voroshilov, Red Air Force Chief Iakov Alksnis, the head of TsAGI Nikolai Kharlamov, Andrei Tupolev, and other dignitaries who gathered to bid the fliers farewell on the aerodrome tarmac.[62] The flight also pointed to the "myth of the Arctic" as a prominent feature of contemporary Soviet culture. In addition to establishing a new world record, the chosen

---

[61] For the authoritative account of the *Cheliuskin* expedition and rescue, see John McCannon, *Red Arctic: Polar Exploration and the Myth of the North in Soviet Russia, 1932–1939* (New York: Oxford University Press, 1998). The adventure served as the basis for numerous documentary and several feature films including the 1936 Lenfil'm release *The Seven Bold Ones* [*Semero smelykh*].

[62] Shabota, "Vospominaniia," 32.

route would carry the crew over the North Pole, thus realizing another Soviet goal: history's first transpolar airplane flight. The record-setting attempt was accompanied by considerable fanfare. In the week leading up to the flight crew's departure, Soviet press organs broadcast news of the impending event to readers throughout the country. Gamely forecasting the success of the endeavor, *Izvestiia* optimistically intoned that "the unprecedented flight will write a new page in the history of Soviet aviation."[63] Party leaders were so confident that the mission would succeed that they approved the release of a postal stamp commemorating the event in advance of the crew's departure.[64] The decision proved premature.

Twelve-hundred miles into the journey, as the ANT-25 was passing over the Barents Sea, Levanevskii was alerted to the presence of oil issuing from the aircraft's lone engine. A common enough occurrence for contemporary aircraft, the oil leak was dismissed as insignificant by copilot Georgii Baidukov. Noting that the plane's temperature and pressure gauges were registering normally, he attributed the leak to excess oil being discharged by a breather especially designed for that purpose. Well acquainted with the aircraft owing to his involvement in its extensive preflight tests, Baidukov counseled that the mission continue as planned. Levanevskii radioed headquarters in Moscow.[65] What transpired next is not entirely clear. According to Anatolii Shabota, the chief mechanic selected by Levanevskii to supervise work on the ANT-25's engine, following a series of exchanges between the pilot and mission control, the airplane was ordered to turn back.[66] Others recall that the decision to abort the mission was made by Levanevskii, in contravention of the recommendations wired him from Moscow. According to Baidukov, a heated exchange quickly erupted between him and his pilot. As Levanevskii reached for his pistol, Baidukov relented, "realizing at that moment that things might end very badly."[67]

That evening, the plane landed at an airfield not far from Novgorod. There, Levanevskii, Baidukov, and Levchenko surrendered their log books to awaiting NKVD officers.[68] The following morning, the crew was interviewed by

---

[63] "Rekordy dal'nosti," *Izvestiia*, 1 August 1935.

[64] Iu. A. Kaminskii, *Kremlevskie perelety* (Moscow: Zhurnalistskoe agenstvo "Glasnost'," 1998), 49.

[65] Kerber, *Stalin's Aviation Gulag*, 118.

[66] Shabota, "Vospominaniia," 35–6.

[67] Kaminskii, *Kremlevskie perelety*, 50. Kaminskii's account is based on personal interviews that he conducted in the 1980s with individuals involved in the various prestige flights of the 1930s. Although he attributes the quote concerning the pistol to Baidukov, the alleged incident does not appear in the story as recounted in Baidukov's own book, *Chkalov* (Moscow: Molodaia gvardiia, 1986). For the English-language edition of this book see, Georgiy Baidukov, *Russian Lindbergh: The Life of Valery Chkalov*. Edited by Von Hardesty (Washington, D.C.: Smithsonian Institution Press, 1991).

[68] NKVD (*Narodnyi komissariat vnutrennykh del*) was the successor to the OGPU.

a group of aviation officials and specialists (including constructor Andrei
Tupolev) who had traveled overnight from Moscow. By all accounts, the
meeting was tense and heated. According to Shabota, Tupolev rebuked
Levanevskii, calling him a "shithead" [*govniuk*] for aborting the flight
against the express advice of the mission specialists. In no mood to be dressed
down, Levanevskii told the airplane constructor to "go fuck himself" before
storming off in anger. Much later, Tupolev would admit his own uncertainty
as to what required more courage: the decision to continue, or the decision
to turn back.[69] Given the prevailing atmosphere of suspicion and repression,
the failure did not bode well for the individuals associated with the flight.
All were subsequently summoned to a group meeting at the Kremlin. There,
in front of the highest-ranking members of the Soviet state, the personal
animosity between Levanevskii and Tupolev redounded to the detriment of
the constructor. Queried by Stalin as to the reasons for the mission's failure, Levanevskii laid the blame squarely at Tupolev's feet. Announcing that
he would never again fly any of the constructor's planes, the pilot claimed
that the ANT-25 was unfit for service. Moreover, he continued, Tupolev
was an "enemy of the people" against whom he wished to make a formal
denunciation.[70] Ashen-faced and shaken, Tupolev grew visibly ill. A physi-
cian was summoned to escort him home. Only the intervention of Georgii
Baidukov appears to have forestalled the constructor's arrest. Speaking in
defense of Tupolev, Baidukov insisted that the ANT-25 was both airworthy
and capable of completing a record-setting flight. For the time being, however, Stalin deferred making a decision, ordering Levanevskii to travel to the
United States to see what aircraft might be obtained from the Americans for
undertaking another transpolar crossing.[71]

The failure of the 1935 mission revealed that, behind the facile displays
of collectivity, heroism, and bravery habitually depicted in popular publications, Soviet pilots, engineers, and aviation officials operated in a contentious
and dangerous atmosphere that pitted individuals against one another in
competition for professional and personal survival. Although this was certainly true of other contemporary Soviet endeavors, the stakes were particularly high for these men given the keen interest in aviation shown by

[69] Kerber, *Stalin's Aviation Gulag*, 119.
[70] Testimony of G. F. Baidukov in Kaminskii, *Kremlevskie perelety*, 52. Kerber reports a similar
turn of events, but does not mention Levanevskii's denunciation.
[71] Levanevskii spent most of the spring of 1936 in the United States. His tour included visits
to the Sikorsky, Wright, and Douglas aviation firms as well as meetings with American
military and naval officials. (NARA Record Group 72, Box 1187, Folder EF 61/A2-14, vol.
2.) He returned to Moscow via Alaska and Siberia aboard a Vultee V1-A seaplane acquired
through Amtorg. Equipped with retractable landing gear, a variable-pitch propeller, and a
Wright Cyclone R-1820-F2 engine, the all-metal, stressed-skin Vultee was a state-of-the art
aircraft. Levanevskii's 10,000-mile flight aboard the U.S-built plane was not publicized in
the Soviet press. Andersson, *Soviet Aircraft*, 319–20.

FIGURE 47. Josef Stalin (*left*) with a group of air-minded Soviet children at Tushino airfield in Moscow, ca. 1936.

Josef Stalin. According to almost every contemporary observer, the dictator was deeply involved in aeronautics, personally interrogating key individuals, gathering information, and issuing decrees that determined the fate of designers, airplanes, and the men who flew them. By the mid-1930s no major decision could be made without Stalin's consent. The affair also revealed the continuing role played by political legitimation in shaping Soviet aviation. Although VVS officials had voiced interest in developing the ANT-25 as a long-range bomber, the airplane was designed and constructed for the express purpose of setting a world record for distance. To this end, it was identical to the *Maxim Gorky*, the foreign tours of the late 1920s, the Great Flight to Tokyo, indeed every major aeronautical event since the founding of the Soviet state. Any technical advances or practical applications resulting from the development of the plane were subordinated to the primary goal of proving the propriety of the Soviet path to modernity. The trouble was, thus far, the ANT-25 had yet to prove anything.

The events of August 1935 were deeply embarrassing. The apparent failure of the plane convinced officials not to publicize future prestige flights in advance of their successful completion. It also left them temporarily uncertain as to the fate of the ANT-25. For the better part of a year, the plane sat idle. Finally, in the spring of 1936, a new crew, consisting of Baidukov, navigator Aleksandr Beliakov, and pilot Valerii Chkalov, begin preparing for a new long-distance mission. To minimize the risk of another high-profile fiasco, this next flight would occur wholly within the borders of the Soviet

FIGURE 48. The ANT-25 *Stalin's Route* in preparation for the flight from Moscow to Kharabovsk, 1936.

Union. Only after the ANT-25 had proven reliable would it be reexposed to the international scrutiny certain to accompany another attempt at a transpolar crossing. In June 1936, Chkalov, Baidukov, and Beliakov were summoned to the Kremlin, where they received their orders directly from Josef Stalin. Standing before a large map of the Soviet Union, Stalin traced the crew's route with the mouthpiece of his pipe. After leaving Moscow, the ANT-25 would fly a meandering course that would take it over Victoria Island, Franz Joseph Land, Severnaia Zemlia, Bukhta Tiksi, Petropavlovsk-na-Kamchatke, and Nikolaevsk-na-Amure. By the time the fliers touched down at their final location (the Far Eastern city of Kharabovsk), the plane would have covered nearly 6,000 miles, nearly half of which lay above the Arctic Circle.

On 20 July 1936, Chkalov, Baidukov, and Beliakov lifted off from Moscow aboard the freshly painted and newly christened ANT-25 *Stalin's Route* [*Stalinskii marshrut*]. Although the airplane that carried the crewmen was the same one piloted by Levanevskii the preceding August, this time it proved successful. After flying for 56 hours and 20 minutes, the crew landed on Udd Island, not far from Nikolaevsk-na-Amure near the Sea of Okhotsk. Only the onset of a storm toward the end of the journey prevented them from reaching the intended destination of Kharabovsk. The crew radioed word of their landing to Moscow. Sometime later they received a telegram, signed by Stalin and other Politburo members, congratulating them on the successful completion of their flight. For the "bravery, courage, endurance, composure,

FIGURE 49. Soviet leader Josef Stalin (*left*) prepares to be greeted by Valerii Chkalov following the return of *Stalin's Route* from Udd Island, 1936.

persistence, and mastery" demonstrated on the flight, each pilot would be granted the title "Hero of the Soviet Union" as well as a substantial monetary award.[72] The adulation was just beginning.

On 2 August, following the completion of a hastily constructed airstrip built under the supervision of regional NKVD agents, the three fliers departed for Moscow aboard the ANT-25. Along the way, they touched down at nearly a half dozen cities, where they were greeted by ever-increasing crowds of local residents and Party officials. *Stalin's Route* finally returned to Moscow's Shchelkovo airfield on the 10th. There, the highest-ranking leaders of the state were on hand to greet the crew members as they disembarked from the airplane. Stalin, too, was present. As he extended his hand in welcome to Chkalov, the pilot embraced the leader of the nation with a kiss. The next morning, a photograph of the encounter appeared on the front page of *Pravda*. It was one of the very few times that a leading Soviet periodical would depict the dictator in such intimate proximity to another human being.[73] Away from the aerodrome, the reception was tumultuous. Tens of thousands of citizens bearing banners, flags, and portraits lined the highway leading from the capital to Shchelkovo Field. Tens of

[72] Baidukov, *Russian Lindbergh*, 154.

[73] *Pravda*, 11 August 1936. Another photograph, published in 1934, had depicted Stalin kissing Otto Schmidt, the leader of the *Cheliuskin* expedition. The image was doctored to make the diminutive dictator appear taller than the Arctic explorer who stood more than six feet, five inches in height. Brooks, *Thank You Comrade Stalin!*, 102, and McCannon, *Red Arctic*, 200, n. 159.

thousands more gathered in various locations throughout the city to take part in official celebrations held to commemorate the "victory of the courageous troika."[74]

The festivities quickly reached a crescendo. On 12 August a mass rally attended by more than 20,000 aviation workers was held in Moscow's Gorky Park. Once again, leading officials were present to fête the three fliers as well as the laborers, engineers, and constructors who had helped build the ANT-25. One after another, speakers stepped up to the rostrum to praise the bravery, fortitude, and discipline of the "bright falcons" who had so gloriously fulfilled the mission entrusted to them by the Party. When it came time for the heroes to address the crowd, each deflected praise away from himself, acknowledging instead the immense contributions made by others. According to Valerii Chkalov, the success of the ANT-25 derived not from the individual efforts of the fliers, but from the collective effort of the Soviet people and the mission's true leader, Josef Stalin:

If it weren't for you, there would be no us. We are your comrades, workers just like you. How were we able to complete our flight? Because Great Stalin guided us. Great Stalin showed us the path! [Applause]. To Great Stalin I want to say: all of us gathered here today will help you to fulfill all that you want and all that you desire for the good of humanity. [Thunderous applause rising to an ovation]. This most inspirational victory belongs to Great Stalin! It is for the great navigator of our path, Comrade Stalin! Hurrah! [Thunderous applause, shouts of "Hurrah!"].[75]

Similar sentiments were echoed by Baidukov and Beliakov, each of whom reiterated the importance of the collective support of "our great, beautiful people [*narod*]" and the leadership of "Great Stalin" in making possible the successful flight.

The fulsome praise observed at the public rally was matched by that of the press. Compensating for the silence that had preceded the outbound departure of the ANT-25, the country's periodicals launched a frenzied round of coverage that explained in the most effusive language imaginable every aspect of "the spectacular flight, the glorious victory of the country of socialism."[76] Inspired by "the beloved leader of peoples, Comrade Stalin" and demonstrating "boldness, daring, persistence, and hardened Bolshevik will," the "three sons of the great land of socialism" were lionized for having accomplished on behalf of the entire nation a task that "proved to every corner of the world the glory of the Great Proletarian Revolution."[77] From the time that the fliers

---

74 "Na puti v Moskvu," *Sotsialisticheskoe zemledelie*, 10 August 1936 and "Na ulitsakh Moskvy," *Krasanaia zvezda*, 11 August 1936.
75 *Slava geroiam!* (Moscow, 1936), 69–70.
76 *Rabochaia Moskva*, 11 August 1936.
77 "Letat' vyshe, dal'she, bystree!," *Krasnaia zvezda*, 18 August 1936; "Slava geroiam – synam velikoi strany sotsialisma," *Rabochaia Moskva*, 11 August 1936; "Rastushchaia moshch' sovetskoi aviatsii," *Sotsialisticheskoe zemledelie*, 18 August 1936; and "Stalinskie sokoly Oktiabria," *Samolet* (November 1936) 11:2.

landed in the Far East until well after their triumphant return to Moscow, stories about the airplane, the aircrew, and the historic mission dominated the press. Entire issues of newspapers and journals were devoted to the accomplishments of Soviet aviation.[78] The furor lasted until 18 August (the "Day of Soviet Aviation") before dissipating as quickly as it had appeared. On the 20th, following a one-day publishing hiatus, the heroic fliers and their airplane were swept from the pages of the country's newspapers by headlines announcing that the show trial of the "Trotskyite-Zinov'evite gang of killers" had begun.[79] The sudden shift in coverage was a stark reminder of the day-to-day realities obscured by prestige flights and similar Potemkin productions. Doubtless, news of the show trial deeply affected Georgii Baidukov. His father, Filipp Kapitonovich, had recently been arrested as an "enemy of the people" for allegedly engaging in "wrecking" the country's railroad industry. Only the success of the ANT-25 spared his life. He was released from NKVD custody as a final reward to his son, the newly minted "Hero of the Soviet Union."[80]

[78] *Rabochaia Moskva*, 18 August 1936.
[79] *Pravda*, 20 August 1936.
[80] Kaminskii, *Kremlevskie perelety*, 79–80.

8

"Higher, Faster, Farther!"

VICTORY

The success of *Stalin's Route* meant that, following a two-year delay, Soviet aviators would again attempt to fly the pole. In late May 1937, Chkalov and Baidukov were summoned by Stalin to a meeting in the Kremlin. There, they were given permission to undertake another transpolar crossing aboard the same ANT-25 that had carried them to Udd the previous summer.[1] Within a week of Chkalov's Kremlin meeting, Mikhail Gromov was informed that he, too, would lead a transpolar flight. Together with copilot Sergei Danilin and navigator Andrei Iumashev, Gromov was charged with setting a new world-distance record aboard a second ANT-25 specially equipped for long-range Arctic flights.

The ANT-25 piloted by Chkalov departed Moscow on 18 June 1937. Following a flight of just over sixty-three hours, the plane landed around 8:30 A.M. at the Pearson Army airfield in Vancouver, Oregon, just north of Portland. The Sunday morning arrival came as a surprise to the commander of the base (and future secretary of state), General George C. Marshall. Aware that the Soviet pilots were attempting a transpolar crossing, he and other American officials expected that the plane would make its scheduled landing in Oakland, California, later in the day. Chkalov, Baidukov, and Beliakov emerged from the ANT-25 hungry, filthy, and exhausted. Following baths and breakfast, they were sent to rest in Marshall's private quarters. As weight restrictions on the overloaded ANT-25 had prevented the crewmen from bringing anything other than the clothes on their backs, Marshall arranged for a local department store to deliver some twenty suits and fifteen pairs of shoes while the fliers slept. (He also tracked down a tailor and three interpreters to help the men select and size their new outfits.) Meanwhile, the Soviet ambassador to the United States, Aleksandr Troianovskii, quickly made his way to Vancouver from Oakland in order to supervise the fliers. Fed, rested, and bedecked in new clothes, the crewmen were finally presented

---

[1] A. V. Beliakov, *V polet skvoz' gody* (Moscow: Voennoe izdatel'stvo ministerstva oborony SSSR, 1981), 189–92. On a training mission at the time, Beliakov did not attend the Kremlin meeting.

to the American newsmen later that day. The following afternoon, Oregon's Governor Charles H. Martin accompanied the fliers on a hastily organized parade through the streets of Portland before hosting a luncheon in their honor at the city's Chamber of Commerce.[2]

Accompanied by Troianovskii, the fliers embarked on a three-week tour of the country. Remarkably similar to the path followed eight years earlier by the *Land of the Soviets*, their itinerary included visits to Portland, San Francisco, Chicago, Washington, D.C., and New York. At each stop the crew was honored with public receptions and subjected to a series of interviews with local journalists. Meetings with Soviet "colonists" and fellow-traveler organizations such as the "Friends of the Soviet Union" rounded out their activities.[3] As Chkalov, Baidukov, and Beliakov prepared to set sail from New York City on 12 July aboard the ocean liner *S. S. Normandie*, Gromov's crew departed Moscow. After passing over the pole they continued on to southern California, where they touched down in the city of San Jacinto on the 14th, having established a new world record by covering more than 6,300 miles in a single flight.

Back in the USSR, the transpolar crossings touched off a new round of public adulation even more excessive than that which had followed the trip to Udd Island. Alongside typically hyperbolic press coverage, scores of poems, short stories, and novels celebrating the discipline and bravery of the Soviet fliers appeared in the wake of the American landings. Printed materials were augmented by the release of feature films such as *Victory* (1938), *Tales of Heroic Aviators* (1938), and *Courage* (1939), which reinforced the pilots' role as positive heroes and disseminated their stories to audiences across the Union. By repeating set anecdotes reflecting on the bravery and daring of the fliers, these productions ensured that a standard narrative would emerge surrounding the personalities and deeds of the Soviet "falcons."[4] Typical was an often retold exchange involving Valerii Chkalov. Queried as to why he preferred the single-engine ANT-25 over multiengine airplanes, the flier replied in nonchalant fashion, "Why bother with four engines? There's just four times the risk of engine failure!"[5] Although not without merit, the

[2] *The Papers of George Catlett Marshall*, edited by Larry I. Bland and Sharon Ritenour Stevens. Vol. 1, "The Soldierly Spirit, December 1880–June 1939" (Baltimore: Johns Hopkins University Press, 1981), 545–7, and Forrest C. Pogue, *George C. Marshall: Education of a General* (New York: Viking Press, 1963), 306–7.

[3] Beliakov, *V polet*, 271–2.

[4] Hans Günther, "Stalinskie sokoly: analiz mifa tridtsatykh godov," *Voprosy literatury* 11/12 (1991), 122–41.

[5] Z. M. Kanevskii, *Zagadki i tragedii Arktiki* (Moscow, 1991), 136–49, cited in John McCannon, *Red Arctic: Polar Exploration and the Myth of the North in Soviet Russia, 1932–1939* (New York: Oxford University Press, 1998), 102; Beliakov, *V polet*, 192; L. L. Kerber, *Stalin's Aviation Gulag: A Memoir of Andrei Tupolev and the Purge Era*. Edited by Von Hardesty. (Washington, D.C.: Smithsonian Institution Press, 1996), 120; and Iu. A. Kaminskii, *Kremlevskie perelety* (Moscow: Zhurnalistskoe agenstvo "Glasnost'," 1998) 91.

statement was hardly original. American Charles Lindbergh had made the same observation to potential patrons as he lobbied to raise money in support of his 1927 trans-Atlantic crossing.[6] Widely reprinted in the press and popular literature as an example of the Soviet flier's daring, the blithe comment typified the affected bravado attributed to the country's positive heroes. Four engines or one, the fact was that, unlike Lindbergh, Chkalov had no choice in the matter. The ANT-25 on which he flew was the only airplane the Soviet Union possessed capable of completing such a flight. And it had been developed only at significant cost and effort.

The construction of the ANT-25 had taken much longer than state officials originally intended. Responding to the directives of a special commission on long-distance flights headed by Klim Voroshilov, the Tupolev design bureau had submitted initial plans for the airplane during the summer of 1931. In keeping with the Soviet proclivity of hastening production tempos, the prototype was rushed to completion. Not surprisingly, its maiden flight on 22 June 1933 proved disappointing. The ANT-25 failed to perform up to its design specifications. As changes were undertaken to improve the aircraft's aerodynamics (including covering its corrugated surfaces with lacquered fabric and altering the engine cowling, cockpit cabin, and rudder to reduce drag) work began on a second ANT-25. Following a series of delays caused by problems with the new M-34R engine, testing resumed on the refurbished planes in the fall of 1934.[7] By the time Levanevskii lifted off on his aborted mission to San Francisco in August 1935, four years had passed. Two more elapsed before the project paid its declared dividends with the prestige flights to the United States.

The devotion of so much time and effort to a single aircraft might have made sense had the ANT-25 program produced a state-of-the-art airplane capable of advancing Soviet military or commercial interests. However, it did not. Although it did set a new world record, the plane was one dimensional and unserviceable. To meet the Party mandate of flying farther than the capitalist West, the Tupolev construction bureau maximized the ANT-25's range by designing it with a highly exaggerated wing aspect ratio. The result, one historian has wryly noted, amounted to an airplane that was little more than a cross between a powered glider and a flying fuel tank.[8] Capable of carrying only a miniscule bomb load and virtually defenseless from

[6] Charles Lindbergh, *The Spirit of St. Louis* (New York: Scribner's, 1953), 26.

[7] Lennart Andersson, *Soviet Aircraft and Aviation, 1917–1941* (Annapolis, MD: Naval Institute Press, 1994), 232, and Kerber, *Stalin's Aviation Gulag*, 113–14.

[8] Alexander Boyd, *The Soviet Air Force Since 1918* (New York: Stein and Day, 1977), 65. "Aspect ratio" refers to the difference between an airplane's wingspan (measured from the tip of one wing to the tip of the other) and chord (the distance, or width, between the front and back edges of each individual wing). High aspect ratios generally increase an airplane's loft, thus maximizing its flight duration. They are, however, also accompanied by an increase in drag that reduces the top speed at which a plane can fly.

FIGURE 50. "Warm greetings to the Stalinist pupils, the courageous and steadfast fliers of our homeland!" This 1937 poster commemorates the world's first nonstop transpolar flight. Pictured (from left to right) are Soviet airmen Valerii Chkalov, Georgii Baidukov, and Aleksandr Beliakov. Courtesy The Hoover Institution.

enemy fighters owing to its poor armament, low ceiling, and slow speed, the military version of the aircraft had no practical value. Moreover, the fully loaded plane was immensely ponderous, requiring nearly twice the distance to attain takeoff speed as did comparably sized aircraft. This necessitated the construction of a special runway two-and-a-half miles in length. Of the thirteen ANT-25s built before the production run was halted in 1937, none saw squadron service.[9] Issues of practicality aside, the aircraft did elevate the stature of Soviet aviation. The three flights undertaken by the two ANT-25s brought unprecedented renown to the country's constructors and pilots.

STALIN'S PROUD FALCONS

The prestige flights accomplished by the country's aircrews in 1936–7 granted aviators pride of place within the pantheon of Soviet positive heroes. The fanfare accorded them in the press and at the public gatherings held to celebrate their accomplishments was only one example of how they occupied the public's imagination in the last half of the 1930s. Fliers were ubiquitous in Stalin's Russia. They appeared on canvas, stage, and currency, in statuary, novels, poems, and in an array of feature films. Their images adorned the walls of Moscow metro stations and hymns of praise were penned in their honor by popular musicians. The popularity of aviators in contemporary cultural productions is not at all surprising given that aviation iconography had been consciously cultivated by Party propagandists for more than a decade. Soviet leaders had long understood that flying was the ideal occupation for representing their most revered values. They used pilots to personalize abstract concepts such as discipline, valor, and technical acuity while glorifying an endeavor essential to the country's economic development, military security, and international prestige.

Of all the Soviet Union's "brave falcons," none was more famous than Valerii Chkalov. Lionized for his role as the lead pilot of two ANT-25 expeditions, Chkalov stood out from his many contemporaries. His life and exploits were the subject of a 1941 feature film and, in keeping with the Soviet fashion of immortalizing heroes, both his hometown (Orenburg) as well as the island Udd were renamed in his honor.[10] Following his untimely death in December 1938, he was accorded the Soviet Union's highest accolades: a state funeral accompanied by an honor guard of Party officials (led by Stalin) followed by interment in the Kremlin wall.

---

9   The majority of these aircraft were used as training planes or as platforms for testing diesel engines. One was modified by the Bureau for Experimental Design (BOK) to serve as a high-altitude research aircraft. The BOK program was dissolved in 1941 following the German invasion. Boyd, *Soviet Air Force*, 66.

10   *Valerii Chkalov* (Len'film, 1941, directed by Mikhail Kalatozov). The southern Siberian city reverted to its original name in 1997. The island, however, remains Chkalov.

FIGURE 51. Pilot Valerii Chkalov, 1936.

The mythology that surrounded Chkalov during his lifetime has led some to envision him as the Soviet equivalent of Charles Lindbergh, whose celebrity eclipsed that of all other American pilots.[11] The comparison is appropriate insofar as it reflects the propensity of both men to serve as incarnations of idealized and entrenched cultural values. Viewed by contemporaries as an emblem of such time-honored national virtues as self-sufficiency, determinism, and dogged independence, the celebrated "Lone Eagle," Charles Lindbergh, was considered to be quintessentially "American." His flight across the Atlantic Ocean was viewed as a symbolic expression of America's ongoing transition from its traditional bucolic past toward a new technologically driven future.[12] This was likewise true of Chkalov. Overcoming vast distances and the forces of nature through the mastery of advanced technology, he personified the ideal Soviet citizen who, through discipline, courage, and loyalty to the Party, was helping to bring about humanity's great socialist future.

---

[11] I have here in mind the American translation of Georgii Baidukov's biographical memoir. Titled *Chkalov* in its Russian–language original, it was rechristened *Russian Lindbergh* on its release in the United States. See Georgiy Baidukov, *Russian Lindbergh: The Life of Valery Chkalov*. Edited by Von Hardesty (Washington, D.C.: Smithsonian Institution Press, 1991).

[12] Kenneth S. Davis, *The Hero: Charles A. Lindbergh and the American Dream* (New York: Doubleday, 1959).

Care must be taken, however, in drawing such a comparison. Although both fliers functioned as receptacles of official and public aspirations, the meanings imparted by the two men in American and Soviet culture were substantially different. Specifically, the association risks overstating the importance accorded the individual by official Soviet culture. Given the tenaciously hagiographic accounts written by his colleagues and historians, it is easy to forget that Chkalov's triumphs were shared experiences. Unlike Lindbergh, who flew alone, Chkalov was but one of three fliers to bring glory to the Soviet Union. Although his position as lead pilot entitled him to official status as the head of the expeditions, his personal contributions to the two flights did not exceed those made by his crewmates. As noted in the previous chapter, it was Baidukov who had been instrumental to the continuation of the ANT-25 program, bravely defending the plane and its constructor following the debacle of August 1935. He played a similarly consequential role in recommending Chkalov to his superiors and then encouraging the pilot to take up the mission. Once underway, Baidukov and Beliakov bore equal responsibility for the fate of the aircraft as the crewmen rotated the helm during the two arduous journeys. Although Chkalov did make a masterful landing on the open terrain of Udd Island, it was Baidukov who brought the plane down at Vancouver's Pearson Field under less than perfect weather conditions.[13]

Chkalov's celebrity also differed from Lindbergh's insofar as it was largely predetermined by Soviet authorities. Although there can be no doubt that he was both skilled and charismatic, Chkalov's rapid rise from obscurity to international renown owed as much to the state's desire to create a particular type of hero as it did to the pilot's proficiency and personality. Among contemporary Soviet fliers, Chkalov was neither the most experienced nor the best suited to attempt a new world duration record. Before his August 1936 flight aboard the ANT-25 *Stalin's Route*, Chkalov had spent almost his entire career flying small single-seat fighter planes (first in the VVS from 1924 until 1930 and thereafter as a test pilot assigned to the Polikarpov OKB). By all accounts he was an accomplished, if occasionally reckless, aviator capable of performing amazing aerial acrobatics and remarkable stunts aboard the fast and nimble airplanes that were Polikarpov's specialty. In May 1935, he was awarded the Order of Lenin for his work with the I-15 and I-16 fighter prototypes.[14]

Given his professional experience, Chkalov's selection as the ANT-25's lead pilot and the resulting accolades accorded him appear contrived. There were far more appropriate candidates for both, most notably Mikhail Gromov. One of the Soviet Union's most decorated pilots, Gromov was much better suited to the task at hand and, perhaps, more deserving of recognition

---

[13] Beliakov, *V polet*, 152–3 and 201–26 and Baidukov, *Russian Lindbergh*, 138–9 and 192–229.
[14] Baidukov, *Russian Lindbergh*, 123.

as the country's preeminent pilot. Adept at the helm of large bomber-type aircraft and with more than a decade's worth of experience undertaking long-distance prestige flights to his credit, Gromov had fulfilled numerous missions similar to those planned for the summers of 1936 and 1937. More important, he was intimately familiar with the ANT-25, having served as its principal pilot since the plane began test flights in 1934. By the summer of 1936 he had logged more hours aboard the aircraft than any other Soviet aviator. In recognition of these facts, Gromov was selected to pilot the second ANT-25 over the pole in August 1937. But it was Chkalov who was selected to go first. And it was Chkalov who was subsequently singled out in the Soviet media as the archetypal socialist aviator and as the "favorite" of Stalin's flier–falcons.

Chkalov's promotion past more qualified colleagues was facilitated by his social origins. The son of an impoverished laborer (his father had worked as a boilermaker before taking up a factory position repairing river vessels), Chkalov possessed ideal credentials to serve as a representative figure of the Soviet system.[15] The same was not true of Gromov who, despite outstanding qualifications and a stellar service record, was ideologically tainted as a descendant of Imperial Russian gentry. This fact weighed heavily in the decision to dispatch Chkalov to the United States ahead of the more senior and experienced pilot.[16] There can be little doubt that it prefigured in the elevation of Chkalov as the epitomic aviator. Even so, Chkalov's rise to glory was not at all unusual. His trajectory mirrored that of other idealized Soviet workers who emerged from obscurity in the mid-1930s to become "ordinary celebrities."[17] Like tractor driver Praskovia Angelina, coal miner Aleksei Stakhanov, and other exemplars of positive heroism, Valerii Chkalov was chosen by Party patrons as a suitable subject for public adulation because he comported with the regime's master narrative. He was socialism's consummate success story: the scion of an illiterate proletarian, transformed through Red Army training and service into a highly skilled, technically adept "new Soviet man." That he would ultimately garner much more attention than other "celebrities" owed as much to his profession as it did to his personality or patrons. As is true today, airplanes in the 1930s captured the public imagination in ways unmatched by tractors or pneumatic drills.

Valerii Chkalov notwithstanding, it was the flight-crew collective [*ekipazh*] rather than individual pilots that figured most prominently in the Stalin-era aviator cult. Like the three-airplane *zveno* [unit] around which the VVS organized the country's military defenses, the three-person *ekipazh* (consisting of pilot, copilot, and navigator) was the essential unit employed to represent the country's aviation cadres. Whereas a single film was made about Chkalov's

[15] *Ibid.*, 22–4.
[16] Kaminskii, *Kremlevskie perelety*, 101.
[17] Sheila Fitzpatrick, *Everyday Stalinism* (New York: Oxford University Press, 1999), 74.

FIGURE 52. Soviet aviators as celebrities. Andrei Iumashev, Mikhail Gromov, and Sergei Danilin pose with American child star Shirley Temple in Los Angeles following their 1937 transpolar flight.

life and deeds, dozens appeared concerning the trials and tribulations of collective aircrews. The same was true of the myriad aviation short stories, novels, and children's books published in the Soviet Union from mid-decade onward. Particularly common were poems like "The Three" and "Stalin's Route," which glorified the cooperative labor of the aircrew. Others, such as "Warriors," served as paeans to the legions of aviators who risked their own lives for the benefit of the country as a whole.[18] Although it was not unheard of for a newspaper to extol the accomplishments of an individual pilot, stories about entire flight crews, or trilogies devoted to all members of a given *ekipazh*, were more common.[19]

None of this, of course, was unique to the Stalinist 1930s. The propensity to portray Russian aviation in terms of collectivist impulses or organizational

[18] "Troe," *Ogonek* (30 September 1936): 15; "Stalinskii marshrut," *Izvestiia*, 16 July 1937; and "Bogatyri," *Pravda*, 28 July 1937.
[19] See, for example, the three article series on Chkalov, Baidukov, and Beliakov published in *Pravda*, 21–23 June 1937 and the individual stories concerning Gromov, Danilin, and Iumashev in *Pravda*, 15 July 1937.

patterns originated during the Imperial era. Then, patrons and the press contrasted the selflessness of fliers such as Mikhail Efimov and Lev Matsievich with the crass individualism and greed of their western counterparts. In the early 1920s, Soviet propagandists voiced similar sentiments, denigrating foreign pilots like Charles Lindbergh as "bourgeois individualists" while proclaiming the moral superiority of their country's collective cadres.[20] During the last half of the 1930s, collectivism remained a central component of Soviet aeronautical culture, with officials advancing the *ekipazh* as an ideologically correct alternative to the individual celebrities encountered in the West. The country's pilots, too, embraced collective celebrity as they ritualistically intoned the importance of selfless contributions to the group in their scripted remarks to the press and public. As Chkalov himself acknowledged before the reception that followed the return from Udd Island,

Here amid the thousands gathered, it is impossible to single out a lone individual from the crew of the ANT-25. Our strength and our victory are the strength and victory of the collective! We are a small collective of three people. Fulfilling Stalin's will, fulfilling your will, we were supported by you and, thus, fulfilled the task.[21]

"Born and raised in factories and plants, in the Party, in the Red Army, and in the Communist Youth Organization," Soviet pilots were said to accomplish their "daily heroics" through the inspiration they derived from the collective cause of building socialism. In stark contrast to the professional sportsmen of Europe and America who undertook flights "merely for monetary gain and personal fortune," Soviet aviators flew "everywhere and anywhere, motivated by an existential joy [*radost' zhizni*] derived from [their] country and epoch."[22] "Collectivism and loyalty to the ideas of Communism" distinguished Soviet fliers from their counterparts in the West as, "inculcated by the values of the Party of Lenin and Stalin," they sought "not personal glory nor gold," but "to serve the cause of human progress."[23]

Collectivist rhetoric was not the only aspect of Stalinist aviation with deep roots in Russian culture. Folkloric motifs (once popular with patriotic imperial journalists, officials, and aeronautical patrons) also figured prominently in the late 1930s as propagandists hearkened back to the imagined past in an effort to portray the miracles made possible by scientific socialism. Encouraged by leading political and cultural figures to use folk culture as a "weapon of class conflict," Soviet writers undertook a broad campaign in the 1930s to resurrect traditional genres such as the tale [*skazka*], short rhyme [*chastushka*], epic [*bylina*], extended poem [*starina*], and funeral lament

[20] See above, pp. 165–6 and 176.
[21] *Slava geroiam*! (Moscow, 1936), 69.
[22] "O radosti zhizni," *Krasnaia zvezda*, 12 August 1936.
[23] "Prazdnik vsego naroda" and M. Vodop'ianov, "Pobediteli stikhii" in *Rabochaia Moskva*, 11 August 1936, and *Izvestiia*, 16 July 1937.

[*plach*].[24] The result was an outpouring of new folkloric works, allegedly gathered from across the Soviet Union and said to represent genuine expressions of the popular will. The vast majority was, in fact, "fakelore," carefully contrived and controlled works of fiction that faithfully copied traditional language, structures, and genres to advance the Party's political agenda.[25]

Aviators figured prominently in Stalinist fakelore.[26] Identified as "falcons" [*sokoly*], "eagles" [*orly*], or "red-winged birds" [*krasnokrylye ptitsy*], they were attributed all the qualities of epic heroes. They were "proud" [*gordye*], "bold" [*smelye*], "fearless" [*besstrashnye*], and "bright" [*iasnye*]. Their motives were always "pure" [*chistye*] and "true" [*vernye*]; their deeds, "miraculous" [*chudesnye*] and "eternal" [*vechnye*]. A "fairytale warrior [*skazochnyi bogatyr'*] alive in the present day," the Soviet pilot was said to be an individual "for whom nothing is impossible and from whom emerges the most miraculous deeds."[27] As the refrain from one of the era's popular songs noted, aviators were "born to make fairytales come true."[28] They were the supreme expression of socialism's progressive powers, the greatest and most revered of the "New Soviet People."

Folklore supplied more than a vocabulary for glorifying aviators. It also provided a narrative template for extolling the exploits of "falcon fliers" that legitimated the Party by underscoring its centrality to the realization of the glorious future. Like the traditional Russian *skazka*, the standard Stalinist aviation narrative was a miraculous tale of trials and transfiguration in which ordinary men (*very* rarely women) were transformed into heroes through the accomplishment of a difficult quest.[29] The tale was told in terms of ritual encounters and rites of passage in which "young eaglets" [*iunye orliata*] became "proud falcons" [*gordye sokoly*] through regimented

---

[24] Iu. M. Sokolov, "Priroda fol'klora i problemy fol'kloristiki," *Literaturnyi kritik* 12 (1934): 127, cited in Frank J. Miller, *Folklore for Stalin: Russian Folklore and Pseudofolklore of the Stalin Era* (Armonk, NY: Sharpe, 1990), 7, and A. L. Toporkov, T. G. Ivanova, L. P. Lapteva, and E. E. Levkievskaia (eds.), *Rukopisi, kotorykh ne bylo: poddelki v oblasti slavianskogo fol'klora* (Moscow: Ladomir, 2002), 403–888.

[25] Miller, *Folklore for Stalin*, and Felix J. Oinas, "Folklore and Politics in the Soviet Union," *Slavic Review* 32 (1973): 45–56. On "fakelore," see Richard Dorson, *Folklore and Fakelore: Essays Toward a Discipline of Folk Studies* (Cambridge, MA: Harvard University Press, 1976).

[26] Numerous authors have commented on the prevalence of folkloric elements in Stalinist flight culture including Günther, "Stalinskie sokoly," 138–40; McCannon, *Red Arctic*, 125–8; and Kendall Bailes, *Technology and Society Under Lenin and Stalin: Origins of the Soviet Technical Intelligentsia, 1917–1941* (Princeton, NJ: Princeton University Press, 1978), 385–6. Conversely, for an analysis of flight symbolism in Russian folklore, see Scott W. Palmer, "Icarus, East: The Symbolic Contexts of Russian Flight," *Slavic and East European Journal* 49(1) (Spring 2005): 19–47.

[27] "Sila i geroizm," *Izvestiia*, 14 July 1937.

[28] See the first epigraph to Part III.

[29] See the numerous Stalinist–era tales summarized in Miller, *Folklore for Stalin*, 138–51.

training at the hands of Party officials. Learning to suppress their naturally reckless ways, the loyal fliers *qua* heroes acquire the wisdom and discipline essential for the completion of their task through the inspirational examples set by their leaders. Airplanes supplied by the omniscient Party replaced the flying carpets and magical birds proffered the folkloric hero by supernatural powers, while Arctic blizzards, violent cyclones, and the expanse of vast space [*prostranstvo*] substituted for sorcerers, dragons, and other evil adversaries. America served as the "Other-Worldly" destination. Invariably, the role of the tsar was played by "Great and Wise Stalin" who, like the folkloric rulers of yore, dispatched his *bogatyri* far and wide across the oceans.

In addition to folkloric imagery, aeronautical fables routinely incorporated paternal and filial motifs. These were used by state propagandists to inspire community and belonging among the public by advancing the idea that the Soviet Union comprised an extended "Great Family."[30] United by close personal relationships, mutual respect, and loyalty, Soviet fliers were described as "friends" and "brothers" who labored out of love for the benefit of their fellow countrymen. Their *ekipazh* was a cooperative "little family." It was an example of the marvels made possible through selflessness, community, and brotherhood; a model for citizens to emulate. As *paterfamilias* of the Soviet "Great Family," Stalin was portrayed as a stern but loving mentor whose wisdom, advice, and instruction the fliers relied on as they eagerly sought guidance in the fulfillment of their duties. He was an inspirational master, a "father and teacher" to his brave young "sons" whom he held to the highest standards but whose lives he considered "far more dear than any machine."[31] The metaphor was completed through the addition of a maternal figure: the "motherland" [*rodina-mat'*] who had given birth to "father" Stalin's heroic flier "sons" and who "embraced them tenderly" on their return from abroad.[32] A new phenomenon in the evolution of Soviet culture, the use of familial rhetoric in the 1930s to promote legitimacy and to foster community revealed yet again the persistence of inherited forms in shaping the content of Soviet aviation. Whereas the mythology of the *rodina-mat'* was deeply entrenched in the country's cultural tradition, pilots' public proclamations of loyalty and love for "our father Stalin" hearkened back to peasants' customary address of the tsar as their own "little father" [*batiushka*], an appellation that held considerable appeal for the Soviet Union's "Red Tsar."[33]

Although less evident than transparent references to falcons, families, and flying carpets, religious themes remained an integral component of Stalinist

[30] Katerine Clark, *The Soviet Novel: History as Ritual* (Chicago: University of Chicago Press, 1981), 114–35.

[31] *Sotsialisticheskoe zemledelie*, 18 August 1936.

[32] Günther, "Stalinskie sokoly," 127.

[33] Simon Sebag Montefiore, *Stalin: The Court of the Red Tsar* (New York: Knopf, 2004), 179.

flight culture. As discussed in Chapter 5, religious imagery and narrative structures were standard devices in early Soviet aviation propaganda. Hoping to supplant the religious faith of the Orthodox Church with the secular ideology of Communism, Party spokesmen portrayed aviators and airplanes as heavenborne agents of enlightenment and salvation. During the last half of the 1930s, religious motifs returned to prominence as pilots resumed their archetypal function as prophets or disciples of the "new religion." Like the saints of the Church who were exalted above average men and women owing to their proximity to God, fliers belonged to a higher cast whose status derived from their close interactions with Josef Stalin. Widely publicized meetings between Stalin and his pilots reinforced the image of aviators as devoted disciples. So did numerous stories and poems that described in religious terms how aviators, "carrying Stalin's name in their hearts," looked to him for guidance and succor.[34] One poem, describing the first flight over the North Pole, portrayed the crew of the ANT-25 invoking Stalin's name in prayer:

> Their lips quietly whispered:
> "Leader and Friend, guide us from afar!
> Against these storms and winds,
> Above these deserts of eternal ice!"[35]

Other publications described how aviators, during their most troubling and difficult times, "derived inspiration from Stalin [who] was always with them." Fliers were said to draw strength and serenity from the knowledge that, even as they journeyed over vast oceans and Arctic wastelands, the Party's leader "lovingly and attentively followed their progress."[36]

Religious associations were even more obvious in phantasmagoric descriptions that ascribed omniscience and other godlike qualities to Josef Stalin. The "eternally wise" and "all-knowing" dictator was depicted as a font of inspiration, energy, and judgment for his followers. He was the "unsleeping always vigilant leader" whose "ever-present hand guided the fliers and the nation" to unrivaled heights.[37] Like the resurrected Christ, Stalin was frequently attributed the radiance of an overpowering, brilliant sun. Chkalov himself remarked on the heavenly glow of the Great Leader, proclaiming that "Where there is Stalin, there is no darkness, only bright light."[38] Still, if Stalin was like a god, he remained personal and attentive to the needs of his worshippers. He cared for them and loved him as if they were his children. And he inspired them to do the same. As Georgii Baidukov reverently

---

[34] "Stalinu," *Samolet* 3 (1936): 5.

[35] Cited in McCannon, *Red Arctic*, 106.

[36] "Muzhestvo, znanie, organizovannost'," *Krasnaia zvezda*, 15 August 1936.

[37] "Velikaia pobeda velikoi strany," *Krasnaia zvezda*, 10 August 1936.

[38] *Slava geroiam!*, 68.

FIGURE 53. "We respond to Stalin's concern for children through a ceaseless struggle for the life and health of every child." Postcard, ca. 1937.

proclaimed, "We live in an epoch of colossal love for one another. And the great love that Comrade Stalin possesses for the people [*narod*] is transmitted to us all."[39]

Even the symbolic elements comprising the Soviet "Great Family" carried religious overtones. Typically interpreted by scholars as a metaphoric statement of the larger nationwide community, the construct of father–Stalin, mother–land, and pilot–son also suggested associations with Christianity's triune "family" of God the Father, the Mother of God, and the Son of God, Jesus Christ. Such a reading helps to clarify at least one of the most bizarre cultural artifacts to emerge from the Soviet Union, a postcard-sized montage produced by Osoaviakhim in the late 1930s (see Figure 53). A compilation of three separate photographic images, the montage depicts Stalin within a halolike circle holding a young child in his arms. Smiling, he looks down toward a young women who is breastfeeding an infant. In between, three airplanes descend from the heavens. The purpose of the odd composition is explained by the printed message: "We respond to Stalin's concern for children through a ceaseless struggle for the life and health of every child."

[39] *Ibid.*, 69–70

A subtext partially qualifies this main point by admitting that "Mother's milk is the best nourishment for a child." Reprising the recurrent message of the 1920s that aviation would ensure the development and prosperity of Soviet citizens, the postcard reminds the viewer of airplanes' continuing role in supplying the countryside with much needed assistance. Dispatched by Stalin, the planes bear baby formula and other nourishment to the most isolated and desolate backwaters of the country. They will ensure the health and well-being of the next Soviet generation, thereby demonstrating the Great Leader's solicitous regard for all of his children.[40]

Although the postcard's transparent use of familial imagery was very much in line with the metaphor of the Stalinist "Great Family," a closer examination reveals the extent to which latent religious associations structured the composition. The montage of photographic images was in fact a montage of iconic forms drawn from the traditions of the Russian Orthodox faith. The snapshot of the fatherly Stalin enclosed by a circle mirrored the standard iconic practice of representing God the Father through the device of a circle (sometimes a semicircle) positioned in the upper-left-hand corner of an icon. More obviously, the photograph of the breastfeeding woman was a "Sovietized" reference to the Mother of God that recalled the more contemporary "Petrograd Madonna" from Kuz'ma Petrov-Vodkin's celebrated painting, *1918 in Petrograd* (1920). The final element of the photographic triptych, the three descending airplanes, corresponded to the three rays or three lines traditionally used by iconographers to represent the descent of the Holy Spirit from the Throne of Heaven. Given their expressed function of distributing food to the country's hinterlands, the airplanes could also be interpreted as a biblical reference to the ravens sent by God to nourish St. Elijah and other Holy Fathers in the desert. The influence of religion extended even to the manner in which the montage was distributed throughout the country. Produced in conjunction with the Maxim Gorky Squadron's 1937–8 agit-flight campaign, these postcards were intended as keepsakes for the cadres of shock-workers invited to fly aboard the squadron's planes.[41] Following their "aerial baptism," workers were handed copies of the image to remind them of the experience and inspire them to still greater acts of

---

[40] The postcard did not lack for cruel irony. The image of Stalin being embraced by the young girl was a reproduction of a well-known photograph, taken at a Kremlin reception, that had first appeared on the front page of *Izvestiia* on 1 May 1936. The girl, Gelya Markizova, was the daughter of Ardan Markizov, second secretary of the Buryat Mongol ASSR. A year after the photograph appeared in print, Stalin demonstrated his "solicitous regard" for young Gelya by accusing her father of spying for Japan and ordering him shot. Shortly thereafter, Gelya's mother, Dominica, was killed as the wife of an enemy of the people. David King, *The Commissar Vanishes: The Falsification of Photographs and Art in Stalin's Russia* (New York: Metropolitan Books, 1997).

[41] RGAE f. 9527, op. 1, d. 1391 (Godovoi otchet po osnovnoi deiatel'nosti agitatsionnoi eskadril'i im. Gor'kogo za 1938 g.), *et passim*.

service, a practice not unlike the Orthodox tradition of presenting small icons to converts following their baptism into the faith.

STALINIST AVIATION ON THE INTERNATIONAL STAGE

Simultaneously with their effort to promote the hero worship of falcon fliers, Party authorities waged a concerted campaign to raise the international profile of the Red Air Force. As discussed earlier, prestige events such as the rescue of the Cheluskintsy and the long-distance flights of the mid-1930s were vital in this regard. State officials employed these orchestrated displays of technological prowess to demonstrate how far the country had developed under the auspices of centralized planning. Record-breaking flights were not, however, the only means used to legitimate the advances overseen by the Party. The growing prominence of the country's aviation cadres was also facilitated by the Soviet Union's presence at international aeronautical exhibitions. Increasingly, Soviet representatives attempted to cultivate wider interest in their aviation programs by displaying domestic successes to foreign audiences across the Continent. In Paris, Copenhagen, Milan, and other venues, exhibit halls and display stands became key components in the drive to convince European public opinion that Party leaders had successfully constructed a technologically advanced and peace-loving socialist state.

The Soviet contribution to the Fourteenth International Aviation Exhibition exemplified the state's growing desire to impress foreign audiences. Held in Paris during the fall of 1934, the exhibition provided thousands of European citizens and officials with an early opportunity to view in person the Soviet Union's most recent accomplishments.[42] Hoping to attract large crowds to their displays and aware that their efforts would be measured against those of the United States and Europe's leading aeronautical powers, the Party commission in charge of overseeing the exhibit entrusted the design of the pavilion to Lazar El Lissitskii, a celebrated architect known throughout Europe for his avant-garde compositions. The choice proved an immense success. Although state representatives found it impossible to compile precise statistics during the course of the two-week event, they observed that the number of people attending the Soviet displays was far higher than that enjoyed by other nations' pavilions. At times, lines to view the Soviet pavilion's individual components ran as many as 200 people deep while at peak

---

[42] During the summer of 1934, the Soviet government had participated in its first international aviation show, a much smaller exhibition in Copenhagen, Denmark. Devoted almost entirely to aviation engines, the Copenhagen venue did not include displays from the United States, Italy, or Holland. See RGAE f. 9527, op.1, d. 706 (Otchet o rabote Sovetskogo pavil'ona na vtoroi mezhdunarodnoi aviavystavke v Kopengagene 17 avgusta–2 sentiabria 1934 g.).

hours of the day the pavilion was completely full of patrons, "necessitating the deployment of up to ten agents to maintain order."[43]

The official report on the Paris experience acknowledged that this overwhelming success was largely attributable to El Lissitskii's innovative design. Both in its external appearance and internal layout, the Soviet pavilion appeared strikingly different from all others.[44] As important, officials noted, the artist had proven particularly adept at displaying the country's aviation program as the product of a collective endeavor. Whereas other nations' pavilions had been cobbled together by individual private firms, "each of whom competed against one another" for the public's attention at the air show, the Soviet entry successfully represented "the country as whole," demonstrating "the accomplishments of our aviation programs as products of the development of socialist construction and the participation in it of the broadest social masses." Although its lavish appearance and composition accounted for much of the public's interest, the pavilion did not lack for substance. Displays devoted to the recently completed Stal'-2 prototype aircraft and the M-34 engine attracted the attention of aviation specialists while exhibits explaining the rescue of the Cheliuskintsy and the ANT-20 *Maxim Gorky* appeared most popular with general audiences. Unlike other participants at the Exhibition, however, the Soviets made no reference to their country's military aviation programs.[45]

Although the public's response to the Soviet pavilion at the 1934 Paris Aviation Exhibition clearly exceeded the expectations of official propagandists, the production was not an unqualified success. Ironically, like the aviation industry itself, its striking appearance could not entirely mask the endemic manufacturing deficiencies that continued to plague the Soviet Union. Officials lamented that in terms of its material quality, the display left much to be desired. The pavilion's Soviet-made components were noticeably inferior to those comprising the Western European displays. Despite cost overruns, poor-quality paint, cheap paper, and substandard construction materials detracted from the attendees' experience and gave the whole enterprise a rather slapdash feel (an impression no doubt exacerbated by organizers' rush to complete the pavilion on the very eve of the Exhibition's grand opening).[46] Further irony could be found in the fate of El Lissitskii's modernist style. Even as the celebrated artist labored to complete the state-sponsored project, his avant-garde approach to architectural design was

---

43 RGAE f. 9527, op. 1, d. 868 (Materialy o rabote Sovetskogo pavil'ona na Parizheskoi aviatsionnoi vystavke 16 noiabria–2 dekabria 1934 g.), ll. 67 and 70.

44 RGALI f. 2361, op. 1, d. 33 (Zapisnaia knizhka s nabroskami chertezhei i risunkov i zapisiami otnosishchimsia k oformleniiu Sovetskogo otdela na Parizheskoi mezhdunarodnoi aviatsionnoi vystavke). A copy of the final schematic design of the pavilion, signed by Lissitskii, can be found in RGAE f. 9527, op. 1, d. 868, l. 1.

45 RGAE f. 9527, op. 1, d. 868, *et passim*.

46 *Ibid.*, ll. 70–1.

under assault by the guardians of official Soviet culture. Intent on harnessing art to the political imperatives of the state, the new Party mandate of social-ist realism imposed a stylistic orthodoxy on artists that would preclude for the foreseeable future truly innovative productions like those championed by El Lissitskii.

If European exhibits provided Soviet officials with a public venue for show-casing their achievements in civilian aviation, developments in Spain soon provided them with an opportunity for measuring the military capabilities of the Red Air Force against potential European opponents. In July 1936, army forces under the leadership of General Francisco Franco attempted a mili-tary coup against the Republican government of Spain. Civil War ensued. Soon after the onset of hostilities, the Fascist states of Germany and Italy dispatched aid and equipment to Franco's Nationalists. The Soviet Union quickly responded in kind, orchestrating the formation of an "International Brigade," consisting mostly of Communist volunteers, to fight alongside Republican loyalists. In October 1936, Stalin ordered an initial shipment of aircraft and other military equipment to bolster the Republicans. More matériel soon followed, as did numerous Soviet "volunteers" – military spe-cialists whose mission was to help train Republican troops. Although the exact number of aircraft sent to Spain remains clouded in secrecy, reliable estimates place the total at around 1,500, some 500 of which were oper-ational at any given time. The force consisted of approximately 1,000 I-15 and I-16 fighters, 200 SB-2 light bombers, and a similar number of R-5 reconnaissance planes. To the dismay of American officials, several airplanes purchased from the United States also appeared in the skies over Spain. Hundreds of Soviet mechanics and military pilots accompanied the planes. By 1937, the Soviet-supplied aircraft accounted for ninety percent of the Republican air force.[47]

Initially, the VVS scored a series of successes. The most notable of these occurred in the spring of 1937 when an air strike launched against Nationalist troops pressing toward Madrid provided the Republican forces enough time to reinforce the capital. However, hampered by shortages of spare parts and a lack of adequate maintenance services, Soviet air supe-riority did not last long.[48] More important, in late 1937 the Germans upgraded their "Condor Legion" with a shipment of Messerschmitt Me-109 fighters and Junkers Ju-87 dive bombers. A full generation ahead of

[47] For figures relating to Soviet planes and pilots in Spain, see Reina Pennington, "From Chaos to the Eve of the Great Patriotic War," 45–6, and Tom Alison and Von Hardesty, "Aviation and the Transformation of Combined–Arms Warfare, 1941–1945," in Robin Higham, John T. Greenwood, and Von Hardesty, *Russian Aviation and Air Power in the Twentieth Century* (London: Cass, 1998), 92–3. The reactions of American officials are preserved in NARA Record Group 72, Box 1187, Folder EF 61/A2–14, vol. 2.

[48] Von Hardesty, *Red Phoenix: The Rise of Soviet Airpower, 1941–1945* (Washington, D.C.: Smithsonian Institution Press, 1982), 50.

the Soviet-designed aircraft, the Messerchmitts and Junkers quickly proved the I-15s and I-16s obsolete. As Soviet losses mounted in late 1937 and early 1938, Stalin grew enraged. In August 1938, he ordered the withdrawal of his air force personnel and equipment from Spain. By the end of the year the Soviet contingent had departed, abandoning the Republicans to Franco's troops.

CRISES AND CATASTROPHE ON THE EVE OF WORLD WAR

The proxy war in Spain coincided with political war at home as Stalin unleashed a new round of purges beginning in the summer of 1936. Unlike the "lesser" waves of arrest and persecution during the 1920s and early 1930s, which had principally targeted "saboteurs" and "wreckers" in industrial, manufacturing, and technical sectors, the "Great Terror" fell disproportionately on old Bolshevik activists, high-ranking Party members, and elements of the state's administrative elite. In August 1936, Mikhail Tomskii, head of the Soviet trade union movement was accused of belonging to an anti-Soviet conspiratorial center. Rather than face death at the hands of state executioners, Tomskii committed suicide. Others were less fortunate. Grigorii Zinov'ev and Lev Kamenev, already serving five-year sentences for their "moral responsibility" in the 1934 murder of the Leningrad Party Chief Sergei Kirov, were brought out of prison and subjected to a second elaborately staged trial for allegedly conspiring to assassinate Stalin and other high-ranking officials. Although the long-time Bolshevik activists begged Stalin for their lives, they were found guilty and shot. Other Party luminaries enjoyed similar treatment. Iurii Piatakov, a prominent figure in the industrialization drive, together with Karl Radek, Grigorii Sokol'nikov, and Leonid Serebriakov, was tried and executed in January 1937. Nikolai Bukharin and Aleksei Rykov, the principal subjects of a spectacular show trial in the spring of 1938, followed. No one seemed immune from the dispensations of Soviet justice. Even NKVD Chief Genrikh Iagoda fell victim to the executioner's bullet. Tried alongside Bukharin and Rykov he, too, was shot. His successor, Nikolai Ezhov, fared no better. Removed from his post in December 1938, he was executed in early 1940.

The arrest of Marshal Mikhail Tukhachevskii in May of 1937 signaled the beginning of the military leadership's end. Accused of plotting to overthrow the Soviet regime, Tukhachevskii was tortured, secretly tried, and summarily shot the following month. He was but one of thousands of Red Army officers to die at the hands of the NKVD. General Iona Iakir, commander of the Kiev Military District, met a similar fate. So, too, did scores of other high-ranking military leaders, including Ieronim Uborevich of the Belorussian Military District, naval commander Romual'd Muklevich, tank commander Innokenti Khalepskii, Avgust Kork of the Frunze Military Academy, Anatolii Gekker, head of Red Army Foreign Liaison, and Ian Gamarnik, chief of the

Red Army's Political Administration.[49] Before the bloodletting ended, Stalin would kill more Soviet generals than would Hitler's *Wehrmacht* in the Second World War. The Terror decimated the Red Army's highest officer ranks as 15 of 16 army commanders, 60 out of 67 corps commanders, and 136 of 199 divisional commanders were dispatched on Stalin's orders.[50] Although recent archival findings have led specialists to downgrade the actual number of casualties resulting from the 1937–8 purges from a previously estimated 35,000 to just under 23,000, the resulting damage to the Red Army's command structure and war readiness was, nevertheless, immense.[51]

The Terror had particularly important ramifications for Soviet military aviation as senior air force commanders numbered among the purge's most prominent victims. VVS Commander-in-Chief Iakov Alksnis, an associate of Tukhachevskii, was arrested in November of 1937 and shot the following summer. A purge of the most senior VVS leadership ensued as Chief of the Air Staff Vasilii Khripin, Air Force Political Director Benedikt Troianker, Zhukovskii Air Force Academy head Aleksandr Todorskii, and large numbers of military district commanders were swept up by the Soviet secret police. By the end of 1939, more than three-fourth of VVS senior officers had been arrested, executed, or relieved of duty.[52] Subsequent commanders fared little better. Alksnis's successor, General Aleksandr Loktionov, a former rifle brigade commander with fewer than four years' experience in the air force, lasted only until September 1939 before being replaced with Iakov Smushkevitch, one-time head of the Soviet air group in the Spanish Civil War.[53]

The purge of Soviet aviation cadres did not end with the military's command and officer corps. Aeronautical designers, engineers, and researchers all fell victim to political repression. TsAGI director and chief of scientific research and construction at VAO, Nikolai Kharlamov, was arrested and executed in 1937. A similar fate befell his successor, M. N. Shul'zenko, in 1940. Employees throughout the aviation industry were dismissed by the thousands as many research, testing, and design organizations lost all or most of their key personnel. Moscow's Aviation Factory No. 1 lost its director, chief and deputy engineers, two design brigade chiefs, and four shop chiefs. Decimated by the losses, some production plants were shut down.[54] The nation's most

---

[49] For a full account of the military purge, see John Erickson, *The Soviet High Command: A Military–Political History, 1918–1941* (New York: St. Martin's, 1962), 449–73.

[50] Ronald Grigor Suny, *The Soviet Experiment: Russia, the USSR, and the Successor States* (New York: Oxford University Press, 1998), 264.

[51] The revised figures are cited in Roger R. Reese, *The Soviet Military Experience: A History of the Red Army, 1917–1991* (New York: Routledge, 2000), 85–92.

[52] Hardesty, *Red Phoenix*, 53–54 and Pennington, "From Chaos to the Eve of the Great Patriotic War," 50–1.

[53] Loktionov was executed in October 1941.

[54] John T. Greenwood, "Aviation Industry, 1917–1997," in Robin Higham *et al.* (eds.), *Russian Aviation*, 138.

prominent and distinguished engineers were not immune from arrest, as evidenced by bomber designers Vladimir Petliakov and Vladimir Miasishchev, both of whom were taken into custody in 1937. Even Andrei Tupolev, whose design bureau had been responsible for the Soviet Union's most celebrated accomplishments of the 1920s and 1930s was hauled in at the end of October 1937. His arrest occurred within three months of Mikhail Gromov's successful transpolar flight to San Jacinto, California, aboard the Tupolev-designed ANT-25. Assigned to the NKVD-run Central Design Bureau No. 29, Tupolev spent several years as a virtual slave laborer of the state. Although he, like Petliakov and Miasishchev, was spared execution, others were less fortunate. Konstantin Kalinin, famous for designing the first delta-wing airplane, was shot for "sabotage" in 1938 after the test-flight crash of his K-4 prototype claimed the lives of four Party members. The purges also claimed the lives of the aviation theorists Aleksandr Lapchinskii, Aleksei Algazin, and A. K. Mednis. According to the testimony of one contemporary aviation specialist imprisoned during the 1930s, as many as 50 leading designers, engineers, and technicians were shot by the end of the decade, while another 100 died in the Soviet prison camp system. Meanwhile, upwards of 300 arrested specialists were put to work in the special technical bureaus administered by the NKVD.[55]

The purges served only to exacerbate further the manifest problems plaguing Soviet aviation. Despite the positive impressions made on Europeans and Americans by prestige flights and exhibition pavilions, during the closing years of the 1930s the country's aviation programs remained mired in crisis. Although the VVS would perform reasonably well in a series of border skirmishes against the Japanese near Lake Khasan and Khalkin-Gol in 1938–9, a woeful performance in the "Winter War'" with Finland (November 1939–March 1940) provided clear evidence of its underlying weakness. Against the lightly armed and vastly outnumbered Finns, the Soviets proved embarrassingly incompetent. Lack of advance preparation, poor planning, inadequate intelligence, and amateurish generalship led to a series of early and decisive defeats. Following the late-December rout of the Red Army at Suomussalmi, Stalin reacted in characteristic fashion, sacking dozens of senior officers and ordering the execution of at least one divisional commander. Although the tide of the war turned following an overhaul of the military's command structure and the massive infusion of men and matériel, nearly 49,000 Soviet soldiers would lose their lives and an additional 158,000 would be wounded before the cessation of hostilities.[56]

The Red Air Force fared no better than the Red Army as the 200 obsolete aircraft deployed by the Finns proved more than a match for the 900-odd

[55] Kerber, *Stalin's Aviation Gulag, et passim.*

[56] This account of the Finnish campaign is based on the excellent short summary contained in David Glantz and Jonathan M. House, *When Titans Clashed: How the Red Army Stopped Hitler* (Lawrence, KS: University Press of Kansas, 1995), 18–23.

planes initially placed at the disposal of Soviet commanders. Inadequately trained Soviet pilots had great difficulty attempting to fly in the inclement weather that predominated during the first two-and-a-half months of the conflict. During this period, many aviation units managed fewer than seven operational days. To offset this problem, the quantity of planes in the theater of operations was soon doubled. Ultimately, such measures proved the difference as the USSR's ability to muster overwhelmingly superior numbers of airplanes and soldiers enabled it to wear down the Finns. Still, the cost of the campaign was steep. By the time the war ended in March 1940, the VVS had suffered the loss of 684 aircraft (240 in air combat) against only 62 lost by the Finns. Blame for this nearly catastrophic failure naturally fell on the head of Iakov Smushkevitch, the recently appointed VVS chief. In August 1940 he was relieved of command. The following year, he was arrested and shot. His successor, Pavel Rychagov, remained in his post for only one year before he, too, fell victim to the executioner's bullet.[57]

If the debacle in Finland revealed that there was less to Soviet military aviation than met the eye, the same was proving true of Soviet civilian aviation. By the end of the decade, Osoaviakhim, the country's largest and most prominent social organization devoted to aeronautics, had ceased to provide any meaningful service to the state. Conditions in Saratov *oblast'* typified the problems that afflicted the organization on a nationwide level. Reports delivered to the local Osoaviakhim presidium during 1937–8 revealed that despite (or perhaps more likely, owing to) repeated efforts to restructure the society's administration, Osoaviakhim continued to suffer from the same organizational maladies that had plagued ODVF and Aviakhim throughout the 1920s. Missing and uncollected membership dues, lack of meaningful programs or activities, disinterest on the part of local members, and "utter organizational chaos" were repeatedly cited as the society's principal achievements.[58] The youth camps and training centers that Osoaviakhim operated throughout the Soviet Union for the ostensible purpose of promoting aviation and civilian defense were in equally deplorable condition. Many lacked basic items such as boots, linens, and eating utensils. Owing to extraordinarily poor sanitary practices in the camps, outbreaks of food poisoning and lice infestation were common.[59] Such miserable conditions led to widespread corruption among the poorly paid and inadequately supported staff members charged with administering Osoaviakhim's programs. Embezzlement and outright theft of the society's property and funds skyrocketed as the

---

[57] Pennington, "From Chaos to the Eve of the Great Patriotic War," 51–2.

[58] TsDNISO f. 6141, op. 2, d. 6 (Zasedanii prezidiuma Saratovskogo oblastnoso soveta Osoaviakhima za 1937–1938 goda), ll. 141, 154–5, *et passim*.

[59] GARF f. 8355, op. 6, d. 6, ll. 55–65, cited in Timothy J. Paynich, "Black–Market Patriotism: Osoaviakhim and Illegal Trading Networks, 1927–1941," 16 (unpublished essay).

decade wore down. The arrest and execution of Osoaviakhim Chief Robert Eideman in 1938 did not solve these issues.

More visible to the public (and, thus, more disconcerting for image-conscious Party leaders) were a series of high-profile aviation catastrophes that occurred at decade's end. Beginning only weeks after the successful transpolar expeditions led by Chkalov and Gromov and continuing until the end of 1938, these accidents hinted at the systemic problems besetting Soviet aviation. In August 1937, an N-209 (DB-A) heavy bomber piloted by Sigizmund Levanevskii disappeared near the North Pole while attempting to complete a flight from Moscow to New York. Despite a seven-month search-and-rescue mission aided by pilots from the United States and Canada, neither the aircraft nor its six-man crew was ever found. The Soviet Union's aviation cadres suffered further blows to their prestige as poor weather conditions, mechanical failure, and pilot error led to several serious accidents during the search. The most spectacular of these occurred on 14 March 1938 when an N-212 under the command of Iakov Moshovskii veered out of control on takeoff and rammed into an N-211 piloted by Mikhail Babushkin. Babushkin's plane crashed into the ocean ice, exploding in a huge fireball. The experienced and highly regarded pilot was killed along with two others. Several more were injured.[60] Even successes were tempered by misfortune, as exemplified by the case of the ANT-37 *Motherland*, a twin-engine bomber dispatched from Moscow to the Far East in September 1938. Charged with setting a new world-distance record, the all-female flight crew (consisting of pilot Valentina Grizodubovaia, copilot Polina Osipenko, and navigator Marina Raskova) was forced down over Siberia after a fire broke out in the airplane's cabin. After spending two weeks in the isolated Siberian taiga, the crew was finally rescued, but not before a midair collision involving two aircraft dispatched to find them added another fifteen deaths to the mounting number of aviation casualties.[61] It was the worst catastrophe to befall Soviet aviation since the 1934 crash of the *Maxim Gorky*. Two months later, on 15 December 1938, Valerii Chkalov was killed while test-flying a Polikarpov I-180. The event set off another round of purges within aviation design and production circles. Although rumors quickly surfaced that the crash was orchestrated by Stalin to dispatch the popular pilot, it seems more likely that Chkalov's death resulted from his own well-known recklessness, coupled with adverse weather conditions and inadequate preparations by engineers who were under pressure to rush the plane into production.[62]

---

[60] RGASPI f. 82, op. 2, d. 620, l. 88.

[61] Prikaz no. 37 NKO SSSR, "Ob avariinosti v chastiakh Voenno–Vozdushnykh Sil RKKA," in *Glavnyi voennyi sovet RKKA, 13 marta 1938 g.–20 iiunia 1941 g.: dokumenty i materialy* (Moscow: ROSSPEN, 2004), 238.

[62] See the comments attributed to the Russian aviation historian D. A. Sobolev, in Von Hardesty's "Introduction" to Baidukov, *Russian Lindbergh*.

FIGURE 54. Viktor Deni and Nikolai Dolgorukov, "Long live the brave falcons of our homeland, the Stalinist pupils and courageous Soviet fliers who know no boundaries in accomplishing their established goals!" In this 1938 poster commemorating the flight of the *Motherland*, a fatherly Stalin looks down on the all–female flight crew – Valentina Grizodubovaia, Polina Osipenko, and Marina Raskova. Courtesy The Hoover Institution.

Questions regarding the quality of Soviet airplanes and air cadres became the subjects of increasing media scrutiny in the West following the return of America's premier aeronautical celebrity, Charles Lindbergh, from a tour of the USSR in the late summer of 1938. Accompanied by his wife, Lindbergh spent two weeks in the Soviet Union as an official observer for the U.S. government.[63] Although facilitated by the U.S. Departments of State and War, such visits were not at all unusual. As early as the 1920s celebrities and intellectuals, together with ordinary citizens from the United States and Western Europe, had begun traveling to the USSR to judge for themselves the degree of success attained by the Soviet "experiment." Typically idealistic, hopeful, and predisposed to a belief in socialism's ability to radically remodel

[63] The trip was Lindbergh's third to the Soviet Union. His first visit (which amounted to brief stops in Leningrad and Moscow) occurred in 1933 as part of a five-and-a-half-month Atlantic survey flight aboard a Lockheed Sirius aircraft. He had visited the Soviet Union a second time during the summer of 1936. As in 1938, this trip was arranged through the United States government as part of a "fact-finding" mission that also took the pilot to several other European countries, including Germany.

society and human behavior, these "political pilgrims" proved immensely valuable in legitimating the Soviet government to audiences abroad. With few exceptions, their published accounts provided Party leaders with a propaganda bonanza as the vast majority returned from Moscow bearing news of the miraculous transformations underway in the "workers' and peasants'" state.[64]

Given their overwhelming success in convincing western visitors of the virtues of Stalinism, Soviet officials' decision to host the Lindberghs' visit in the summer of 1938 is perfectly understandable. Notwithstanding Charles Lindbergh's well-publicized disdain for Communism, Party leaders could reasonably expect that the flier might be won over to a more charitable view of the Soviet Air Force and the regime that had built it. At the very least, even qualified statements of approbation on Lindbergh's part would help to discredit foreign notions that the Soviet Union's industrial and military accomplishments amounted to something less than had been officially advertised. Following their arrival in Moscow on 17 August, the couple was treated to a tightly scripted program that included tours of seven different aviation establishments (among them a military academy, engine and airframe factories, an experimental laboratory, research facilities, and a flying school). Additional trips to museums and the ballet, the metro, several factories, a collective farm, and a youth camp rounded out the Lindberghs' visit.

To the ultimate chagrin of Party officials, efforts to convince Lindbergh that the Soviet Union had reached parity with the West in terms of its aviation programs and industrial capacity proved unsuccessful. Although struck by the scale of the airplane factory that he visited in Moscow, Lindbergh correctly observed that "most of its machines and all of its best ones had been imported from the United States and Germany." The factory's workers impressed the airman as "neither highly trained nor skillful" while "the bombers under construction were inferior in design to those being built in America, Germany, and England." Subsequent visits to other aeronautical installations reinforced Lindbergh's general impression that the Soviet Air Force was noteworthy only for its "mediocrity." The dilapidated structures and poorly organized factories that he saw suggested that the country's actual accomplishments did not match official claims. On 30 August, he departed the USSR convinced that in terms of research laboratories, engines, and airplanes Soviet preparations were "inadequate for the conditions of modern war." Ultimately, he concluded, the Soviet Air Force was "no match for the German *Luftwaffe* in either quality or quantity."[65]

---

[64] Paul Hollander, *Political Pilgrims: Travels of Western Intellectuals to the Soviet Union, China, and Cuba, 1928–1978* (New York: Oxford University Press, 1981); on the pilgrimages to the USSR in the twenties and thirties, see 102–78.

[65] Charles A. Lindbergh, *Autobiography of Values* (New York: Harcourt, 1992), 163–7.

Lindbergh arrived in Great Britain in mid-September following an extended stopover in Prague and a side trip to Paris. Sometime later, in a private dinner conversation with Lady Astor at Cliveden, he was alleged to have commented that the Soviet Air Fleet was "without leadership and in a chaotic condition" whereas the *Luftwaffe* was well-enough equipped to "defeat the combined air fleets of Britain, France, the Soviet Union, and Czechoslovakia." Lindbergh's remarks were summarized in a mimeographed London scandal sheet called *The Week*, which purported to provide the "secret history" of current British and world affairs.[66] Occurring against the backdrop of the unfolding Munich Crisis, the comments did not place Lindbergh in good stead with public opinion makers. His subsequent decision to travel to Berlin in early October (where, at Hitler's personal order, he was awarded the Service Cross of the German Eagle with Star) produced surprise and indignation among the mainstream European and American press. Increasingly the airman came under fire for what appeared to be his pro-Nazi sympathies. The *New York Times*, which for years had turned a blind eye to Stalinist atrocities, devoted considerable space to Lindbergh's floundering European popularity. Left-wing publications in Paris and elsewhere attacked him as a Hitlerite stooge. Not surprisingly, the Soviet reaction was even more hostile. In the wake of Lindbergh's published comments to Lady Astor and his trip to Berlin, *Pravda* countered with a 10 October 1938 article excoriating the "has-been flier" as a "toad," "lackey," and "hired liar who has fulfilled the tasks of his [Nazi] masters" in an attempt to weaken the prestige of Soviet aviation.[67] Less than one month later, in a public speech before a packed house at Moscow's Bolshoi Theater, Soviet Premier Viascheslav Molotov repeated these insults, labeling Lindbergh a "paid liar" and "Fascist agent."[68]

Unknown to the public at the time was that Lindbergh's observations were very much in line with the independent assessments reached earlier by American military officials. One of the more revealing reports had been submitted by Thomas D. White, the Army lieutenant on hand to observe the public unveiling of the *Maxim Gorky*. During the summer of 1934, White had flown from Moscow to the Crimea aboard a Douglas O-38F airplane, gathering first-hand information on the status of the Soviet Union's domestic aviation network. Although admitting that he did not yet have "sufficient experience over Soviet air routes to explode the Soviet air myth," White indicated his clear impression that Soviet officials had significantly exaggerated their level of aeronautical development. Numerous frustrating attempts to have

[66] Davis, *Hero*, 380.

[67] "Novyi 'rekord' Charlza Lindberga," *Pravda*, 10 October 1938.

[68] *Pravda*, 9 November 1938. Nine months later, as the newly appointed People's Commissar of Foreign Affairs, Molotov would append his signature to the Soviet Non–Aggression Pact with Nazi Germany.

his plane properly serviced by local personnel while en route revealed that Soviet ground crews lacked rudimentary knowledge of standard maintenance and safety measures. The experience led White to conclude that the country's efforts were best characterized by "bureaucratic machinations, inertia, and inefficiency." No less telling were physical conditions at the airfields that he visited. "At each airport," he noted, there "exists a new but rapidly deteriorating and extremely badly built aerodrome office and waiting room. Except for miscellaneous wooden shacks and steel drums of gasoline stored in various states of disorder no other buildings or facilities exist at any of the airports visited. There are no hangars, no gas trucks, gasoline reservoirs or stationary pumps."[69] White's critical assessment was verified in May 1935 by Staff Sergeant John C. Cook, who undertook a series of ten separate assessment flights aboard Soviet domestic passenger aircraft for the U. S. Air Corps. The experience proved exceedingly unpleasant as the sergeant was constantly forced to contend with uncomfortable and overloaded aircraft, dilapidated and filthy airports, and interminable delays. Issues of comfort aside, Cook, as White before him, was shocked by the lax safety measures that he observed as well as the poor condition of the improperly maintained aircraft on which he flew. The series of flights aboard domestic passenger aircraft led him to observe that the Soviets' efforts "cannot compare with even the poorest of the American airways."[70] The subsequent observations of Major George E. Huthsteiner, a U.S. military attaché based in Latvia, revealed that as many as four years later few improvements had been made. Reporting on the condition of the Soviet Air Force in May of 1939, Huthsteiner concluded,

Most of the [air force] personnel are poorly trained, and it is estimated that about one quarter of the first line planes will remain inactive during an emergency due to the shortage of qualified pilots and observers. There is also a shortage of spare parts and facilities which will seriously hamper military operations. The technical personnel is insufficient. According to the statement of a well-informed aviation expert, the Red Air Forces will practically cease to exit after three months of a major war unless there is a radical change for the better.[71]

In at least one critical respect Huthsteiner's assessment proved incorrect. Following the German invasion on 22 June 1941, the Soviet Air Force practically ceased to exist after only three weeks.

The qualified successes and less mitigated failures of Soviet aviation during the 1930s were not the immanent results of a hypercentralized economy,

---

[69] NARA, "Correspondence of the Military Intelligence Division Relating to General, Political, Economic, and Military Conditions in Russia and the Soviet Union, 1918–1941" (Microfilm Publication M1443), MID 2090, roll 20, frame 1036.

[70] *Ibid.*, frames 953–956. The quote appears on frame 956.

[71] *Ibid.*, frame 555.

nor were they unique outgrowths prompted by a headlong rush toward industrialization. Although the scope and scale of "Stalinist" aviation far exceeded anything imagined in the 1920s or 1910s, the manner in which the Party attempted to realize its air-minded aspirations and the symbolic language that it employed to advertise its achievements were indebted to cultural precedents deeply imbedded in the nation's history. In every major respect, the approaches to aeronautical development undertaken during the decade demonstrated the indissoluble link between Russia's present and past.

Reprising the longtime strategy of borrowing from abroad to jump-start development at home, Soviet experts ventured West (especially to the United States) in search of aviation materials and expertise. Benefiting from the liberal trade policies of American corporations and the lax security standards of the U.S. government, they secured the acquisition of leading-edge technologies indispensable to the modernization of their own industries. The transfer of technology was accompanied by the transfer of technique as delegations of pilots, engineers, and graduate students were dispatched to observe and to master the latest production procedures developed by foreign firms. Beginning in 1931 and continuing throughout the decade, Soviet delegations maintained a constant presence in American factories and enterprises. What they could not obtain openly they secured surreptitiously through an extensive espionage network that operated virtually unchecked in industries across the United States.

In the hope of more effectively exploiting the resources acquired abroad, the state strengthened its monopoly on the aviation industry. Mirroring the consolidation and militarization of civil organizations during the 1920s that had produced Osoaviakhim, the state centralized all aeronautical enterprises by conjoining civilian and military production into the bureaucratic mega-agency Glavaviaprom. In time, all major decisions related to aviation would be made at the very highest levels of the Soviet state. Initially, these strategies paid quick dividends as designers and technicians managed qualitative and quantitative improvements that far exceeded previous levels of indigenous production. Even so, the Soviet Union continued to lag behind the West. In a pattern identical to the Imperial experience, Soviet technicians struggled to duplicate imported engines and airframes while foreign manufactures continued to produce major new breakthroughs. Although new generations of Soviet aircraft emerged as the 1930s progressed, their development depended on recurrent infusions of foreign technology. Despite every effort, the Soviet Union could not "overtake and surpass" its ideological opponents. Its aviation industry was incapable of self-generating growth.

Institutionalized dependence on the West was further exacerbated by Communist Party officials' sense of urgency. Emphasizing the need for haste in the confrontation with capital, state leaders forced production tempos and imposed excessively high quotas in a desperate race to prepare for impending ideological Armageddon. The time allotted for the design and construction of new airplanes was drastically reduced from the standards established by western aviation firms. Although this ensured that new aircraft would emerge at a relatively rapid rate, it had a deleterious effect on planes' durability and airworthiness. Hastily constructed prototypes, like the ANT-14, were commissioned for service before being equipped with necessary components while production models often failed to meet the performance specifications forecast by designers.

Sharing with their Imperial forbears an iconic vision of flight, Soviet officials recognized aviation as both an agent and a symbol of industrial modernization. They looked to the airplane as a sign of their progress and as a means of facilitating the rapid transition to socialism. The aerial behemoth *Maxim Gorky* reflected this propensity. Intended as a marker and means of Party-mandated enlightenment, the ANT-20 represented the colossal strides made under socialism at the same time that it contributed to a collective sense of community. Pilots, too, served as icons of the air-minded Soviet state. Allegedly distinguished from their western counterparts by their altruism and self-sacrifice, they symbolically expressed officially sanctioned values such as loyalty, discipline, and collectivity while providing ordinary citizens with role models to emulate. Although the language used to describe their exploits was deeply indebted to Russia's religious and folk traditions, they were upheld as quintessential examples of the modern "New Soviet Person."

Unable to fulfill immediately the utopian promises made to their populace, Soviet leaders relied on compensatory symbolism to bridge the divide between their rhetoric and reality. Expecting that the next crash campaign (or the one after that) would finally provide the nation with its longed-for transcendent act, Party leaders marked time with Potemkin displays that enhanced their prestige, but conferred few concrete benefits. The record-setting ANT-25 was but one case in point. Developed at considerable expense over a period of six years, the aircraft achieved its goal of establishing a new world-distance record. Beyond that, it had no value. Incredibly slow, poorly armed, and incapable of carrying freight, the airplane was useless for military or civilian applications. Still, it attracted the attention of the state's foreign adversaries, raising concerns (albeit false) of the Soviet Union's industrial and military might.

Ironically, at the very height of its reputation abroad, the Red Air Force faltered. First in Spain, then in Finland, the repercussions of the Party's misguided policies became all too evident. The "victories" achieved under Stalin's leadership proved largely spurious. Crippled with obsolescent planes, outdated tactics, and an officer corps decimated from terror, the VVS proved hollow in the nation's time of need. Paralleling the experience of the Imperial Air Fleet in 1914, the Soviet Red Air Force was subjected to crushing defeat during the opening weeks of war in June 1941. Like their tsarist predecessors before them, Party leaders had fallen victim to ideological illusions. Taking false comfort in projected visions of grandeur, they had come to believe their own exaggerated rhetoric. The Soviet people would pay a terrible price for this hubris.

9

Red Phoenix

OPERATION BARBAROSSA

The beginning of "Operation Barbarossa," Adolf Hitler's plan to vanquish the Soviet Union and thereby secure mastery over the European continent, was marked by spectacular success. In the predawn hours of Sunday, 22 June 1941, advanced bomber detachments of the German *Luftwaffe* passed over the eastern frontier of Nazi-occupied Poland en route to ten major airbases located behind Red Army front lines. This initial contingent of aircraft was soon followed by a full-scale aerial assault as a German air force, comprising 500 bombers, 270 dive bombers, and 480 fighters, subjected Soviet positions to incessant bombardment. Wave on wave of German airplanes struck at sixty-six separate airfields that served as bases for nearly three fourths of Soviet combat aircraft. Caught unprepared, and capable of mounting only token resistance, the VVS suffered catastrophic defeat. By noon on the 22nd, nearly 890 combat aircraft had been destroyed, the vast majority of these while still on the ground. Before nightfall, 921 more airplanes were added to the tally. During the second twenty-four hours of hostilities an additional 1,000 aircraft were destroyed. Devastation continued in the days and weeks that followed. By 9 July, the Soviet Air Force had lost at least 3,985 airplanes, according to official figures. In contrast, *Luftwaffe* combat losses amounted to only 150 aircraft.[1]

Following the suppression of the enemy's air capabilities, German strategy called for the *Wehrmacht* to advance into the Soviet Union along three main lines: Army Group South toward Odessa, Kiev, and the Crimea; Army Group North through the Baltic States en route to Leningrad; and Army Group Center toward the Soviet capital, Moscow. According to the plans drawn up by Hitler and his generals, the first phase of operations would focus on the annihilation of Red Army forces stationed in the Ukrainian and Baltic regions. From there, the Soviet military would be pushed deep into Russia,

---

[1] Von Hardesty, *Red Phoenix: The Rise of Soviet Air Power, 1941–1945* (Washington, D.C.: The Smithsonian Institution Press, 1982), 11–15, and John T. Greenwood, "Soviet Frontal Aviation during the Great Patriotic War, 1941–1945," in Robin Higham, John T. Greenwood, and Von Hardesty (eds.), *Russian Aviation and Airpower in the Twentieth Century* (London: Cass, 1998), 65.

beyond the Ural Mountains, leaving Germany proper safe from the prospect of retributive bombing. Ultimately, the surviving remnants of Bolshevism would be isolated beyond the Volga River behind a defensible border stretching from the Caspian Sea northward to the Urals and Arkhangel'sk on the Arctic Ocean.[2] To accomplish this monumental task, German military planners had amassed a monumental force. Comprising an estimated 3,350 tanks, 7,200 artillery pieces, 2,770 airplanes, and more than 152 divisions totaling 3.8 million men in uniform, theirs was the largest invading army in human history.[3]

The decimation of the Red Air Force during the opening phase of Operation Barbarossa and the ensuing rout of the Red Army exceeded even the most optimistic expectations of German planners. So, too, did the rapidity of the German advance. The complete collapse of the Soviet military set the stage for the *Wehrmacht*'s lightning-quick deployment deep into Russian territory. Having attained absolute surprise and air superiority within the first seventy-two-hours of conflict, Hitler's army was free to maneuver at will along the entirety of its 1,800-mile Eastern Front. By 1 July, the German Army had overrun and occupied the Baltic states of Lithuania and Latvia. Eight days later, Białystok and the Belorussian capital Minsk fell. Smolensk followed on 16 July. Entire Soviet Army groups numbering hundreds of thousands of soldiers were destroyed by the advancing Germans in a series of spectacular encirclement maneuvers. At Smolensk alone, the Red Army lost over 417,000 men.[4]

The advance abated only toward the end of July when Hitler, fearing that his panzer tank groups might outrun their supply lines, temporarily called a halt to the offensive in order that his troops might rest and refit. The respite did not last long. The offensive resumed in full force toward the end of August. German strategy, however, had now changed. Believing that the capture of the Soviet Union's industrial and agricultural centers was far more important than occupying the capital, Hitler turned his attention away from Moscow. Over the vocal opposition of his leading generals, he ordered the diversion of Army Group Center's panzers to support a two-pronged late-summer offensive toward Leningrad in the north and the Ukraine in the south. The decision proved an immense tactical success. Aided by Germany's Finnish allies, Army Group North soon reached the outskirts of Leningrad. By 8 September, the city's 3 million inhabitants were surrounded. Nine hundred days and 1.5 million civilian lives would pass before the siege was lifted. Meanwhile, in the south, the onrushing panzers quickly occupied the

---

[2] Roger R. Reese, *The Soviet Military Experience: A History of the Red Army, 1917–1991* (New York: Routledge, 2000), 100.

[3] David M. Glantz and Jonathan M. House, *When Titans Clashed: How the Red Army Stopped Hitler* (Lawrence, KS: University Press of Kansas, 1995), 31.

[4] *Ibid.*, 53.

ancient city of Kiev (18 September), encircling and destroying in the process four Soviet field armies totaling more than 665,000 men. The Red Army's Southern Front had effectively disintegrated.

At the end of September, with Leningrad isolated and panzers bearing down on Rostov, the *Wehrmacht* resumed its push toward Moscow. Now, however, the German Army faced two opponents. As Soviet resistance intensified, the weather grew inclement. The first snowfall in early October was followed by the *razputitsa* (literally "time without roads"), the in-between season that strikes Russia each fall and spring, bringing heavy rains that turn unpaved roads into impassable mire. The Nazi offensive slowed to a crawl. When rain turned to snow in early November, the *Wehrmacht* regained momentum, but the advance toward Moscow was exacting increasingly high costs. The German Army faced a precarious situation. Its forces were strung out along a 1,500-mile front, its supply lines overextended, and its troops were not properly equipped to contend with the oncoming winter. In retrospect, Hitler's late-summer decision to divert forces from Army Group Center had proved a major strategic blunder. The two-month diversion had given the Red Army precious time to regroup and fortify its positions. When the Battle of Moscow was joined in early November, the *Wehrmacht* was forced to contend with a now battle-hardened opponent and temperatures hovering near minus twenty degrees Fahrenheit.

The drive toward Moscow brought advanced units of the German Army to within fifteen miles of the city before stalling. On 5 December, the Red Army struck back. Reinforced by troops called up from Siberia and the Far East, the Soviet military launched a major counteroffensive aimed at relieving the capital and reversing its long string of crushing defeats. Shocked by the tenacity of their Soviet opponents and unprepared for one of the harshest Russian winters in almost a century, the Germans were thrown back almost 200 miles. In the process, they lost several hundred thousand men. For the first time in its history, Hitler's *Wehrmacht* had suffered a major defeat. It would not be the last. The Soviet stance at the gates of Moscow was an augur of things to come. Although the war's most decisive battles remained to be fought, time was no longer on Germany's side. The Battle of Moscow marked the beginning of the end of the Nazi Third Reich.

RUSSIA'S WAR

The German invasion could hardly have come at a worse time for the Red Army and Air Force. Caught in a period of institutional transition and still reeling from the bloodletting unleashed by the 1937–8 purges of the officer corps, the Soviet military proved disastrously unprepared for battle. Despite enjoying numerical superiority in terms of tanks and airplanes, Soviet equipment was vastly inferior to that fielded by the Germans. The lightly armored and obsolete T-26 tank that formed the bulk of the Red Army's mechanized divisions in 1941 was no match for the German Mark III and Mark IV Panzers. Likewise, the VVS posed little threat to the *Luftwaffe* in the war's opening stages. Although an estimated 9,576 combat aircraft made it the largest in the world, the Red Air Force, like the numerous aviation "achievements" hailed by propagandists during the preceding two decades, was something of a Potemkin production.[5] The majority of Soviet planes were obsolescent and poorly maintained. Meanwhile, many Soviet fighter pilots had as few as four hours' flying time in their aircraft. Although the VVS would later achieve technical parity with the *Luftwaffe* thanks to the introduction of the advanced MiG-3 fighter, the Il-2 "Shturmovik" ground-attack plane, and the Pe-2 dive bomber, too few had been deployed to make a difference by June 1941. Moreover, the transition to the new equipment was marked by characteristic confusion. In the opening days of the conflict, the Red Air Force's new Su-2 bombers (whose deployment had been kept secret from Soviet fighter pilots) came under attack from Soviet airmen and antiaircraft batteries.[6] In time, the exigencies of war and a Herculean effort by the country's engineers and factory workers would decisively tip the balance in favor of the Soviet Union, but not before the country paid a catastrophic price for the mistakes of the 1930s.

With the outbreak of war, the Soviet High Command dissolved into complete disarray. Four hours after the beginning of the invasion, the commissar of war, Marshal Semen Timoshenko, responded to the German onslaught by issuing orders for Soviet troops to go on the offensive, using "all their strength and means [to] attack enemy forces and liquidate them in the areas where they have violated the Soviet frontier." However, the order continued, the Red Army was prohibited from crossing the frontier "unless given special authorization." This nonsensical command was followed the same evening by a second even more unrealistic directive that instructed forward units to launch an immediate counteroffensive against the Germans. Aware of the actual situation, but fearing retribution from above, subordinate commanders compounded the mounting crisis by passing the order on to the front. In the days that followed, tens of thousands of soldiers were sacrificed in ill-planned actions against vastly superior forces.[7]

The chaos and confusion that gripped the Red Army at the outset of the war was, to a considerable extent, an outgrowth of the ideologically

[5] For recent assessments of the size, strength, and readiness of the Red Air Force in 1941, see David M. Glantz, *Stumbling Colossus: The Red Army on the Eve of World War* (Lawrence, KS: University Press of Kansas, 1998), 184–204, and M. I. Mel'tiukhov, "22 iiuniia 1941 g.: Tsifri svidetel'stvuiut," *Istoriia SSSR* 3 (March 1991): 16–28.

[6] Alexander Werth, *Russia at War, 1941–1945* (New York: Dutton, 1964), 139; Alexander Boyd, *The Soviet Air Force Since 1918* (New York: Stein and Day, 1977), 113; and Hardesty, *Red Phoenix*, 24–5.

[7] John Erickson, *The Soviet High Command: A Military–Political History, 1918–1941* (London: St. Martin's, 1962), 587, and Glantz and House, *When Titans Clashed*, 51.

inspired myopia and incompetence that plagued the highest ranks of the country's government. In this regard, Josef Stalin was particularly culpable. The "Father of the Soviet Peoples" greeted news of the German invasion with surprise and incredulity. In the weeks leading up to 22 June, he had dismissed numerous reports of an impending German attack as nothing more than lies and provocations. Believing that Hitler was too sensible to open a front in the East while still at war with the British, Stalin elected to ignore the mounting signs of danger reported by foreign diplomats and his own intelligence agents. He continued to fulfill assiduously the terms of the Non-Aggression Pact that he had forged with Hitler in 1939, ostensibly to buy time to strengthen the Soviet military. The launch of Operation Barbarossa demonstrated the artlessness of Stalin's foreign policy. The rapid collapse of the Red Army proved empty the militaristic rhetoric of the 1930s. Shaken by the disastrous turn of events, the "Great Leader" abandoned his post. Perhaps expecting that his subordinates would hold him accountable for the debacle or that the regime would be overthrown by a popular revolt, he fled to the seclusion of his summer house outside of Moscow. According to some accounts, he endeavored to relieve his mounting fear by drinking heavily.[8] Several days later, having regained his composure and confidence, he returned to the capital and assumed command of the war effort.

Considerable time and a great many lives passed before the Red Army mounted its first serious opposition to the Germans at the gates of Moscow. In the meantime, Stalin hoped to forestall collapse by demanding that the military not give ground. Soviet territory would be held to the last drop of blood. His refusal to approve General Georgii Zhukov's recommendation that the Red Army retreat from Kiev to a defensible position behind the Dnepr' River led to the encirclement and loss of more than 665,000 men in mid-September.[9] In a frantic effort to slow the rapidly advancing German Army, Stalin ordered that military commanders impose draconian measures on their own troops. Discipline would be maintained through coercion and drastic punishments. "Deserters," "traitors," and those who "abandoned weapons and battle-stations" were subjected to summary execution at the hands of special NKVD detachments deployed behind the front lines.[10]

---

[8] Peter Kenez, *A History of the Soviet Union from Beginning to End* (Cambridge: Cambridge University Press, 1999), 139, and Ronald Grigor Suny, *The Soviet Experiment: Russia, the USSR, and the Successor States* (New York: Oxford University Press, 1998), 310–11. For an alternative interpretation of Stalin's activities in the wake of the invasion, see Steven J. Main, "Stalin in June 1941: A Comment on Cynthia Roberts," *Europe-Asia Studies* 48(5) (1996): 837–9.

[9] Reese, *Soviet Military Experience*, 101.

[10] John Erickson, *The Road to Stalingrad: Stalin's War with Germany* (New York: Harper & Row, 1975), 176. For an overview of the NKVD's "shadow army," see David Glantz, *Colossus Reborn: The Red Army at War, 1941–1943* (Lawrence, KS: University Press of Kansas, 2005), 157–77.

Similar measures were enacted on the home front, where the situation was no less bleak. In mid-October, with the Germans relentlessly pressing their attack on Russia's heartland, preparations were undertaken by the government to abandon Moscow. Panic ensued. To forestall complete disorder, the state directed that looters and panic-mongers be shot. For good measure, orders were also given to shoot every tenth apartment manager.[11]

Had Soviet authorities been forced to rely solely on coercion and terror to stop the German advance, it is doubtful that the regime would have survived the war. Stalin was most assuredly aware of this. When he finally delivered his first wartime radio broadcast to the public on 3 July, the tone and language of his speech was wholly uncharacteristic. Addressing his audience as "brothers and sisters," Stalin implored the country's citizens to rally behind the cause of the "all-people's patriotic war against the German–Fascist forces." Allied with Europe and America, he declared, the USSR would wage a successful struggle for "independence and democratic freedom" that would free those currently "groaning under the yoke of German Fascism" and liberate the Soviet motherland from its occupying forces.[12] Absent from Stalin's speech were references to "class war," "proletarian internationalism," and other rhetorical fetishes long favored by Party leaders. Throughout the remainder of the conflict, as Soviet propagandists endeavored to inspire citizens to further acts of bravery and heroism, they invoked names and images from the Russian past, rallying them by appealing to their sense of tradition, their Russian patriotism, and their love of the *rodina-mat'*. The strategy was not that unusual. During the preceding two decades propagandists had routinely co-opted long-standing symbols and customs in an effort to legitimate the Party and its programs. Still, the effective abandonment of Marxist rhetoric for the duration of the war was an implicit admission that attempts to promote social unity and cohesion through appeals to class consciousness, worker solidarity, and Party loyalty had failed.[13]

Whatever the value of propaganda and terror in advancing the country's war effort, it was the strength of the Soviet people that secured victory over Germany. Despite the manifest incompetence of military and state officials at the outset of the War, the soldiers of the Red Army fought with tenacity and courage. During the darkest days of the summer of 1941, desperate Air Force pilots adopted the last-ditch tactic of *taran*, intentionally ramming their aircraft into German bombers after having exhausted their ammunition (a technique pioneered during the First World War by the Imperial aviator Petr Nesterov).[14] In the months and years that followed their stand at the gates of

---

[11] Richard Overy, *Russia's War* (New York: Penguin, 1997), 97–8.

[12] Cited in Suny, *Soviet Experiment*, 311.

[13] John Barber and Mark Harrison, *The Soviet Home Front, 1914–1945: A Social and Economic History of the USSR in World War II* (London: Longman, 1991), 69–70.

[14] See Chapter 2, p. 68. According to official Soviet sources, more than 200 instances of *taran* were carried out by Soviet pilots during the war. See Hardesty, *Red Phoenix*, 27–30.

Moscow, soldiers and pilots continued to display uncommon valor. Ordinary citizens, too, contributed mightily to the cause. Beginning in July of 1941, they preserved the country's productive capacity (and thereby guaranteed ultimate victory) by dismantling and evacuating thousands of factories and industrial enterprises to the East where they were reassembled beyond the reach of German bombers.

Faced with the barbarism of the Nazi invaders, Russian men and women endured terrible deprivations in the defense of their homeland. Their collective sacrifice is all the more poignant, given the barbarism inflicted on them by their own government. Before, during, and after the war, Soviet officials were profligate with human life. Even after 1942, when the tide of battle had shifted in their favor, the casual waste of lives continued as military leaders used human decoys, ordered frontal assaults on armored lines, and punished their own men for alleged cowardice.[15] After the war, soldiers who had suffered unimaginable horrors in German POW camps returned home only to find themselves charged as "traitors" and "Nazi collaborators." Hundreds of thousands were dispatched to prison camps in Siberia and the Far East. Although victory was finally achieved in the spring of 1945, it came at a terrible price. By the time that the Red Army occupied Berlin, the Soviet Union had suffered the deaths of nearly 28 million citizens, soldiers and civilians combined.[16]

RED PHOENIX

The fortunes of the Red Air Force during the Great Patriotic War mirrored those of the Red Army and the country as a whole. In the opening days and weeks of the conflict, the VVS suffered grievous losses as inexperienced and unprepared pilots flying obsolete planes were sent into battle by incompetent commanders to face a more tactically and technologically advanced opponent. By early December 1941, the Soviet Air Force teetered on the edge of annihilation. That it staved off collapse testified to the discipline and tenacity of ordinary Soviet citizens. That it was reborn in the course of the conflict testified to a variety of factors, many of which were not directly influenced by the Soviet people and their leaders.

Much of the Red Air Force's ultimate success derived from rapid increases in the production of airplanes, parts, and engines after late 1942. The country's industrial sector proved remarkably resilient during the war. Between 1942 and 1945, the Soviet aviation industry attained levels of production unprecedented in its history. Increases in output were matched by significant improvements in the quality and durability of Soviet airplanes. At the outset of the war, Soviet fighter and bomber pilots, flying obsolete I-15s, I-16s,

[15] Catherine Merridale, *Night of Stone: Death and Memory in Twentieth-Century Russia* (New York: Penguin, 2000), 215.
[16] Barber and Harrison, *Soviet Home Front*, 206–7.

FIGURE 55. Ilyushin Il-2 "Shturmovik" aircraft in flight. Photo courtesy Von Hardesty.

and TB-3s, found themselves unable to cope with the faster and more nimble German fighters. By early 1943, however, the production in quantity of the next generation of Soviet aircraft meant that, at the very least, the performance gap between the two adversaries had been significantly reduced. Moreover, the arrival in quantity of the Il-2 "Shturmovik" fighter bomber provided the Soviet Army with a reliable aerial "tank killer" that enabled it to blunt the offensive potential of Hitler's panzers.

Relative to the best planes produced by American, British, and German factories, Soviet aircraft were not the most technically advanced, but they were durable and increasingly effective as the war ground on. By essentially forgoing efforts at research and development in order to focus on refining a handful of highly reliable, but less complex, models, Soviet factories proved capable of producing serviceable aircraft in sufficiently large numbers. By late in the war, the build quality of Soviet planes finally surpassed that of the *Luftwaffe* as the Germans came to rely increasingly on poorly motivated slave laborers. Thus, as the conflict progressed, Soviet airplanes came to more closely match (and in some cases surpass) those fielded by Germany. More important, they arrived in increasingly large numbers. In the end, the VVS and the country as a whole weathered the brunt of the German offensive before overwhelming the *Wehrmacht* by dint of greater manpower and superior production capacity.

The VVS also benefited from a fundamental shift in organization and tactics that helped transform it into a more useful and effective military arm. At the outset of the War, Soviet fighters were organized into tight three-plane groups [*zveno*] whose assigned task of supporting small army units dictated that they be stretched out along the length of a front. Conversely, the country's sizable contingent of bombers was concentrated into separate squadrons of nine aircraft that flew in close "wedge" or "line" formations to maximize defensive firepower and reduce losses. These poorly coordinated deployments revealed the considerable extent to which the country's military commanders had failed to understand the principles of modern air combat. They contributed greatly to the widespread destruction of Soviet aircraft in the opening weeks of battle as fighters were frittered away in ineffective front-line engagements while slow and vulnerable bomber formations were destroyed en mass by German interceptors and antiaircraft batteries.[17]

The organizational and tactical transformation of the Red Air Force began in the spring of 1942 following the replacement of VVS Commander General Pavel Zhigarev with Aleksandr Novikov, a young and talented officer who had earned Stalin's regard for successfully organizing air operations around Leningrad. Novikov understood well the Red Air Force's deficiencies. He set out to rectify these by combining an indigenous operational style with the proven techniques developed by the Germans. Insisting on concentrating available aircraft in order that they might carry out wide-ranging and devastating aerial strikes, Novikov oversaw the creation of more flexible combined air armies composed of fighters, bombers, and ground-attack planes. Closely controlled from a central command structure (thanks to reorganized radio communications and the gradual introduction of radar), the Red Air Force was increasingly used in well-coordinated offensive attacks on German air bases and ground units. In short order, Novikov's efforts helped to close the performance gap between the VVS and the *Luftwaffe*.[18]

Success also depended on factors largely beyond the control of Soviet commanders. Demonstrating one of the few tangible benefits derived from the prewar infatuation with Arctic flying, VVS planes and pilots proved much better adapted to operating in extreme environments. They also benefited from better equipped, permanent airfields, and secure supply lines. The resolve of Red Air Force pilots was another key to victory. As already noted, their willingness to adopt the desperate tactic of *taran* helped forestall the German advance in the opening phase of Operation Barbarossa. Similarly, the examples set by pilots like Nikolai Gastello served to inspire countless other Red airmen to acts of bravery and personal sacrifice. In the opening days of the war, Gastello directed his damaged plane into an advancing

[17] Hardesty, *Red Phoenix*, 26.
[18] *Ibid.*, 126.

column of tanks, sacrificing himself in an effort to forestall the German advance.[19]

The rebirth of the Soviet Air Force was further abetted by the considerable contributions of airplanes, spare parts, and other materials supplied by the country's wartime allies, the United States and Great Britain. Particularly significant were American shipments of A-20 "Havoc" light bombers and P-40 "Warhawk" and P-63 "Kingcobra" fighter aircraft. Considered obsolete by the Allied air forces, the P-39 "Airacobra" also proved immensely successful on the Eastern Front as both a "tank buster" and a fighter interceptor.[20] Three of the Soviet Union's top four aces, Aleksandr Pokryshkin, Nikolai Gulaev, and Georgii Rechkalov, recorded the majority of their combat victories while flying these airplanes. America's all-purpose military and civilian workhorse, the C-47 (DC-3), also proved invaluable. Produced in the USSR under license as the Li-2, it comprised the bulk of Soviet air transport capacity until well after the war.[21] Although the approximate 18,303 planes obtained from the United States and Great Britain amounted to only 15.6% of the 117,501 combat aircraft produced indigenously by Soviet factories between 1941 and 1945, they nevertheless represented a vital injection of capable aircraft. No less important, the Allies ensured that Soviet-built planes were able to fly and fight as the United States provided more than half of the aviation fuel and explosives used by the VVS during the war.[22]

Allied contributions of airplanes and aeronautical supplies represented only a small portion of the immense aid shipments that arrived in the Soviet Union via Lend-Lease. The Western Allies (overwhelmingly led, of course, by the United States) delivered a staggering amount of armaments, vehicles, communication equipment, and raw materials, all of which made possible the Soviet war effort. Front-line communications were facilitated by the shipment of 35,000 radio stations, 380,000 field telephones, and 956,000 miles of telephone cable.[23] The reconstruction and maintenance of the Soviet supply system was guaranteed by the arrival of more than half a million vehicles, including 77,900 jeeps, 151,000 light trucks, and over 200,000 Studebaker army trucks. Generally of higher quality and durability than Soviet-produced models, these vehicles accounted for fully one-third of

[19] Rosalinde Sartori, "On the Making of Heroes, Heroines, and Saints," in Richard Stites (ed.), *Culture and Entertainment in Wartime Russia* (Bloomington, IN: Indiana University Press, 1995), 181.

[20] Dmitriy Loza, *Attack of the Airacobras: Soviet Aces, American P-39s, and the Air War Against Germany*. Translated and edited by James F. Gebhardt. (Lawrence, KS: University Press of Kansas, 2001).

[21] Robert A. Kilmarx, *A History of Soviet Air Power* (New York: Praeger, 1962), 160 and 231.

[22] Overy, *Russia's War*, 197.

[23] Hubert P. van Tuyll, *Feeding the Bear: American Aid to the Soviet Union, 1941–1945* (Westport, CT: Greenwood, 1989), 156–7.

FIGURE 56. Georgii Rechkalov, the Soviet Union's third-ranking World War II ace with fifty-five recorded "kills," alongside his American-made P-39 "Airacobra." Photo courtesy Von Hardesty.

Soviet ground transport. In addition, more than half (56.6%) of the rails used during the war were supplied by American factories, as were 1,900 locomotives and 11,075 railway cars. The latter were particularly valuable given the Soviet Union's meager wartime production of train engines (92) and rolling stock (1,087). The western assistance program also helped sustain Soviet industrial production by supplying the country's factories with more than $500 million in machine tools and equipment, 2.25 million tons of steel, and some 339,000 tons of copper. The arrival of more than 261,000 tons of aluminum, representing the equivalent of two years' Soviet production at 1945 rates, made possible the Red Air Force's belated conversion to all-metal aircraft late in the conflict.[24]

From the end of the Great Patriotic War in 1945 until the collapse of the USSR in 1991, official Soviet histories of the war dismissed Lend-Lease as having had little or no influence in shaping the Red Army's victory. More recent reevaluations by both western and Russian scholars clearly reveal that this was not the case. The material contributions made by the Allies were very substantial, a fact privately admitted by Josef Stalin during and after the war. In a series of taped interviews suppressed until after the collapse of the Soviet Union in 1991, Nikita Khrushchev reported having heard Stalin

[24] John T. Greenwood, "Aviation Industry, 1917–1991," in Higham *et al.* (eds.), *Russian Aviation*, 147–8.

FIGURE 57. American Lend-Lease airplanes bearing Soviet insignia await shipment to the USSR from Ladd Field, Alaska. 9 July 1944. Photo courtesy Von Hardesty.

comment on several occasions that, without western aid, the country "would not have been able to cope with Germany one-on-one" owing to the substantial industrial losses that occurred in the war's opening months. Likewise, Marshal Georgii Zhukov, chief architect of the Soviet Army's victory, was secretly recorded in 1963 acknowledging that the military "could not have continued the war" without Lend-Lease.[25] Although such revelations do not in any way diminish the immense contributions of the country's own citizens, it seems reasonable to conclude that, "without western supplies, the Soviet Union not only could not have won the Great Patriotic War, but even could not have resisted German aggression."[26]

A NEW LOCUS OF LEGITIMACY

The victory over Nazi Germany provided Soviet propagandists with a virtually inexhaustible source of epic battles, patriotic deeds, and heroic personalities from which they could craft their postwar *oeuvre*. By the close of the conflict in May 1945, more than 10,000 citizens had been designated

[25] The comments attributed to Stalin and Zhukov are cited in Overy, *Russia's War*, 195.
[26] B. V. Sokolov, "Lend Lease in Soviet Military Efforts, 1941–1945," *Journal of Slavic Military Studies* 7 (1994): 581.

"Hero of the Soviet Union," the country's highest official honor.[27] These heroes came from all walks of life and from every region of the country. Their ranks included young and old, soldiers and partisans, men and women, those still living, and a great many dead. During the war, their inspirational deeds were preserved in essays, verse, and song as a means of instilling hope and maintaining the fighting spirit of the general populace. Afterward, the stories of their lives (and, all too often, their sacrifices) were expanded into popular novels and feature films. These productions provided a new locus of legitimacy for Party leaders who now pointed to the victory over fascism as the definitive demonstration of the Soviet system's power and strength.

As had been true in the decades leading up to 1941, aviators played a prominent role in the heroic mythology that emerged from the Great Patriotic War. Although the falcon fliers, world records, and international expeditions of the 1930s did not disappear from the country's collective memory, these individuals and exploits were, necessarily, eclipsed by the personalities that emerged and the events that transpired over the front lines of the battle against Germany. As in the United States and Great Britain, fighter pilots were a special source of inspirational heroism. Every citizen knew the names of the country's best fliers, men like Ivan Kozhedub and Aleksandr Pokryshkin who survived the onslaught of the German invasion to record sixty-two and fifty-nine kills, respectively, making them the highest-ranking aces among all Allied pilots. The numerous books published by and about them after the war were read by millions. Like Chkalov before them, they came to serve as exemplars of the ideal Soviet citizen. Disciplined, dedicated, and fearless in flight, they were iconic figures used by the state to inspire others to greatness.

Still more inspiring was the extraordinary story of aviator Aleksei Maresev. Shot down in April 1942, Maresev survived the crash of his plane, only to suffer severe injuries to both of his feet. Unable to walk, he crawled between the German and Soviet front lines for eighteen days before being rescued by a band of partisans. Rushed to a Moscow military hospital, the fighter pilot's career appeared at an end when doctors were forced to amputate his gangrenous feet. Amazingly, Maresev overcame his disability. Only weeks after the lifesaving surgery, he had learned to walk (and sometime later, dance) on his two prosthetic devices. Within a year, Maresev had become so adept that he was allowed to resume flying. He subsequently returned to active military service where he went on to record seven more kills. In August 1943, Maresev was awarded the title "Hero of the Soviet Union." A book-length account of his experiences titled *The Story of a Real Man* was published in 1946. Two years later, a feature film bearing the same title appeared, as did a three-act opera by Sergey Prokofiev.[28] During the conflict,

---

[27] Sartorti, "On the Making of Heroes," 176.

[28] B. N. Polevoi, *Povest' o nastoiashchem cheloveke* (Moscow, 1946). The book was translated into more than twenty languages, appearing in an English version in 1949.

FIGURE 58. P. Sudakov, "Glory to the flier-heroes!" Poster, 1942. Courtesy The Hoover Institution.

and in the years to follow, countless novels and movies about the wartime exploits of Red Air Force pilots would find receptive audiences throughout the Soviet Union. Similar to the twenty-odd aviation films released during the decade preceding the war, these features served as vehicles for transmitting to Soviet citizens Party-sanctioned messages of loyalty, patriotism, and faith in the system.[29]

Although the cultivation of wartime fliers as iconic figures introduced few new themes to those featured in the 1920s and 1930s, the war did alter Soviet aviation culture in at least one respect. Increasingly, hero fliers took on female forms. Largely invisible in the country's prewar aeronautical discourse, women aviators now rose to prominence for their contributions to the defeat of Nazi Germany. In certain respects, their active participation in the war was an understandable response to the critical manpower shortage induced by the military debacle that followed the invasion. Hoping to shore up the ranks of an air force that had lost eighty percent of its planes and a great many pilots in the opening weeks of war, Soviet officials proved amenable to the idea of mobilizing the state's female reserves to stave off collapse. In late 1941, Marina Raskov (a participant in the all-female flight of the ANT-37 *Motherland* in 1938 and the country's most well-known female pilot) initiated the formation of three women's air regiments from among the ranks of the country's few female civilian flight instructors. One of these, the 588th (46th Guards) Night Bomber Regiment (the "Night Witches") figured prominently in the decisive Battle of Stalingrad. In other instances, female aviators were attached to predominately male air regiments or incorporated into mixed-gender crews in which many performed with merit and distinction. The most renowned of the Red Air Force's female fighter pilots was Liliia Litviak. Known to her contemporaries as "The White Rose of Stalingrad," Litviak recorded twelve kills before being shot down in August 1943. In recognition of her achievements, she was posthumously elevated into the ranks of the country's wartime pantheon as one of ninety women (out of the 10,000 total citizens) designated a "Hero of the Soviet Union."[30] Representing only a tiny fraction of the Soviet Union's military pilots, female fliers nevertheless proved as capable and courageous as their male counterparts.[31]

In addition to contributing to victory over Nazi Germany, aviators helped shape postwar Soviet culture by providing state leaders with new stories and

[29] Peter Kenez, *Cinema and Soviet Society, 1917–1953* (Cambridge: Cambridge University Press, 1992), *passim*.

[30] Kazimiera Jean Cottam, *Women in War and Resistance: Selected Biographies of Soviet Women Soldiers* (Nepean, Ontario: New Military Publishing, 1998).

[31] For the authoritative account of female aviators' contributions to the Soviet war effort, see Reina Pennington, *Wings, Women, and War: Soviet Airwomen in World War II Combat* (Lawrence, KS: University Press of Kansas, 2001).

FIGURE 59. Soviet World War II ace Liliia Litviak recorded twelve "kills" in less than one year of combat flying. Photo courtesy Reina Pennington.

sagas that could be used to inspire and unify the populace. Together with the soldiers of the Red Army and the partisan fighters who had operated in German-occupied territory, the men and women of the Soviet Air Force played the parts of martyrs and saints within the burgeoning cult of the

Great Patriotic War.[32] Like the "ordinary heroes" of the 1930s, who had been used to legitimate Soviet socialism by serving as exemplars of Party-inspired progress and development, the extraordinary deeds of wartime citizens were subsequently exploited as proof of the socialist system's durability and strength. Increasingly, the war became the defining moment in Soviet history, eclipsing the Bolshevik takeover of October 1917 and the industrialization campaign of the 1930s as the principle source of the regime's legitimacy. Calling on citizens to make sacrifices in the present to secure prosperity in the future, leaders and propagandists pointed to 1941–5 in an effort to inspire renewed confidence in the system and to explain away the lingering deficiencies that continued to plague the country.

THE LASTING LEGACY OF DEPENDENCE

The developmental patterns witnessed in the late Imperial and early Soviet eras continued during the years that occupied and followed World War II. As earlier, the modernization of the USSR's civilian and military air fleets relied heavily on western materials, technology, and expertise. The enormous influx of equipment that arrived via Lend-Lease was instrumental to the modernization of the Soviet Union's postwar aviation industry. Equally important, Lend-Lease was accompanied by critical transfers of advanced technical and scientific knowledge as some 15,000 Soviet officials and engineers visited American factories and military installations between 1942 and 1945.[33] Continuing practices begun in the 1920s and 1930s, these representatives exploited American openness to obtain information regarding cutting-edge technologies and production techniques indispensable to the modernization of Soviet aviation and military industries. As one contemporary American official noted in the late 1940s, the United States had offered the Soviet Union much of its most advanced military and technical information, "never losing an opportunity to give the Russians equipment, weapons, or information which we thought might help our combined war effort."[34] Alongside American largess, the war witnessed the massive expansion of Soviet covert operations as the country's official representatives, diplomatic and consular agencies, purchasing commissions, spies, and U.S.-based sympathizers engaged in widespread and effective industrial espionage activities. The result was an "orgy of information grabbing" that enabled Stalin's government to surreptitiously acquire from the United States industrial plant designs, photographs of the technical processes involved in deploying aviation fields, motor parts, fine precision drills, top-secret

---

[32] Nina Tumarkin, *The Living and the Dead: The Rise and Fall of the Cult of World War II in Russia* (New York: Basic Books, 1994).

[33] Overy, *Russia's War*, 197.

[34] John R. Deane, *The Strange Alliance* (New York: Viking Press, 1947), 50.

blueprints relating to jet propulsion, atomic secrets, and even fissionable materials.[35]

The single most important contribution made by the United States to the postwar fortunes of the VVS involved its involuntary support of the Soviet strategic bombing program. As discussed earlier, Soviet planners and designers had devoted considerable time and resources to the production of long-range heavy bombers during the 1930s. Despite their efforts, however, they had achieved only disappointing results. What little progress they did make was largely erased by the military purges of 1937–8 as the country's leading strategic bombing theorists were subject to arrest and execution. Moreover, military operations against Germany did little to advance Soviet bombing capabilities. The destruction of nearly all of the country's multi-engine bombers in the opening days of the war, coupled with Red Army commanders' overriding emphasis on frontal air operations, meant that the tactical deployment of aircraft in support of ground operations, rather than strategic bombing, dominated the country's wartime aviation efforts.[36] Still, the heavy damage inflicted by the Western Allies' air forces on German industry between 1943 and 1945 (and the August 1945 detonation of two American atomic bombs in Japan) clearly indicated that strategic bombing would play a central role in future conflicts. Hoping to jump-start the Soviet Union's strategic aviation program, Stalin made several formal requests during the war for the shipment of British and American four-engine bombers via Lend-Lease. The requests were refused.[37] As luck would have it, Stalin did not need the Allies' assent. On 29 July 1944, an American B-29 was forced to land near the Soviet city of Vladivostok, having run low on fuel after a mission over Japanese-occupied Manchuria. In November, two more B-29s crash-landed in Siberia following raids on the Japanese mainland. The crews were interned for over a month and subjected to extensive interrogation by Soviet agents.[38] Although Stalin's government eventually released the airmen, it did not surrender their aircraft. Instead, they were handed over to Soviet teams of designers, engineers, and technicians who began the arduous process of reverse-engineering the planes and their subsystems under the direction of Andrei Tupolev. More than 105,000 individual parts were measured and checked for material specifications and functions, the manufacturing processes of the components were determined, tolerances and fits were evaluated, and then everything was translated into Soviet equivalents.[39]

[35] Kilmarx, *History of Soviet Air Power*, 209–13.

[36] Greenwood, "Soviet Frontal Aviation," 62–90.

[37] David Holloway, *Stalin and the Bomb: The Soviet Union and Atomic Energy, 1939–1956* (New Haven, CT: Yale University Press, 1994), 234.

[38] Curtis E. LeMay and Bill Yenne, *Superfortress: The Story of the B-29 and American Air Power* (New York: McGraw-Hill, 1988), 167.

[39] Ulrich Albrecht, *The Soviet Armaments Industry* (Chur, Switzerland: Harwood Academic, 1993), 23.

FIGURE 60. An American B-29 "Superfortress" is dismantled by Soviet technicians. The successful attempt to reverse-engineer the aircraft made possible the production of the Soviet Tu-4 heavy bomber. Photo courtesy Von Hardesty.

On 3 July 1947, just less than three years after the landing of the first B-29 near Vladivostok, the Soviet version of the American aircraft, the Tu-4, made its inaugural test flight.

The acquisition of the B-29 was a technological windfall that had immense and lasting repercussions on the subsequent development of Soviet aviation. At the time of its operational debut in early June 1944, the B-29 was by far the largest and most powerful military airplane in the world. With a length of 99 feet and a wingspan in excess of 141 feet, the "Superfortress" dwarfed the world's next-largest bomber, the American B-17. Weighing over 70,000 pounds when standing empty, the B-29 was also the heaviest production craft built to date. Nevertheless, it possessed a bomb-load capacity of 20,000 pounds and was capable of reaching a top airspeed of 365 miles per hour. Powered by four 2,200-horsepower Wright 3350-R Double Cyclone engines, the plane could fly over 5,800 miles at an altitude of 30,000 feet and a cruising speed of 253 miles per hour. As impressive as its immense size, lift capacity, and range were the numerous highly advanced technological innovations incorporated into the plane. The "Superfortress" was the first aircraft in history to have pressurized crew compartments, a centralized fire control system, radar-assisted navigation and bombing sets, and computerized remote-control guns. Developed at a cost of some $3 billion, it was also the most expensive military weapon constructed to date. Its price tag surpassed even that of the atomic bomb on which the U.S. government spent a mere $2 billion.[40] Although historians have devoted far more attention to the Soviet Union's concurrent, surreptitious acquisition of American atomic secrets, the seizure of the B-29 was arguably no less important to Soviet military and diplomatic fortunes during the first years of the Cold War. At the time, the B-29 was the only aircraft in the world capable of delivering a nuclear weapon. In the absence of the Soviet Tu-4 variant, "Stalin's bomb" would have been practically useless.

Soviet efforts to reverse-engineer the American bomber proved, in the main, successful. Still, the results underscored the inherent limitations imposed by the long-standing practice of pursuing development through the acquisition and adaptation of advanced foreign systems. Virtually every aspect of the Tu-4 was inferior to the B-29. The plane's supercharged engines and variable pitch propellers did not function properly. Numerous engine fires resulted from the Soviet engineers' inability to copy precisely the plane's complex cooling system. Meanwhile, gunners and pilots struggled with poor visibility because Soviet industry could not reproduce the advanced Plexiglas used in the B-29's window panes. Revisiting experiences with German Junkers aircraft during the 1920s and 1930s, the Soviet variant also proved much heavier and less maneuverable than the American aircraft. By the time the first batch of Tu-4s was ready for deployment in 1950, the B-29 platform had become obsolete, its American manufacturer Boeing having shifted to production of the much larger and faster B-47.[41] Even so, the effort to copy the "Superfortress" provided the Soviet engineers and technicians with critical insights into America's most advanced technological systems and design innovations. The plane left a lasting imprint on Soviet aviation. For more than four decades following the issue of the Tu-4, a considerable amount of B-29 technology would continue to be incorporated into Soviet military and commercial aircraft.[42]

Foreign "assistance" continued to play a vital role in Soviet aviation fortunes long after 1945. The country's most important advances continued to be made possible by aircraft and expertise obtained from abroad. In the immediate postwar era, considerable help came from occupied Germany where the Soviet Union benefited from the largest and most advanced pool of scientific and technical expertise ever obtained by means of armed conflict. By May 1945, nearly eighty percent of Germany's aircraft production centers had fallen into Soviet hands. Factories such as the Junkers facility at Dessau, the Siebel plant in Halle, and the Heinkel plants in Oranienburg and Rostock-Warnermünde were stripped and their equipment shipped East. Thousands of German specialists trapped in the Soviet occupation zone were

---

[40] These figures represent the actual costs in 1945 dollars.
[41] Albrecht, *Soviet Armaments Industry*, 24.
[42] Bill Gunston, *Aircraft of the Soviet Union: The Encyclopedia of Soviet Aircraft Since 1917* (London: Osprey, 1983), 13, and Greenwood, "Aviation Industry," 148–9.

also seized. On the night of 21–22 October 1946, a well-planned and neatly executed operation successfully netted nearly all of the German armament resources housed in the Soviet-occupied Eastern Zone. As a result of the clandestine operation (ironically code-named "Osoaviakhim"), between 10,000 and 15,000 aviation technicians, scientists, and skilled workers, together with their wives, children, and nearest relatives, were rounded up by Soviet NKVD agents and army units, packed into trains, and deported to the Soviet Union.[43] Their contributions proved critical to the development of subsequent generations of Soviet aircraft and engines.[44] The country's postwar aviation programs received yet another significant boost when, to the dismay of American officials, the British Labor government approved the sale of more than four dozen Rolls-Royce turbines to the USSR, including twenty-five copies of the "Nene II" (considered at the time the world's most advanced aviation power plant). These engines proved invaluable to the Soviet jet industry. Thanks to the British, by the early 1950s Soviet designers were able to produce MiG-15 fighters capable of competing with American F-86s in the skies over Korea. Ultimately, nearly three-fourths of Soviet military combat aircraft produced during the decade would be outfitted with Soviet versions derived from the Rolls-Royce turbojets.[45]

The chronic inability to keep pace with the West continued to characterize Soviet aerospace efforts as interests shifted from the skies above the earth to the vast reaches of outer space. Although the brilliance demonstrated by Soviet technicians in adapting borrowed and stolen technology enabled the USSR to score stunning propaganda victories in 1957 with the launch of the world's first intercontinental ballistic missile and the world's first artificial satellite, *Sputnik*, the command economy continued to lag far behind its American rival in terms of technical and scientific ingenuity, productivity, and innovation. Ironically, the methods chosen by Soviet leaders to showcase their space programs served only to underscore their system's inherent limitations. Unable to match the American accomplishment of manned lunar landings, the Soviet state instead turned to the device of long-duration orbits as a means of demonstrating prowess in space. Beginning with Yuri Gagarin's first liftoff into orbit in 1961 and continuing until the eve of the USSR's collapse in 1991, Soviet cosmonauts (both male and female) repeatedly set world records for the longest time spent in orbit. Although there is no doubt that these missions were vital in advancing scientific understanding, there can also be little doubt that they were motivated by compensatory symbolism. Clearly reminiscent of the long-distance flights undertaken by Stalinist

---

[43] Norman M. Naimark, *The Russians in Germany: A History of the Soviet Zone of Occupation, 1945–1949* (Cambridge, MA: Belknap Press of Harvard University, 1995), 220–8.
[44] Boyd, *Soviet Air Force*, 206, and Albrecht, *Soviet Armaments Industry*, 33.
[45] Derek Leebaert, *The Fifty-Year Wound: The True Price of America's Cold War Victory* (Boston: Little, Brown, 2002), 44–5, and Kilmarx, *History of Soviet Air Power*, 228–9.

aviators during the 1930s, the long-duration orbits were outwardly impressive feats of human fortitude that provided cover for the regime's technical incapacity vis-à-vis the United States.

Unable to keep pace with technological innovations critical to economic prosperity and military security, the Soviet leadership increasingly relied on espionage and theft in a desperate attempt to narrow the rapidly growing divide between their country's capabilities and American achievements. In 1970, at the behest of the State Committee on Science and Technology and the Military Industrial Commission, the KGB created an operational arm known as "Line X" through which it launched a massive campaign to pass on western research and development secrets to Soviet scientists and technicians. Using the cover of trade and cultural exchanges that mushroomed under détente, the Soviet government revisited the strategy employed so successfully between 1925 and 1945 of stationing technicians, agents, and other "advisors" in major American and European firms. Between the beginning of the program in 1970 and the early 1980s, Line X provided the Soviet Union with an intelligence pipeline not seen since the heyday of Lend-Lease. Drawing materials from such important defense contractors as General Dynamics and Westinghouse, and aviation giants Boeing, Lockheed, and McDonnell Douglas, the program served as the basis for perhaps as many as half of all major Soviet defense industry projects during that period. It also helped to modernize elements of the country's decrepit industrial infrastructure, including metallurgy, power generation, and engineering. The KGB obtained so many thousands of American blueprints and products that it appeared, in retrospect, as if Soviet military and civil sectors had simply substituted American and European firms for their own research and development labs.[46]

In the end, however, even these efforts proved insufficient. By the mid-1980s, the highest echelons of the Communist Party leadership had become painfully aware that the strategy of borrowing from abroad to facilitate development at home had failed to reduce the rapidly widening scientific, technological, and economic gaps separating the Soviet Union from its global competitors. Incapable of keeping pace with (let alone surpassing) western ingenuity and productivity in such critical new fields as computing, microelectronics, and telecommunications, and unable to maintain an adequate standard of living for its own people, the Soviet Union's status in the world was in steep decline. As was true of the workers' paradise prophesized by Bolshevik revolutionaries in 1917, the industrial autarky promised by Stalin in the 1930s had proven an ideological chimera. Mikhail Gorbachev's subsequent efforts to reform the system through *perestroika* only served to hasten the collapse by inadvertently calling into question the legitimacy of the Soviet "experiment."

[46] Leebaert, *Fifty-Year Wound*, 397–400 and 525–7.

And yet, even as the Soviet Union entered into the final stages of inexorable decline, the country's aerospace engineers demonstrated the powerful pull of the past. In the spring of 1984, they embarked on a grandiose program intended to shatter world records and enhance the country's prestige through the design and production of the world's largest aircraft. Revisiting the strategy employed by the Tupolev construction bureau during the 1930s, the approach chosen by the Kiev-based Antonov design team called for enlarging the dimensions of an already existing model, the An-124 cargo transport aircraft. They would produce the new plane by expanding the An-124's airframe and wings and lengthening its cabin while adding two more wheel sets and two additional engines (for a total of six). Their efforts culminated, on 21 December 1988, with the maiden flight of the prototype Antonov-225. Measuring 275 feet in length, possessing a wingspan of 290 feet, and capable of transporting a 250-ton payload, the An-225 heavy-lift cargo aircraft dwarfed all competitors. Its success was short-lived. Following a triumphal appearance at the June 1989 air show at Le Bourget outside Paris, the aircraft was mothballed, a victim of the economic dislocation that followed in the wake of the Soviet Union's collapse. After more than a decade in storage, the Ukraine-based Antonov Corporation subsequently attempted to revive the An-225 program, spending some $30 million to modernize the airplane with updated systems imported from Europe. At present, the ultimate fate of the airplane-behemoth and, more generally, Russian aviation remains unclear. What does seem clear, however, is that the future of Russian aviation will be closely tied to its past.

Conclusion
Aviation Culture and the Fate of Modern Russia

In certain key respects, Russians' responses to the arrival of the airplane during the first decade of the twentieth century mirrored those in evidence across the continent of Europe. Like their counterparts in Great Britain, France, and Germany, Russian citizens and statesmen greeted the airplane with excitement and wonder. As in London, Paris, Berlin, and elsewhere, the residents of cities such as St. Petersburg and Moscow flocked to airfields and aerodromes in the tens of thousands to watch with rapt attention the flying "tsars of the air." Celebrating machine-powered flight as a triumph of human genius, Russians contemplated the airplane's role in transforming the contemporary world. They ruminated on its meaning as an instrument of peace and as a weapon of war while revering the Promethean pilots who dared challenge the natural order. In these ways, Russians proved little different from their European neighbors. At the dawn of the aviation age, they, too, succumbed to a "passion for wings."

Even so, Russians' eager embrace of the airplane remained unique. Whereas for Western European and American audiences, the airplane symbolized power and progress in the present, for Russians, it represented a portent of the future. Consciously aware of their continuing backwardness relative to the West, Russian citizens saw the airplane as a sign of things to come, a hopeful icon of their unrealized potential that might serve as a means for transcending the past. The key to fulfilling humanity's centuries-old dream of flight, the airplane also appeared the key to Russians' dreams of modernity. By mastering machine-powered flight, many believed, Russia would finally assume its rightful place as the most cultured and advanced of the European states.

Reprising an approach often attempted in the nation's history, Imperial statesmen and citizens looked to the West in order to accomplish their aeronautical visions. They borrowed strategies and images developed abroad in the hope of fostering air-mindedness at home. They established air clubs and air shows on the basis of European models, they trained pilots in France's leading flight schools, and they relied on foreign factories for the acquisition of an air fleet. Their efforts paid quick dividends. By the eve of the First World War, Imperial Russia boasted the world's second largest air force. Thanks to the independent efforts of its greatest aviation genius, Igor

282

Sikorsky, the country also boasted the world's largest airplanes. Sikorsky's aerial giants, the *Russian Warrior* and the *Il'ia Muromets*, were engineering marvels. Ground-breaking aircraft that transformed aviation design, they demonstrated Russians' ability to achieve theoretical breakthroughs in the face of the inherent obstacles posed by industrial backwardness.

The best efforts of private citizens and public spokesmen notwithstanding, Imperial Russia's aviation glory was only fleeting. The results of the First World War quickly proved illusory the country's recent gains. In doing so, the conflict underscored the fundamental disjuncture between the rhetoric and reality of Imperial aviation. Keenly aware of the achievements of foreigner fliers, Russian spokesmen had responded to Europeans' success in the years that preceded the outbreak of war by extolling the particular virtues of their country's own heroes. Attributing "Russian" qualities such as self-sacrifice and collectivity to the nation's native pilots, they upheld Mikhail Efimov, Lev Matsievich, and Petr Nesterov among others as morally superior to their counterparts in the West. In similar fashion, they embellished Russian contributions to world aviation, exaggerating the significance of only marginal accomplishments while reinventing history to conceal the country's relative failings. A key element in the emerging Russian culture of flight, compensatory symbolism, like the iconic vision of the airplane, would define Russian air-mindedness for generations to come.

The Bolshevik Party's consolidation of power in the years immediately following 1917 revealed the persistence of continuity amid change in Russia's history. Although distinguished from their Imperial forebears by their utopian Marxist credo, Soviet leaders conceived similarly the issues and challenges they faced in their quest to forge a "dictatorship of the air." They shared their predecessors' belief that they could telescope development by imposing from above state-directed modernization. Similar to Imperial patrons who promoted state-sponsored aeronautical clubs as a means of facilitating concord between the autocratic state and society, Soviet leaders looked to "voluntary" organizations to reconstitute social networks destroyed by revolution and civil war. Through the promotion of ODVF and its successors, Party officials aimed to create an air-minded culture while generating public support for their revolutionary agenda. The methods that they employed in the pursuit of these ends revealed the contradictions inherent in their approach to social engineering. Subordinating practical considerations to the theoretical mandates of forced modernization, Party leaders quickly abandoned the pretense of volunteerism. The result was the exponential growth of aeronautical "pseudo-organizations" that conscripted citizens to labor on behalf of Party-dictated goals. Inefficient and ineffective, "compulsory volunteerism" undermined long-term efforts to promote genuine air-mindedness by suppressing local initiative. It also foreshadowed the numerical fetishism and bureaucratic centralism that would dominate the Stalinist 1930s.

Soviet leaders shared as well their Imperial forebears' iconic understanding of flight. Cognizant of aviation's unrivaled symbolic resonance and convinced of its utility in facilitating modernization, they embraced the airplane as an emblem and instrument of the socialist future. Co-opting and inverting traditional sacred forms in support of aviation, they advanced aeronautical images and themes to legitimate their political authority while promoting the airplane as a "new religion" capable of effecting prosperity and progress. Even as they labored to foster domestic faith in aviation, they looked abroad for solutions to their modernizing dilemmas, relying, as had their predecessors, on western firms and governments to provide essential equipment and technological expertise. When reality failed to conform to their air-age ambitions, they too resorted to the rhetoric of compensatory symbolism, devising Potemkin displays to mask recurring deficiencies. Through the orchestration of international prestige flights, they consciously cultivated images of competency and strength while gathering the technical intelligence necessary to keep pace with the West.

During the decade of the 1930s, the scale and scope of Soviet "aerofication" increased dramatically as the Party undertook its "great break" with the past. Committed to the rapid realization of the world's foremost industrial society and fed by fears of foreign encirclement and war, Party leaders embarked on a frenetic crusade to realize once and for all their dreams of technological dominance. Few resources were conserved and fewer lives were spared as the industrialization campaign reached its frenzied crescendo. The strategy produced very quick results. Production surged, unemployment evaporated, and colossal new construction projects were undertaken during the course of successive Five-Year Plans. In short order and in large numbers, new aircraft and engines emerged from Soviet factories, bringing the air force of the USSR into numerical parity with its capitalist adversaries for the first time in history. As the United States and Western Europe descended deeper into economic depression, and as Soviet propagandists heralded the achievements of the planned economy, it increasingly appeared that modernizing Russia had finally turned its back on the past. The future, it seemed, now belonged to the workers' and peasants' state. The reality, however, was somewhat different.

Despite their apparent success in aviation, the industrial and cultural revolutions carried out under Stalin merely intensified and extended the trends of the 1920s. As earlier, pilots were depicted as instruments and symbols of the future in language indebted to the traditions of the past. Heralded for their "Soviet" qualities of collectivity, self-sacrifice, and loyalty, they were described in folkloric terms as "falcons" and "*bogatyri.*" Likewise, even as the country's aviation engineers proved increasingly adept, the Soviet Union continued to rely on importations from the West. During the course of the 1930s, the state greatly expanded its efforts at industrial espionage. Hundreds, if not thousands, of agents were dispatched to leading western aviation firms to obtain vital information through purchase and theft. These measures helped close the technological gap between the USSR and the West in key areas, but they did not free the country from dependence. Revisiting the experiences of the 1910s and 1920s, foreign manufacturers continued to develop innovative airframes and engines while Soviet technicians worked to perfect designs acquired from abroad.

In addition to institutionalizing dependence on the West, Stalinist development institutionalized inefficiency, redundancy, and waste. Although the centralization of the aviation industry under the auspices of Glavaviaprom significantly improved the rate at which new airplanes were developed and produced, it limited innovation and undermined quality control as design teams were increasingly subject to the whims of political authorities. The emphasis placed on production tempos throughout the decade meant that planes were frequently rushed into service, oftentimes before they had been proven airworthy or, as in the case of the ANT-14, before they were even complete. Meanwhile, the Party's predominant concern with proselytizing socialism led to the development of aircraft that had little practical value. The behemoth ANT-20 and the record-setting ANT-25 were the most prominent cases in point. Driven by Party leaders' desire to maintain political legitimacy, the two planes were intended to symbolize the colossal strides made under socialism while diverting attention from state-sponsored famine and terror.

With the coming of war in 1941, the achievements of the 1930s were proven largely hollow. Equipped with outmoded airplanes and tactics and weakened by the recent purge of its leading officers, the Soviet Air Force collapsed in the opening weeks of the war. Only the heroic effort of the country's citizens and the influx of material aid from its wartime allies forestalled utter collapse. Although the VVS survived the catastrophe of 1941–2 to emerge victorious in 1945, its rebirth and subsequent success was indebted to the West. Captured B-29 bombers, kidnapped German technicians, and the critical purchase of advanced British turbojets revisited the developmental patterns of 1909–41. Reprising a strategy first employed by Peter the Great, Soviet officials relied on infusions of foreign technology in an effort to close the gap with the West. On occasion, the country's engineers improved on these systems, constructing world-class combat aircraft (such as the MiG-15) that matched, and in some cases surpassed, the planes of their adversaries. Still, despite passing its most harrowing test in defeating Nazi Germany, the Soviet system proved increasingly incapable of adjusting to a changing world. Like the numerous airplanes that emerged to great fanfare and celebration during the course of the 1920s and 1930s, the Soviet Union emerged from its greatest victory already obsolescent.

Scholars who point to the military victory against Nazi Germany in 1945 (or, for that matter, the literacy and electrification campaigns of the 1920s or the space programs of the 1970s) as evidence that Soviet socialism did not lack for redemptive successes ignore the larger point. The Soviet Union was not founded to repel foreign fascists. The tsarist order was not deposed to bring light bulbs to rural reading rooms. Millions of citizens were not murdered so that cosmonauts could experience zero gravity. Dedicated to the conquest of Russia's backwardness and poverty, the architects of the Soviet state aimed to transcend both the past and the present. They endeavored to lead a world revolution that would accomplish the ends of history by unleashing unparalleled prosperity and equality. Their goal was not merely to match the West, but to best it. Through the rational application of "scientific" laws, Lenin, Stalin, and generations of their adherents believed that they could "overtake and surpass" Europe and the United States. They would catch up with (and then conquer) the capitalist world through planned development and social engineering. Their purpose was not to achieve economic parity, but to create an earthly paradise.

Of course, sacrifices would have to be made along the way, a fact that Soviet leaders readily acknowledged. Both before and after the conflict with Germany, adequate housing, decent consumer goods, and other creature comforts were postponed so that heavy industry (the backbone of military production) might flourish. As justification for their citizens' discomfiture, Party hierarchs pointed to the constant prospects of foreign invasion and the eternal presence of internal "enemies." Threats of war were constantly embellished, and at times invented, to condition the population to accept the Party's direction and to steel them for the coming conflict with the West. As collective compensation for personal penury, new heroes and holidays were devised to provide citizens with cause for public celebration and to encourage them toward private acts of "heroism" that might benefit the state. Modern-day equivalents of ancient Rome's bread and circuses, these attractions diverted attention from the Party's irrational ideology and the country's continuing backwardness vis-à-vis the capitalist world.

Measured against the standards proclaimed by its citizens and statesmen and compared with the prosperity achieved by the West, twentieth-century Russia failed early and often. It did so for many reasons, not the least of which was the inability of its leaders to make reality conform to their ideals. Far from establishing the world's most advanced society, Russia's chosen path to modernity institutionalized obsolescence. There are few better examples of this than the fate of its aviation programs. Inspired by the publicity generated by prestige flights in the 1930s and subsequently abetted by the Red Army's victory over Nazi Germany in World War II, aviation has long been considered a Russian success story. As this study has attempted to show, a closer examination reveals the extent to which official rhetoric belied reality. Although not without noteworthy achievements, the history of Imperial and Soviet aviation culture epitomizes the debilitating limitations imposed by Russians' visions of development and reveals recurrent patterns in the history of the nation that have worked to forestall its parity with the West.

Bibliography

Archival Sources

Gosudarstvennyi arkhiv Rossiiskoi Federatsii (GARF)

fond 102 — Delo proizvodstva osobogo otdeleniia
fond r-7577 — Obshchestvo druzei vozdushnogo flota (ODVF)
fond r-8355 — Obshchestvo sodeistviia oborone aviatsionnomu i khimicheskomu stroitel'stvu SSSR (Osoaviakhim)
fond r-9404 — Obshchestvo druzei aviatsionnoi i khimicheskoi oborony i promyshlennosti SSSR (Aviakhim)

Rossiiskii gosudarstvennyi arkhiv ekonomiki (RGAE)

fond 4372 — Gosudarstvennaia planovaia komissiia pri SNK SSSR (Gosplan)
fond 9527 — Glavnoe upravlenie grazhdanskogo vozdushnogo flota (GUGVF) pri Soveta Ministerov SSSR
fond 9574 — Uchrezhdenie vozdukhoplavaniia v SSSR
fond 9576 — Osobaia aviatsionnaia vozdukhoplavatel'naia agitatsionnaia eskadril'ia im. Maksima Gor'kogo pri Kollegii GUGVF
fond 9577 — Vsesoiuznoe obshchestvo grazhdanskogo vozdushnogo flota (Dobrolet). Glavnoi inspektsii vozdushnogo flota, 1923–30

Rossiiskii gosudarstvennyi arkhiv literatury i iskusstv (RGALI)

fond 2361 — El Lissitskii (Lissitskii, Lazr Makarovich)

Rossiiskii gosudarstvennyi voenno-istoricheskii arkhiv (RGVIA)

fond 1 — Kantseliariia voennogo ministerstva
fond 802 — Glavnoe inzhenernoe upravlenie
fond 873 — Vserossiiskii aero-klub
fond 2000 — Glavnoe upravlenie general'nogo shtaba

Rossiiskii gosudarstvennyi voennyi arkhiv (RGVA)

fond 29 — Upravlenie voenno-vozdushnykh sil
fond 33987 — Sekretariat predsedatelia Revvoensovet SSSR
fond 33988 — Sekretariat zamestitelia predsedatelia Revvoensovet SSSR
fond 33989 — Sekretariat vtorogo zamestitelia predsedatelia Revvoensovet SSSR

Tsentr dokumentatsii noveishei istorii Saratovskoi oblasti (TsDNISO)

fond 2639   Fraktsiia VKP(b) Nizhe-Volzhskogo kraevogo soveta
Osoaviakhima
fond 6141   Saratovskii oblastnoi sovet Osoaviakhima

National Archives and Records Administration (Washington, D.C.)

Record Group 38   Office of the Chief of Naval Operations, Division of Naval
Intelligence (General Correspondence, 1929–42)
Record Group 72   Records of the Bureau of Aeronautics
Record Group 373   Records of the Defense Intelligence Agency

Microfilm Publication M1443

"Correspondence of the Military Intelligence Division Relating to the General, Political, Economic, and Military Conditions in Russia and the Soviet Union, 1918–1941" (MID 2090, rolls 20 & 22)

Yale University Russian Archives Project

"Materials on Soviet–German Military Cooperation"

Periodicals

English-language periodicals

> *New York Sun*
> *New York Times*
> *San Francisco Chronicle*
> *Seattle Post-Intelligencer*
> *The Times of London*

Aviation Journals

Aero
Aero i avtomobil'naia zhizn'
Aero-sbornik
Aeromobil'
Aviadrug
Aviatsiia i khimiia
Aviatsiia i vozdukhoplavanie
Avtomobil' i vozdukhoplavanie
Avtomobil'naia zhizn' i aviatsiia
Daesh motor
Daesh Sibiri krasnye kryl'ia
K sportu!
Krasnye kryl'ia
Kryl'ia
Novosti vozdukhoplavaniia
Samolet
Sevastopol'skii aviatsionnyi illiustrirovannyi zhurnal

Tekhnika vozdukhoplavaniia
Tiazhelee vozdukha
V tsarstve vozdukhe
Vestnik vozdukhoplavaniia
Vestnik vozdukhoplavaniia i sport
Vestnik vozdushnogo flota
Vozdukhoplavanie
Vozdukhoplavanie i sport
Vozdukhoplavatel'
Vozdushnyi flot
Vozdushnyi put'
Zaria aviatsii
Zavoevanie vozdukha
Zhurnal aerodroma

General Periodicals

Birzhevoi den'
Birzhevyia vedomosti
Gazeta kopeika
Golos Rusi
Izvestiia KPSS
Kino, teatr, sport
Kinonedelia
Komsomol'skaia pravda
Krasnaia niva
Krasnaia zvezda
Krest'ianskaia gazeta
Krokodil
Leningradskaia pravda
Literaturnaia gazeta
Moskovskiia vedomosti
Niva
Nizhegorodskii listok
Novaia Rus'
Novoe vremia
Novyi zritel'
Ogonek
Peterburgskaia gazeta
Peterburgskii kur'er
Peterburgskii listok
Pravda
Priroda i liudi
Rabochaia Moskva
Rabochii zritel'
Ranee utro
Rech'
Rodina
Rossiia
Russkoe slovo
Russkoe znamia
Sankt Peterburgskiia vedomosti

Sine-fono
Sinii zhurnal
Smena
Sotsialisticheskoe zemledelie
Sovremennoe slovo
Sovremennyi mir
Sportivnaia zhizn'
Svet
Trud
Utro Rossii
Vechernee vremia
Vecherniaia Moskva
Vestnik znaniia
Zaria vostoka
Zemshchina
Zhizn' dlia vsekh

Primary Sources

Adamovich, P. *Krasnye orly*. Moscow, 1923.
Anoshchenko, A. *Voina v vozdukhe*. Moscow, 1923.
Aviakhim v derevne. Moscow: Mosaviakhim, 1925.
Aviaugolok: materialy. Moscow: ODVF, 1925.
Barsh, G. Z. *Vozdukhoplavanie v ego proshlom i v nastoiashchem*. St. Petersburg, 1906.
Berezov, R. and A. Glagolev. *O popovskoi zabote, o saranche i o samolete*. Moscow: ODVF, 1925.
Biulleten' Aviakhima posviashchennyi pereletu Moskva–Mongoliia–Kitai i uchastiiu sovetskikh planeristov v ronskikh planernykh sostiazaniiakh v Germanii. Moscow, 1925.
Bobrov, N. S. and A. Arkhangel'skii. *Samolet Maksim Gor'kii*. Moscow, 1933.
Bobrov, N. S., ed. *Kryl'ia sovetov: sbornik rasskazov i vospominanii*. Moscow, 1928.
Bobryshev, I. T. *Na "kryl'iakh" po Evrope: pis'ma s puti*. Moscow: Molodaia gvardiia, 1930.
Borozdin, N. *Zavoevanie vozdushnoi stikhi*. Warsaw, 1909.
Chto takoe aeroplan i kakaia ot nikh pol'za. Moscow, n.d.
Dnevnik vtorogo vserossiiskago vozdukhoplavatel'nago s"ezda. Moscow, 1912.
Dubenskii, D., ed. *Vozdukhoplavanie*. St. Petersburg, 1911.
Dva goda ODVF: torzhestvennoe zasedanie 6 Aprelia 1925. Moscow, 1925.
Eskadril'ia "Lenin." Moscow: ODVF, 1924.
Frank, M. L. *Istoriia vozdukhoplavaniia i ego sovremennoe sostoianie*. St. Petersburg, 1910.
———. *Vozdukhoplavanie: istoriia aviatsii*. St. Petersburg, 1911.
Garri, A. N. *Evropa pod nogami: ocherki*. Moscow: Izdatel'stvo federatsiia, 1930.
Glagolev, A. F., compiler. *Aviakul'tury v rabochii klub: material po aviarabote v rabochikh klubakh*. Moscow: ODVF, 1925.
———. *Avia-agit-doklad: konspekt*. Moscow: ODVF, 1925.
Iatsuk, N. A. *Aviatsiia i ee kul'turnoe znachenie*. Moscow, 1923.
Kol'tsov, M. E. *Khochu letat'*. Moscow, 1931.
Krasnyi vozdushnyi flot na sluzhbe revoliutsii: boevye epizody. Moscow, 1923.
Kritskii, Pavel. *Podvigi Russkikh aviatorov*. Moscow, 1915.
Lapchinskii, A. N., ed. *Krasnyi vozdushnyi flot: iubileinyi sbornik, 1918–1923*. Moscow: Glavnoe upravlenie Vozdukhflot, 1923.
Maiakovskii, V. V. *Polnoe sobranie sochenenii*. 13 vols. Moscow, 1955.
Masal'skii, Konstantin. *Sochineniia*. St. Petersburg, 1843.
Mikhailov, F. *Vozdushnye sily nashikh vragov*. Ural: ODVF, 1924.

Naidenov, V. F. *Russkoe vozdukhoplavanie i istorii i uspekhi.* St. Petersburg, 1911.

Prozorovskii, N. P. *Gorod pod udarom.* Moscow, 1934.

"Pribytie vozdushnago shara v Olimp." *Zerkalo sveta* 103 & 104 (1787): 819–23 & 819–37.

Raevskii, A. E. *Zolotye gody avio-sport.* Moscow, 1924.

Rasskazy, stikhi, chastushki. Perm: Perm ODVF, 1925.

Riazanov, N. *Prikliucheniia Egora Poddevkina na samolete.* Khar'kov: Ukrvozdukhput', 1924.

Rodnykh, A. A. *Istoriia vozdukhoplavaniia i letaniia v Rossii: letanie i vozdukhoplavanie v starinu.* St. Petersburg, 1911.

———. *Kratkii ocherk po istorii russkago vozdukhoplavaniia.* 2nd ed. St. Petersburg, 1910.

Russkii morskoi i vozdushnyi flot sooruzhennyi na dobrovol'nyia pozhertvovaniia: illius-trirovannyi ocherk deiatel'nosti vysochaishe uchrezdennago osobago komiteta po usileniiu voennago flota na dobrovol'nyia pozhertvovaniia. St. Petersburg, 1913.

Ruzer, L. *Vozdukhoplavanie: ego istoriia, uspekhi i budushchee.* St. Petersburg, 1910.

Rynin, N. A. *Vserossiiskii prazdnik vozdukhoplavaniia.* St. Petersburg, 1910.

Sergeev, A. V. *Piat' let stroitel'stva i bor'by vozdushnogo flota, 1917–1922.* 2 vols. Moscow, 1926.

Slava geroiam! Moscow, 1936.

Stamat'ev. *Vozdukhoplavanie.* Odessa, 1910.

Stobrovskii, N. G. *Nasha strana–rodina vozdukhoplavaniia.* Moscow: Voennoe izdatel'stvo ministerstva oborony soiuza SSSR, 1954.

Torzhestvennoe zasedanie ODVF, 26 aprelia 1923 g. Moscow, 1923.

Trinadtsatyi s"ezd RKP(b): Stenograficheskii otchet. Moscow, 1924.

Trotskii, L. D. *Aviatsiia–orudie budushchego.* Ekaterinburg, 1923.

———. *Perspektivy i zadachi voennogo stroitel'stva.* Moscow, 1923.

———. *Zadachi Dobrokhima.* Khar'kov, 1924.

Trotsky, Leon. *Problems of Everyday Life and Other Writings on Culture and Science.* New York: Monad Press, 1973.

Veigelin, K. E. *10–15-go iiulia 1911. Perelet S. Peterburg–Moskva.* St. Petersburg, 1911.

———. *Zavoevanie vozdushnogo okeana: istoriia i sovremennoe sostoianie vozdukhoplavaniia.* St. Petersburg, 1911.

Velizhaev, A. *Dostizhenie sovetskoi aviapromyshlennosti za 15 let.* Moscow, 1932.

Vozdukhoplavanie. St. Petersburg: IVAK, 1912.

Vozdukhoplavanie: kratkii istoricheskii ocherk. St. Petersburg, 1904.

Vozdukhoplavanie za 100 let. St. Petersburg, 1884.

Vozdushnyi flot-sila Rossii. Moscow, 1913.

Zarzar, V. A. *Grazhdanskaia aviatsiia kapitalizma i sotsializma.* Moscow, 1932.

———. *Grazhdanskaia aviatsiia SSSR i ee piatiletnii plan.* Moscow, 1929.

———. *Vtoraia piatiletka grazhdanskogo vozdushnogo flota.* Moscow, 1932.

Zheliabuzhskii, I. A. *Zapiski Zheliabuzhskago s 1682 g. po 2 iiulia 1709 g.* Compiled by F. O. Tumanskii. St. Petersburg, 1840.

Zhikharev, S. P. *Zapiski sovremennika s 1805 po 1819 god.* St. Petersburg, 1859.

Secondary Sources

Adas, Michael. *Machines as the Measure of Men: Science, Technology, and Ideologies of Western Dominance.* Ithaca, NY: Cornell University Press, 1989.

Albrecht, Ulrich. *The Soviet Armaments Industry.* Chur, Switzerland: Harwood Academic, 1993.

Alexander, John T. "Aeromania, 'Fire-Balloons,' and Catherine the Great's Ban of 1784," *The Historian* 58 (1996): 498–516.

Andersson, Lennart. *Soviet Aircraft and Aviation, 1917–1941.* Annapolis, MD: Naval Institute Press, 1994.

Aviatsiia i vozdukhoplavanie: annotirovannyi katalog knig. Moscow: Put' Oktiabria, 1937.

Baidukov, G. F. *Chkalov.* Moscow: Molodaia gvardiia, 1986.

Baidukov, Georgiy. *Russian Lindbergh: The Life of Valerii Chkalov.* Edited by Von Hardesty. Washington, D.C.: Smithsonian Institution Press, 1991.

Bailes, Kendall. *Technology and Society Under Lenin and Stalin: Origins of the Soviet Technical Intelligentsia, 1917–1941.* Princeton, NJ: Princeton University Press, 1978.

Ball, Alan. *Imagining America: Influence and Images in Twentieth-Century Russia.* New York: Rowman and Littlefield, 2003.

Barber, John and Mark Harrison. *The Soviet Home Front, 1941–1945: A Social and Economic History of the USSR in World War II.* London: Longman, 1991.

Beliakov, A. V. *V polet skvoz' gody.* Moscow: Voennoe izdatel'stvo ministerstva oborony SSSR, 1981.

Benvenuti, Francesco. *The Bolsheviks and the Red Army, 1918–1922.* Cambridge: Cambridge University Press, 1988.

Bilstein, Roger E. *Flight Patterns: Trends of Aeronautical Development in the United States, 1918–1929.* Athens, GA: University of Georgia Press, 1983.

———. *Flight in America: From the Wrights to the Astronauts.* Baltimore: Johns Hopkins University Press, 1984.

Biushgens, G. S., ed. *Aviatsiia v Rossii.* Moscow: Mashinostroenie, 1988.

Bonnell, Victoria. *Iconography of Power: Soviet Political Posters Under Lenin and Stalin.* Berkeley, CA: University of California Press, 1997.

Boyd, Alexander. *The Soviet Air Force Since 1918.* New York: Stein and Day, 1977.

Brooks, Jeffrey. "Public and Private Values in the Soviet Press, 1921–1928," *Slavic Review* 1 (1989): 16–35.

———. *Thank You, Comrade Stalin!: Soviet Popular Culture From Revolution to Cold War.* Princeton, NJ: Princeton University Press, 2001.

Bunyan, James. *The Origin of Forced Labor in the Soviet State, 1917–1921: Documents and Materials.* Baltimore: Johns Hopkins University Press, 1967.

Carr, E. H. *The Interregnum, 1923–1924.* New York: Macmillian, 1954.

Chkalova, V. V. *Chkalov bez grifa "sekretno."* Moscow: Poligrafresursy, 1999.

Clark, Katerina. *The Soviet Novel: History as Ritual.* Chicago: University of Chicago Press, 1981.

Clowes, Edith, Samuel D. Kassow, and James L. West, eds. *Between Tsar and People: Educated Society and the Quest for Public Identity in Late Imperial Russia.* Princeton, NJ: Princeton University Press, 1991.

Cochrane, Dorothy, Von Hardesty, and Russell Lee. *The Aviation Careers of Igor Sikorsky.* Seattle, WA: University of Washington Press, 1989.

Conquest, Robert. *Harvest of Sorrow: Soviet Collectivization and the Terror-Famine.* Oxford: Oxford University Press, 1986.

———. *Stalin: Breaker of Nations.* New York: Penguin, 1991.

Coopersmith, Jonathan. *The Electrification of Russia, 1880–1926.* Ithaca, NY: Cornell University Press, 1992.

Corn, Joseph J. *The Winged Gospel: America's Romance With Aviation, 1900–1950.* New York: Oxford University Press, 1983.

Cottam, Kazimiera Jean. *Women in War and Resistance: Selected Biographies of Soviet Women Soldiers.* Nepean, Ontario: New Military Publishing, 1998.

Courtois, Stéphane, Nicholas Werth, Jean-Louis Panné, Andrzej Paczkovski, Karel Bartošek, and Jean-Louis Margolin. *The Black Book of Communism: Crimes, Terror, Repression.* Translated by Jonathan Murphy and Mark Kramer. Cambridge, MA: Harvard University Press, 1999.

Daniels, Robert V. *The Conscience of the Revolution: Communist Opposition in Soviet Russia.* Cambridge, MA: Harvard University Press, 1960.

Davies, R. W. and Stephen G. Wheatcroft, *The Years of Hunger: Soviet Agriculture, 1931–1933*. New York: Palgrave Macmillan, 2004.

Davis, Kenneth S. *The Hero: Charles A. Lindbergh and the American Dream*. New York: Doubleday, 1959.

Deane, John R. *The Strange Alliance*. New York: Viking Press, 1947.

Delear, Frank J. *Igor Sikorsky: His Three Careers in Aviation*. New York: Dodd, Mead, 1969.

Dmitroff, James. "The Confluence of Aviation and Russian Futurism, 1909–1914." Ph.D. dissertation, University of Southern California, 1998.

Dorson, Richard. *Folklore and Fakelore: Essays Toward a Discipline of Folk Studies*. Cambridge, MA: Harvard University Press, 1976.

Douhet, Giulio. *The Command of the Air*. Translated by Dino Ferrari. New York: Coward-McCann, 1942.

Duz', P. D. *Istoriia vozdukhoplavaniia i aviatsii v Rossii: period do 1914 g*. Moscow: Mashinostroenie, 1979.

_____. *Istoriia vozdukhoplavaniia i aviatsii v Rossii: iiul' 1914 g.–oktiabr' 1917*. Moscow: Mashinostroenie, 1986.

Efimov, Boris. *Desiat' desiatiletii: o tom, chto videl, perezhil, zapomnil*. Moscow: Vagrius, 2000.

Eksteins, Modris. *Rites of Spring: The Great War and the Birth of the Modern Age*. New York: Doubleday, 1989.

Erickson, John. *The Soviet High Command: A Military–Political History, 1918–1941*. London: St. Martin's, 1962.

_____. *The Road to Stalingrad: Stalin's War with Germany*. New York: Harper & Row, 1975.

Finne, K. N. *Igor Sikorsky: The Russian Years*. Edited by Carl J. Bobrow and Von Hardesty. Translated by Von Hardesty. Washington, D.C.: The Smithsonian Institution Press, 1987.

Fitzpatrick, Sheila. *Everyday Stalinism*. New York: Oxford University Press, 1999.

_____. *Stalin's Peasants: Resistance and Survival in the Russian Village After Collectivization*. Oxford: Oxford University Press, 1994.

Fritzsche, Peter. *A Nation of Fliers: German Aviation and the Popular Imagination*. Cambridge, MA: Harvard University Press, 1992.

Gershchenkron, Alexander. *Economic Backwardness in Historical Perspective*. Cambridge, MA: Harvard University Press, 1962.

Glantz, David M. *Stumbling Colossus: The Red Army on the Eve of World War*. Lawrence, KS: University Press of Kansas, 1998.

_____. *Colossus Reborn: The Red Army at War, 1941–1943*. Lawrence, KS: University Press of Kansas, 2005.

Glantz, David M. and Jonathan M. House. *When Titans Clashed: How the Red Army Stopped Hitler*. Lawrence, KS: University Press of Kansas, 1995.

Glavnyi voennyi sovet RKKA, 13 marta 1938 g.–20 iiunia 1941 g.: dokumenty i materialy. Moscow: ROSSPEN, 2004.

Goldstein, Laurence. *The Flying Machine and Modern Literature*. London: Macmillan, 1986.

Golomstock, Igor. *Totalitarian Art in the Soviet Union, the Third Reich, Fascist Italy and the People's Republic of China*. London: Collins Harvill, 1990.

Graham, Loren R. *The Ghost of the Executed Engineer: Technology and the Fall of the Soviet Union*. Cambridge, MA: Harvard University Press, 1993.

_____. *Science in Russia and the Soviet Union: A Short History*. Cambridge: Cambridge University Press, 1993.

_____. *What Have We Learned About Science and Technology from the Russian Experience?* Stanford, CA: Stanford University Press, 1998.

Grazhdanskaia aviatsiia SSSR v dokumentakh partiinykh, gosudarstvennykh i pravitel'stvikh organov. Moscow: Vozdushnyi transport, 1982.

Gunston, Bill. *Aircraft of the Soviet Union: The Encyclopedia of Soviet Aircraft Since 1917.* London: Osprey, 1983.

Günther, Hans. "Stalinskie sokoly: analiz mifa tridtsatykh godov," *Voprosy literatury* 11/12 (1991): 122–41.

Günther, Hans, ed. *The Culture of the Stalin Period.* New York: St. Martin's, 1990.

Hardesty, Von. *Red Phoenix: The Rise of Soviet Air Power, 1941–1945.* Washington, D.C.: The Smithsonian Institution Press, 1982.

Hart, Clive. *The Prehistory of Flight.* Berkeley, CA; University of California Press, 1985.

_____. *Images of Flight.* Berkeley, CA: University of California Press, 1988.

Heller, Mikhail and Aleksandr Nekrich. *Utopia in Power: The History of the Soviet Union from 1917 to the Present.* New York: Summit Books, 1986.

Higham, Robin. *Air Power: A Concise History.* New York: St. Martin's, 1972.

Higham, Robin and Jacob W. Kipp, eds. *Soviet Aviation and Air Power: A Historical View.* Boulder, CO: Westview, 1977.

Higham, Robin, John T. Greenwood, and Von Hardesty, eds. *Russian Aviation and Air Power in the Twentieth Century.* London: Cass, 1998.

Hollander, Paul. *Political Pilgrims: Travels of Western Intellectuals to the Soviet Union, China, and Cuba, 1928–1978.* New York: Oxford University Press, 1981.

Holliday, George D. *Technology Transfer to the USSR, 1928–1937 and 1966–1975: The Role of Western Technology in Soviet Economic Development.* Boulder, CO: Westview, 1979.

Holloway, David. *Stalin and the Bomb: The Soviet Union and Atomic Energy, 1939–1956.* New Haven, CT: Yale University Press, 1994.

Holquist, Peter. *Making War, Forging Revolution: Russia's Continuum of Crisis, 1914–1921.* Cambridge, MA: Harvard University Press, 2002.

Husband, William. *"Godless Communists:" Atheism and Society in Soviet Russia, 1917–1932.* DeKalb, IL: Northern Illinois University Press, 2000.

Ingold, Felix. *Literatur und Aviatik: Europäische Flugdichtung, 1909–1927.* Basel: Birkhäuser Verlag, 1978.

Istoriia otechestvennoi grazhdanskoi aviatsii. Moscow: Vozdushnyi transport, 1996.

Iumashev, A. B. *Rekord dal'nosti.* Moscow: K. S. Volodina, 2002.

Kamenskii, Iu. A. *Kremlevskie perelety.* Moscow: Zhurnalistskoe agenstvo "Glasnost'," 1998.

Katyshev, G. I. and V. P. Mikheev. *Kryl'ia Sikorskogo.* Moscow: 1992.

Kenez, Peter. *The Birth of the Propaganda State: Soviet Methods of Mass Mobilization, 1917–1929.* Cambridge: Cambridge University Press, 1985.

_____. *Cinema and Soviet Society, 1917–1953.* Cambridge: Cambridge University Press, 1992.

_____. *A History of the Soviet Union from Beginning to End.* Cambridge: Cambridge University Press, 1999.

Kennett, Lee. *The First Air War.* New York: Free Press, 1991.

Kerber, L. L. *Stalin's Aviation Gulag: A Memoir of Andrei Tupolev and the Purge Era.* Edited by Von Hardesty. Washington, D.C.: The Smithsonian Institution Press, 1996.

Kern, Stephen. *The Culture of Time and Space, 1880–1918.* Cambridge, MA: Harvard University Press, 1983.

Khan-Magomedov, Selim. *Rodchenko: The Complete Work.* Edited by Vieri Quilici. London: Thames and Hudson, 1986.

Kilmarx, Robert A. *A History of Soviet Air Power.* New York: Praeger, 1962.

King, David. *The Commissar Vanishes: The Falsification of Photographs and Art in Stalin's Russia.* New York: Metropolitan Books, 1997.

Klehr, Harvey and John Earl Haynes. *Venona: Decoding Soviet Espionage in America.* New Haven, CT: Yale University Press, 1999.

Klyuchevsky, Vasili. *Peter the Great.* Boston: Beacon Press, 1958.

Koenker, Diane, William Rosenberg, and Ronald Grigor Suny, eds. *Party, State and Society in the Russian Civil War: Explorations in Social History.* Bloomington, IN: Indiana University Press, 1989.

Kopelev, Lev. *Education of a True Believer.* Translated by Gart Kern. New York: Harper & Row, 1980.

Koroleva, E. V. and V. A. Rudnik. *Soperniki orlov.* Odessa, 1976.

Kotkin, Stephen. *Magnetic Mountain: Stalinism as a Civilization.* Berkeley, CA: University of California Press, 1995.

Krasnyi vozdushnyi flot v grazhdanskoi voine v SSSR, 1918–1920 g.: materialy voennoistorich-eskoi konferentsii, provedennoi v TsDSA 8 dekabria 1967 g. Moscow, 1968.

Kriukova, S. S., ed. *Krest'ianskie istorii: rossiiskaia derevnia 1920-kh godov v pis'makh i dokumentakh.* Moscow: ROSSPEN, 2001.

Leebaert, Derek. *The Fifty-Year Wound: The True Price of America's Cold War Victory.* Boston: Little, Brown, 2002.

LeMay, Curtis E. and Bill Yenne. *Superfortress: The Story of the B-29 and American Air Power.* New York: McGraw-Hill, 1988.

Leonard, Raymond W. "The Kremlin's Secret Soldiers: The Story of Military Intelligence, 1918–1933." Ph.D. dissertation, University of Kansas, 1997.

Liakhovetskii, M. B. *Aviatsiia v delakh i dumakh Il'icha.* Kiev, 1969.

Lindbergh, Charles. *The Spirit of St. Louis.* New York: Scribner's, 1953.

————. *Autobiography of Values.* New York: Harcourt, 1992.

Linz, Susan, ed. *The Impact of World War II on the Soviet Union.* Totowa, NJ: Rowman and Allenheld, 1985.

Lotman, Iu. M., B. A. Uspenskii, and L. Ia. Ginsburg, eds. *The Semiotics of Russian Cultural History.* Ithaca, NY: Cornell University Press, 1985.

Loza, Dmitriy, *Attack of the Airacobras: Soviet Aces, American P-39s, and the Air War Against Germany.* Translated and edited by James F. Gebhardt. Lawrence, KS: University Press of Kansas, 2001.

Main, Steven J. "Stalin in June 1941: A Comment on Cynthia Roberts," *Europe-Asia Studies* 48(5) (1996): 837–9.

Malia, Martin. *The Soviet Tragedy: A History of Socialism in Russia, 1917–1991.* New York: Free Press, 1994.

Mandryka, A. P. *Aero-mekhanicheskie laboratorii Peterburga.* Leningrad: Nauk, 1980.

McCannon, John. *Red Arctic: Polar Exploration and the Myth of the North in Soviet Russia, 1932–1939.* New York: Oxford University Press, 1998.

McDaniel, Tim. *Autocracy, Capitalism, and Revolution in Russia.* Berkeley, CA: University of California Press, 1988.

McReynolds, Louise. *The News Under Russia's Old Regime.* Princeton, NJ: Princeton University Press, 1991.

Mel'tiukhov, M. I. "22 iiuniia 1941 g.: tsifri svidetel'stvuiut." *Istoriia SSSR* 3 (March 1991): 16–28.

Merridale, Catherine. *Night of Stone: Death and Memory in Twentieth-Century Russia.* New York: Penguin, 2000.

Meyer, Alfred G. "The War Scare of 1927." *Soviet Union/Union Soviétique* 5(1) (1978): 1–15.

Miller, Frank J. *Folklore for Stalin: Russian Folklore and Pseudofolklore of the Stalin Era.* Armonk, NY: Sharpe, 1990.

Montefiore, Simon Sebag. *Stalin: The Court of the Red Tsar.* New York: Knopf, 2004.

Morozov, K. N. *Partiia sotsialistov–revoliutsionerov v 1907–1914 gg.* Moscow: ROSSPEN, 1998.

Morrow, John H. Jr. *The Great War in the Air: Military Aviation From 1909 to 1921.* Washington, D.C.: The Smithsonian Institution Press, 1993.

Naimark, Norman M. *The Russians in Germany: A History of the Soviet Zone of Occupation, 1945–1949.* Cambridge, MA: Belknap Press of Harvard University Press, 1995.

Noggle, Anne. *A Dance with Death: Soviet Airwomen in World War II.* College Station, TX: Texas A&M University Press, 1994.

Nove, Alec. *An Economic History of the USSR, 1917–1991.* London: Penguin Books, 1992.

Odom, William E. *The Soviet Volunteers: Modernization and Bureaucracy in a Public Mass Organization.* Princeton, NJ: Princeton University Press, 1973.

Oinas, Felix J. "Folklore and Politics in the Soviet Union." *Slavic Review* 32 (1973): 45–58.

Overy, Richard. *Russia's War.* New York: Penguin, 1997.

Palmer, Scott W. "On Wings of Courage: Public Air-Mindedness and National Identity in Late Imperial Russia." *Russian Review* 54 (1995): 209–26.

———. "Peasants into Pilots: Soviet Air-Mindedness as an Ideology of Dominance." *Technology and Culture* 41 (2000): 1–26.

———. "Icarus, East: The Symbolic Contexts of Russian Flight." *Slavic and East European Journal* 49 (2005): 19–47.

The Papers of George Catlett Marshall, edited by Larry I. Bland and Sharon Ritenour Stevens. Vol. 1, "The Soldierly Spirit, December 1880–June 1939." Baltimore: Johns Hopkins University, 1981.

Paris, Michael. *From the Wright Brothers to Top Gun: Aviation, Nationalism and Popular Cinema.* Manchester, U.K.: Manchester University Press, 1995.

Parrott, Bruce. *Politics and Technology in the Soviet Union.* Cambridge, MA: MIT Press, 1983.

Paynich, Tim. "Black-Market Patriotism: Osoaviakhim and Illegal Trading Networks, 1927–1941." Unpublished essay.

———. "Accidents, Discipline, and Willing Disbelief: Osoaviakhim, 1934–1936." Paper presented at the National Conference of the American Association for the Advancement of Slavic Studies. Pittsburgh, Pennsylvania. 23 November 2002.

Pendo, Stephen. *Aviation in the Cinema.* Metuchen, NJ: The Scarecrow Press, 1985.

Pennington, Reina. *Wings, Women, and War: Soviet Airwomen in World War II Combat.* Lawrence, KS: University Press of Kansas, 2001.

Peris, Daniel. *Storming the Heavens: The Soviet League of the Militant Godless.* Ithaca, NY: Cornell University Press, 1998.

Pisano, Dominick and F. Robert Van der Linden. *Charles Lindbergh and the Spirit of St. Louis.* New York: Abrams, 2002.

Pogue, Forrest C. *George C. Marshall: Education of a General.* New York: Viking Press, 1963.

Polevoi, B. N. *Povest' o nastoiashchem cheloveke.* Moscow, 1946.

Popov, V. A., ed. *Vozdukhoplavanie i aviatsiia v Rossii do 1907 g.: sbornik dokumentov i materialov.* Moscow, 1956.

Reese, Roger R. *Stalin's Reluctant Soldiers: A Social History of the Red Army, 1925–1941.* Lawrence, KS: University Press of Kansas, 1996.

———. *The Soviet Military Experience: A History of the Red Army, 1917–1991.* New York: Routledge, 2000.

Rudenko, S. I. *Lenin i aviatsiia.* Moscow, 1970.

Saburov, N. N. *Bor'ba partii za ustanovlenie ekonomicheskoi smychki rabochego klassa s trudiashchimsia krest'ianstvom, 1921–1925 gg.* Leningrad: Izdatel'stvo Leningradskogo universiteta, 1975.

Sanborn, Joshua A. *Drafting the Russian Nation: Military Conscription, Total War, and Mass Politics, 1905–1925.* DeKalb, IL: Northern Illinois University Press, 2003.

Sankov, V. E. *U istokov aviatsii.* Moscow, 1976.

Scanlan, James P. and Loren R. Graham. *Technology, Culture, and Development: The Experience of the Soviet Model.* New York: Sharpe, 1992.

Shabota, A. M. "Vospominaniia o Sigizmunde Aleksandroviche Levanevskom." Unpublished manuscript in possession of author.

Shavrov, V. B. *Istoriia konstruktsii samoletov v SSSR do 1938 g.* Moscow, 1986.

Shumikhin, V. S. *Sovetskaia voennaia aviatsiia, 1917–1941*. Moscow, 1986.

Sibley, Katherine A.S. "Soviet Industrial Espionage Against American Military Technology and the U.S. Response, 1930–1945." *Intelligence and National Security*. 14(2) (Summer 1999): 94–123.

Siegel, Katherine. *Loans and Legitimacy: The Evolution of Soviet–American Relations, 1919–1933*. Lexington, KY: University of Kentucky Press, 1996.

Sobolev, D. A. and Iu. V. Rychkov, eds. *Vsemirnaia istoriia aviatsii*. Moscow: Veche, 2002.

Sobolev, Dmitrii. "Tragediia 'Maksima Gor'kogo.'" *Rodina* 8 (August 2004): 51–4.

Sokolov, A. K., ed. *Golos naroda: pis'ma i otkliki riadovykh sovetskikh grazhdan o sobitiakh, 1918–1932 gg*. Moscow: ROSSPEN, 1997.

Sokolov, B. V. "Lend Lease in Soviet Military Efforts, 1941–1945." *Journal of Slavic Military Studies* 7 (1994): 567–86.

Stites, Richard. *Revolutionary Dreams: Utopian Vision and Experimental Life in the Russian Revolution*. Oxford: Oxford University Press, 1989.

Stites, Richard, ed. *Culture and Entertainment in Wartime Russia*. Bloomington, IN: Indiana University Press, 1995.

Stoecker, Sally W. *Forging Stalin's Army: Marshal Tukhachevsky and the Politics of Military Innovation*. Boulder, CO: Westview, 1998.

Stone, David R. *Hammer and Rifle: The Militarization of the Soviet Union, 1926–1933*. Lawrence, KS: University Press of Kansas, 2000.

Suny, Ronald Grigor. *The Soviet Experiment: Russia, the USSR, and the Successor States*. New York: Oxford University Press, 1998.

Sutton, Antony C. *Western Technology and Soviet Economic Development, 1917–1965*. 3 vols. Stanford, CA: Hoover Institution Press, 1968–73.

Tauger, Mark. "The 1932 Harvest and the Famine of 1933," *Slavic Review* 50 (Spring 1990): 70–89.

Thomas, Lowell and Lowell Thomas, Jr. *Famous First Flights That Changed History*. Garden City, NY: Doubleday, 1968.

Toporkov, A. L., T. G. Ivanova, L. P. Lapteva, and E. E. Levkievskaia, eds. *Rukopisi, kotorykh ne bylo: poddelki v oblasti slavianskogo fol'klora*. Moscow: Ladomir, 2002.

Tumarkin, Nina. *The Living and the Dead: The Rise and Fall of the Cult of World War II in Russia*. New York: Basic Books, 1994.

Vance, Jonathan. *High Flight: Aviation and the Canadian Imagination*. Toronto: Penguin, 2002.

Van der Linden, F. Robert. *Airlines and Airmail: The Post Office and the Birth of the Commercial Aviation Industry*. Lexington, KY: University of Kentucky Press, 2002.

Van Tuyll, Hubert P. *Feeding the Bear: American Aid to the Soviet Union, 1941–1945*. Westport, CT: Greenwood, 1989.

Vitarbo, Gregory. "The Power, Strength, and Future of Russia: Aviation Culture and the Russian Imperial Officer Corps, 1908–1914." (Ph.D. dissertation, University of Michigan, 1999).

Von Geldern, James. *Bolshevik Festivals, 1917–1920*. Berkeley, CA: University of California Press, 1993.

Von Hagen, Mark. *Soldiers in the Proletarian Dictatorship: The Red Army and the Soviet Socialist State, 1917–1930*. Ithaca, NY: Cornell University Press, 1990.

Ward, John W. "The Meaning of Lindbergh's Flight." *American Quarterly* 10 (1958): 3–16.

Werth, Alexander. *Russia at War, 1941–1945*. New York: Dutton, 1964.

West, James L. and Iurii A. Petrov, eds. *Merchant Moscow: Images of Russia's Vanished Bourgeoisie*. Princeton, NJ: Princeton University Press, 1998.

White, Stephen. *The Bolshevik Poster*. New Haven, CT: Yale University Press, 1988.

Wilson, Timothy. "A Story Untold: The Imperial Russian Air Force, 1909–1917." (Ph.D. dissertation, Pennsylvania State University, 2001).

———. "Broken Wings: The Curtiss Aeroplane Company, K-Boats, and the Russian Navy, 1914–1916." *The Journal of Military History* 66 (October 2002): 1061–83.

Wohl, Robert. *A Passion for Wings: Aviation and the Western Imagination, 1908–1918*. New Haven, CT: Yale University Press, 1994.

———. *The Spectacle of Flight: Aviation and the Western Imagination, 1920–1950*. New Haven, CT: Yale University Press, 2005.

Young, Glennys. *Power and the Sacred in Revolutionary Russia: Religious Activists in the Village*. University Park, PA: Pennsylvania State University Press, 1997.

Zelnik, Reginald, ed. *Workers and Intelligentsia in Late Imperial Russia*. Berkeley, CA: University of California Press, 1999.

Zhabrov, A. A. *Annotirovannyi ukazatel' literatury na russkom iazike po aviatsii i vozdukho-plavaniia za 50 let, 1881–1931*. Moscow, 1931.

Index

Note: *Italic pages are related to figures*